1765 John Newbery publishes *The Renowned History of Little Goody Two Shoes, Otherwise Called Mrs. Margery Two Shoes*, authorship attributed to Oliver Goldsmith. This highly moral tale is considered the first novel in English for children; it is a small step away from the didacticism of the *New England Primer*.

1783-1789 *The History of Sanford and Merton*, by Thomas Day, is published. Like *Goody Two Shoes*, this fictional work contains thinly disguised moral lessons. Such books, which supposedly made didacticism palatable, are misguided attempts to follow Jean–Jacques Rousseau's ideas: to aid the child in his natural quest for knowledge and morality by exposing him to literature describing exemplary behavior.

1806 *Tales from Shakespeare*, by Charles and Mary Lamb, appears in England.

1824 *Household Stories*, by Jacob and Wilhelm Grimm, is translated into English.

1846 Publication in England of Charles Kingsley's *The Heroes*, stories taken from the Greek myths.

1865 Lewis Carroll's *Alice's Adventures in Wonderland* appears in England, followed by *Through the Looking-Glass* (1871) and *The Hunting of the Snark* (1876).

1868 Louisa May Alcott's *Little Women*, a nondidactic novel of everyday life of four girls, is published in the United States.

1876 Publication in the United States of Mark Twain's *The Adventures of Tom Sawyer*, followed by *The Adventures of Huckleberry Finn* (1884), both boyhood classics and examples of the healthy trend in children's literature away from moralizing and didacticism.

1882 Robert Louis Stevenson's *Treasure Island* is published, followed in 1885 by his *A Child's Garden of Verses*.

1889 Andrew Lang's *The Blue Fairy Book* appears, followed by the Red, Green, and Yellow books.

1894 Publication of Rudyard Kipling's *Jungle Book*.

1908 Kenneth Grahame's *Wind in the Willows* is published.

A New Look at Children's Literature

William Anderson   San Fernando Valley State College

Patrick Groff   San Diego State College

Bibliography compiled by   **Ruth Robinson**   Senior Children's Library Los Angeles Public Library

Wadsworth Publishing Company, Inc., Belmont, Calif.

ISBN–0–534–00177–7
L. C. Cat. Card No. 70–185928
Printed in the United States of America

1 2 3 4 5 6 7 8 9 10—76 75 74 73 72

Preface

Children's literature has become a major field of study. Those involved with the young—teachers, librarians, and parents—feel a great responsibility to select the best books for children and to guide young readers in understanding and appreciating great writing. Books are chosen for children by adults, and pleasurable literary experiences are usually organized for children by adults. A child's introduction to this source of entertainment and meaning is one of the most important parts of his intellectual growth; therefore, the evaluation of new books and a reexamination of old ones is a large part of the responsibility of the adult who works with children.

The job of understanding children's books demands certain critical skills and perceptions. If one cannot judge books himself, he is forced to rely on the opinions of others, which may be dated and are seldom directly applicable to individual needs and circumstances. The critic seeking books for a certain audience will make better choices of books if he is able to synthesize his own viewpoint than if he relies on a lengthy approved booklist compiled by someone else.

Literary criticism has been largely neglected as a viable approach to analyzing children's literature. Most writers on this subject imply that children's books do not fit into the mainstream of literature and that they therefore demand a unique kind of appraisal. Too often such critiques fail to discuss the elements of literature—plot structure, character development, and analysis of style—or they descend into the coy, the sentimental, or the gushy. Such analysis does not lead the student to understand, finally, how one approaches a book to see whether it succeeds or fails as a work of art.

The major premise of *A New Look at Children's Literature* is that children's literature is not limited to children's books of the last 200 years and that it is fully a part of the mainstream of literature. Further, the critical doctrines of those who evaluate adult literature—from Aristotle to Northrop Frye—are as valuable and relevant to children's literature as they are to adult literature. In fact, we find that most distinctions between good adult literature and good children's literature dissolve under careful scrutiny; the main difference between the two is not in their essential nature but in the age level of the largest number of readers.

Hence, evaluating and understanding children's literature has direct kinship to the critical reading of any work of literature.

A New Look at Children's Literature surveys the various doctrines of literary criticism and demonstrates how they work. We start with the most general concepts of literature and move into more specialized concerns. Part One, "Children's Literature: Basic Concepts," acquaints the student with fundamental elements of literature—structure, plot, character, style, and archetype—and demonstrates them using examples from widely available works which are perhaps already familiar to the student.

Part Two, "Types and Uses of Children's Literature," presents a survey and analysis of the subdivisions of the field: mythology, folklore, and related forms; fantasy; prose fiction; poetry; picture books and picture storybooks; biography; and information books. In this section we emphasize helping the student reach an awareness of the essence of each kind of writing and its interrelationship with other forms. The familiar theme of the orphan child, for example, is shown in its various forms from mythology to modern children's novels.

In Part Two, we see that some forms of children's literature require extra-literary critical considerations, and we discuss them separately: picture books require consideration of both illustrations and text; biography calls for an examination of historical accuracy, which is not normally part of the literary critic's job; and information books require critical appraisal of their factual accuracy in areas outside the usual knowledge of a literary critic.

Part Three, "Teaching Literature to Children," presents a rationale for devising a curriculum for literature in the elementary schools and some means of implementing the study of literature.

Part Four, "Books for Children," contains a 500-title annotated bibliography of good books for children, a list of children's book awards, and a list of periodicals which contain reviews of children's books. The text refers frequently to examples listed in the bibliography; the student should read some of these books on his own to try out the critical concepts he has learned.

Many thanks are due to family and friends who have offered encouragement, time, help, and enthusiasm to the project. We are deeply grateful to those who have made this work more pleasant—and, indeed, possible. We also want especially to thank Paul Olson, Director of the Tri-University Project in Elementary Education at the University of Nebraska. During the academic year 1967–1968, we were College Participants in this project. While the blizzards swirled around Andrews Hall, our Monday afternoon seminars with Paul Olson were our initial inspiration for this book. We also wish to thank reviewers Leland B. Jacobs, Teachers College, Columbia University; Sam Sebesta, University of Washington, Seattle; and Jerome Cushman, University of California, Los Angeles. It has been a rewarding study; we hope it will prove as gratifying for new students of the field as it has been for us.

William Anderson
Patrick Groff

Contents

Part One
Children's Literature:
Basic Concepts

1 Approaching Children's Literature: Basic Concepts

Literature contains every kind of experience, character, and language; its scope and range are virtually limitless. By opening the pages of a book, we can discover all of the representations of the human mind. In literature, gods and goddesses stand side by side with cowboys; battles with sea monsters occupy equal time with space flights; planets of the outer galaxies achieve the same clear focus as cars seen through a window opening onto a city street. In the literary cosmos, the totally alien becomes the completely familiar. Perhaps these lines by Blake best describe the imaginative insights of literary experience:

> To see a World in a Grain of Sand
> And a Heaven in a Wild Flower,
> Hold Infinity in the Palm of your Hand
> And Eternity in an Hour.[1]

Literature offers many pleasures. The action we find in books not only entertains us, it also deeply involves us in its own form and dimensions. Because literary portrayal takes place within certain structures and patterns, which give a shape and order to life, literature interprets and organizes experience in its depiction of action. Reality, which otherwise might appear bewildering and chaotic, can be known and understood when seen in the forms of literature. In providing this unique manner of grasping the meaning of existence, literature replaces blindness with vision and creates a picture of the world.

Those who bring children and literature together—teachers, librarians, or parents—introduce the young to their cultural heritage as well as to a new way of seeing the world. Their goal is to evoke in children the same sense of dis-

---

[1] William Blake, *Complete Writings* (London: Oxford University Press, 1966), p. 431.

2

covery and pleasure in books Keats described after he first felt the impact of reading Chapman's translation of Homer:

> Then felt I like some watcher of the skies
>   When a new planet swims into his ken;
> Or like stout Cortez when with eagle eyes
>   He star'd at the Pacific—and all his men
> Look'd at each other with a wild surmise—
>   Silent, upon a peak in Darien.[2]

Our central concern is to explore the many possibilities of guiding children in their experiences with literature, of aiding them in their discoveries of the "realms of gold."

First, we must ask, "What is children's literature?" If we limit the field to books written especially for children within the last two hundred years, we narrow the range of investigation excessively and destructively. Children's literature should not be separated from literature in general for many reasons. One of our main assumptions is that rigid definitions of what is and is not children's literature should be avoided. Children's literature, like all other kinds of literature, is a portrayal of life and mind in language.

Naturally, some of the logical and emotional limitations of childhood will occasionally rule out some kinds of literature. But what once seemed clearly inappropriate for a young audience is no longer so. Television and movies, among other contemporary forces, have phenomenally increased the sophistication of children's awareness of such once taboo subjects as sexuality, violence, death, revenge, and crime. We can now reconsider previously sharply defined boundaries of children's literature from the viewpoint that children are not blank slates of innocence, ignorant of many kinds of so-called adult reality. This is not, of course, to argue complete license in children's literature. It is rather to admit the obvious: children, although not "little adults," are not so bereft of experience with the real world that all aspects of adult life must be filtered out of their literature. Such censorship, never particularly effective, stems from a misguided trend begun in the seventeenth century to use children's literature as a didactic tool to teach children moral lessons they probably would ignore when they grew up.

If we examine the larger history of literature, we find two great traditions: the oral and the written. From the earliest times of civilization, children have been a part of the audience of oral literature, exposed to the same works as adults. As one example, the epic, dating from the beginnings of Western civilization, was sung and chanted to an audience of children and adults long before it was

---

[2] John Keats, *Complete Poems and Selected Letters* (New York: The Odyssey Press, 1935), p. 45.

written down. Similarly, the Greek myths, like those of other cultures, took on the form of familiar stories and folktales that have been told and retold from one generation to the next, and they are still of equal interest to children and to adults. Seen in historical perspective, children and adults always have been equal partners in their enjoyment of spoken literature. This is still true today.

Oral literature is the oldest form of children's literature and is of special value and interest to children. Even a child of three has an almost miraculous comprehension of the spoken word. It is by no means necessary to wait for a child to learn to read before he is exposed to literature. Naturally, at first a child will find some words perplexing. The small child may share the same kind of difficulty Edward Bear (Pooh) encounters in *Winnie-the-Pooh* when he tries to find out from Owl how to help his friend Eeyore regain his lost tail:

> "Halloo, Pooh," he said. "How's things?"
>
> "Terrible and Sad," said Pooh, "because Eeyore, who is a friend of mine, has lost his tail. And he's Moping about it. So could you very kindly tell me how to find it for him?"
>
> "Well," said Owl, "the customary procedure in such cases is as follows."
>
> "What does Crustimoney Proseedcake mean?" said Pooh. "For I am a Bear of Very Little Brain, and long words Bother me."
>
> "It means the Thing to Do."
>
> "As long as it means that, I don't mind," said Pooh humbly.
>
> "The thing to do is as follows. First, Issue a Reward. Then——"
>
> "Just a moment," said Pooh, holding up his paw. "*What* do we do to this —what you were saying? You sneezed just as you were going to tell me."
>
> "I *didn't* sneeze."
>
> "Yes, you did, Owl."
>
> "Excuse me, Pooh, I didn't. You can't sneeze without knowing it."
>
> "Well, you can't know it without something having been sneezed."
>
> "What I *said* was, 'First *Issue* a Reward.'"
>
> "You're doing it again," said Pooh sadly.
>
> "A reward!" said Owl very loudly. "We write a notice to say that we will give a large something to anybody who finds Eeyore's tail."
>
> "I see, I see," said Pooh, nodding his head.[3]

But Pooh learns quickly from his friends. His comprehension of language grows steadily through conversation. So too, the verbal skills of the child between two and five, who has been called a "linguistic genius" by the Russian psychologist Chukovsky,[4] develop with more rapidity and complexity than at any other time of life. Even very small children respond to literature that is read aloud to them. It is estimated that older children in the first grade have listening vocab-

---

[3] From the book *Winnie the Pooh* by A. A. Milne with decorations by E. H. Shepard. Copyright 1926 by E. P. Dutton & Co., Inc. Renewal 1954 by A. A. Milne. Published by E. P. Dutton & Co., Inc. and reprinted with their permission.

[4] Kornei Chukovsky, *From Two to Five* (Berkeley: University of California Press, 1968), p. 1.

ularies of twenty thousand words,[5] thus making a great deal of literature accessible when presented orally to them. The advantages of such early encounters with literature are clear: the child not only participates in the pleasures of literature but his own language growth is also enriched through exposure to the language of literature.

As in all literature the oldest traditions of children's literature are oral. In a sense, therefore, there are two histories of children's literature. There is first that vast body of literature that children have always been a part of through attendance with adults in religious services and theatrical presentations, and now through the media of television, radio, records, and movies. A televised version of, say, *Moby Dick* places that work within the literary awareness of the children who see it. *Moby Dick,* like *The Odyssey,* or *The Adventures of Huckleberry Finn,* is not exclusively children's literature. Such works, and the list would be practically endless, belong to whoever hears or reads them; and both children and adults have formed the audience for them.

Secondly, there is the tradition of books written solely for children. Printed books written especially for children appeared relatively late. Although some didactic works had been published early—hornbooks, and other religious and moral documents—it was not until the eighteenth century with the works of Charles Perrault and John Newbery that the modern trend toward books intended only for children was firmly established. From the middle of the eighteenth century until the present, there has been a greatly increasing supply of books for children, until now in the 1970s it is likely that from 3500 to 4000 new titles will appear each year in the United States alone.

Frequently, however, there is a difference between children's books and children's literature. Common sense tells us that of the thousands of books published for adults each year, ranging from hacked-out pornography to serious fiction, not all can be equally good literature. Hopefully the best survive and the bad sink into oblivion. So too, of all the titles that appear in children's book lists, many are not good literature, while others will become classics. Children's books are almost always selected by adults. In recognizing the importance of literature to the intellectual and emotional life of the child, it is also necessary to recognize the responsibility to find the best literature to present to them.

The quesion then arises, "What is good literature?" From the time of Plato to the present, thinkers, philosophers, and scholars have concerned themselves with this difficult problem. The number of different answers offered is almost equal to the number of those who have considered the matter. But throughout the history of literary criticism, the most widely accepted approach to the problem has been to consider and to describe the essential characteristics of works commonly held to be good. The critic, therefore, starts with a point of reference and works from his understanding of these exemplary works toward formulating

---

[5] Paul Hanna and Jean Hanna in "The Teaching of Spelling," in *Readings on Contemporary English in the Elementary School.* Iris M. Tiedt and Sidney W. Tiedt, eds. (Englewood Cliffs, N.J.: Prentice-Hall, 1967).

a sense of how to look at a newly encountered piece of writing. A critic must be flexible, widely knowledgeable, and very sensitive in his responses to literature. We expect a critic to be almost infallible in his instincts. No one ever is, of course, so we find, instead of certainty, that some approaches to literature have been less prone to error than others. Because literary criticism is not a precise science, there sometimes are no clear answers. But the importance, need, and fascination of the critical study of literature are undeniable.

From the history of literary criticism, we see that the most important aspects to examine in a work are its form and language. From these two dominant concepts, many other related matters emerge, such as plot, tone, character development, symbolism, thematic unity, style, structure, and archetype. These concerns are common to all literary endeavors, and indeed the list could be much longer. In this chapter, we will explore these universal and basic concepts before turning to the unique and distinctive features of the various genres or types of literature. Our approach will be descriptive, exploring exemplary works to form some basis for further generalizations. Not all books fit the same molds, obviously. But when discussing one literary work, there is, almost inevitably, a transfer of concepts to other works. That is our notion here—that by close scrutiny of certain books you will be able to understand others on your own. And so, on to some basic concepts.

Structure   Structure is essentially how the literary work is put together: its broad shape; its limits of time, place, and action; the relationships among its parts and how these fit together to make the total statement of the work. Any piece of literature, from the longest epic to the brief haiku of seventeen syllables, has a definite structure which cannot be altered without changing the overall effect of the work as a whole. The most general term used to describe structure is *plot*. The plot is the complete action of the story, narrative, or poem, including the time, places, and characters portrayed. From the time of the Greeks it has been assumed that a plot should have an organic unity—that all its parts should be necessary members of the whole.

For the plot to create unity, how it begins and how it ends are of great importance. Aristotle says of plot in *The Poetics*:[6]

> A whole is that which has a beginning, a middle, and an end. A beginning is that which does not itself follow anything by causal necessity, but after which something naturally is or comes to be. An end, on the contrary, is

---

[6] Aristotle places plot in a position of importance even greater than that of character, because the plot is the dimension within which characters are portrayed.

that which itself naturally follows some other thing, either by necessity, or as a rule, but has nothing following it. A middle is that which follows something as some other thing follows it. A well constructed plot, therefore, must neither begin nor end at haphazard, but conform to these principles.[7]

Consider how the formulas at the beginning and end of some fairy tales agree with Aristotle's description of plot. The familiar "Once upon a time . . ." serves to create a beginning which does not have to follow any single event, although it is in some fashion related to prior experience. It is as though experience is a continuum delineated by intervals that are complete within themselves. Beginning a story at just the right point on the continuum means finding the spot where the action portrayed can stand by itself, without necessarily having to be seen in any additional context. When you find yourself waiting at the movies until the next feature starts so you can see the whole of the plot, you are waiting for the right beginning. And the fairy tale ending of ". . . lived happily ever after," or the cinematic riding off into the sunset, implies that whatever was going on in the earlier parts of the plot has been settled or resolved. Whatever new problems may arise will be another story and on another part of the continuum from the one which is now completed.

To look at a specific example, "The Elves" from *Household Stories* by the Brothers Grimm, begins as follows:

> There was once a shoemaker, who, through no fault of his own, became so poor that at last he had nothing left but just enough leather to make one pair of shoes.[8]

As a beginning for this brief tale, the first sentence indicates that what is to follow is a break with the past. The shoemaker's time of poverty will be the concern of the plot, not his former prosperity. It is also evident that it is no fault of the shoemaker that he is poor. And, the expectation for the middle of the plot is to find out what happens to the leaher for the one pair of shoes now that the shoemaker is poor.

The story moves quickly to its middle section; elves come in during the night and make a beautiful pair of shoes which the shoemaker sells for enough profit to buy more leather. The middle then continues with the elves making shoes by night for the shoemaker to sell by day. Finally, the shoemaker and his wife discover who their benefactors are and decide to reward them with Christmas

---

[7] Walter Jackson Bate, *Criticism: the Major Texts* (New York: Harcourt, Brace and Company, 1952), p. 24.

[8] The Brothers Grimm, *Household Stories*. tr. Lucy Crane (New York: Dover Publications, 1963), p. 171.

suits. The elves are so delighted with their gifts that they decide to give up cobbling (at least for this shoemaker), and they never come back to work for him again.

The middle of the plot is over, and the ending is reached:

> From that time they were never seen again; but it always went well with the shoemaker as long as he lived, and whatever he took in hand prospered.[9]

This plot portrays the time the shoemaker had elves as helpers. When the little men leave, that association ends, and the plot concludes, happily, as it turns out, for the shoemaker who continues to prosper. The plot thus has an organic unity.

As another example in children's literature of Aristotle's theory of plot unity of beginning, middle, and end, Maurice Sendak's *Where the Wild Things Are* begins:

> The night Max wore his wolf suit and made
>   mischief of one kind
> and another
> his mother called him "WILD THING!"
> and Max said "I'LL EAT YOU UP!"
> so he was sent to bed without eating anything.[10]

This start for the story points to a middle that will describe what happens once Max is upstairs. Here the beginning of the story is complete and needs no prior causal necessity. Because no mention is made of what kind of mischief Max had been up to, the story is thus about what happens after he is sent upstairs, not about what naughtiness caused his banishment.

The plot of *Where the Wild Things Are* progresses directly to its middle section, which grows organically from the beginning as seen in the story's next line: "That very night in Max's room a forest grew." It appears that Max has fallen asleep and in a dream conjures up a realm where he meets Wild Things, or monsters, which he can tame by staring directly into their yellow eyes. Max achieves the same mastery over the monsters that his mother has exercised over him, giving him a sense of strength and identity. The monsters want Max to stay with them, but delicious odors draw the boy back to his own room (or wake him up) to the ending of the plot. His mother has left his supper, still warm, on a table for him. The plot ends here, because its middle part is now

---

[9] *Ibid.*, p. 172.
[10] From *Where the Wild Things Are* by Maurice Sendak. Copyright © 1963 by Maurice Sendak. Reprinted by permission of Harper & Row, Publishers.

resolved. The monsters of the dream are no longer necessary, because Max has been forgiven for his mischief, which restores to him his identity of loved son. Tomorrow's mischief will be another story; today's has ended.

The beginning of a plot typically will set up the problems or conflicts that the middle and end will resolve, as in these opening lines of *Charlotte's Web* by E. B. White:

> "Where's Papa going with that ax?" said Fern to her mother as they were setting the table for breakfast.
>
> "Out to the hoghouse," replied Mrs. Arable. "Some pigs were born last night."

Fern stops her father on his way to kill the runt pig. Illustration by Garth Williams. From Charlotte's Web *by E. B. White. Copyright, 1952, by E. B. White. Reprinted by permission of Harper & Row, Publishers.*

> "I don't see why he needs an ax," continued Fern, who was only eight.
>
> "Well," said her mother, "One of the pigs is a runt. It's very small and weak, and it will never amount to anything. So your father has decided to do away with it."[11]

The entire novel is the account of how Fern and Charlotte the Spider rescue Wilbur the Pig. The beginning of the plot needs no "prior causal necessity," because it begins with the birth of the runt pig whose very existence is the problem of the plot. Saving his life creates the middle part of the action. Notice that a theme of death is introduced in these first lines of the novel. The development of the plot is also a resolution of Wilbur's fears about death: his early abject terror changes to a sense of acceptance of death as a part of the cycle of nature. The beginning of *Charlotte's Web* clearly creates the expectations the rest of the novel fulfills: the problems implicit and explicit in the first lines see their solution by the end of the story.

Now try your own hand at examining the beginning, middle, and end of a plot. Without reading more than the first passage from Perrault's *Cinderella* given below, see how many details and problems are established in the beginning of the story:

> Once upon a time there was a gentleman who married as his second wife the proudest and haughtiest woman who had ever been seen. She had two daughters with a disposition like her own, who resembled her in everything. The husband had for his part a young daughter who was of unparalleled sweetness and goodness—she got this from her mother, who was the best person in the world.
>
> The marriage ceremony was no sooner over than the stepmother gave free rein to her bad disposition. She could not endure the little girl's good qualities, which made her own daughters seem even more hateful.[12]

Several problems established in this beginning are:

1. The vulnerability of the good Cinderella because she is an orphan;
2. An implied weakness of character in the father, who had the bad sense to marry a proud and haughty woman;
3. Thus, the absence of a strong hero at this point in Cinderella's life—such a hero, like the prince, will be needed to save the situation;

---

[11] From *Charlotte's Web* by E. B. White. Copyright, 1952, by E. B. White. Reprinted by permission of Harper & Row, Publishers.

[12] From *Twelve Dancing Princesses*, edited by Alfred and Mary David. Copyright © 1964 Alfred David & Mary Elizabeth David. Reprinted by arrangement with The New American Library, New York, N.Y.

4. The stepmother's jealousy, which will create a conflict between Cinderella and her stepsisters.

These problems, and perhaps others, are those with which the middle of the plot must deal. Cinderella goes to the ball through the efforts of her fairy godmother, who serves as a substitute for the dead mother, taking care of the first problem. At the ball, she gains the favor of the prince, introducing a strong male figure into the action, thus offering a solution to the second and third problems. The prince's love for Cinderella finally rescues her from the control of the evil stepmother (fourth problem), and the end of the story resolves the conflict between Cinderella and the stepsisters:

> Then the two sisters recognized her for the beauty they had seen at the ball. They threw themselves at her feet to ask her forgiveness for all the harsh treatment they had made her suffer. Cinderella raised them up, kissed them, told them she forgave them with all her heart, and begged them to love her forever.
>
> Dressed as she was, she was led to the palace of the young prince. He found her more beautiful than ever, and a few days later he married her. Cinderella, who was as good as she was beautiful, had her two sisters come live at the palace and married them the same day to two great lords of the court.[13]

Cinderella has now become the princess and the sisters have been reconciled with each other, leaving behind them the proud and evil stepmother, thus making all turn out happily. Any further portrayal or narrative of Cinderella and her stepsisters would require a new plot, because it would be beyond the limits established at the beginning of this one.

There is a similarity between the limits of a plot and the shape of a canvas on which a painting is made. For example, see if you can guess which two famous paintings fit the shapes of the canvases shown on page 12 with only a few sketchy details of the images given.

If you guessed both, you did so from only a few very rudimentary details of form and line. This would argue that the shape of the canvas is of great importance to the effect of the painting. Furthermore, it is obvious that all the details of the painting must fit the proportions of the canvas and be contained within its limits. Moving the *Mona Lisa's* face to the right or left would change the effect of the painting just as the meaning of *The Last Supper* would be changed if Jesus were moved to the edge of the canvas and thus to the foot of the table. So too, the beginning and end of the plot are of great importance to

---

[13] *Ibid.,* pp. 152–153.

the effect the narrative achieves through its structure as a whole, through its unity of beginning, middle, and end.

To demonstrate the difference between an organically unified plot and one which is not, a comparison of two versions of the Sleeping Beauty story will show how one achieves a compressed, dramatic effect and the other an anticlimactic and banal ending. In many respects, Perrault and The Brothers Grimm tell the same tale. But notice the difference in plot unity as seen below.

<table>
<tr><td>

Briar Rose
by
The Brothers Grimm

1. Long awaited birth of the princess.
2. Christening feast to which the king invites only twelve of the thirteen wise-women in his country because he owned only twelve gold plates.
3. The twelve guests begin to give gifts, of virtue, beauty, wealth, etc.

</td><td>

The Sleeping Beauty
by
Charles Perrault

1. Long awaited birth of the princess.
2. Christening feast to which the king invites all but one of the good fairies, having forgotten her because of her long seclusion in a tower.
3. The fairies begin offering gifts of beauty, angelic disposition, etc.

</td></tr>
</table>

4. The thirteenth, in revenge for not having been invited, bursts in and places a curse of death on the princess in her fifteenth year.

5. The twelfth wisewoman, not yet having given her gift, softens the curse to a sleep of 100 years.

6. On her fifteenth birthday, the princess discovers a locked tower, enters, and finds an old woman spinning there.

7. The princess pricks her finger while attempting to spin the wheel and falls asleep. All in the castle also fall asleep and a thorn hedge grows up around the palace.

8. The 100 years pass and a prince comes, determined to see Briar Rose, although he is warned that many others have died trying to get through the hedge.

9. When he approaches, the thorns turn to roses, a path opens, he enters, kisses Briar Rose, and she and all the rest of the people in the castle awaken. The prince marries Briar Rose and they live happily ever after.

4. The uninvited fairy bursts in and, in anger that the king has no golden case like those he gave the other fairies to give her, pronounces the curse of death on the princess from a spinning wheel.

5. The youngest fairy, although unable to erase the curse, changes it to a sleep of 100 years.

6. When she is almost sixteen, the princess discovers a tower in which an old woman is spinning.

7. The princess pricks her finger while attempting to spin and falls asleep. The good fairy returns from distant lands and puts everyone else in the castle to sleep for 100 years. A dense forest grows up around the castle.

8. The 100 years pass and a prince comes, determined to see the Sleeping Beauty.

9. The brambles open before him and he enters the palace and kneels beside the sleeping princess. She awakens and they fall in love. Everyone in the castle also awakens and the prince and the Sleeping Beauty are married at once.

10. The prince returns to his own home but visits the Sleeping Beauty two or three days a week, until after two years they have a son named Day and a daughter named Dawn. The prince is reluctant to bring his wife home because he fears that his mother, descended from a race of ogres, will eat his children.

11. The old king dies, and the prince, now king and no longer fearing his mother, brings Sleeping Beauty, Dawn, and Day to live in his castle.

12. When the new king leaves to wage a war, the ogre queen orders Day, Dawn, and the Sleeping Beauty, in turn, to be served for dinner. Each time, however, a friendly steward substitutes an animal disguised by elaborate sauces.

13. The ogress finds the hidden three, however, and orders them thrown into a pit of snakes.

14. The king returns and the ogress, in shame, throws herself into the pit and dies.
15. After a period of seemly grief for his mother, the king and queen live happily ever after.

From the details of the two plots given above, it is possible to demonstrate that the two stories have the following shapes.

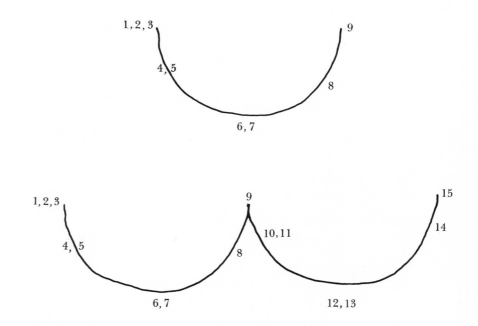

In *Briar Rose,* the action begins on a highpoint of expectancy and potential as the princess is born to the king and queen. However, there is an immediate decline in the fortunes of the characters, when the thirteenth wisewoman's revenge becomes a problem at the christening feast. The fortunes of the characters worsen as the plot progresses to the princess' fifteenth birthday when the prophecy of the twelfth wisewoman is fulfilled: the princess pricks her finger and falls into a sleep of 100 years.

After the princess and the entire court fall asleep, the action remains at this low point until the prince arrives. The entrance of the prince serves to counteract the harmful inadequacies of the king in the earlier part of the story. As the prince demonstrates his bravery, and the favor of the gods is shown by the opening of the thorn hedge, the final resolution of the plot is reached through the marriage of Briar Rose and the prince. Now a strong hero is in control of the action and good fortune is restored.

In Perrault's plot of *The Sleeping Beauty,* the same progress is apparent in the first part of the story, from points 1 to 9, as the narrative also moves from the birth of the princess through the ill-fated christening scene to the sleep and finally to the prince's arrival. After the prince's father dies, however, a separate story begins in the Perrault version, with a plot that is not clearly related to the earlier plot of the "Sleeping Beauty." The only clear continuity between the two stories is the presence of some of the same characters in each. Thus the second plot is a tenuous addition to the first story, and it tends to elongate the tale beyond the natural limits of the first plot. It is possible, therefore, to argue that instead of one organic unity in Perrault's "Sleeping Beauty," there are in fact two loosely related stories.

Subplot and episode

Within the broad outlines of a plot, the inner parts of the narrative must fit together to constitute a unity. Typically, novels consist of smaller units such as subplot and episode that complement each other and the main story line to add up to an organic whole. Indeed, the smaller units will serve to highlight the main theme of the plot. *The Wind in the Willows,* by Kenneth Grahame, for example, is constructed with complementary plot divisions. In this novel, various characters go through adventures that in some sense contrast with each other. Several episodes, for instance, show the generosity and friendliness of the character Rat. One such example is his kindness and hospitality to the field mice, who entertain him and Mole with Christmas carols, when they are caught in a snow storm in the Wild Wood and find refuge in Mole's old house. In every scene in which Rat interacts with the other characters, his actions are trusting and sympathetic. In contrast, when Toad deals with the other characters, he continually dupes and betrays them for his own selfish purposes. As these episodes accrue, Rat looks all the more noble because he is compared with Toad, just as Toad becomes more ridiculous because of the inevitable comparison with Rat and other good characters such as Mole and Badger. The subplot of Toad's automobile journeys, which always end in disaster and near ruin, are contrasted with the subplot of Rat's journeys with Mole on the river to recover the lost Otter, to save the lost Mole from the Wild Wood, and even to rescue Toad himself. Here actions in the subplot make comments upon other portions of the narrative.

When the limits of the plot are properly set and all of its inner parts add to the total effect, a world is created that has a meaning and organization seldom possible in the real world. Literature, like other human symbol systems for understanding experience—such as time and geometry—selects events from reality or creates them from the imagination and places them within a context of form and structure to create meaning. A good plot with boundaries of beginning and end, which contains a harmonious unity, builds a world not found in ordinary experience. Literature thus makes sense out of chaos by its arrangement of reality.

Characters

Within the plot, characters interact with each other and with the nature of the world created by the plot. Although certain literary works make minimal use of explicit characters, there is always some action, and this is always somehow relevant to human life whether it describes the acts of several generations of a family or only a star falling. There is always at least one personality involved in the action, either experiencing it, causing it, or writing it as an author who is at some distance from the action, relating it in retrospect. These presences in literature are the characters in the story who breathe the air of the plot, fit the atmosphere of their world, and speak the language of their time and place.

And there are no limits to the kinds of characters in children's literature. The most fantastic or realistic character finds his audience. At one end of the scale quite ordinary persons like ourselves, like people who appear every day in the newspapers, can be figures and actors in narratives. Such works of literature are realistic in their presentation of characters. For example, Louise Fitzhugh's *Harriet the Spy* presents many factual details of Harriet's life on 87th Street in Manhattan. This is a child living in the real world that you and I know. The author describes the subway she takes, her favorite dessert when she goes out (she likes egg creams), what her father says when he comes home from a hard day at work. These details, along with the topical references to New York City, make the authenticity, the reality, of the character completely believable. She is drawn from the real world, like the one in which you and I live. A character in a novel such as *Harriet the Spy,* like other realistic novels, is completely credible in terms of the actual world, just as in William H. Armstrong's *Sounder,* a portrayal of a poor black family in the South, the characters are real types, living in a believable world where the usual expectations of cause and effect continue to operate.

However, such characters from the contemporary real world are in the minority in children's literature. It is from the creations of fantasy that most characters are derived. In fairy tales and folk tales, for instance, the princes and princesses, the kings and queens, trolls, witches, and goblins are remote from ordinary life. They are either all evil or all good, either totally ugly or ethereally beautiful, unlike human beings. In addition to the mythical fairy tale characters, there is a great cast of animal characters in children's literature—Mole, Rat, Toad, and Badger in *The Wind in the Willows;* Charlotte A. Cavatica the Spider, Wilbur the Pig, and Templeton the Rat in *Charlotte's Web;* the Tortoise, Hare, Fox, and Crow in Aesop's *Fables,* and so on. These animal characters actually represent human types and exhibit human characteristics: the slow tortoise, the selfish pig, the crafty fox, and the rapacious wolf. Invented characters also abound: elves, goblins, dwarves, and hobbits in Tolkien; and the Mushroom people in Cameron's *The Wonderful Flight to the Mushroom Planet.* Characters need not come from animate nature: the fabulous automobile in Ian Fleming's *Chitty Chitty Bang Bang,* a guardian spirit and guide to adventure with the license plate of **GEN II,** is a car which can take the responsibility of becoming a hydrofoil when necessary; it can volunteer as a radar sensor to track down gangsters who have kidnapped the children of the family; it is, in fact, modern technology's answer to the fairy godmother of the folk tale.

Anything from an angel to a stone can become a character in a story if endowed with life and made accessible to the imagination. A stone which remains forever simply a stone can never become a character because such a stone lacks personality. So too, an angel or a fairy, seen only from afar so that its personality does not emege, can never become a viable and gripping character. Without some vitality or energy that transmits itself to the reader, an object remains merely a stage setting and not a mover in the action or a participant in the world created by the plot.

The question then arises, "How do characters become vital and alive within a plot?" One of the primary means to develop character is description. The writer gives the reader details of how the character dresses, how he moves, how he looks to others in the story. In *Harriet the Spy,* Ole Golly the governess is described this way:

> Ole Golly had on her outdoor things. Ole Golly just had indoor things and outdoor things. She never wore anything as recognizable as a skirt, a jacket, or a sweater. She just had yards and yards of tweed which enveloped her like a lot of discarded blankets, which ballooned out when she walked, and which she referred to as her Things.[14]

This competent creature with her no-nonsense shoes and sensible tweeds forms a bulwark of responsibility and good sense in the novel.

Later, Harriet and Ole Golly go out to visit the governess' ancient mother, who is described as follows:

> The fat lady stood like a mountain, her hands on her hips, in a flowered cotton print dress and enormous hanging coat sweater. Probably the biggest sweater in the world, thought Harriet; probably the biggest pair of shoes too. And her shoes were a wonder. Long, long, black, bumpy things with

---

[14] From *Harriet the Spy* by Louise Fitzhugh. Copyright © 1964 by Louise Fitzhugh. Reprinted by permission of Harper & Row, Publishers.

Ole Golly's mother in Harriet the
Spy. *Illustration by Louise Fitzhugh.
Copyright © 1964 by Louise Fitzhugh.
Reprinted by permission of Harper
& Row, Publishers.*

high, laced sides up to the middle of the shin, bulging with the effort of
holding in those ankles, their laces splitting them into grins against the
white of the socks below.[15]

Finally it becomes clear that Ole Golly's purpose in bringing Harriet to see
the fat lady is to show her what becomes of a person who refuses to accept the

challenges of the adventures life has to offer, a recurrent theme throughout the novel as Harriet puts aside the vicarious role of spy and becomes a participant in life. For Harriet to grasp this point, she must become aware that Ole Golly's mother is gluttonous and indeed dropsical, as indicated by her fat ankles. Of all the descriptive details that could be given, those of the ankles are the most telling in the characterization of the mother.

In a narrative poem, as in fiction, the characters similarly emerge from the description of their appearance. In *The Highwayman,* the Hero is presented in these visual terms:

> He'd a French cocked-hat on his forehead, a
> bunch of lace at his chin,
> A coat of the claret velvet, and breeches of
> brown doeskin:
> They fitted with never a wrinkle; his boots
> were up to his thigh!
> And he rode with a jewelled twinkle,
> His pistol butts a-twinkle,
> His rapier hilt a-twinkle, all under the
> jewelled sky.[16]

This chivalrous, gallant, daring young man is the hero, in love with Bess, the landlord's daughter. The two are betrayed by the villain, Tim the Ostler, whose stealth and treachery are revealed by his description:

> . . . his face was white and peaked,
> His eyes were hollows of madness; his hair like moldy hay.[17]

Tim's description reveals his madness, secretiveness, and hatred in opposition to the openness, bravado, and gallantry of the Hero.

Closely allied to the description of the character's appearance is his status in society. King, princess, prince, stepchild, or stepmother are roles that give the character a specific part to play in the action. Stepmothers are seldom generous in fairy tales; princes are invariably heroic and noble; witches are rarely kind or helpful; and persons of very humble origin such as cobblers, woodcutters, or hunters usually are reliable and kindly. These characters form fixed images in

---

[15] *Ibid.,* p. 14.

[16] Alfred Noyes, *The Highwayman,* in *The Golden Treasury of Poetry,* Louis Untermeyer, ed. (New York: Golden Press, 1965), p. 131.

[17] *Ibid.,* p. 131.

our imagination through their repeated association with the same roles in folk or fairy tales. They need little description since they are archetypes from the past. Characters in the present and those from some imaginary worlds, as we shall see in the chapter on fantasy, usually require much more detail and description.

For a child to identify with a character, to see him as a living creature, vivid, detailed description is of paramount importance. Illustrations are as useful as

Max in his bedroom. Illustration by Maurice Sendak. From Where the Wild Things Are *by Maurice Sendak. Copyright © 1963 by Maurice Sendak. Reprinted by permission of Harper & Row, Publishers.*

descriptions and status identifications to illuminate and convey character. (A later chapter deals at length with the use of illustrations in children's literature.) A dynamic picture gives an immediate feeling for the characters portrayed. This is especially important for younger children who may not grasp all of the sub-

The forest begins to grow in Max's bedroom. Illustration by Maurice Sendak. From **Where the Wild Things Are** *by Maurice Sendak. Copyright © 1963 by Maurice Sendak. Reprinted by permission of Harper & Row, Publishers.*

tleties in a rich, verbal description of character. Again, characters can be drawn from any source, from the real world or a world invented by the author. But they must be accessible to the imagination of the reader. Such a successful illustration of character can be seen in Maurice Sendak's *Where the Wild Things Are*. Max, when we first see him, has on his face an understandable look of defiance because he is being sent to bed with no supper. In the next illustration, he is patting his foot in great satisfaction, because of his emerging fantasy of the forest in which he will prove himself against the Wild Things—and show himself above such mundane matters as parental punishment.

Mr. Toad ready to begin another adventure. Illustration by E. H. Shepard (Copyright 1933, 1953 Charles Scribner's Sons; renewal copyright © 1961 Ernest H. Shepard) is reproduced by permission of Charles Scribner's Sons from The Wind in the Willows *by Kenneth Grahame.*

In *The Wind in The Willows,* as another instance, Mr. Toad's inflated self-esteem and self-love, which lead him to refer to himself continually as "Handsome Mr. Toad," are apparent in the illustration in which he is just about to embark on another of his misadventures by stealing an automobile that was left in the inn yard.

An illustration or a detailed description of a character provides the reader with external information about the person he is to become more intimately acquainted with in the progress of the plot. As in real life, a character's appearance and his surroundings convey a sense of the outer man, yet they reveal very little insight into the real person. It is that inner part of the character we want to probe in literature. The characters in literature, even though fantastic creations of the imagination, must be related to the significance of our own lives. If they are not a part of the world accessible to the imagination, a world into which one is drawn by the writer, the reader fails to identify with the characters and he remains at a distance, lessening the literary experience.

Thus, in the creation of a meaningful character in literature, it is necessary to go to more subtle means than mere description or illustration through a photograph or drawing of the character. The essence of a character is his action in the plot: a character is what he does. When a world is created through the dimensions of a plot, the figures or actors on that stage show their inner motivation and meaning through their actions. And like persons in real life, some characters are capable of grand accomplishment, while others are not. There is a range of characterization through action, from the superhero, like Heracles who conquers all obstacles, down to the villain or the lowest kind of character, like the wicked stepmothers and stepsisters in fairy tales. Actions of characters in literature place them in a hierarchy of heroism, truth, virtue, or, contrastingly, in positions of evil and villainy.

This hierarchy of action is a part of a universal portrayal of heroes of which Joseph L. Henderson, in *Man and His Symbols,* says:

> The myth of the hero is the most common and the best known myth in the world. We find it in the classical mythology of Greece and Rome, in the Middle Ages, in the Far East, and among contemporary primitive tribes. It also appears in our dreams. It has an obvious dramatic appeal, and a less obvious, but nonetheless profound, psychological importance.[18]

In children's literature, the range of characterizations in the hierarchy, like that of all literature, places the superhero at the top. Heracles is the son of Zeus and a mortal woman. In his progress as a hero, Heracles is assigned 12 incredibly difficult tasks to prove himself worthy of his role. He must perform such labors

---

[18] Joseph L. Henderson, "Ancient Myths and Modern Man," in *Man and His Symbols,* Carl Jung, ed. (Garden City, N.Y.: Doubleday & Co., 1964), p. 110. Reprinted by permission.

as first killing the Nemean lion—whose skin is invulnerable to stone, brass, and iron—to lastly dragging the dog Cerberus up from the underworld. In fulfilling these tasks, through his great cunning, strength, and also through the aid of the gods and goddesses, he finally is admitted to his full status of godhood. He is a character at the top of the scale of potentiality, since his beginnings were half divine, but through his own efforts he becomes a member of the pantheon of gods.

In the portrayal of heroes, there is a sense of difference among various alternatives, of different levels of nobility of motive. Heracles, like epic heroes, comes close to the top. An example of one at the bottom of the scale is the stepmother in *Snow White,* who is punished for attempting to murder her stepdaughter by being forced to dance in red hot iron shoes until she falls dead. Love and noble energy elevate characters in the hierarchy; envy and pride cast them to the bottom.

The question of individual action against an obstacle is another aspect of the same type of characterization. In comparison with Heracles or the fairy tale prince heroes, Peter Rabbit, although lovable, is not a heroic character in his very near brush with death in Mr. McGregor's garden. He is punished by being sent to bed with no supper. The level of his aims, goals, and ambitions, and his inability to fulfill them, place Peter Rabbit's character as hero on a lower plane than Heracles.

To pursue the interaction of plot and character, one of the forms a plot can take is that of journey, quest, test, and succeeding or failing to achieve a goal. It is the hero who performs or fails within the structure of the plot. If the quest within the plot is worthy and noble, such as the rescue of a maiden from a tower, or the restoration of the Greek order (Ulysses' goal), then the character within that framework has before him grand possibilities of heroic action. If, on the other hand, the quest is on a lower level—such as Peter Rabbit stealing lettuce—the character is obviously on a lower plane than that of Ulysses.

Once the reader has a vision of a character's externals—his appearance; his occupation; his tastes and attitudes; his age; where he lives; what he does in his leisure time—then the interpretation can become more sophisticated. If to these is added the sense of purpose and motivation from within the character that will drive him forward in the action of the plot, the reader and the author get together in a value system. It is here that liking or disliking a book usually comes about. If the writer is successful, the reader becomes a part of the world which has been created for him. If there is a great variation in value systems, or if the reader does not identify with the plot, then a book fails.

One major problem in judging children's books is to discover whether or not the world of the book matches, meets, adds to, or speaks to the life-style of the child. The sensitivity of the teacher, parent, or librarian determines this. Every human being comes from a different cultural environment. Although we can make great pronouncements about Western culture or Eastern culture, the books one is interested in must add to one's own home and neighborhood experiences. The reason we cannot give formulas for judging books from this viewpoint is because no two authors of a book on children's literature can know all the cultural variants in the United States. This is where you, as a guide, will function. This is where your knowledge of the life-style of your children governs the selection of books for them.

Back to characterization. Another perspective of a character is gained through his language, his speech patterns as revealed in narrative, a language suited to the world of the plot. Speech, along with description and action, reveals a character. Various attitudes and kinds of personality can be associated with a dialect. Through a dialect, the author can delineate a character with a certain kind of personality.

Two examples from *The Hobbit* show the use of dialect to enhance the picture of a character. In this novel, when Bilbo Baggins and the dwarves set out on their journey to restore the golden treasure, they observe and overhear three trolls sitting around their campfire:

> Obviously trolls. Even Bilbo, in spite of his sheltered life, could see that: from the great heavy faces of them, and their size, and the shape of their legs, not to mention their language, which was not drawing-room fashion at all.
>
> "Mutton yesterday, mutton today, and blimey if it don't look like mutton again tommorrer," said one of the trolls.
>
> "Never a blinking bit of manflesh have we had for long enough," said a second. "What the 'ell William was athinkin' of to bring us into these parts at all, beats me—and the drink runnin' short, what's more," he said jogging the elbow of William, who was taking a pull on his jug.
>
> William choked, "Shut yer mouth!" he said as soon as he could. "Yer can't expect folk to stop here forever just to be et by you and Bert."[19]

Although these are trolls who are complaining of their lack of a human to add to their stew, the Cockney dialect (*blimey, blinking, yer, et*) creates a picture of dissipated, snarling, pirate types with a jug of grog between them. Tolkien, by giving the trolls a human dialect, makes them more accessible to the imagination than the usual stock figure of the troll, as in, for example, *The Three Billy Goats Gruff*, where the monster has no really distinctive speech pattern nor is presented in rich descriptive detail.

Later in *The Hobbit*, another imaginary creature enters the action, the slimy troglodyte Gollum, who has his own personal dialect:

> Suddenly up came Gollum and whispered and hissed:
>
> "Bless us and splash up my preciousness! I guess it's a choice feast; at least a tasty morsel it'd make us, gollum!" And when he said *gollum* he made

---

[19] J. R. R. Tolkien, *The Hobbit* (Boston: Houghton Mifflin Co., 1966), p. 46. Reprinted by permission of Houghton Mifflin Company.

a horrible swallowing noise in his throat. That is how he got his name, though he always called himself "my precious."[20]

It comes as no surprise that a character who calls himself "my precioussss" presents no threat to Bilbo, and that he will he unable to keep the born adventurer Baggins from getting the ring away from him.

As another example of how the language of a character reveals his personality, consider these words of the White Rabbit in *Alice in Wonderland*:

The White Rabbit. Illustrated by John Tenniel.

[20] *Ibid.*, pp. 79–80.

The Duchess! The Duchess! Oh my dear paws! Oh my fur and whiskers! She'll get me executed, as sure as ferrets are ferrets! Where *can* I have dropped them, I wonder![21]

This is a fop who is so caught up in his worry about being late for the Duchess' party that he cannot find his gloves. If, for the moment, we compare him with Heracles when he fulfilled the labors of the gods, it is obvious that the rabbit's excessive concern over being late for the party characterizes him as a parvenu social climber. The rabbit is the man invited to fill the vacant place at the table: he is never the main guest. The rabbit, one can assume, is tolerated as an extra body at a social gathering. And all of this is gleaned merely from what he says.

Other characters in *Alice in Wonderland* reveal themselves through their speech. In the chapter called "A Mad Tea Party," Alice has the following conversation with the March Hare, the Mad Hatter, and the Dormouse:

> ... "Why is a raven like a writing-desk?" "Come, we shall have some fun now!" thought Alice. "I'm glad they've begun asking riddles—I believe I can guess that," she added aloud. "Do you mean that you think you can find out the answer to it?" said the March Hare. "Exactly so," said Alice. "Then you should say what you mean," the March Hare went on. "I do," Alice hastily replied; "at least—I mean what I say—that's the same thing, you know." "Not the same thing a bit!" said the Hatter.
>
> "Why, you might just as well say that 'I see what I eat' is the same thing as 'I eat what I see'!"
>
> "You might just as well say," added the March Hare, "that 'I like what I get 'is the same thing as 'I get what I like'!"
>
> "You might just as well say," added the Dormouse, which seemed to be talking in its sleep, "that 'I breathe when I sleep' is the same thing as 'I sleep when I breathe'!"

Here the March Hare and the Hatter reverse everything that Alice says. Their reliance on illogic in their language shows them as creatures of Wonderland and characterizes them as members of a world where the ordinary rules of discourse and logic are overthrown and nonsense prevails.

Dialogue between characters makes them viable in the reader's imagination. They speak in their own language and terms, as characters do in the movies or on television, where various regional dialects represent different characters. For instance, Texans, with their diphthongs, usually are seen as ingenuous and vulnerable; British accents are associated with refinement and breeding; French accents suggest worldliness and glamour; and a Midwestern twang is the key

---

[21] Lewis Carroll, *Alice's Adventures in Wonderland* (New York: New American Library, 1960), p. 38.

to a hard-bitten, stolid character. Thus, one way to evaluate the completeness and characterization of literature is to consider the extent the author uses dialogue and dialect to create effect and a vivid sense of presence.

As a further example of this technique of creating vitality in literature through the characters' language examine this passage from Scott O'Dell's *Island of the Blue Dolphins:*

> My leg hurt so much by the time I had reached the house that it was hard for me to crawl under the fence and move aside the heavy rock. For five suns I could not go out because my leg had swollen so badly and I had no herbs with which to treat it. I had enough food to eat, but on the third day the water in the basket ran low. Two days later the basket was empty. It was necessary then for me to go to the spring in the ravine.[22]

This speech's stark sentences show a person with no leisure for more ornamented expression, one who gives a sense of being at the edge of survival. The phrase "for five suns" indicates that the character is an American Indian, complementing the overall theme of the book, which is the oppression of Indian by the white man. The speech also reveals a character who is extremely rational, with no frivolity of nature, and who therefore will have the strenth of will to conquer the problems of surviving totally alone in the hostile wilderness.

Apart from the construction of character through description, illustration, action, and speech pattern, it is also possible to rely on the symbolic nature of a character. In fables and in other stories, animals, for example, can be characterized by the details of their existence in nature—how they survive, how they look, how they behave. Because turtles are slow, rabbits fast but unpredictable, oysters pleasant but helpless, cats mysterious, such traits often characterize animals in a children's story. The personality of the animal projected on the basis of his true natural attributes makes it possible to ascribe human thoughts and significance to creatures who, in fact, do not possess them. The author or reader observes the correspondence between the appearance and nature of an animal and translates that symbolic possibility into the action of a narrative, which is an imaginative creation. When we read of the tortoise and the hare or of the characters Rat, Badger, Mole, and Toad in the *Wind in the Willows,* we are encountering animal characters who symbolize certain kinds of human actions such as vanity, perseverance, honesty, and generosity.

Characterization and plot are two of the three most important aspects of literature. But the foremost determinant of literary effectiveness is language. Only through language can literature communicate; whether written or spoken, the essence of literature is always verbal. And the consideration of the kinds and uses of language to create the effects literature achieves is called *style.*

---

[22] Scott O'Dell, *Island of the Blue Dolphins* (Boston: Houghton Mifflin Company, 1960), p. 86. Reprinted by permission.

Style

The author's choice among the almost infinite possibilities of vocabulary and syntax a language offers determines his style and his effect upon his audience. "Proper words in proper places makes the true definition of style,"[23] according to Swift. The wide choice of words and their position in a sentence allows the author to create an immense panorama of tones, moods, images, and finally the composite world of his literary expression.

Even in the simple comparison of the two statements, "The dawn came" and "Came the dawn," different effects are achieved through the differences in syntax, or how words are put together. The first statement is more direct and declarative than the second. Because poetry uses reversed syntax more often than prose, the statement "Came the dawn" is said to be in a more "poetic" style than "The dawn came." And even with the same syntax, a change in vocabulary will create a different effect: "The morning came" is somewhat the same statement as "The dawn came," but the word "dawn" seems more "poetic" than the word "morning" because "morning" is a more general term; the special kind of expression associated with poetry is usually more precise.

A statement, whatever its literal meaning, can create strikingly different effects through variations, either in vocabulary, syntax, or both. For example, the following hypothetical cosmetic ads say basically the same thing—"Dye your hair red." But each statement arouses different feelings due to their different connotations, or associated meanings:

> Be Red-haired!
> Be Titian-haired!
> Be Carrot-topped!
> Be Copper-headed!
> Be Ravishing-red!

The first statement is rather plain and factual. The second, however, has a connotation which is both grand and artistic, associated with the painter Titian, who used a certain hue of red, which is to be associated with the splendor of the hair. This statement connotes a kind of aloof glamour, perhaps that of a goddess. The third statement has an altogether different connotation: the head of hair is compared to the lowly carrot, the color of which is more orange than the color of the hair. Somehow this statement denigrates the beauty of the hair, demeaning it by association with a commonplace object. The fourth statement would be even less appealing as a description, since a Copperhead is a snake. The fifth statement is what the ad writer probably would use. Here he creates a sexual allure for red hair. He makes it pleasant to say, or poetic, by using alliteration and thereby creates a name women won't forget at the cosmetic counter, which may also give him a copyright to or exclusive use of the term if the ad proves successful. The advertising copywriter

---

[23] Quoted in Ross Winterowd, *Rhetoric: A Synthesis* (New York: Holt, Rinehart and Winston, 1968), p. 86.

clearly would be lost without a clear understanding of the connotative value of language.

The connotations and effect of certain styles are often associated with the particular form of literature in which they appear. For instance, prose fiction and epic poetry do not always use the same syntax and vocabulary. For example, consider these two passages:

Epic (Beowulf)	*Prose fiction (The Boy Who Took Care of the Pigs)*
Then over the sea-waves, blown by the wind, the foam-necked boat traveled, most like a bird, until at good time on the second day the curved prow had come to where the seafarers could see land, the seacliffs shine, towering hills, great headlands. Then was the sea crossed, the journey at end. Then quickly the men of the Geats climbed upon the shore, moored the wooden ship; mail shirts rattled, dress for battle. They thanked God that the waveway had been easy for them.[24]	Juanito, the boy who took care of the pigs, was six years old. His father and mother were very poor. They all lived in a small house made of mud and stones. It had a straw roof. Inside, there was only one room and there was no floor. The ground was their floor. They cooked and they kept themselves warm with a fire which they made every day in the middle of the room.[25]

It is apparent that the word order in the epic differs from that of prose fiction. Also, the vocabulary of the two passages is not the same. The style, then, of each clearly adds to its intended effect. The effect of the epic passage is of solemn grandeur; the passage from the short story is almost like a newspaper report because of its direct, simple syntax and vocabulary.

The lines from the epic also show a greater use of figurative language than those of the short story. Such expressions from the epic as *wave-way* (meaning *sea*) and *foam-necked* (meaning that the waves break against the prow of the ship), are uses of language which give a heightened visual impression of the scene. They are of descriptive value because they point to special aspects of the view the writer describes.

Figurative language is based upon similarities. Metaphors, the direct comparison of two objects, such as those in the opening of *The Highwayman,* create vivid descriptions by associating one part of the scene with a similar and corresponding image:

---

[24] Reprinted from *Beowulf,* A New Prose Translation by E. Talbot Donaldson. By permission of W. W. Norton & Company, Inc. Copyright © 1966 by W. W. Norton & Company, Inc.

[25] Reprinted from *The Boy Who Could Do Anything,* text © 1942, renewed 1969, by Anita Brenner, a Young Scott Book, by permission of Addison-Wesley Publishing Company.

> The wind was a torrent of darkness
>   among the gusty trees,
> The moon was a ghostly galleon
>   tossed upon cloudy seas,
> The road was a ribbon of moonlight
>   over a purple moor. . . .[26]

The wind's sound is compared with the sound of a river; the moon looks like a ship and the sky like the ocean; the road looks like a ribbon. These metaphors say much more than "It was dark and the moon was shining while the wind blew."

The language the author uses to portray the entire sensual experience of a scene or action in literature relies upon all of the connotative and affective qualities of language and their power to affect the reader. Because feelings are nonverbal experiences and as such are difficult to communicate to others, analogies, comparisons, and images for them are needed so the reader can sense the flavor of a moment. As an example of this, in *The Wind in the Willows,* spring is associated with rebirth, reawakening, new life, and the power of nature. Such feelings, intangible in themselves, become immediate to a reader when described in language that creates or conjures a visual and sensually accessible scene. In chapter III, *The Wild Wood,* Mole sits dreaming of the springtime and summer that have passed. In his imagination, he plays back over the entrance of spring; his feelings are told by the author in language that evokes a similar mood in the reader:

> The pageant of the river bank had marched steadily along, unfolding itself in scene-pictures that succeeded each other in stately procession. Purple loose-strife arrived early, shaking luxuriant tangled locks along the edge of the mirror whence its own face laughed back at it. Willow-herb, tender and wistful, like a pink sunset cloud, was not slow to follow. Comfrey, the purple hand-in-hand with the white, crept forth to take its place in the line; and at last one morning the diffident and delaying dog-rose stepped delicately on the stage, and one knew, as if string-music had announced it in stately chords that strayed into a gavotte, that June at last was here. One member of the company was still awaited; the shepherd-boy for the nymphs to woo, the knight for whom the ladies waited at the window, the prince that was to kiss the sleeping summer back to life and love.[27]

The language of this descriptive passage compares the entrance of summer to a religious–dramatic presentation in the theatre. The words "pageant," "march,"

---

[26] Noyes, *The Highwayman,* p. 131.
[27] Kenneth Grahame, *The Wind in the Willows* (New York: Charles Scribner's Sons, 1954), p. 45. Reprinted by permission.

and "stately procession" in the first sentences set the tone of the movement of minor characters in the action first and then later the most important as the full company moves onto the stage. There is first "purple loosestrife," then "willow-herb," then "comfrey," all described in terms of the colors of their costumes as they move onto the stage. Purple and white convey the religious undertones of the scene and equate the sanctity of nature with the sanctity and power of a religious drama. Music is suggested in the gavotte which heralds the entrance of summer. And, as in the theatre, where the most important character in a processional enters last, summer follows all the preludes to his entrance. As a concept, summer is perhaps vague and illusory to the imagination. But as represented in the visible images of this passage, it becomes a dramatic character: here in this passage, after the progress of the others, the first sign of spring is the early blossoming of various flowers. Finally, as the pastoral setting is developed, the shepherd-boy enters—the "knight" and the "prince." As the shepherd-boy and the knight and the prince are identified with summer, the kiss of the prince and knight will re-awaken the maiden earth from her sleep of winter. Within this passage, then, rather than saying "Summer has arrived," there is a sense of the feeling of the entrance of the hero, of the arrival of the main character in the theatre, of the promised happiness of the entrance of a lover, and of the power he will have to restore "life and love." Associating the prince, shepherd, and knight with summer creates the necessary connotation to give this scene power.

Style, then, by the choice of associated meanings, allows the author to make the scene before the reader as visible as that seen on a stage. Indeed, the scene presented by a writer is usually more immediate, because of the greater sensitivity of the literary artist's perceptions and arrangement of them into the symbols of language. Art clarifies the vision of the world by heightening the perceptions that the senses ordinarily may distort or ignore.

In a descriptive or an evocative passage in literature, the progression of objects described also will create a feeling equal to or greater than that of actually taking part in an experience in the real world. In Chapter 3 of *Charlotte's Web*, the reader enters a barn with Fern and Wilbur:

> The barn was very large. It was very old. It smelled of hay and it smelled of manure. It smelled of the perspiration of tired horses and the wonderful sweet breath of patient cows. It often had a sort of peaceful smell—as though nothing bad could happen ever again in the world. It smelled of grain and of harness dressing and of axle grease and of rubber boots and of new rope. And whenever the cat was given a fish-head to eat, the barn would smell of fish. But mostly it smelled of hay, for there was always hay in the great loft overhead. And there was always hay being pitched down to the cows and the horses and the sheep.[28]

---

[28] White, *Charlotte's Web*, p. 13.

When approaching a barn, the broad outlines of its shape and its general appearance will be the first impressions made on the senses. Here the description begins with this general, overall glimpse of the barn as "large" and "old." Standing before it, the first sense impression would probably be that of the smell, and the two most dominant smells of a barn are hay and manure, as in the first line of the description above. Because it takes a moment to separate one smell from another, the description moves from the overriding smell of hay and manure to the more subtle odors of "the perspiration of tired horses and the wonderful sweet breath of patient cows." This gives a sense of the spatial and temporal dimensions of looking at the barn first, then moving closer, waiting, and then moving on through its doors. The smell of cows' breath may even be imaginary, but its description evokes the real experience of standing in the barn and perceiving its surroundings. As the description moves on to an interpretation of the odors—a "sort of peaceful smell, as though nothing bad could ever happen," the barn takes on the guise of a place of sanctuary and safety. The barn becomes the world of the plot in *Charlotte's Web,* and the description of the barn goes on to give more and more details of the smells of the barn: the "smell of the grease," "the boots," and "the fish-head given the cat," create a sense of the daily life and movement and existence and activities carried on in the barn. Later in this same chapter, more and more visual details are added to those of smell, and a list of the kinds of objects seen in the barn is given:

> ladders, grindstones, pitch forks, monkey wrenches, scythes, lawn mowers, snow shovels, ax handles, milk pails, water buckets, empty grain sacks, and rusty rat traps.[29]

This kind of cataloging and compression of visual and sensual detail actually involves the reader in the world that is the setting for the plot, characters, and action. For the feeling of literature to transmit itself to the reader, this power and feeling in language must be apparent. Otherwise, the world and experiences contained in a book will remain flat and one dimensional.

Style provides an infinity of moods, tones, and evocative possibilities; it separates the great writer who can exploit the riches of language from the poor writer who remains on its periphery. As an exercise, the reader can turn directly to many of the books listed in Part IV's bibliography. By comparing different genres—poetry, prose, fiction, informational books, and so on—and even several versions of the same folk tale, the reader can sharpen his own sense of style.

---

[29] *Ibid.,* p. 14.

Archetype   Perhaps the greatest discovery of modern literary criticism is the universal and universally apparent patterns of imagery, of structure, of character, and of plot that continually reappear in all literature. Studies of the folk tales of many cultures show striking similarities of form, plot, and character. In many cases, the tales are so diverse that one could never have been the source of the other. Studies of myths also reveal universal concerns, kinds of execution, and values in all cultures. We call these universal patterns of form and structure *archetypes*. Indeed, modern psychology is built on the premise that human thinking works in universal patterns of imagery, leading to the conclusion that all humans look at the world in similar ways.

In literature the archetype is of special force in creating an affective response. Archetypes are deeply and necessarily related to the way humans think, and what it means to be human. The psychologist Jung describes archetypes as part of the symbol-making propensities of man.

Such symbolic structures in literature are closely allied to the natural and universal human desire to characterize and organize life into meaningful images and symbols. Archetypes in literature go directly to the heart of the matter—creating an understanding of reality.

Because the developing intellect of the child is itself striving toward a definite picture of the world, archetypes are of special value in childhood literature. The fact that fairy tales and folk tales are closely related to older myths, which themselves are of a metaphysical and religious character, explains the concentration of archetypes in these forms. Childhood literature, when a part of the great traditions of symbol making, puts the child in touch with what all peoples from the beginning of the human experience have seen as the picture of reality.

There are many archetypes. To describe them all is beyond the scope of this book, but the concept itself can be described in general terms, with specific examples emerging as we probe more deeply into the various genres of literature. Northrup Frye has demonstrated that the most basic characteristic of archetypes is to create a direct relationship between the seasons and human experiences. He gives the following four phases of archetypal structure:

1. The dawn, spring, and birth phase. Myths of the birth of the hero, of revival and resurrection, of creation, and (because the four are a cycle) of the defeat of the powers of darkness, winter and death. Subordinate characters: the father and the mother. The archetype of romance and of most dithyrambic and rhapsodic poetry.
2. The zenith, summer, and marriage or triumph phase. Myths of apotheosis, of the sacred marriage, and of entering into Paradise. Subordinate characters: the companion and the bride. The archetype of comedy, pastoral, and idyll.
3. The sunset, autumn, and death phase. Myths of fall, of the dying god, of violent death and sacrifice, and of the isolation of the hero. Subordinate characters: the traitor and the siren. The archetype of tragedy and elegy.
4. The darkness, winter, and dissolution phase. Myths of the triumph of these powers; myths of floods and the return of chaos, of the defeat of the hero, and Gotterdämmerung ["Twilight of the Gods"] myths. Subordi-

nate characters: the ogre and the witch. The archetype of satire (see, for instance, the conclusion of *The Dunciad*) .[30]

In the portrayal through archetypes, spring is linked with portrayals of youth, of rebirth, of beginnings; summer with triumph; autumn with tragedy; winter with death. Let's consider a few examples of such characterizations. Consider this use of springtime in the Prologue to *The Canterbury Tales* of Chaucer, quoted here from a special edition for children by A. Kent Hieatt and Constance Hieatt:

> When the showers of April bathe the earth and nourish a fresh crop of grass and flowers, and when the west wind stirs the new leaves budding on the trees, the birds return to us from their winter homes and make the warm days merry with their music. This is the time, too, when people long to journey to distant shores and to make pilgrimages to faraway holy places in strange lands.[31]

Here the rebirth of the grass and flowers is analogous to the travellers' desire to make pilgrimages. Further, the pilgrimages the travellers are about to undertake are to thank their patron saints for having helped them through the winter phase of sickness and death; spring brings the defeat of the powers of sickness, or winter, in the same way the earth buds once more into spring. As the new life of the year begins, so those who have survived winter once more long to make their journey.

If we take another look at *The Wind in the Willows,* we see this same use of spring as the archetype of beginnings:

> Spring was moving in the air above and in the earth below and around him, penetrating even his dark and lowly little house with its spirit of divine discontent and longing. It was small wonder, then, that he [Mole] suddenly flung down his brush on the floor, said "Bother!" and "O blow!" and also, "Hang spring-cleaning!" and bolted out of the house without even waiting to put on his coat. Something up above was calling him imperiously. . . .[32]

Mole's initiation into the world outside is equated with the reawakening of earth. His sudden decision to leave his hole and to embrace the world above is characterized by using the archetype of spring—his new awareness of life is as great as

---

[30] Northrop Frye, in "The Archtypes of Literature" in *Fables of Identity* (New York: Harcourt Brace Jovanovich, Inc., 1963) , p. 16. Reprinted by permission.

[31] Used by permission of Golden Press from *The Canterbury Tales* of Geoffrey Chaucer translated by A. Kent Hieatt and Constance Hieatt. Copyright 1961 by Western Publishing Company, Inc.

[32] Kenneth Grahame, *The Wind in the Willows,* p. 1.

the power with which the life of nature begins again. Think how the author might have demeaned Mole's entry into adventure if he had written instead something like "Mole decided to go upstairs for a quick smoke and a coffee break." This would have created an entirely different—and less exalted—impression. Something as large as nature, indeed perhaps larger, has called Mole to itself. And surely the dark hole in which he has always lived can be seen as a kind of blindness, or hiding from experience (the choice of a mole for this character is thus no accident) . Mole under the ground is like a seed in the earth—spring calls them both to life and action.

Two more examples of the use of season archetypes are seen here:

It was the spring of hope, it was the winter of despair.
—Charles Dickens, *A Tale of Two Cities*

My way of life
Is fall'n into the sere, the yellow leaf. . . .
—Shakespeare, *Macbeth*

Dickens equates spring with hope, and winter with despair. The defeated Macbeth sees himself as in the autumn of life, the tragic phase of the archetype.

Why are archetypes important to the critic of children's literature? First, because of the ancient nature of the archetype as a way of looking at the world, these patterns of imagery are of vital force in the human tradition. Also, because of their deep psychological nature they stir real emotional responses. Further, because they are so important a tool to the literary artist, so widely and richly used, their recognition is necessary to the interpretation of literature. They are a real part of the symbolism of literary art—learning to see them is an additional way of reaching the whole experience of literature.

To continue the exploration of archetypes, let us introduce an alternative term, *motif*. Both archetypes and motifs are recurrent images, characters, themes, situations, and structures that appear in all literature. From the beginnings of Western literature, for example, the forest has represented a place of danger and evil. Consider how in fairy tales (*Hansel and Gretel* and *Little Red Ridinghood*, to name only two) the forest is a place where one encounters the dangerous witch or wolf—how in the darkness of the trees pitfalls and threats to security lurk.

Notice how the motif of the forest adds to the richness of *Where the Wild Things Are*. When Max has been sent upstairs, he dreams of a forest which grows up in his room. When the boy has gone "in and out of weeks" to "where the Wild Things are," he sees a collection of monsters which at first look like rolling eyes and sharp claws. We know from fairy tales that in the forest children meet wolves and other enemies. But Max has a different experience with the monsters.

We can appreciate its difference from the fairy tale forest only if we first know the archetype of the forest as a place of danger. Here the motif of the forest is changed. Instead of being eaten alive by them, Max becomes friends with the monsters, or Wild Things, by staring into their eyes. By asserting that he is a Wild Thing himself, he becomes master of the situation. His dream concept of himself[33] allows him, first, to restore his self-image to full strength after his bruising encounter with his mother when she sent him to bed, and second, helps him to see the controversy between himself and his mother in a different perspective. When he stares down the Wild Things, he gains the same control over them that his mother has over him. But when they repeat his very phrase by saying they will eat him up, he realizes this is not the way to show love. Also implicit in his relationship of master to the Wild Things is that as the master he is benevolent. Later events in the story prove his mother equally so.

The Wild Things very much want Max to remain—indeed they offer him the same invitation that he gave to his mother, that of eating him alive. Here Max probably can see that his use of this phrase to his mother was not loving. The dream seems to interpret Max's actions for him. Similarly, even a child can realize that we talk to ourselves in our dreams and often see the world differently when we think back on our dreams than we would otherwise.

The terrors of the forest are exorcised—Max finds himself restored to harmony and love at the end of the episode when his mother brings him his supper. The forest is the archetype of the place where the dangerous confrontation between reality and self must take place. If you can win in the forest—and it is through the archetype we know from the fairy tale that we realize the dangers of the woods—then you can win in the real world. In this story, as in the fairy tale, the way one wins in the forest is through courage and love.

Small children are aware of frightening places—dark rooms, the night, anywhere that mysterious noises seem to threaten one from every corner. They are also aware of how love in the form of a parent is what restores the safety and security of the known. The meaning of the tale about Max is enriched through the use of archetype. The forest is a place of real terror in its traditional use as motif or archetype. That Max achieves a victory over the monsters is quite a triumph over evil. Because it is his own assertion of identity that tames the monsters, we can see that his identity is strong.

Similarly, in *The Wind in the Willows,* the Wild Wood represents a frightening place in which there are continual mysterious rustlings among the leaves. It is the power of friendship among Badger, Rat, and Mole that drives away the weasels who are the cause of the noise. And, to portray the victory over darkness and fear, the story ends in summer, the archetype of triumph and fulfillment:

---

[33] The notion that dreams are essential as (1) fulfillment of wishes and desire, and (2) revealers of self is common knowledge among modern readers. Psychoanalysis, for example, is predicated on this. And, in the twentieth century, literature and psychology are closely linked. Browse through Freud's *The Interpretation of Dreams.*

> Sometimes, in the course of long summer evenings, the friends would take a stroll together in the Wild Wood, now successfully tamed so far as they were concerned; and it was pleasing to see how respectfully they were greeted by the inhabitants.[34]

In both stories the forest serves as motif and archetype of the unknown and dangerous.

Archetypal Plots

In plots there are similar and recurrent situations and circumstances that are archetypes and motifs. A theme which seems to reappear again and again is that of rags-to-riches, a plot motif we associate with *Cinderella.* Another recurrent plot is that of the hero who journeys into the unknown, encounters a monster or other peril, saves himself from this danger, and finally returns home wiser than when he left. The plot of Potter's *Peter Rabbit* follows this motif. The major source of archetypes and motifs in plots is folklore; Chapter 2 treats the types of archetypes and motifs in folklore more fully.

Archetypal Characters

These archetypal plot themes find their representation in corresponding archetypal characters. Cinderella is so associated with the motif of the orphan who through virtue rises in the world that her name is a symbol for this kind of success. A comparison can be made to the *Mona Lisa;* just as she symbolizes enigmatic calm, Cinderella similarly indicates virtue rewarded. In fables, various animal characters are archetypes of the human actions they symbolize: the ant is industry; the fox is cunning; and the wolf and the tiger are the threats encountered in the wild woods.

These motifs and themes, universal in literature both for children and adults, give further proof of the continuity and fullness of the family of literature. Archetypes also serve as a constant strand through the development of literary awareness, from first encounters as youngsters to the mature understanding that grows from a lifetime of reading.

An examination of the plot in terms of unity and structure will focus attention upon what is discrete from the story. An awareness of the archetypes and motifs used by a writer gives the added dimension of the literary tradition behind the work. If, for example, a writer uses thorn imagery, he probably will be doing so with reference to the archetypal image of thorns as worldly obstacles, as apparent in Jesus' crown of thorns or in the thorn hedge around Sleeping Beauty's castle.

---

[34] Kenneth Grahame, *The Wind in the Willows,* p. 258.

Such uses of tradition in literature add a great richness to the statement a single literary work can make. A book written today can become a meeting-place of much that has been thought or said in the past—for instance *Where the Wild Things Are* and *The Divine Comedy,* which begins in a forest, share the archetype of the forest. Archetypes and motifs place childhood literature in the great traditions of Western literature.

Summary

In Part One of *A New Look at Children's Literature,* we have surveyed a number of the concepts useful in examining literature. In summary, these are language, plot, character, and archetype. With these basic concepts in mind, we shall proceed to the various special types of literature. While we are examining the literature itself, it will also be appropriate to consider how such works might be presented to children. Thus, in the chapters to follow there will be some mixing of pedagogy with literary criticism. After all, if a question arises whether children can absorb certain literary concepts, why not deal with it on the spot?

As we said at the beginning, literature is a vast area to cover. We make no claim of analyzing or even noting every title that has appeared for children. The absurdity of such an undertaking is obvious. What we intend is to inculcate in an adult, who is in turn going to work with children, a really effective critical method of understanding how good literature works.

For additional studies of literary criticism see *The Anatomy of Criticism* by Northrop Frye; *Criticism: The Major Texts,* edited by Walter Jackson Bate; *Theory of Literature* by Renee Wellek and Robert Penn Warren.

For histories of children's literature, see *Children's Books in England: Five Centuries of Social Life* by F. J. Harvey Darton and *A Critical History of Children's Literature* by Cornelia Meigs, *et al.*

For additional works on children's literature, see *Children and Books* by May Hill Arbuthnot; *Children's Literature in the Elementary Classroom* by Charlotte Huck and Doris Kuhn; *A Critical Approach to Children's Literature* by James Steel Smith; *Books, Children and Men* by Paul Hazard; and *Only Connect,* a series of essays edited by Sheila Egoff.

Part Two
Types and Uses of Children's Literature

2 Mythology, Folklore, and Related Forms

Myth, folk tale, fairy tale, fable, epic, and romance

mythology and folklore spring from an innate human need to interpret and organize experience into the shape and structure of narrative, parable, and image. This fact has become increasingly evident as anthropologists have delineated the many interrelationships that exist among the various mythologies of the world. *The Golden Bough* by Sir James Frazer, *Man and his Symbols* by C. G. Jung, and *The Savage Mind* by Claude Levi-Strauss, among other studies, argue the universality of mythmaking and the strikingly similar concerns and directions in the various myths of the world.

Certain literary critics, notably Jessie L. Weston in *From Ritual to Romance,* Maud Bodkin in *Archetypal Patterns in Poetry,* and Northrop Frye in *The Anatomy of Criticism,* have come to see, largely through the influence of anthropologists, that mythology and folklore are the origin and source of most literary forms and structures. Literature and mythology are two modes of representing human experience which bear the closest kind of relationship to each other.

That there is this universal quality to mythmaking, the origin of literature, argues for the importance of these kinds of representations to human existence. And the fact that mythology and folklore are so prominent in children's literature has actually formed the basis for the first really effective and critical understanding of literature for children. Mythology as the source of literature, coupled with the appeal that myths hold for children, indicates that children's literature is fully in the mainstream of man's symbol-making process.

Myth, folk tale, fairy tale, fable, epic, and romance are of central concern in this book. In this chapter we will consider these traditional forms sequentially— in order to demonstrate their kinship in terms of archetypes and motifs and also to explore further the broader history of children's literature. We will begin with a discussion of myth and mythology, describing essential characteristics, and then explore the significance of mythology in terms of culture, religion, literature, and childhood. Later, we will examine each of the other kinds of literature.

Myth is to be defined as a complex of stories—some no doubt fact, and some fantasy—which, for various reasons, human beings regard as demonstrations of the inner meaning of the universe and of human life. Myth is quite different from philosophy in the sense of abstract concepts—consisting of vivid, sensually intelligible narratives, images, rites, ceremonies, and symbols.[1]

Myth as representation

This definition of myth conveys the manner in which myths are philosophy (and science) in parable.[2] Whereas in philosophy one works with abstract concepts that remain intangible—such as Justice, Virtue, Truth—myth quite literally fleshes out these ideas into the personages of gods, goddesses, and other characters who act out their essential meanings in the context of a story or narrative. Hence, wisdom, only an abstraction to the philosopher, in Greek mythology becomes the the goddess Athena, a woman sprung from the forehead of Zeus, the highest of the gods. As she appears in the Greek myths, dramatically interacting with gods and mortals alike, she portrays the highest mental power, that of the foremost of the gods. What remains remote and sensually nonexistent to the philosopher becomes, in myth, sensually intelligible—felt, seen, heard, known, and familiar. What would otherwise remain unnamed, inaccessible, and vague becomes interesting, viable, and immediate in the parable of a myth.

As a narrative, myth operates on the fundamental assumption that behind the impenetrable face of reality there is pattern, order, causality, will, meaning, and design. Myth posits that there is a life force behind nature that shows purpose, direction, and the power to execute and fulfill a grand scheme. This is why the gods and goddesses of myths, the concrete personages of the concepts of reality, are always associated with religion. Myths "show the inner meaning of the universe" and portray that meaning in vivid, concrete images and action.

In providing a representation of the meaning of the universe, myths organize into the remarkably complete structure of a mythology. In a culture, a myth will not stand single and unique, but will rather hold a clear, logical relationship to the other myths of the culture, thus creating a holistic, all-encompassing picture of nature and of man. Myths form a full vision of life in a pantheon (Gr. *pan*, all; *theo*, a god) ; a complete collection of gods and goddesses forms a comprehensive view of reality. Levi-Strauss calls a mythology a "semantic universe," a structure· of meaning whereby a culture achieves emotional security regarding the baffling forces of physical and human nature.

Several semantic problems can impede a complete understanding of myth, and at this point, some of the difficulties with the term *myth* should be explored. Once misconceptions about myth have been exposed, one can see better the true grandeur of the subject. The first problem encountered in discussing mythology is a tendency to equate the words *myth* and *falsehood*. In ordinary English usage we often call a *lie* a *myth*. We may say of a braggart, "His wealth was all just a

---

[1] Alan Watts, *Myth and Ritual in Christianity* (New York: Vanguard Press, Inc., 1954) . Reprinted by permission.
[2] Geoffrey Parrinder, *African Mythology* (London: Paul Hamlyn, 1967) , p. 15.

myth." This confusion may arise from the fact that myths are not literally true, although they may have some remote basis in fact. As used in this chapter, *myth* derives from the Greek *mythos*, a speech or story, with the special distinction of metaphysical and religious value. Myth as story and narrative is not demonstrably true in scientific terms; myths spring from the imagination, which has its own kind of logic. *Myths* involve a representation of the unknown by projecting a set of other-worldly characters of gods and goddesses along with other imaginative constructs to explain the meaning of the world.

A second difficulty with the term *myth* arises from this first confusion of *myth* with *lie*. Because of the low value we place on falsehood, one tends to resent having cherished beliefs and faiths called myths. Furthermore, as members of an advanced technological society, we may feel uneasy with anything not scientifically demonstrable. We may feel that perhaps the Greeks needed myths because they lacked our scientific sophistication. This is, however, to undervalue the role of the imagination in human life, and, further, it is to be blind to the realities of myth as the dominant source of culture. Myth is neither false nor unimportant. Indeed, we shall see in the course of this chapter that scientific thought is actually at the mercy of the myths of a culture.

Types of myths

There are in general three kinds of myths:

1. Creation myths that explain the origins of the universe and of man.
2. Exemplary or hero myths that show a model of behavior through the portrayal of a hero.
3. Nature myths that account for the operations of the physical environment.

Let us examine some examples of these kinds of myth.

Creation Myths

Creation myths generally begin with the concept of a chaos or void out of which emerges some first primal cause and formation of matter. The forces of creation are associated with specific gods or goddesss in narrative. Three examples of creation myths will be discussed: the Greek creation myth, the Norse creation myth, and a Central American and Mexican Indian creation myth. In the following discussion of the myths, look for the archetypal patterns.

In the Greek creation myth, as told by Hesiod in *The Theogony,* out of void there appeared first the Mother Earth, named Gaea. Other figures also emerged from the void: Eros (love), Erebus (night), and Hemera (day). In the progressive birth of the universe, the most important child of Gaea was Uranus, the sky. Uranus became the husband of Gaea and the father of various races of beings on the earth. This part of the narrative can be seen as a representation of the visual relationship of earth and sky. The sky embraces the earth, and like a husband makes her fertile and fecund with plants engendered and nourished by his rain.

But Uranus has a dual nature in his relationship with earth—at times the gentle and loving gift of rain is changed to the raging storm of apparent battle and hatred. The myth, then, has explained not only the origins of earth and sky, but also why the sky is sometimes peaceful and sometimes turbulent. And, the image of earth and sky as lovers is entirely apt and appropriate compared to the fluctuations of calm and storm that we see in earthly marriages, explaining why nature varies between the poles of peace and anger. In the original account, the story progresses as pure narrative, without any kind of interpretive intrusion.

As the myth continues, the theme of conflict between earth and sky, or Gaea and Uranus, continues. Uranus becomes horrified by his progeny—first, there is the race of Titans; next come the Cyclopes, who are one-eyed monsters; finally come the Giants, who each have fifty heads. It is possible to interpret the children of earth and sky as mountains (Titans), volcanoes (Cyclopes), and trees (Giants with fifty heads), and as they multiply, Uranus fears that they seem ready to impale their father. To protect himself, Uranus thrusts the children back into Mother Earth through storm or lightning, which would erode the earth and level the mountains and trees. Thus, in the logic of the myth, fear for his own safety causes Uranus to wage war on his children and wife, echoing the conflict of earth and sky observable in nature. Clearly, Mother Earth and her children must have won the final battle with Uranus, because all the mountains and trees have reemerged from their mother.

In the myth, Mother Earth persuades Cronus, her last born son, to mutilate his father Uranus. Following Cronus' victory over his father, nature now has achieved an uneasy kind of peace; the sky is somewhat tamed. But not without a price. The Furies, or guilt, rise from the blood of Uranus. Thus, although Earth wins the battle with sky, guilt is the result. Therefore, the state of the universe into which man will finally emerge in the progress of the myth is a place of disquiet and peril, where man is vulnerable to the retribution of the Furies. Or put another way, man is liable to guilt. Original sin?

In the construct of the Greek creation myth, observable details from real life are applied to the perplexing problems of nature and reality—namely how the earth came into being, why nature shows such instability between turbulence and rest, and how human life seems beset by the devastating problems of guilt and anxiety that the Furies symbolize.

After the conflict between Uranus and Cronus (time), successive groups of gods, with Zeus at the top of the hierarchy, are born to various personages in the mythology.

Finally Mother Earth gives birth to the first race of men. These first men are called the golden race and closely resemble the gods; they live in eternal spring. This race die away, however, and are replaced by the silver race. The silver race make the seasons and thus no longer live only in spring. They are the first to build houses. Next come the bronze race, who inherit the seasons from the silver race, but who leave behind them a legacy of war and weapons. Finally the iron race are born. To Zeus, this race of men seem ignoble in comparison with those preceding them, and he decides to destroy them.

Zeus sends a flood to destroy the iron race, but he is thwarted in his attempt to extinguish mankind by one of the gods, Prometheus the Forethinker, who warns two of the best of the iron race, Deukalion and Pyrrha, to build a strong ship to last out the flood. When Zeus sees that Deukalion and Pyrrha are good, he allows them to live. Prometheus then steals fire from Zeus' altar, bringing hideous punishment upon himself, but not before he has taught the new iron race how to fashion tools from iron with the aid of the stolen fire.

Thus, the iron race, aided by forethought and the ability to make tools as well as weapons, inherit the earth. But still, those who are the descendants of Deukalion and Pyrrha are not at the level of the first golden race. They are in a lesser state, having also inherited, in a sense, the worst legacies of the silver and bronze races. The meaning, then, is that with the aid of mind and industry (Prometheus and fire) man can overcome his lower nature and make for himself a culture to control the destructive forces of nature and of man himself.

The Norse creation myth similarly begins with a chasm in which there are two realms, the northern, icy Niflheim, the land of death, and the southern Muspelheim, a place of fire. These two domains are connected by twelve rivers which flow between them, changing to ice as they reach the northern end. The fire from Muspelheim finally melts the ice and from the water is born Ymir, the first Giant. After the creation of the first Giant and the frost maidens, who become the mothers and wives of Ymir's sons, the theme of parent–child conflict is again in evidence. Odin kills his grandfather, Ymir, and from his body are created the earth and sky—the sea is made from his blood, the earth from his body, and the heavens from his skull. Then the first humans are made—the man from an ash tree and the woman from an elm. The creation of the universe continues as the area within Ymir's skull is peopled with the lowly dwarfs—workers and craftsmen—and by the ethereal elves, who are artists and protectors of beauty.

Within the center of the universe is the tree called Yggdrasil which supports the whole structure. Its roots are nourished in a well guarded by three Norns, Urda (the past), Verdandi (the present), and Skuld (the future). Yggdrasil is threatened by a serpent, who gnaws continually at its roots, even though it is protected by Mimir the wise. But the Norse creation myth also contains a prophecy that after the final destruction of this world, another, greater by far, will arise in its place.

In the Norse myth, as in the Greek, there is a theme of conflict between parent and child, between ugliness and beauty, and between good and evil. Although man is capable of overcoming pain through love, human life is carried out in an atmosphere of conflict and struggle between opposing forces. Neither mythology portrays human life in an idealized paradisical form. Indeed, the theme of a lost paradise is a dominant archetype in world mythologies.

In a creation myth from a different culture, that of the Central American and Mexican Indians, there was at first complete silence and boundlessness. In the beginning the gods Tepeu and Gucumatz meditated separately and alone. The Heart of the Sky, Hurakan, sets creation into motion, and Tepeu and Gucumatz form the earth and progressively populate it with the various animals. Finally the gods decide to create men, beginning with men of clay. The clay race prove, however, to be breakable by the buffeting of nature. Next the gods carve men from wood, making creatures who, although durable, nevertheless lack the mind or soul with which to praise the gods. They are destroyed in a flood. The crow and the coyote are enlisted to find the perfect substance from which man should be made. The answer is yellow maize, following logically from observable facts in nature because, after all, this is what sustains life. Once the first men are made, it is indeed evident that they are perfect. Too perfect—because the gods soon become jealous of the threat of these beings. The Heart of the Sky, however, saves man by breathing a cloud into his mind, limiting his visionary capacity and thus protecting him from competition with the gods.

Man in these three mythologies, as in many others, is shown as a creature who has fallen away from an initial paradise, just as the universe itself has descended from initial perfection into a state of conflict. The concept of a lost paradise accounts not only for the polarities of good and evil, only too apparent in reality, but more particularly, these portrayals of the first stages of the universe and of man show a great potential in man's character that can be realized through his own actions. Such aspirations to return to the primeval mythic perfection of man before his fall into the world where his vision is limited, where his forethought is weak, and where he is threatened by the destruction of the tree of wisdom, are shown in the myth of the hero. The hero represents the image of man's potential.

Hero Myths

In the Greek myths, the portrayal of the hero is in the form of a story of great adventure, of test, of trial, and of ultimate victory over almost insuperable obstacles. The great journeys and many escapades of the heroes generate, in fact, the structure and pattern of almost all later storytelling. From the myth to the epic to the folk tale, the hero, because of his stature, established by his parentage and by his actions, is able to survive an amazing number of miraculous brushes with disaster. Such episodes form the plot of the hero myth and also of the folk tale and the epic.

The character of the hero, as in all literature, is revealed through a description of his parentage, his appearance, through his actions, and through his success in dealing with the problems that present themselves to him, as can be seen in the Greek myth of Perseus.

Perseus is born to Danäe after she has been visited by Zeus in a shower of gold while she is in prison. Perseus is therefore half divine, like Heracles, the child of Arcmene and Zeus. The semidivine child has great possibilites for transcending the human condition. He is above the usual restrictions placed upon mortals.

Danäe's father has heard a prophecy that his daughter will bear a son who will kill him, recalling the earlier myth of Cronus and Uranus. Fearing to kill Danäe and Perseus, he sends the two away to sea in an ark from which they are rescued in a land where Perseus grows up to fulfill his destiny as a hero. The archetype of the story of the divine child who is cast out to sea and rescued by a protective guardian is one which occurs in numerous mythologies. The semidivine child is seemingly always within the favor of the gods and he always receives their attention and help.

When Perseus has grown to manhood, he is forced to present a wedding gift to the king who rescued him and his mother from the sea. In a rash moment, Perseus promises that he can win the head of the Gorgon Medusa for the present. Medusa is a creature cursed with snakes for hair and with a terrifying ugliness that turns all who look upon her into stone. With the necessary help from the goddess Athena, aid to which Perseus is entitled because of his kinship to the gods, he obtains a pair of winged sandals from the Stygian Nymphs by first stealing the single eye and tooth the three share among themselves, thus forcing them to give him what he needs for his journey. Suitably equipped, Perseus leaves on his quest to win the head of Medusa. When he finds Medusa, Athena guides his hand, and by looking at Medusa's shield instead of her face he saves himself and cuts off her head. In returning home with it, he escapes several attempts on his life by holding up the head and petrifying his enemies with fright. Thus he is enabled, among other adventures, to rescue the beautiful Andromeda who was chained to a rock as a sacrifice to a sea monster. Perseus finally returns to his first home and eventually becomes king upon the death of his grandfather.

In this story the first element is that of the charisma and power of the hero. This is first indicated by his semidivine nature, because he is the son of a god. Second, the hero's destiny has the apparent blessing of the gods, as seen in his rescue from attempts to kill him. The hero also shows great purpose and undertakes a quest to fulfill a noble task. In the case of Perseus this is seen in the killing of the Gorgon Medusa and the freeing of Andromeda from the rock. He has the power to do all of these things, and in fulfilling his quest, accomplishes a grand destiny.

The Greek hero Theseus also shows an early propensity for his role as hero. As an infant, Theseus is left in a distant country by his father, Aegeus, who must return to Athens to defend his throne. The father leaves his son a sword and his sandals, symbols of office, under a rock. He tells Theseus' mother that when the boy can lift the rock he must come to Athens to aid his father. When

Theseus is eighteen, he is able to lift the rock, thus demonstrating his emergence as a hero. He goes to the aid of his father and in the course of his journey kills all of the miscreants and villains he meets on the way—Sinis, who ties unwary travelers to bent pine trees and rips them in two, and Procrustes, who urges his tired guests to lie down on a bed to which he fits them by stretching or cutting off their hands and feet.

After these adventures, when Theseus arrives in Athens, he frees his father from the spell of a witch and then immediately leaves for Crete to conquer the Minotaur, a monster who has carried away many Athenian youths. The Minotaur is enclosed in a labyrinth made by the master craftsman Daedalus, from which no one can escape. When Theseus is placed in the maze, the king's daughter, Ariadne, gives him a ball of string, one end of which he leaves at the maze's entrance and follows back again to safety, after he has killed the Minotaur. Theseus then takes Ariadne with him and returns home to Athens.

Here, again, the hero has a quest he must fulfill, a role for which he is fated and aided in by the gods, and in the course of which he encounters numerous adventures that are, in a sense, a test of his strength, courage, and purpose. In the course of overcoming lesser obstacles, Theseus is made capable of the final great one killing of the Minotaur. And like the fairy tale prince, he is rewarded with marriage to the Princess Ariadne.

Jason, like Perseus and Theseus, comes to his role as hero through the favor of the gods and goddesses. The child Jason is threatened with murder by his uncle, Pelias, the usurper of his father's kingdom but is saved and spirited away by a Centaur, a creature half horse and half man, who raises and trains the young prince in a manner suitable to his future role as king. Jason finally sets out to seek his fortune. At a river bank he meets an old woman whom he carries across, only to find that she is the goddess, Hera, the wife of Zeus. She discovers that he is her chosen one because he now wears only one sandal, which also reveals his identity to Pelias, the usurper king.

In order to test his courage and, doubtless, expecting to be rid of Jason, Pelias commands him to embark upon a quest to bring home the golden fleece from Colchis, an ornament stolen from the magic ram. With a company of heroes, Jason leaves for Colchis and encounters many adventures similar to those of the other heroes described above. In one of the stories of Jason and his crew, their ship must sail between blue rocks that clash together and crush every ship trying to pass through them. Jason overcomes this obstacle by sending a heron through first and darting between the rocks when they rebound after attempting to close on the bird. In this incident, Jason shows the same kind of cunning Heracles demonstrates when he diverts a river to clean out the Augean stable.

The heroes reach Colchis. But here Jason's career goes in a different direction from that of Perseus and Theseus. Jason falls under the spell of the witch–goddess, Medea, who helps him steal the golden fleece from her father in return for taking her back to Greece with him. After they have stolen the fleece from its sacred garden, Medea and Jason are pursued at sea by her father, the king.

But Medea stops the pursuit by killing her brother and scattering pieces of his body in the ocean, knowing that her father will stop to gather them for decent burial.

Medea's crime betrays the nobility of Jason's quest. By allowing himself to come under the witch's spell, the rest of Jason's life is spent under a shadow of tragedy. He and Medea finally wander to Corinth, where Jason decides to marry the princess Glauce, to become king. Medea, in vengeance, kills their two children and disposes of Glauce by giving her a magic wedding dress which burns her to death the instant it is put on. This particular motif also appears in the folk tale "Snow White" when the stepmother is given red-hot iron shoes in which to dance to her death.

If the hero does not fulfill his quest by passing tests at a heroic level, then tragedy results for him. The dominant hero in Central American and Mexican myth is Quetzalcoatl, the plumed serpent, a creature who is half snake and half bird, making him an emblematic figure composed of the earth, represented by the serpent, and of the flowing characteristic of the air, represented by the upper bird part of him.

Quetzalcoatl brings to man the knowledge of how to plant maize. Just as Prometheus brought the gift of fire, forethought, and tool-making ability to mankind, Quetzalcoatl also teaches cultivation and brings wisdom. But Quetzalcoatl is not the same kind of hero as Perseus and Theseus. He is rather more like Jason in that an inherent weakness finally disqualifies him from his role of hero. He has an enemy, Tezcatlipoca, who drives him away from earth by changing himself into a jaguar. The battle between the two recalls the idea implicit in creation myths of the embattled and turbulent nature of human existence.

But although Quetzalcoatl leaves earth and becomes the evening star, his importance lies in his symbolization of man's condition and his potential. Recall the Mexican creation myth in which the final race of man is made of maize; it is clear that Quetzalcoatl is a hero to man by bringing the grain that sustains life. Also, he symbolizes the heroic nature of man in his wing-like upper body, which stands for the soul, yet is attached to the earthbound snake body, a symbol for the physical nature of human beings. To consider Quetzalcoatl in terms of the quest and test motif, his quest is to bring the arts of agriculture to man. In his test, however, in the battle with his enemy, he is not a hero since he cannot overcome all obstacles of the mortal world. He is a weaker hero than Perseus, Theseus, or Heracles because the forces of evil are too great for him. He cannot surmount them.

When we consider these four heroes together—Perseus, Theseus, Jason, and Quetzalcoatl—we see again the hierarchy of heroes in terms of worldly effectiveness, of their divine mission, of the heavenly aid they receive, and of their transcendence over human problems which gives a sense of the possibilities inherent in life.

A different kind of hero is the spider Anansi, in African mythology. Instead of being a hero at the top of the scale like Perseus or Heracles, Anansi signifies a different kind of action, a different kind of example of the interaction between being and reality. For the most part, Anansi is a trickster who survives by stealth and cunning. In one Anansi story, God sends for the conceited Anansi and, laughing at him, sends him out to find "something." With no more knowledge of what he is to find than this, Anansi leaves to discover the "something" which is the goal of his quest. The spider borrows a cloak, flies back to heaven, perches on a tree outside of God's house, and overhears God telling a guest that the "something" is the sun, moon, and darkness. Anansi finds out from the python where to find the sun, moon, and darkness, and he brings them back to God in a bag. As he pulls the sun out, it blinds everyone, and that is how blindness came into the world—through the treachery of Anansi.

In this story the hero does not play the role of direct confrontation—by cutting off the head of Medusa—or enact the divine mission of bringing corn to man. Instead, Anansi represents the precarious position of man in his dealings with the unknowable forces of nature around him. Anansi represents wit, cunning, cleverness, and intrigue. As a spider in the jungle, he symbolizes what would probably be the most effective kind of human behavior for those who live there, that of adapting to the colors and tapestry of the environment instead of the direct and open confrontation more suited to the open plains where there is no place to hide. As a hero, then, Anansi suits the needs of the jungle culture.

Thus, in each of these hero myths, there is an example of how life should be lived, how man should or should not conduct himself in dealing with reality. There is, on the one hand, the possibility of the most heroic kind of action, exemplified by the hero Perseus. But there is also the admonition that heroism must be coupled with morality and conscience as seen in the case of Jason, who betrays his great destiny through his association with the crimes of Medea. As an image of man, Quetzalcoatl would indicate that a man must be hopeful in his nature; he must be both air and earth, bird and serpent, tree and ground. Anansi, in turn, can use cleverness in dealing with reality, but nevertheless falls into the trap of vanity; through his own conceit he brings destruction and loss to himself and others. He symbolizes false pride in his desire to outwit God. Later in this chapter, when we turn to the heroes of folk and fairy tales, we shall see the same range of possibility in the hero and also the same causes for his downfall. In a fairy tale, love and heroism conquer pain and death. As in hero myths, the heroes of the folk tale stand or fall if they are blessed by the gods, engaged in a noble quest, able to pass the tests placed in their way, and if they are inherently of good moral purpose and a loving nature.

Nature Myths

As in the myth of Quetzalcoatl, who brings corn and a knowledge of cultivation to the Indians of Mexico, associated with the hero are the return of the seasons and the fertility of the fields, along with the knowledge of those arts which make life prosperous and full. Prometheus brings tool-making and forethought; Quetzalcoatl brings the cultivation of corn. In Egyptian mythology the Hero, Osiris, is associated with the rebirth of the seasons.

In the myth of Osiris and Isis, his wife, Osiris brings man awareness of all the arts of civilization and agriculture. Following this time of prosperity and fertility, Osiris' jealous brother Seth, in the familiar pattern of brother against brother, tricks Osiris into lying down in a chest which Seth covers over with melted lead and throws into the river. The chest, like the ark of Perseus or the crib of Moses, floats unharmed and lands in a distant kingdom. There, a magical tree grows up around it and protects it from harm. Isis finally finds the body of Osiris, restores him to life, and takes him back to Egypt, which has been beset by war and famine ever since his departure. When Osiris returns, Egypt prospers again.

But Seth, the evil brother, cuts Osiris into fourteen pieces and throws him into the river. At once the springtime is over and war and death again control nature. Isis, however, again restores Osiris to life by searching for the pieces of his body in the river. Here the death of the hero is equated with winter and his rebirth with springtime. The cycles of nature are also equated with the freedom and happiness of the gods and goddesses as in the Greek myth of Demeter and Persephone.

In this myth, Pluto, the lord of the underworld, falls in love with Persephone and steals her away to Hades with him. Demeter, the goddess of springtime, wanders grief-stricken looking for her lost daughter, and in her distraction does not renew the seasons. After the earth has become almost barren, Zeus makes a bargain between Demeter and Pluto for the return of Persephone. Pluto, however, persuades Persephone to taste a pomegranate, an act that links her eternally with the underworld.

Finally, a compromise is reached in which Persephone remains with her mother on earth for two-thirds of the year and spends one-third of it with Pluto. During the time that Demeter is separated from her daughter, the seasons languish from the lack of her care. When Demeter and Persephone are rejoined, the mother in her great joy reawakens the earth.

Nature myths, although they explain such large issues as the return and absence of the seasons, can also deal with very minor aspects of the physical world. Of the many *pourquoi* stories that describe how various facts of nature came into being, one American Indian legend explains how the opossum lost the hairs on his tail.[3] Opossum meets raccoon and says to him, "What a fine tail you have there." Raccoon answers, when asked how the opossum can get similar rings on his tail, "All you have to do is to put some rings made out of tree-bark on your tail and then stick it in the fire. The longer you leave it in, the lovelier will the rings be." When the opossum does this, he loses all the hair on his own tail, and forever after hides in shame because of the joke he has become to the other animals.

---

[3] Vladimir Hulpach, *American Indian Tales and Legends* (Prague: Paul Hamlyn, 1965), p. 147.

From this survey of various kinds of myths, it is evident that men in all cultures create a structure through mythology within which an understanding of nature and reality is achieved. Nature operates in a certain fashion, and man relates to it after patterns of behavior exemplified in the stories of his mythology.

Myths not only define a culture, they provide the most compelling forces within a society. Myths create belief and influence action more than scientific doctrine because myths are governed by the power of emotion; they speak to the deepest passions of man. Indeed, this very depth of feeling with which myths are held lends credence to the statement: "War is the clash of mythologies."[4]

Myth, childhood, and culture

During his early years, the child becomes part of a cultural tradition through assimilation of the myths of his society. It is not a genetic heritage to be a member of a culture but rather the absorption of a myth-system. As Ruth Benedict shows in *Patterns of Culture,* myths rather than biology define a culture. The child adopts the myths of his culture, his family, and his education. It is, therefore, of great importance to the developing intellect of the child to perceive, enjoy, and experience the vast stores of narrative and image available to him in the mythologies of the world.

Furthermore, the kind of thinking a child is capable of before the age of 11 is more compatible with mythic representation than it is with the abstract concepts of science. As an example of the essentially mythic thinking of a child, consider the following from Piaget's *The Child's Conception of the World:*

> When d'Estrella looked at the clouds he imagined them to have been made by God's big pipe (d'Estrella referred to God as the "great strong man, hidden behind the hills, who used to throw the sun into the air every morning") . . . . Why?—Because he had often noted with childish admiration the eddies of smoke rising from a pipe or cigar. The fantastic shapes of the clouds as they floated by in the air would often fill him with wonder. What powerful lungs God must have! When it was misty the child supposed it must be God's breath in the cold morning. Why?—Because he had often observed his own breath in such weather. When it rained he was quite sure God must have taken a large mouthful of water and spat it out from his huge mouth in the form of a shower. Why?—Because he had frequently remarked the skill with which the Chinese of San Francisco thus watered the linen to bleach it.[5]

---

[4] Mark Schorer, *The Politics of Vision* (New York: Vintage Books, 1959), p. 26.
[5] Jean Piaget, *The Child's Conception of the World* (New York: Humanities Press, Inc., 1948).
Reprinted by permission.

In this passage there is the essence of mythic representation that endows nature with life and purpose—and a sense that there is a discoverable answer to the "why" for things. Furthermore, the mythic quality of correspondences between the known and the unknown—the linking of cigar smoke to the similar smoke-like appearance of the clouds—is told in a narrative form with the character of God performing the actions of smoking, breathing, and spitting water like the Chinese laundrymen. In addition to being a "linguistic genius," the child is also a natural myth-maker.

Folklore

Mythology is associated with religion, with belief, and with passionate involvement by the members of a social structure. Folklore contains many of the elements of mythology as an explanation of reality, as a guide to exemplary behavior, and as a statement on the nature of things. But folklore does not involve such deep-seated and religious fervor as mythology. Folklore is mythology translated into literature.

The material of folklore in its purest form is the oral transmission of stories about various characters acting in plots similar to myth. In folk tales can be found the mythic archetypes of journey–quest–test; of the importance of the hero; of the loss of paradise; and of the ultimate triumph of love over suffering. And, just as it is apparent that similar narrative patterns are seen in myths, so similar motifs and themes reoccur in all folklore. For example, the folklorist Stith Thompson has shown that the Cinderella rags-to-riches motif appears in almost all American Indian folk tales. As in the recurrent patterns of mythology, the many similarities of parable and structure among the folklores of the world argue for their innate character in the human experience.

The folk tale is at the core of children's literature because of its oral nature. In the home, the folk tale has from earliest times been the first literary experience of children. As Elizabeth Cook says in *The Ordinary and the Fabulous:*

> Until the end of the eighteenth century traditional 'fairy tales' formed, almost by accident, the greater part of storytelling for very young children: uneducated nurses and servants told children the old stories they had been told themselves, because they were the only stories they knew.[6]

As it happens, this was a happy accident because the material of the folk tale is, as Erich Fromm calls it, a "Forgotten Language," so close to the essence of

---

[6] Elizabeth Cook, *The Ordinary and the Fabulous* (Cambridge, England: Cambridge University Press, 1969), p. 1. Reprinted by permission.

the human experience that modern psychoanalysis is in large part based upon the recapture of folkloristic formulations of the images of life. Folklore is a body of stories which arises from all peoples in their daily endeavor and in their representation of reality.

Folk tales and fairy tales build a world that is a product of the imagination. They abound with characters such as elves, fairies, dwarfs, goblins, witches, and other magical emissaries from the other world—characters who are very like the gods and goddesses of mythology. The traits of the mythic hero like Perseus or Theseus are seen in the fabulous strength of a Paul Bunyan or in the skill and cleverness of a Febold Feboldson of the Nebraska plains.

Folk tales and fairy tales achieve their esthetic force by their similarity to the established modes of representation—plot, characterization, and often the style of myths. They make their impact upon the audience through their kinship to the older, more religious narrative of the myths. The magical events in the folk tale become believable because they are a further extension of the mythology of a culture. The world of a mythology is also the world of a folklore. Just as mythology creates a "semantic universe," folk tales create what Tolkien calls a "secondary world." And in folk and fairy tales no further advice is necessary for "literary belief" than the formula "Once upon a time. . . ."

Because folk tales and fairy tales are transmitted orally, it was late in the history of literature that they were collected, written down, and thus made available to persons in other cultures and in later times. Today, recognizing that the great importance of the folk tale is its closeness to the daily lives of all mankind, folklorists insist upon collecting stories in their purest form. By making a tape transcription of a tale, told by a selected informant in a culture, all of the basic flavor of the story is kept. In this manner, by collecting and preserving the story in its native form, all of the devices of spoken language appear in the performance. To be absolutely scrupulous, the folklorist must not tamper with the story in any way. He is merely the recorder and collector. If he does not have tape equipment, he must record the story in the phonetic alphabet so as not to deprive the story in any way of the effect of its natural dialect and setting. Such meticulous accuracy is a modern development, however, and only in recent times have technology and scholarship provided the means for it.

In children's literature, one of the first great collections of folk tales published was that of Charles Perrault, in 1697, popularly called *Tales of Mother Goose*. These stories were published in a translation from the original French into English by John Newbery in 1729. The next great collection of folk tales was the German *Household Stories* of the Grimm Brothers, published in the early nineteenth century and translated into English in 1823. Next came Hans Christian Andersen's various collections called *Fairy Tales*. And later appeared Andrew Lang's collections of folk tales, *The Blue Fairy Book* (1889), followed by the red, green, and yellow books. None of these collections meets the standards of modern scholarly accuracy. But they were the germinal force in inspiring myriad other collections of folk and fairy tales for children. When writers borrow from mythology and folklore, they are no longer folklorists, but become writers of fantasy; this was often true of Hans Christian Andersen.

Folklore is studied both by the anthropologist and the literary critic. But they approach the subject in different ways. The anthropologist seeks the record of a civilization. The literary critic searches for themes and modes of narrative, characterization, plot, and style. In examining folk tales as literature, numerous dominant plot situations and characterizations are apparent. Of the many that might be cited, five are suggested here as the most helpful to the student of children's literature:

1. The test and quest of the hero on a journey
2. The threatened maiden
3. The orphan child
4. The animal story
5. The trickster

Here our examination of mythology will be useful as the transfer of thematic material from mythology to folklore becomes evident. The first of the archetypes, that of the hero's test and quest, is seen in the myths of Perseus, Theseus, and Jason. All of the mythic heroes embark on journeys, encounter obstacles which test them in the course of their travel, and finally succeed or fail to fulfill their quest. Andromeda, in the myth of Perseus, the maiden chained to the rock to be sacrificed to a dragon, is like the threatened maiden Rapunzel, or Beauty in *Beauty and the Beast*. The various sons in the Greek myths who were deprived of their fathers—Perseus, Theseus, and Jason—are orphans just like Cinderella and Snow White, who lost their mothers. The stories of Anansi, the spider in African mythology, like those about the coyote and crow in American Indian mythology, endow animals with the same kind of humanized traits as seen in *Brer Rabbit* and *The Three Little Pigs*. Prometheus, who steals from the gods and tricks Zeus out of destroying man, is like the cunning fox of fables and the clever animals in the *The Bremen Town Musicians*.

But merely to codify and classify folk tales is not our intention here. Many folk and fairy tales fit all five categories, and others defy all labels. As you examine other folk tales and fairy tales on your own, however, explore to see how many of them *do* fit the patterns described above. The importance of the plot structures these kinds of stories typify is seen in their wide use in other forms of literature, such as fantasy, which borrow the already established pattern of mythic and folkloristic archetype. Myth has been painstakingly examined here to demonstrate the foundations of later evolutions of children's literature. The reappearance of the structures, images, and characters in later works relies upon the most primal forces of symbol-making. Thus a modern writer has at his command what Shelley called "The best and happiest moments of the happiest and best minds."[7]

---

[7] Percy Bysshe Shelley, *A Defense of Poetry* (Albuquerque: The University of New Mexico Press, 1966), p. 294.

To return to the five themes of folklore described above, a further theme which links all of them is the portrayal of a hero. All stories depend upon the representation of a hero, whether animal or prince. The orphan who has lost a parent typically awaits the advent of a hero, a strong male figure to rescue him from unhappy circumstances. The threatened maiden also awaits a hero to slay the dragon, to place the kiss on her brow, or to release her from her bondage in a tower. And the hero can be the prince or he can be an animal. The guardian wolf in *Prince Ivan, the Firebird, and the Gray Wolf,* a Russian folk tale by Afanasiev, is just as much a hero as the Prince in *The Sleeping Beauty.* Furthermore, in the hierarchy of heroes, the trickster, although of a lower level than the superhero, is nevertheless a part of the representation of heroes in myth and folklore.

To explore the necessity of a hero, let us turn to *Briar Rose* by the Brothers Grimm. In Part I, we examined the plot structure of *Briar Rose* and compared it with the version by Charles Perrault. In probing the plot of *Briar Rose,* the first problem that presents itself is the character of the king. Of all the members of a society, the most important is the ruler: he is to the culture what the gods are to all mankind. The king in *Briar Rose,* to celebrate the birth of the long-awaited princess, has a feast to which he invites only twelve of the thirteen wisewomen in his country. The reason for the omission of the thirteenth is that the King owns only twelve golden plates, emblematic of his inadequacy as a ruler. Each wisewoman bestows a desirable gift on the princess. One gives virtue, another beauty, another riches; and there is no indication in the text that the thirteenth would have been any less generous than the others if invited.

By excluding the thirteenth wisewoman, the king is, in effect, negligently depriving his daughter, and by extension, his people, of the gift this goddess could bestow. In the manner of justice apparent in myth, an offense against the pantheon of gods brings a curse—in this case, that the princess will die on her fifteenth birthday. The king further shows himself as weak when he foolishly attempts to outwit the prophecy by destroying the spinning wheels in his kingdom and secondly, by being absent from the castle on the day his daughter most needs him—her fifteenth birthday.

After the prophecy has been fulfilled and all the court lies in the same sleep as winter, the second part of the story brings the advent of the noble hero prince of great courage who is a contrast to the king. His quest is to see Briar Rose, and his test will be whether he has the courage to go through the hedge of thorns. He says, "I am not afraid; I will forth to see the beautiful Briar Rose." Like Perseus, Theseus, and Jason, he has the gods' favor; the thorn hedge turns into roses and opens before him. When he awakens the princess, it is like the return of spring, as in the nature myths described earlier in this chapter. With a weak king, the action can only worsen, and only the advent of the strong hero can save it. *Briar Rose* shows the typical fairy tale plot which is like the myth: a questing hero saves the threatened maiden.

In comparing the two versions of the *Sleeping Beauty,* we saw how the Grimms achieved an "organic unity" while Perrault exceeded the limits of a well-defined ending. As another instance of how the Grimms achieved a greater internal plot logic than Perrault, let us consider two versions of Cinderella by these authors. Perrault's is by far the better known. In his story, the threatened maiden, who is also an orphan child, is first aided by a fairy godmother who appears out of nowhere. The motivation for her entrance into the plot is only vaguely suggested; we are told nothing of her place in the story, except that she happens to have the magical powers to give Cinderella the famous pumpkin carriage and glass slippers.

In the Grimms' version, however, as Cinderella's mother lies dying, she says to her daughter:

> Dear child, be pious and good, and God will always take care of you, and I will look down upon you from heaven, and will be with you.[8]

The orphan child is then introduced to the unhappy situation of her father's remarriage to a proud and haughty woman with the two vain daughters. Her salvation comes not from the gratuitous entry of a fairy godmother, but from her innate goodness and piety—and from the influence of her mother in heaven. This becomes evident in the rest of the story. Cinderella's father goes to a fair, and after the two stepsisters have asked him to bring them back fine clothes and jewels, Cinderella modestly asks only for the first twig that rubs against his hat. He returns with a hazel branch which Cinderella plants on her mother's grave:

> She thanked him, and went to her mother's grave, and planted this twig there, weeping so bitterly that the tears fell upon it and watered it and it flourished and became a fine tree. Aschenputtel [Cinderella] went to see it three times a day, and wept and prayed, and each time a white bird rose up from the tree, and if she uttered any wish the bird brought her whatever she had wished for.[9]

The white bird, like the dove which is a symbol of love and peace, appears in the story as a messenger from Cinderella's mother, linking the first statement of the mother with the continuing action of the narrative, as the bird remains in the story as Cinderella's aid and guardian until she is at last married to the Prince. At their wedding, two doves from the grave perch on her shoulders and pluck out the eyes of the hypocritical stepsisters as they march on either side of the bride. The fact that the evildoers are punished for their actions in the Grimms' version is also more logical in terms of character development than the sudden and not quite believable repentance of the stepsisters in Perrault's version.

One objection which may be raised against the Grimms' version, even though it is a more tightly integrated and dramatic presentation, is the self-mutilation the stepsisters perform when they cut off their heels and toes to attempt to fit the

---

[8] The Brothers Grimm, *Household Stories*, Lucy Crane, trans. (New York: Dover Publications, 1963), p. 118.
[9] *Ibid.*, p. 119.

slipper. Let it be remembered, however, that in mythology, the evildoer's punishment and suffering is not tempered by mercy. Prometheus is chained to a rock where a vulture comes each day and eats of his liver. Satan is cast into a burning lake; Loki in Norse mythology is condemned to having poison drip eternally into his mouth. The sharp retribution to the evil stepsisters in Grimm is more in keeping with the mythological foundation of folklore than the pale and unmotivated change of character in Perrault.

Considering the style of old folk tales, translation from one language to another is often a problem. Most of the folk tales available for children in English originated in other languages. Perrault wrote in French, the Grimms in German, Andersen in Danish. Sometimes the translator has not always been faithful to the original.[10] In a good translation, as much of the mythic flavor of a folk tale as possible must be preserved. The images and archetypes of mythology are a major device of style in folk tales. Consider the two translations of the Grimms' *Snow White* given next:

---

[10] A comparison of a key passage in various translations of "The Sleeping Beauty" reveals certain discrepancies. One of the most widely used translations, by Lucy Crane, mistranslates the word *Zauberspruch* in the tower scene as "evil prophecy." This mistranslation, among others, distorts the meaning of the encounter with the old woman by forcing her to be identified as the thirteenth *Frau*. The translation by Gudrun Thorne-Thomsen, if more accurate than the Crane, is vacuous and insipid. The best translations are by Margaret Hunt and by an anonymous translator. The passage in the tower is given from several texts to show the differences. There is no reason why the same rigor of translational accuracy should not be demanded for children's literature as for adult literature, especially when an accurate translation will convey more of the superb drama of the original than a "watering down," whatever reasons might be given for the latter.

I. The German:

In dem Schloss Steckte ein
verrosteter Schlüssel, und
als es umdrehte, sprang die
Thuer auf, and sass da in
einem kleinen Stübchen eine
alte Frau mit einer Spindel
und spann emsig ihren Flachs.
'Guten Tag, du altes Mütterchen,'
sprach die Konigstochter, 'was
machst du da?' 'Ich spinne,'
sagte die Alte und nickte mit
dem Kopf.

'Was ist das für ein
Ding, das so lustig herum-
springt?' sprach das Mädchen,
nahm die Spindel und wollte
auch spinnen. Kaum hatte sie
aber die Spindel angerhurt, so
ging der Zauberspruch in Erfullung
und sie stach sich damit in
den Finger.

In dem Augenblick aber, wie sie
den Stich empfand, fiel sie auf
das Bett nieder, das da stand, und
lag in einem tiefen Schlaf.

II. Accurate English. tr. Margaret Hunt
     (London, George Bell: 1905).

A rusty key was in the
lock, and when she turned
it the door sprang
open, and there in a little
room sat an old woman with
a spindle, busily spinning
her flax.
"Good day, old dame," said
the King's daughter; "what
are you doing there?" "I am
spinning," said the old woman
and nodded her head.

"What sort of thing is that,
that rattles round so merrily?"
said the girl, and she took
the spindle and wanted to spin
too. But scarcely had she touched
the spindle when the magic
decree was fulfilled, and she
pricked her finger with it.

And, in the very moment when
she felt the prick, she fell
down upon the bed that stood
there, and lay in a deep sleep.

Once upon a time in deep winter, when the snowflakes were falling like feathers from the sky, a queen was sitting at a window with a black ebony frame, and she was sewing. And as she looked up from her sewing at the snow, she pricked her finger with the needle, and three drops of blood fell upon the snow. And because the red looked so beautiful against the white snow, she thought to herself, "If I might have a child as white as snow, as red as blood, and as black as the wood in the frame." Soon after that she bore a little daughter, who was as white as snow and as red as blood and

It was the middle of winter, and the snow-flakes were falling like feathers from the sky, and a queen sat at her window working, and her embroidery frame was of ebony. And as she worked, gazing at times out on the snow, she pricked her finger, and there fell from it three drops of blood on the snow. And when she saw how bright and red it looked, she said to herself, "Oh that I had a child as white as snow, as red as blood, and as black as the wood of the embroidery frame!"

Not very long after she had a daughter, with a skin as white as snow, lips as red as blood, and hair as black as ebony, and

---

III. tr. by Gudrun Thorne-Thomsen in *Told Under the Green Umbrella* (New York: Macmillan, 1938).

. . . In a very lonesome spot she saw a tower. She climbed the winding staircase, pushed open the door, and entered a little tower room. There sat an old woman twirling a stick between her hands, and a long soft white thread ran through her fingers.

"Good day, dear Granny," said the Princess, "And what is it you are doing?" The old woman only smiled mysteriously and shook her head, as if she did not hear. "Let me try to make a thread as soft and smooth as yours," now begged the Princess, and without waiting for an answer she held out her hands. The old woman placed the spindle in the Princess' hand—for you must know this old woman was spinning with the spindle and distaff; and all aglow with joy at the work the King's daughter laughed. Then all at once she pricked her finger—and fell asleep. . . .

IV. tr. unnamed (New York: John C. Winston Co., 1924) Grimm's *Fairy Tales*.

From a room at the top came a curious humming noise, and the Princess, wondering what it could be, pushed open the door, and stepped inside.

There sat an old woman, bent with age, working at a strangely shaped wheel. The Princess was full of curiosity.

"What is that funny-looking thing?" she asked.

"It is a spinning-wheel, Princess," answered the old woman, who was no other than the wicked fairy in disguise.

"A spinning wheel—what is that? I have never heard of such a thing," said the Princess. She stood watching for a few minutes, then she added:

"It looks quite easy, May I too do it?"

"Certainly, gracious lady," said the wicked fairy, and the Princess sat down and tried to turn the wheel. But no sooner did she lay her hand upon it than the spindle, which was enchanted, pricked her finger, and the Princess fell back against a silk-covered couch—fast asleep.

V. *Household Stories by the Brothers Grimm.* tr. by Lucy Crane. (New York: McGraw-Hill, 1966).

She climbed the narrow winding stair which led to a little door, with a rusty key sticking out of the lock; she turned the key, and the door opened, and there in the little room sat an old woman with a spindle, diligently spinning her flax.

"Good day, mother," said the Princess, "what are you doing?"

"I am spinning," answered the old woman, nodding her head.

"What thing is that that twists round so briskly?" asked the maiden, and taking the spindle into her hand she began to spin; but no sooner had she touched it than the evil prophecy was fulfilled, and she pricked her finger with it. In that very moment she fell back upon the bed that stood there, and lay in a deep sleep.

had hair as black as ebony, and therefore she was called Snow White. And when the child was born, the queen died.[11]

she was named Snow-White. And when she was born the queen died.[12]

Both versions are accurate to the letter of the German original. But the version on the left preserves the literal meaning of the original and also seems to flow in a more normal English syntax. How do you react to the two passages? Examine some of the devices of style in this passage, notice the figurative language comparing the snow flakes with feathers. Also, notice the use of the number three, a magical number, like thirteen, in folklore. And the theme of the orphan child is obvious.

But folk tales need not deal only with main characters of great nobility like those treated above. The trickster of mythology has his counterpart in folk tales like *The Bremen Town Musicians,* where clever animals trick a robber into believing he has been set upon by devils, thus forcing him to give up his cabin to them. So too, in "noodle" tales, the focus of the plot is upon the droll and humorous "putdown" of clumsy and stupid types who always end up the loser. *The Wise Men of Schilda* by Otfried Peussler is one such collection, and *When Shlemiel Went to Warsaw & Other Stories* by Isaac Bashevis Singer is another. The fact that in Yiddish a *shlemiel* is a clumsy lout indicates the direction this form of folk tale takes. Such a story from Turkish is *Hilili and Dilili* by Barbara K. Walker.

Fables

The talking animals and objects from nature seen in mythology and folklore make a reappearance in the brief narratives called fables. A fable is a tersely styled tale of a single incident in which animals and objects from nature stand for abstract concepts of human action in order to portray a moral lesson. From India, there are three great collections of fables: *The Jataka Tales, The Fables of Bidpai,* and *The Panchatantra.* And, from Greece, we have the famous *Fables of Aesop.* The later French *Fables of Jean de la Fontaine* are translations of a Roman version of Aesop.

In the brief action portrayed in a fable, there will usually be a dialogue between two creatures or other objects in nature, in which each figure in the action stands for a moral concept. Two examples serve to illustrate this point:

The Fox and the Crow

A Fox once saw a Crow fly off with a piece of cheese in its beak and settle on a branch of a tree. "That's for me, as I am a Fox," said Master Reynard, and he walked up to the foot of the tree. "Good-day, Mistress Crow," he

---

[11] From *Twelve Dancing Princesses,* edited by Alfred and Mary David. Copyright © 1964 Alfred David & Mary Elizabeth David. Reprinted by arrangement with The New American Library, New York, N.Y.

[12] The Brothers Grimm, *Household Stories,* Lucy Crane, trans. (New York: Dover Publications, 1963), p. 213.

cried. "How well you are looking to-day: how glossy your feathers; how bright your eye. I feel sure your voice must surpass that of other birds, just as your figure does; let me hear but one song from you that I may greet you as the Queen of Birds." The Crow lifted up her head and began to caw her best, but the moment she opened her mouth the piece of cheese fell to the ground, only to be snapped up by Master Fox. "That will do," said he. "That was all I wanted. In exchange for your cheese I will give you a piece of advice for the future—

"Do not trust flatterers."[13]

The Tree and the Reed

"Well, little one," said a Tree to a Reed that was growing at its foot, "why do you not plant your feet deeply in the ground, and raise your head boldly in the air as I do?"

"I am contented with my lot," said the Reed. "I may not be so grand, but I think I am safer."

"Safe!" sneered the Tree. "Who shall pluck me up by the roots or bow my head to the ground?" But it soon had to repent of its boasting, for a hurricane arose which tore it up from its roots, and cast it a useless log on the ground while the little Reed, bending to the force of the wind, soon stood upright again when the storm had passed over.

"Obscurity often brings safety."[14]

In *The Fox and the Crow* the fox stands for cunning and the proud crow represents vanity. The fox's cleverness enables him to trick the crow into dropping the piece of cheese by playing upon her false pride in her voice. Obviously, a crow is anything but musical, but her vanity makes her vulnerable to the flattery of the fox. So too, in *The Tree and the Reed,* we see vanity humbled at the same time that modesty is rewarded. These two fables represent a universal theme of folklore: the triumph of love, modesty, piety, and self-knowledge over pride, envy, and egotism. Most fables involve only animals, although some include human beings.

One problem that a child has with fables is the allegorical nature of the characters. The characters in a fable have no inner life, nor are they intended to be any more than a representation of an abstract concept. They are not intended to portray how animals really are. Fables are contrived literary works that require the reader to break a code, which is the correspondence of animal with concept. Regardless of one's own experience with turtles or rabbits or other animals, he must set aside those preconditioned associations and accept that in the fable, a tortoise represents perseverance, a rabbit represents frivolity, a fox, cunning. There is a certain algebraic quality to fables. For this reason, children younger

---

[13] Charles W. Eliot, ed., *Folk-Lore and Fable* (New York: P. F. Collier & Son, 1909), pp. 12–13. This material reprinted with the kind permission of Crowell Collier and Macmillan, Inc.

[14] *Ibid.,* pp. 25–26.

than eight have difficulty breaking the code. Because they lack the ability to think abstractly that mathematical thinking requires, small children also may find it difficult to understand just how the crow or the tree or the reed in the fable is different from real trees, reeds, or crows. But fables provide a valuable literary experience in their allegory, in their irony, and in their extension of the themes of mythology and folklore.

Epic and romance

The epic and the romance, like the other forms of literature in this chapter, concern themselves with the portrayal of a hero. The epic hero is slightly higher in the hierarchy than the hero of the romance. Indeed, the heroes of the Greek epics *The Iliad* and *The Odyssey* are often drawn from the hero myths discussed earlier in the chapter. The epic hero rises to the same superhuman potentials as the semi-divine Heracles, Perseus, and Theseus. The epic hero is so extrahuman in his nobility that Aristotle, in *The Poetics,* expressed the fear that ordinary human beings would find it impossible to achieve a sympathetic identification with such a demi-god. The romance hero is portrayed in a slightly more human-ized setting, and thus is made more acceptable to mortals.

The epic hero, drawn from the highest level of the hero in mythology, repre-sents the grandest potential of human aspirations. He is ever-noble, always en-gaged in the worthiest of quests, and fully confident in his ability to overcome every obstacle encountered in fulfilling his destiny. In *The Iliad* and *The Odyssey,* the two dominant heroes are Achilles and Odysseus, who act within the familiar mythic plot structure of journey–quest–test.

The plots of these two epics are set within the entire background of the Trojan War. The war occurs because Paris, son of the King of Troy, has stolen the Greek Helen away from her husband, King Menelaus. This offense against Greek society is answered with the full military might of Greece. The motive of the journey is evident. And in the course of the many battles that follow at Troy, heroes are needed. *The Iliad* recounts the ten years' struggle of the Greeks against the Trojans. *The Odyssey* tells of the return of Odysseus to his home in Ithaca. Behind the immediate plots of the two epics is the cycle of leaving Greece, going to Troy, and returning home.

In the course of their journey home, Odysseus and his men must surmount many challenges to their heroism. They must resist the temptation to become Lotus-Eaters (or dope addicts); they must defeat the Cyclops, a one-eyed mon-ster; escape the lures of Circe, an enchantress who turns men who fall in love with her into pigs; and so on throughout numerous adventures in which they are saved from doom by the efforts of the hero, Odysseus.

Odysseus' own kingdom has been threatened by his absence. Odysseus' wife, Penelope, has been visited by a crowd of suitors. She has managed to postpone choosing one of the suitors as her husband by a clever ruse: she tells them that she must finish weaving a tapestry. Penelope weaves by day and unweaves by night; the tapestry is never completed.

When Odysseus returns home, he shows he is a worthy hero. Only he can string the bow with which he slays the suitors. The same kind of divine favor is apparent in this act as in the thorn hedge's opening before the Prince in *Briar Rose*. And with the return of the hero to his kingdom, peace is restored at last, just as springtime and prosperity return to nature with the advent and rebirth of a hero in nature myths.

In *Beowulf*, the oldest epic in the Anglo-Saxon tradition, the hero is portrayed in this same setting of journey and quest. The hero leaves his home with the Geats to assist the Danish King Hrothgar in ridding himself of the attacks of the monster, Grendel. Beowulf engages the monster in hand-to-hand combat and wrenches off Grendel's arm and shoulder. He has further battles with Grendel's mother and later with a dragon who robs and plunders the land of the Geats.

The style of the epic is solemn and grand in keeping with the seriousness of the problems within the plot (the salvation of a nation, the return of a hero, the preservation of a world order). Homer ornaments his lines with much figurative language to give a heightened visual sense of the great scenes and battles of the epic. For another example of such language, return to the *Beowulf* example in Part I. In most versions retold and rewritten for children, however, the language has been simplified to meet the reading level of the child. But when read aloud, in a good verse translation of the original, the full flavor of the style and music of the epic can become part of the child's experience with language.

The romance hero, as seen in *Sir Gawain and the Green Knight*, is also engaged in a journey and quest. Gawain must defend the honor of King Arthur's Court by accepting the Green Knight's challenge to a duel. But although all the magical and fantastical elements of the epic, myth, and folk tale are present in the romance, Gawain is nonetheless shown in more human detail than other heroes. One of Gawain's tests on his journey to find the Green Knight is to resist the temptations of the lady of a castle he visits in the course of his travels. Although such seduction is somewhat akin to the Circe episode in *The Odyssey*, the worldliness of the romance hero nevertheless may place him on a less exalted plane of characterization than the heroes of the epic. He must fight only one man, and the motivation for the quest is more for honor than for the survival of a civilization. However closely related in plot and in characterization the epic and the romance may be, they differ in the scope of the action portrayed and the importance of the quest.

Summary   In surveying mythology, folklore, and related forms, we have established a foundation from which we can proceed to later forms of literature. It will become evident as we continue that the plot structure, characterization, and archetypes of older forms of literature constantly reappear in children's literature. In a sense, it is tempting to assert that the best of modern literature has its origins in the oldest forms of literature which, we have demonstrated, originate in mythology.

To suggest the impact these stories can have upon the imagination of a child, we offer William H. Armstrong's testimony, given as the author's note to his novel *Sounder:*

> Fifty years ago, I learned to read at a round table in the center of a large, sweet-smelling, steam-softened kitchen. My teacher was a gray-haired black man who taught the one-room Negro school several miles away from where we lived in the Green Hill district of the county. He worked for my father after school and in the summer. There were no radios or television sets, so when our lessons were finished he told us stories. His stories came from Aesop, the Old Testament, Homer, and history.
>
> There was a lasting, magnificent intoxication about the man that has remained after half a century. There was seldom a preacher at the white-washed, clapboard Baptist church in the Green Hill district, so he came often to our white man's church and sat alone in the balcony. Sometimes the minister would call on this eloquent, humble man to lead the congregation in prayer. He would move quietly to the foot of the balcony steps, pray with the simplicity of the Carpenter of Nazareth, and then return to where he sat alone, for no other black people ever came to join him.
>
> He had come to our community from farther south, already old when he came. He talked little, or not at all, about his past. But one night at the great center table after he had told the story of Argus, the faithful dog of Odysseus, he told the story of Sounder, a coon dog.
>
> It is the black man's story, not mine. It was not from Aesop, the Old Testament, or Homer. It was history—*his* history.
>
> That world of long ago has almost totally changed. The church balcony is gone. The table is gone from the kitchen. But the story remains.[15]

"The story remains." What more need be said?

For other studies of mythology see *The Uses of Myth,* edited by Paul Olson; *Man and His Symbols* and *Essays on a Science of Mythology* by C. G. Jung, et al.; *The Greek Way* and *The Roman Way* by Edith Hamilton. Collections of myths other than those outlined in Part IV are *The Greek Myths* by Robert Graves; *Mythology* by Edith Hamilton; *Myths of the World* by Padraic Colum.

For studies of folklore see *The Folktale* by Stith Thompson; *American Folklore* by Richard Dorson. Dorson has made numerous other collections of folk tales besides those outlined in the Bibliography. We should also specially mention *The Forgotten Language* by Erich Fromm.

---

[15] From *Sounder* by W. H. Armstrong. Copyright © 1969 by William H. Armstrong. Reprinted by permission of Harper & Row, Publishers.

3 Fantasy

the literary artist can depict two worlds in his creations. His inspiration and portrayal can be drawn from the real world, which functions according to the commonly accepted notions of the natural sciences, physics, and other scientific and demonstrable descriptions of reality. Or the writer can turn inward into his own imagination, and construct from his personal fantasies and dreams a universe and experience which, although believable itself, does not conform to the dictates of how the real world operates. In building a plot from imaginary circumstances that do not appear in nature, the writer constructs what Tolkien calls a Secondary World, one that is a portrayal of what the mind might conjure, not what actually exists.

Here we make a distinction between the writer of prose fiction and the creator of fantasy. Of course, the portrayals and plots of both kinds of writing are drawn from the writer's imagination. But the writer of prose fiction attempts to match the real world in his work; the fantasy writer presents a world that is real only within the limits of the plot itself. In fantasy we find a succession of events that are startling and provocative in their strangeness. In prose fiction characters and situations correspond to the usually accepted notions of the nature of reality. In fantasy, contrary to our perceptions of the real world, Alice can fall down a rabbit-hole and remain unharmed; fantasy frogs are transformed from slimy nuisances into interesting talking and acting figures in a narrative; and fantastic trips to outer space are accomplished. The fantasy author constructs his own world from his imagination. Those who strive for conformity with the known workings of human conduct, real aspects of nature, and visible and demonstrable facts of human existence are prose fiction writers.

The first question that comes up in discussing this difference is, "What is the real world?" Clearly, one man's reality is another man's madness. And it might be asserted that what exists in the imagination is as much a part of nature as rocks, mountains, and trees. But without pursuing the timeless question of what reality is, we can see the difference between the two kinds of writing as we explore their unique characteristics. We can hope to agree that at a certain point in time, some kinds of action are impossible and that certain kinds of literary characters— like those of mythology and folklore—cannot exist in nature. Their appearance in stories—in the form of talking animals, gods and goddesses, and superheroes— is a creation of the imagination.

No single person can be designated as the creator of a myth or a folktale. These stories, although at times collected by specific persons, like the Grimms or Andrew nevertheless spring from what Jung calls the "collective unconscious." ...ical parables appear spontaneously in a cultural tradition and represent a ...ing held by the body of a civilization. In literature, however, a single author ...amed as the originator or maker of a story. Although himself the product of ...ural and literary tradition, the artist draws his images of experience from his ...n unique imagination and personality. If his material is drawn from his mind, ...hindered by the rules of nature, he has exercised a quality of artistry that ...eates a world not found in ordinary human experience.

The writer of fantasy surmounts the bounds of reason and, in effect, generates ...world from within his own genius. Here again, the artist is different from the ...ientist. A scientist seeks to discover what actually exists in nature; the artist ...uilds a world beyond the reality of nature. As Blake states it, an artist sees "a ...orld in a Grain of Sand," "A Heaven in a Wild Flower." As a further statement ...of the essential difference between the artist and the scientist, Sir Philip Sidney ...ys, in his *Apology for Poetry,* that the writer:

> ...disdaining to be tied to any such subjection, [as the scientist must follow] lifted up with the vigor of his own invention, doth grow in effect another nature, in making things either better than nature bringeth forth, or, quite anew, forms such as never were in nature, as the Heroes, Demigods, Cyclops, Chimeras, Furies, and such like: so as he goeth hand in hand with nature, not enclosed within the narrow warrant of her gifts, but freely ranging only within the zodiac of his own wit.[1]

Fantasy is the construction of a world beyond the limits of the observable face of nature and which further portrays a realm into which the mind of the reader may enter.

To produce this desired state where the imagination of the reader joins with that of the author to enter a world which is "true" and pleasurable while one is inside it, the writer of fantasy must produce a plot that compels the reader's belief. Various techniques and devices have been used to accomplish an acceptance of otherwise improbable, indeed bizarre, plots and characters. In examining a number of exemplary works of fantasy, a sense of the landscape of what Tolkien calls a "Perilous Realm" that "cannot be caught in a net of words"[2] will emerge.

When the writer sets out to create in literature a world that contradicts the reader's own tenets of reality, he has before him the task of structuring an experience that will overwhelm any feeling of disbelief. To do this, the writer provides a set of circumstances which within their own terms, granted a few initial assumptions, proceed logically one from another. The beginning of a fantasy plot must attract the reader by laying the foundation for imaginative acceptance.

---

[1] Sir Phillip Sydney, *An Apology for Poetry* in *The Norton Anthology of English Literature,* Vol. I, ed. by Myron H. Abrams (New York: W. W. Norton & Company, Inc., 1962), p. 426.

[2] J. R. R. Tolkien, *On Fairy Stories* in *The Tolkien Reader* (New York: Ballantine Books, 1966), p. 10.

Briefly stated, fantasy in children's literature uses the plot devices of the dream fantasy; the myth of the machine; a remote setting either in time or in space; science fiction, which can combine all elements; and also direct borrowings of characters and plots from mythology and folklore. Some fantasy uses many such devices to assert its credibility. But each in its own way is a separate means to convince the reader of the truth of what he meets. The reader of good fantasy never stops to ask if what he is shown actually happened; his involvement is such that he never questions the probabilities of character and action.

Each of the devices of fantasy will be explored in turn, not, however, with the intention of exposing the sleight of hand or the craft behind the magician's pulling a scarf out of his ear. Rather the sense of the wonder is increased by awareness of the artistry involved in the creation. Random free association lacks coherence—fantasy organizes its experience into the shape and communication of plot and character in language.

Dream fantasy

Long before Freud's time it was evident that in sleep the mind is liberated from the pressures and restrictions of the waking world and is free to conjure its own fancies. And because everyone has experienced the succession of images in dreams, which differ so from the images of the visible daylight world, the suggestion that events told in a plot transpired in a dream lends them credibility. We all know that in a dream anything goes. In the Middle Ages, the dream fantasy was a common device to portray the miraculous visions of saints as they communed with heaven. The literary artist, then, makes use of the unknown world of sleep to persuade the reader to accept as probable what happens in his story. As a literary device, the writer of fantasy can place his narrative within the context of a dream to give himself license and setting for unlikely happenings.

Indeed, the reality of a dream can be more compellingly true than what is experienced when awake. Sleep allows the psyche to "range freely within the zodiac" of itself. And what is found there takes on a vivid sense of truth. So much so that Keats, after his own fantasy experience in *Ode to a Nightingale,* questions whether he lives in sleep more fully than when awake.

Following his imaginative union with the song of the bird, he asks:

> Was it a vision, or a waking dream?
> Fled is that music:—Do I wake or sleep?

Similarly, Coleridge, when trying to recreate his "Vision in a Dream," the "stately pleasure-dome" of *Kubla Khan,* says of the fantasy that vanished when he awoke:

Could I revive within me
Her symphony and song,
To such deep delight 'twould win me,
That with music loud and long,
I would build that dome in air
That sunny dome! those caves of ice!
And all who heard should see them there,
And all should cry, Beware! Beware!
His flashing eyes, his floating hair!
Weave a circle round him thrice,
And close your eyes with holy dread,
For he on honey-dew hath fed
And drunk the milk of paradise.

In addition to providing the fantasy writer with the setting for his unique images and scenes, the dream device allows him to make comments on the actual world. A truism of dreams is that in sleep the mind acts out its own wishes to satisfy needs the waking personality represses. And puzzling aspects of reality are probed in dreams to achieve a picture of external experience. In fantasy, then, the dream gives the writer the means to make a representation of the actual world that, in a sense, is a comment upon its working. The dream is often a mirror held up to the world to see what has been distorted or missed in the waking state. What happens in Wonderland, in Looking-Glass House, or with the Wild Things is an interpretation of the waking world.

In children's literature, the two most enduring classics of dream fantasy are Lewis Carroll's *Alice's Adventures in Wonderland* and *Through the Looking-Glass.* Written as entertainments for an actual child, Alice Liddell, these two books create a world of the author's own imagining. Wonderland and Looking-Glass House, which form the settings for the fantasies, are occupied by talking animals, by a cat who can become invisible, by a garden party of playing cards, and by chessmen who become characters in the narrative.

In both books, the plot begins with Alice falling asleep to give the framework of a dream to the fantasy. As we first see her in *Alice in Wonderland,* she is "beginning to get very tired of sitting by her sister on the bank, and of having nothing to do . . . ." Alice falls asleep. But the last thing she sees before dozing off is a rabbit hopping by. The rabbit immediately is transposed into her dream world; she then follows it down its hole. Reality thus merges into the dream world, the real world is left behind, and other kinds of adventures are possible. The plot begins with this device to assure the credibility of the action to follow.

As Alice follows the rabbit down its hole, she falls in dream fashion—that is, slowly and with the assured objectivity with which she asks "I wonder what latitude or longitude I've got to?" Throughout the book Alice never fears for her safety in the sense of feeling panic or terror—this would make it a nightmare, and she would awaken. Again and again events point up her safety even when she seems to be threatened. She lands safely at the bottom of the hole; she finds

The Cheshire Cat. Illustration by John Tenniel.

there many ways to change her size; she escapes drowning in the Pool of Tears; she finally is able to break the code of Wonderland logic and acquit herself well at her trial for stealing the Queen of Hearts' tarts. Furthermore, she takes her favorite character from the waking world into her dream to serve as a guardian spirit in the same sense as a fairy godmother. When first faced with the problem of getting out of the Pool of Tears, she wishes that her beloved cat Dinah were there. Soon she meets the Cheshire Cat with the enormous grin, who serves as a protective and benevolent influence in helping Alice find her way through Wonderland, and who is, in fact, a surrogate Dinah.

Alice's inner feelings as a child in a world of Victorian adults are expressed by her discoveries of the numerous foibles and fallacies of society—feelings she probably could not verbalize when awake. The characters in Wonderland include the extinct Dodo, the Mad Hatter, and the Queen of Hearts, all of whom represent echelons of nature and society in an immense panorama of types. In her encounters with them, Alice thus ranges over her own experiences with education and with society. When she and the others want to dry themselves after emerging from the Pool of Tears, they are given a typical history lesson by the Mouse and quickly find that the arid prose has marvelous drying abilities. At the mad Hatter's Tea Party, the manners of the tea table are reversed, and Alice sees the characters acting in as unrefined a manner as she probably suspects adults would like to. Hostility and violence, studiously suppressed in the adult social world, run rampant in Alice's dream as her own perceptions of reality come out of hiding. The Queen of Hearts' croquet party is a parody of a high society function as seen through the eyes of a child. The accepted adult conventions of etiquette and behavior are satirized in the croquet game in which flamingoes are used for mallets and hedge-hogs serve as the balls. This portrayal of a party makes just as much sense as much of what actually does happen at adult gatherings. Alice has a cold gaze in her dream which strips through pretension and falsity to uncover underlying motives and attitudes. The dream replays Alice's experiences with the real world of parents, manners, social protocol, governesses, education, and the universally encountered agents of morality. She is free to follow the advice of the Cheshire Cat to "Call it what you like." In many ways, she prepares herself for her reentry into the waking world where we measure out our lives in coffee spoons, and often waste our lives in false social endeavors. By the end of the book, Alice has gained a new perspective on social mores and customs.

Within its own terms, the plot of *Alice's Adventures in Wonderland* also contains the familiar journey–quest–test motif of myths and folk tales. In her dream journey, Alice quite literally explores herself—she encounters numerous obstacles and her self-assurance grows as she overcomes them. Just as Odysseus must face the threat of Scylla and Charybdis (the octopus and the whirlpool), Alice must solve the problems of size; face the riddles and rudeness of the mad Duchess, the Mad Hatter and the Hare; and finally win her own trial with the Queen of Hearts, who continually shouts "Off with their heads!" By being able to pass Wonderland's tests she achieves a role and identity of her own, just as the heroes of mythology and folklore similarly reach their stature through the tests they confront.

In the early part of her adventures, Alice tells the Caterpillar when he asks "Who are you?":

> "I—I hardly know, Sir, just at present—at least I know who I *was* when I got up this morning, but I think I must have been changed several times since then."

In contrast to her indefinite approach to this crucial question at the beginning of the fantasy, Alice reaches a level of identity so strong that when the Queen of Hearts proclaims, "Sentence first—verdict afterwards," she replies:

> "Stuff and nonsense!" . . . "The idea of having the sentence first!"
> "Hold your tongue!" said the Queen, turning purple.

"I won't!" said Alice.

"Off with her head!" the Queen shouted at the top of her voice. Nobody moved.

"Who cares for you?" said Alice (she had grown to her full size by this time) . "You're nothing but a pack of cards!"

By coming to grips with the threats to her own identity presented by the falsities and confusions of the adult world, Alice achieves a measure of security and control over what is essentially chaotic.

The major thrust of the satire in *Alice* is aimed at the overemphasis Victorian society placed on certainty, its smug assurance of its grasp of reality, and its clear dictates of behavior. But in Wonderland, the honored constructs of logic and politeness are overthrown to suggest that what may seem certain and clear perhaps is false. While sanity is valued in the real world, madness is the keynote of Wonderland. But because the types in Wonderland have their obvious counterparts in the real world, a clear statement is made about the apparent sanity of the society of the actual world. By portraying discernible aspects of the real world in a setting of nonsense and madness, Carroll points up the absurdities of much conventionally accepted truth.

For example, consider the sophism, or fallacious argument, the Cheshire Cat uses to convince Alice that he is mad:

"To begin with," said the Cat, "A dog's not mad. You grant that?"

"I suppose so," said Alice.

"Well, then," the Cat went on, "You see a dog growls when it's angry, and wags its tail when its pleased. Now *I* growl when I'm pleased, and wag my tail when I'm angry. Therefore I'm mad."

Although a reversal of the real world, by placing madness in the place of sanity and supplanting logic with illogic, Wonderland clearly makes a comment on the waking realm of Alice's daily life.

The style reflects the reversals of ordinary logic through the use of puns, riddles, syllogisms, and sophisms. All of these devices add to the ambiguity and uncertainty of the discourse. In Wonderland, even several contradictory meanings of words are exploited to support the theme of uncertainty as truer than certainty. The puns, such as "sole" for "soul," make communication the difficult task which in fact it is. Smugness must give way to the perceptions Carroll offers in his treatment of the real world through the vehicle of Wonderland.

Alice's journey, of course, takes place within her own interpretation and view of reality. The plot begins when she falls asleep, its middle is the dream first inspired by the glimpse of the rabbit, and the end occurs when she awakens. Within the narrative, the author creates almost all the events from an omniscient point of view. Carroll is the transcriber and reporter of what happens in Alice's dream. It is not Alice herself who tells the story; it is the author who relates what happens. The author in such a point of view does not instruct the reader what to think about what takes place in Alice's dream. Instead of overtly stating his intentions, Carroll narrates the action in the third person from the beginning. If Carroll had chosen to have Alice report her adventures in the first person, she would have had to tell the dream to her sister upon awakening, creating a distance from the actual experience and thus losing immediacy.

Alice's Adventures in Wonderland involves a number of statements about the real world. Wonderland is the reverse of what happens during wakefulness. The technique of showing reality by contrasting it with its opposite matured in Carroll's mind, until, apparently, he saw that Wonderland was, in a sense, a mirror he had been holding up to the daily world. The metaphor becomes fully realized in *Through the Looking-Glass*. To make a comment on the mores and foibles of the real world as he had done in *Wonderland,* Carroll used the mirror image, which shows everything in reverse but which gives personal insight, forming the perfect symbol for his explorations.

At the beginning of the novel there are two poems, one which serves as an author's preface and another which serves as a dedication to Alice Liddell. In each one, Carroll calls his work a fairy tale. Thus, from the outset several expectations are established—first, one is assured that nothing bad will happen to Alice—the fairy tale heroine is always safe from harm in the end. But, more subtly, in all fairy tales the main character achieves an identity he works out through the course of the plot. The Sleeping Beauty becomes the queen; Cinderella becomes the wife of the prince; Snow White is awakened from her sleep of death to become the wife of the prince.

Through the Looking-Glass portrays Alice six months after her adventures in Wonderland. At the beginning of the novel, Dinah, the guardian spirit in the form of the Cheshire Cat in Wonderland, has had two kittens, a black one and a white one. As we first see Alice in *Through the Looking-Glass* she is playing with the black one. For the moment she has set aside the chessmen with which she had been playing. As she holds the kitten, she falls asleep. In the dream that follows she decides to step through the mirror over the fireplace, to probe behind the mysteries of what we see in the mirror. If one looks into a mirror, he sees himself. But there is still within the illusion the feeling that there is something behind the mirror. It is that metaphor that *Through the Looking-Glass* uses to show the other side of the real world. There is the face, which is the actuality, but behind it lies some meaning unknown to the waking mind. Once through the mirror:

> ...she began looking about, and noticed that what could be seen from the old room was quite common and uninteresting, but that all the rest was as different as possible. For instance, the pictures on the wall next the fire seemed to be all alive, and the very clock on the chimney-piece (you know you can only see the back of it in the Looking-Glass) had got the face of a little old man and grinned at her.

Thus Alice enters through the mirror and immediately encounters chessmen on the other side; these are the remnants of her last waking moments, like the rabbit in *Wonderland*. The last associations in the waking state transpose themselves into the dream. She picks up the chessmen and places them on a table she finds there. This terrifies them because she is invisible to them. Alice, is at first, an intruder into the mirror world; when she first sees the poem about the Jabberwock, it appears in mirror language to her and she must hold it up to the looking glass in order to read it. First she sees:

.YXↃOWЯƎᗺᗺAႱ

'Twas brillig, and the slithy toves
Did gyre and gimble in the wabe:
All mimsy were the borogoves,
And the mome raths outgrabe.

and then she sees it this way:

JABBERWOCKY.

'Twas brillig, and the slithy toves
  Did gyre and gimble in the wabe:
All mimsy were the borogoves,
  And the mome raths outgrabe.

She cannot read in Looking-Glass House until she becomes a part of its world. When she involves herself with what is behind the face of the mirror, or when she achieves an association with the true meaning of the objects of reality, she floats into their realm just as she fell down the rabbit-hole. In so doing, she first enters the Garden of Live Flowers. The garden here recalls the first scene of *Wonderland* where she wanted to go through a minuscule door to enter a garden. A garden is an archetype for paradise, the Garden of Eden. But in both books, paradise has been lost—there is a threatening puppy in *Wonderland*, and in *The Looking-Glass* she meets rude and insulting flowers.

In *Through The Looking-Glass,* Alice is at a more mature stage of perception than she was earlier. In the course of her journey in Wonderland, she was continually faced with the question "Who are you?" She never gave any particularly good answer. Now, however, she is able to control the discourse with the flowers and to assert herself on a plane of higher security and identity.

The tone of this passage reveals the punning and thus bantering nature of the dialogue with the flowers:

"How it is you can all talk so nicely?" Alice said, hoping to get it into a better temper by a compliment. "I've been in many gardens before, but none of the flowers could talk."

"Put your hand down, and feel the ground," said the Tiger-Lily. "Then you'll know why."

Alice did so. "It's very hard," she said; "but I don't see what that has to do with it."

"In most gardens," the Tiger-Lily said, "they make the beds too soft— so that the flowers are always asleep."

The flowers in the garden do not treat her with any great politeness, yet they are not as rude as the characters in Wonderland. We also see that between her experiences in Wonderland and Looking-Glass House she has achieved a greater awareness of the world around her; she is no longer baffled by the oblique language of the characters.

The first important character Alice meets in the garden is the Red Queen, who serves the same role of guardian and protector the Cheshire Cat did in *Wonderland*. One of Carroll's major devices now becomes apparent: he has transposed the chess game Alice was playing before she fell asleep and entered the Looking Glass world into the dream; the characters of Looking-Glass House are chessmen. The Red Queen begins to escort Alice in her journey, which has two meanings: first of all it is the journey of a pawn (a character in the game, who is also called a lily) across to the other side. But this is also the motif of the fairy tale journey away from home to the fulfillment of a quest. We combine this with the dream framework of the fantasy, and see Alice's journey as a realization of self, as all dreams are. The realm she has entered is a combined simulation of the real world: a chessboard, a mirror, and a dream. The chessboard's lines and columns are represented in *Through the Looking-Glass* by brooks and hedges. Carroll has adopted three themes which he juxtaposes with each other in the course of the narrative. First, there is the sense of identity, or the discovery of one's outer meaning, gained by looking into a mirror; next, there is the fairy tale journey that provides the fulfillment of one's role; and finally there is the actual movement of men on a chessboard.

This can be reinforced by recalling that in the 1933 Paramount film *Alice in Wonderland,* which combines both Wonderland and Looking-Glass House into one plot, the scriptwriters added a line in which the Red Queen tells Alice as they enter the world of the chessboard, "Life is a game of chess." The chess game becomes a metaphor for life in the sense of someone directing the actions of the game. The names of the chess pieces—queen, king, pawn, and so on—add to the image of humans in the hands of fate, just as the pieces on the board are manipulated by the players of the game. Fate is to life what the players are to the chessmen, and the fate of one's life from birth to death is like the journey of the chessmen from one side of the board to the other. If a piece is removed from the board before reaching the final square on the other side, this is like dying early. But, inasmuch as all this takes place in Alice's own dream, she is both player and pawn. And because it is a fairy tale plot, we know that no harm will come to her in her progress across the board. Winning the game in the terms of the fairy tale, the mirror, and the chess game means becoming Queen Alice as she checkmates the Red King, or in other words as she achieves her own identity by fulfilling her quest to become a person. It is only when she enters the chessboard that she becomes visible to the other characters. This means that when Alice begins to participate in life, which the chessboard represents, she becomes able to communicate with others.

Now the game begins. Alice is given the role of pawn. The pawn in chess is also called the lily; the lily symbolizes purity and innocence because of its whiteness. As Alice changes from lily, on one side of the board, to queen, on the other, she checkmates the Red King and progresses from immaturity to maturity. In the journey across the board toward the other side, toward identity, Alice encounters several characters in different episodes, just as on Odysseus' journey to Troy and his return to Ithaca he encounters many adventures. The squares on the chessboard have been designated by Carroll as geographic locations. On an actual board, they are merely black and white squares. But in Looking-Glass House they are topographical locales bounded by rivers and hedges. In each square there is a special landscape to provide the setting for the journey motif. This combination of chess game and journey links the episodes of the plot. Although separate from each other in most visual details, the image of the chessboard and Alice's travels from one place to the next create the unity of the plot. But Alice's travels are governed by the rules of chess. She can only move as a pawn moves. In one scene, a train carries her from one square to the next, juxtaposing the real trip, the fairy tale journey, and the chess game.

In each segment of the journey, Alice encounters a different aspect of the society of the waking world. On the train journey, she finds an exaggerated materialism where each puff of the smokestack is worth a thousand pounds. When the conductor asks for her ticket, he says language is worth a thousand pounds a word. In the illustration on the page, a caricature of Disraeli makes a comment on the commercialism and materialism of Victorian England.

Moving from the train, she comes to the house of Tweedledee and Tweedledum, twins who are mirror images of each other. The sign which points to their house is "TO TWEEDLEDUM'S HOUSE" and "TO THE HOUSE OF TWEEDLEDEE." By reversing the word order of the second part of the sign, an initial sense of their mirroring of each other is given. In several of the episodes an entertainment is presented by the characters. First there was "Jabberwocky," now Tweedledee and Tweedledum recite *The Walrus and the Carpenter:*

> 'The time has come,' the Walrus said
>   'To talk of many things:
> Of shoes—and ships—and sealing-wax—
>   Of cabbages—and kings—
> And why the sea is boiling hot—
>   And whether pigs have wings.'

Alice in the train with the gentleman in white (Disraeli). Illustration by John Tenniel.

This verse shows the mischievous tone of *Through the Looking-Glass* in its mixing together all echelons of society and types in nature: cabbages and kings, shoes and ships, the sea and pigs. It is indicative of Carroll's range of characters and human types and disavows any sense of solemn reverence toward the upper levels of society, such as "real" kings, or the Queen of Hearts and the Duchess from *Wonderland*. The poem reinforces the general tone of the fantasy.

Returning to the image of the dream, while Alice is with Tweedledee and Tweedledum she sees the Red King, which means in the progress of the game that he is on the next square. He is asleep, which means that it is not his turn to move in the chess game. An important question is asked about the dream world:

> "He's dreaming now," said Tweedledee: "and what do you think he's dreaming about?"
>
> Alice said, "Nobody can guess that."
>
> "Why, about *you!*" Tweedledee exclaimed, clapping his hands triumphantly. "And if he left off dreaming about you, where do you suppose you'd be?"
>
> "Where I am now, of course," said Alice.

"Not you!" Tweedledee retorted contemptuously. "You'd be nowhere. Why, you're only a sort of thing in his dream!"

Is he in your dream, or are you in his? This is another part of Carroll's technique of making a statement about the problems of certainty. Are you a Chinese sage dreaming that you are a butterfly or are you a butterfly dreaming that you are a Chinese sage? The same illogic and nonsense of *Wonderland* continues in all of Tweedledee's statements as he answers Alice's questions by "Contrariwise."

As the narrative continues Alice meets the White Queen, who exemplifies the recurrent stylistic device of the pun. The White Queen cannot arrange her shawl. She has this problem on her mind. When Alice meets her she asks, "Am I addressing the White Queen?"

"Well, yes, if you call that a-dressing." the Queen said. "It isn't *my* notion of the thing at all."
Alice thought it would never do to have an argument at the very beginning of their conversation, so she smiled and said, "If your Majesty will only tell me the right way to begin, I'll do it as well as I can."
"But I don't want it done at all!" groaned the poor Queen. "I've been a-dressing myself for the last two hours."

Events occur backwards in the Looking-Glass. Just as the Queen of Hearts called for sentence first, verdict afterwards in *Wonderland,* the same reversal of causality is seen in *Through the Looking-Glass.* The Queen begins by screaming, then pricks her finger, then opens her brooch. But there is certain logical validity to this:

"Take care!" cried Alice. "You're holding it all crooked!" And she caught at the brooch; but it was too late: the pin had slipped, and the Queen had pricked her finger.
"That accounts for the bleeding, you see," she said to Alice with a smile. "Now you understand the way things happen here."
"But why don't you scream now?" Alice asked, holding her hands ready to put over her ears again.
"Why, I've done all the screaming already," said the Queen. "What would be the good of having it all over again?"

Perhaps the most famous character in Looking-Glass House is Humpty-Dumpty. He also betrays the expectations of meaning in the real world. He is an egg, without seams, without discernible top or bottom. This differs considerably from what we expect of characters in the real world, who have heads, necks, and bodies. Again the question of identity arises when Humpty asks Alice, "Tell me your name and your business." He is dissatisfied with her answer, and continues, "What does it mean?" The problem of meaning in communication intensifies, as seen in the following conversation:

> "I don't know what you mean by 'glory,' " Alice said.
> Humpty Dumpty smiled contemptuously. "Of course you don't—till I tell you. I meant 'there's a nice knock-down argument for you!' "
> "But 'glory' doesn't mean 'a nice knock-down argument,' " Alice objected.
> "When *I* use a word," Humpty Dumpty said, in rather a scornful tone, "it means just what I choose it to mean—neither more nor less."

Played in the Paramount film version by W. C. Fields, all of the arrogance of Humpty's character emerges. He is a creature of false pride and a lack of awareness that is a source of *dramatic irony*. Alice knows from the outset that Humpty will fall, because she is familiar with the nursery rhyme. But Humpty remains confident that the king's promise will be fulfilled should he fall. When the audience knows something the character himself is ignorant of, the irony of his vanity takes on the added quality of comedy.

When he falls, as indeed he must, all the king's horses and all the king's men enter the scene. Here Carroll moves us from chess square to chess square and also from episode to episode by moving to the next scene when all the soldiers come to try to put Humpty Dumpty together again.

Alice has a conversation with the lion and unicorn, recalling the extinct dodo of the first chapter of *Wonderland*. Then she encounters the White Knight, a chess piece, but also a character from romance and from chivalry. The White Knight is much like Don Quixote in that he is completely inept in practical affairs. Although a lovable creature, he fails to reach the stature of high romance, because, for one thing, he cannot keep from falling off his horse.

As Alice progresses across the chessboard, she reaches the other side and checkmates the Red King, thus becoming Queen Alice. The square she then moves to becomes a castle, which she enters for the traditional feast to welcome the advent of the hero in the fairy tale. But in *Through the Looking-Glass,* the celebration turns into a nightmarish parody, with the candles growing to the ceiling and all of the food taking on personified life, forbidding her to slice and eat it. When Alice places the blame on the Red Queen and begins to shake her, she awakens to discover that she is holding the black kitten and shaking it. The fantasy ends with Alice asking:

> "Now Kitty, let's consider who it was that dreamed it all. This is a serious question, my my dear, and you should not go on licking your paw like that —as if Dinah hadn't washed you this morning! You see, Kitty, it must have been either me or the Red King. He was part of my dream, of course—but then I was part of his dream, too! *Was* it the Red King, Kitty? You were his wife, my dear, so you ought to know. . . ."

The dream is as real to Alice as the actual world of her own room and the kitten.

In this treatment of a mirrored vision of identity moving from one side of the chessboard to the other, of changing from a lily-pawn to Queen Alice, or as the archetypal motif of the journey which fulfills the quest, Carroll has presented a compressed statement about growing up. The encounters with adult customs in *Through the Looking-Glass* are not so shocking to Alice as they were in *Wonderland*. After all, she is now older and has all those earlier experiences behind her. The sense of herself that she gained in *Wonderland* now comes to her service in Looking-Glass House. In both of these books there has been a place, a *locus,* in which the fantasy occurred. First it was Wonderland, now it is Looking-Glass House. Both plots have been made believable because of the device of the dream. In a dream, whatever happens does so within the limitless power of the sleeping mind to build remarkable and fantastical images. And the device of the dream allows for a portrayal of identity associated with dreams.

The myth of the machine

The writer of fantasy achieves credibility for his creations through the device of the dream. But, although a classic, *Alice* is not the sole criterion of fantasy. Another way one can engage the reader's belief in the products of imagination is through the various myths that we hold in our culture. One of these is the myth of the machine. The great advances in technology over the past century and a half have shown an almost miraculous series of inventions, of machines that can perform all kinds of functions. If we think of what we take for granted in daily life, television sets, computers, copying machines, phonographs, kidney machines, rocket ships—obviously the list could be endless—these devices would appear to some to be at the same level of miracle as a visitation of a god from Olympus would be to the Greeks. Just compare these aspects of our daily lives with what was possible a hundred years ago. A sense emerges that in the future many more such machines will be invented.

It was said that the Director of the United States Patent Office during the 1830s resigned his job because he thought that all that could be invented already had been, and that therefore he was no longer needed. But if we look at this anecdote from our twentieth century vantage point, we see that although at the moment we seem to have a plenitude of machines to serve all our needs, in 2071 more and more seemingly miraculous machines will be equally commonplace. Thus our great expectations of new ways of life and new inventions of machines give the writer of fantasy another device to invest his creation with credibility. An example of using such a machine in a fantasy is *Charlie and the Chocolate Factory* by Roald Dahl. This book concerns a young boy named Charlie Bucket who lives in a town where there is an "ENORMOUS CHOCOLATE FACTORY," owned by Mr. Willy Wonka, who is called the greatest inventor and chocolate maker that has ever been. Mr. Wonka's factory has machinery that can

...make marshmallows that taste of violets, and rich caramels that change color every ten seconds, and little feathery sweets that melt deliciously the moment you put them between your lips, can make chewing gum that never loses its taste, and candy balloons that you can blow up to enormous sizes before you pop them with a pin and gobble them up.[3]

In this fantasy of the magical events at the chocolate factory, again, a locus is established for the story just as Wonderland and Looking-Glass House served the same purpose. The factory takes on a mysterious quality when the iron gates before it are closed for ten years and nothing but shadows can be seen working behind the frosted windows. No workers are ever seen to enter or to leave it, but better and better candies keep emerging. Dahl's use of the myth of the machine makes it believable that a machine to make miraculous candies could be invented.

Another example of the myth of the machine as a device of fantasy is seen in Ian Fleming's *Chitty Chitty Bang Bang*. After receiving a great deal of money for his invention of a candy, Commander Potts decides to buy a car for his family. As he looks around at various new ones, he finally discovers at the back of an old garage an abandoned "Twelve-cylinder, eight-liter, supercharged *Paragon Panther*. They only made one of them, and then the firm went broke. This is the only one in the world."[4] The car immediately attracts the attention of the entire family, and they buy it. After much work, it is in running order and receives its name of Chitty Chitty Bang Bang from its distinctive exhaust noise.

When repaired, at first it functions in a normal manner. But when the family leaves to go on a picnic, they get caught in a traffic jam. The car now begins to take on a personality. A knob on the dashboard lights up and says "PULL!" When there is no response from the driver, the knob then reads "IDIOT!" Finally the angry knob says "PULL, IDIOT!" When obeyed, the car puts out wings, the fan blade goes through the radiator and becomes a propellor, and it flies over all the other cars. The family goes to an island in the English Channel for their picnic, and when threatened by the rising tide, the car becomes a hydrofoil and saves their lives. After various other adventures, gangsters kidnap the children of the family; Chitty Chitty Bang Bang becomes a radar sensor and leads the parents to the captive children.

In another extended use of the myth of the machine, Ray Bradbury in *The Martian Chronicles* projects the reader into the year 2026 and gives the following picture of household machines:

In the kitchen the breakfast stove gave a hissing sigh and ejected from its warm interior eight pieces of perfectly browned toast, eight eggs sunnyside up, sixteen slices of bacon, two coffees, and two cool glasses of milk.

---

[3] Roald Dahl, *Charlie and the Chocolate Factory* (New York: Alfred A. Knopf, 1964), p. 14. Reprinted by permission.
[4] Ian Fleming, *Chitty Chitty Bang Bang* (New York: Random House, 1964), p. 25.

"Today is August 4, 2026," said a second voice from the kitchen ceiling, "in the city of Allendale, California." It repeated the date three times for memory's sake. "Today is Mr. Featherstone's birthday. Today is the anniversary of Tilita's marriage. Insurance is payable, as are the water, gas, and light bills."

Somewhere in the walls, relays clicked, memory tapes glided under electric eyes.[5]

In this land of make-believe, a feeling of credibility is given to such improbable events by the fantasy writer's use of certain beliefs and notions that are held in common by the members of modern society.

Science fiction

From the beginning of the seventeenth century, one of the most passionately held beliefs in Western culture has been that science can uncover all the mysteries of nature. While prior to this time it was believed that the sun orbited around the earth, Galileo, using the telescope, was able to prove that quite the opposite was true. This brought about an entirely new way of looking at the world. Instead of explaining reality in terms of mythological characters, such as those of the Greek pantheon or in other of the creation myths described in Chapter 2, the mode of explaining reality changed. No longer content to see nature in terms of gods and goddesses, demonstrable evidence—the scientists' documented experiments—became the desired description of the universe. Indeed our deeply rooted belief in science as the key to understanding nature has grown steadily over the centuries. In the hundred years after Galileo, man became so captivated with the notion of science as the sole means of knowing reality that this period is often called the Age of Reason or the Enlightenment.

In modern culture we must admit that we have a similar fascination with science and that we regard artistic representation as having a somewhat lesser value. Perhaps we feel less comfortable with what seems more fanciful than the empirical data of science.

As an extreme example of the promises a scientist held out to his culture, let us look at Sir Isaac Newton's scientific method, which he claimed would lead us to know:

... what is the first Cause, what Power he has over us, and what Benefits we receive from him, so far our Duty towards him, as well as that towards one another. . . .[6]

---

[5] Ray Bradbury, *The Martian Chronicles* (New York: Doubleday & Company, Inc.), p. 106. Copyright 1946 by Ray Bradbury, reprinted by permission of the Harold Matson Company, Inc.
[6] Isaac Newton, *Opticks*.

Later in the same century, Alexander Pope composed an epitaph for Newton which said:

> Nature, and Nature's laws lay hid in night:
> God said, Let Newton be! and all was light.[7]

High praise, and an example of the belief in the almost omnipotent power of science.

Steadily since then our scientific knowledge of the world around us has grown immensely. Darwinism, the theory of relativity, and the expanding universe have all influenced man's conception of himself in the universe.

The writer of fantasy has this religiously held belief in science to use as a foundation to lend credibility to his own imaginative creations. And sometimes the portrayals of the science fiction writer do not turn out too far from reality, after all. For instance, Robert Heinlein's 1947 novel *Rocket Ship Galileo* was the basis for a movie called *Destination Moon* made in 1950. When *Apollo* landed on the moon in 1969 it was startling to see how similar the movie's moon land- scape, derived from the science fiction writer's description, was compared to what we actually saw on television. Here the literal came into direct contact with the imagined. Therefore, insofar as the creations of the imagination have their own reality, man had been to the moon long before the actual touchdown of *Apollo*. And even in the sixteenth-century Italian epic *Orlando Furioso,* a character named Astolfo had made a voyage to the moon—not by spaceship but via a hippogriff, a mythical creature.

Science fiction fantasy can build on the style and format by which scientific data are presented. If we believe our knowledge of scientific concepts will grow, then we must concede the possibility that more and more miraculous machines can be invented. The science fiction writer plays upon this faith. By various manipulations of time, place, and setting, the writer can persuade the reader of the credibility of his representation. He can use machines, he can use concocted or real scientific data, and he can place his action in a remote future in outer space. In such a context, the probability of events is never questioned by the reader.

Eleanor Cameron's *The Wonderful Flight to the Mushroom Planet* has a con- temporary setting in California. An ad appears in the local newspaper seeking a spaceship made by two boys who will then apply to a Mr. Tyco M. Bass.

The setting is at first realistic and current. Although this 1954 novel was written before the day of actual space flights, prior experience with V-II rockets during World War II and the numerous flying saucer fads during the 1940s lends believability to the idea of a ship such as that built by David and

---

[7] Pope, *Epitaph Intended for Sir Isaac Newton.*

Chuck, the two main characters of the story. At every step of the narrative, Cameron gives a rationale for the possibility of the flight. Details are given of how the ship is made, of Mr. Bass—the visitor from Basidium, the Mushroom Planet—working out trajectories and carefully spelling out the details of the flight and telling the boys that they must take a mascot along. As it turns out, what is missing on the Mushroom Planet is sulphur, which is necessary for the inhabitants' health. Mr. Bass, with a kind of clairvoyance, knows that David and Chuck will take their pet hen, Mrs. Pennyfeather, with them as their mascot and that her eggs will contain the needed sulphur.

But what remains unbelievable about *The Wonderful Flight to the Mushroom Planet* is the ready permission which David's mother gives him to go on the space flight:

> "But of course you must go, David. If Mr. Bass says his people are in danger, there is no reason you shouldn't try to help them, though it may be very difficult. What did you say the name of the satellite is?"[8]

Although certainly within the spirit of doing a "good deed," it is scarcely within character for a mother to willingly allow her child to go on a journey to outer space.

This book's style lends itself to very young readers. But the problem of matching the language which a child can decode or read on his own with that required to achieve an aesthetic effect can be seen. In the passage quoted below, the two boys, David and Chuck, have left the earth's atmosphere and pass through the outer rings of stars. Here is David's reaction:

> High in the mountains, David had seen the stars sparkle as he had never seen them in the city. But now he knew that neither he nor any other earthbound creature had ever seen them in their true glory. And because he would have liked his mother and father to behold this sight too, he thought of them.[9]

This shows a vexing problem in children's literature. If the book is to be read by the child on his own, perhaps it is desirable that the syntax and vocabulary be held at this extremely simple level. Yet, let us consider the effect which is inherent in this passage. This is not a routine trip to the grocery store; the

---

[8] Eleanor Cameron, *The Wonderful Flight to the Mushroom Planet* (Boston: Little, Brown and Co., 1954) , p. 86. Reprinted by permission.

[9] *Ibid.,* p. 86.

boys in the space ship have left the earth's atmosphere and they are passing through rings of stars around the earth. Is this conveyed in the language above in any terms more than mere reportage? Hasn't the author simply told the reader what to think about the scene instead of evoking a full experience similar to those the children might have had? Compare the flat, unevocative language of the passage above to the richness of detail and sharing of experience which we see in this poem:

The Skyrocket

How sheer the arc I took, vagrant in speed,
Self-circling star, and breathed upon my flight,
Higher and slow and then again to height
Past summer bonfires, over the house the trees.

Gathering suspense in the attempt to thrust
Beyond all earth! Then, sudden gasp and stop.
Elate, I puffed in fire and golden drops
Till the one brightness spread to nebulous.

And I, a single fleck, fall into dark
While strewn about, my sister selves
A shower of small and dimming lights,
Sift lower and lower
And pale and flake and disappear in calm.

—Ann Stanford[10]

Of course it is true that the language of poetry is not the language of prose. Nevertheless, what the literary artist hopes to do beyond reporting events or beyond narrating action is to create tone, setting, mood, and instill feeling in the reader. Literature is a presentation of feeling, thought, and action in language. To come to life from the page, an experience must vibrate from the words. If the intensity of the language is missing, the reader's response likewise will be limited, nonexistent, or negative. Cameron's book is not a bad one—it simply misses realizing the material's potential. To leave earth and travel into space! That material has a built-in effect which can only be called sublime. But in this book the scene does not reach that aesthetic level.

Another science fiction work on a more mature level of sophistication is Madeleine L'Engle's *A Wrinkle in Time*. Three children, Meg and Charles Wallace and their friend Calvin, are enlisted by three magical creatures—Mrs. Which, Mrs. Whatsit, and Mrs. Who—to aid them in their battle against the Black Thing which stands for the powers of darkness and evil. The science fiction device, indicated in the title *A Wrinkle in Time,* is in effect a shift to a

---

[10] From *The Weathercock* by Ann Stanford. Copyright © 1957 by Ann Stanford. All rights reserved. Reprinted by permission of The Viking Press, Inc.

fifth dimension which allows the characters to travel beyond the speed of light, a phenomenon called *tessering,* which is an actual scientific term.

Seen at first as tramps on earth, the three Mrs. Ws, change shape and form as they travel throughout the universe. They are characterized by distinctive speech patterns—Mrs. Which stutters; by idiosyncracies of dress and life-style—Mrs. Whatsit looks like a tramp; and by what they say—Mrs. Who is a great quoter from all sources and epochs of literature and philosophy. In one of her meta-morphoses, Mrs. Whatsit changes from tramp into something quite different:

> Her plump little body began to shimmer, to quiver, to shift. The wild colors of her clothes became muted, whitened. The pudding-bag shape stretched, lengthened, merged. And suddenly before the children was a crea-ture more beautiful than any Meg had even imagined, and the beauty lay in far more than the outward description. Outwardly Mrs. Whatsit was surely no longer a Mrs. Whatsit. She was a marble white body with power-ful flanks, something like a horse but at the same time completely unlike a horse, for from the magnificently modeled back sprang a nobly formed torso, arms, and a head resembling a man's, but a man with a perfection of dignity and virtue, an exaltation of joy such as Meg had never seen.[11]

This description elevates Mrs. Whatsit to a goddess. Her appearance suggests Athena, or wisdom, who is portrayed as the body of a woman carrying the shield of the warrior. There is more than a subtle hint that Mrs. Whatsit com-bines the best of both sexes into the image of a hero.

As seen in hero myths, the nature of the quest will largely determine the seriousness and the tone of the plot. Ridding the universe of the powers of dark-ness in *A Wrinkle in Time* is more important than helping the Mushroom Peo-ple regain their green color. The voyage through space has a secondary quest—to locate Meg and Charles' father. This search makes the children's mother's acceptance of Mrs. Whatsit believable. In Cameron's book it was not credible that David and Chuck would be given permission so easily to leave earth and fly to Basidium. However, in *Wrinkle,* Mrs. Whatsit mentions the code word, *tessering,* which allows Mrs. Wallace, a scientist like her husband, to realize that she is speaking to an emissary from her husband. She and Dr. Wallace had been experimenting with the tesseract in order to free the universe from the powers of darkness.

The three goddesses from space are matched by the three children from earth. Just as each of the Mrs. Ws has her own special gift and power, each child in turn possesses a personal quality which is significant in the plot. Charles Wallace is clairvoyant and later shows a quality which provides both a resistance and an attraction to the power IT, the source of evil on the planet Camazotz. Of the three, only Charles Wallace possesses a complex enough neurological system to scorn

---

[11] Madeleine L'Engle, *A Wrinkle in Time* (New York: Farrar, Straus & Giroux, Inc., 1962), p. 30. Reprinted by permission.

IT at first but later to become a mouthpiece for the disembodied brain. Calvin O'Keefe has a power of communication which at times saves the other members of the plot from fatality.

But as the various characters finally gather on the planet Ixchel, which becomes symbolic of protectiveness and understanding, Meg's special quality, trust, emerges. The characters on Ixchel lack eyes. They understand reality through extrasensory perceptions, but on the surface are gray and dull in appearance. Like the blind prophet Tiresias, lacking actual sight but possessing inner vision, the creatures of Ixchel represent wisdom which is not deceived by outward appearances.

Indeed these characters are probably in the vein of the frog prince theme, or the beast who is actually a handsome prince from mythology and folklore:

> [They] were the same dull gray color as the flowers. If they hadn't walked upright they would have seemed like animals. They moved directly toward the three human beings. They had four arms and far more than five fingers to each hand, and the fingers were not fingers, but long waving tentacles. They had heads, and they had faces. But where the faces of the creatures on Uriel had seemed far more than human faces, these seemed far less.[12]

Although they are outwardly ugly, a marvelous fragrance emanates from these creatures as the Wallaces and Calvin come to trust them and become part of their world. Like the Beauty who finds the love of the Beast to be greater than his physical appearance, the characters on Ixchel bring out the special quality of Meg, who now emerges as the dominant character in the novel.

It is now from Meg's point of view that the story is told, and her own special quality begins to emerge. Gradually, Aunt Beast—Meg's guardian spirit on Ixchel—initiates Meg into her best quality, trust. But it is a trust tempered by the careful and sceptical examination of the facts that is a result of Meg's earlier mathematical precocity. Meg and Aunt Beast form a relationship which had not been possible between Meg and her peers on earth. Because Meg had been ahead—at least in math—of other children in school, she had been like the ugly duckling. The jeers of the other children, the cruelty of teachers and principals, and the feeling that she was not pretty robbed Meg of the outward demonstration of love and trust now possible. Aunt Beast does not scold her— and because Beast has no eyes, Meg forgets her feelings of awkwardness about her looks. She overcomes the frustration of the bright child who is not allowed the freedom of his own identity. Aunt Beast gives Meg complete acceptance, and this creates in her the security to develop love within herself which becomes necessary to solve the problems of the plot.

Earlier the group had visited the planet Camazotz, which was ruled by a central intelligence in a Kafkaesque conformity controlled by IT, much like the

---

[12] *Ibid.,* p. 173.

tyrannical computer in many other science fiction stories. Charles Wallace has been mesmerized by IT and is under its power. The others must rescue him. They meet in conference on Ixchel to decide how to do this. Mrs. Which, the oldest goddess, tells Meg that she has not yet presented her with a gift. Before this, Mrs. Whatsit gave the gift of communication to Calvin, and Mrs. Whosit gave some magical spectacles to Meg to help her through the transparent column where Dr. Wallace was imprisoned. Finally,

> . . . seeming to echo from all around her, came Mrs. Which's unforgettable voice. "I hhavee nnott ggivenn yyou mmyy ggifftt. Yyou hhave ssomethinngg thatt ITT hhass nnott. Thiss ssomethinngg iss yyourr onlly wweapponn. Bbutt yyou mmussttt ffinndd itt fforr yyourrssellf."[13]

Reminiscent of the wise women in *Briar-Rose,* Mrs. Which gives Meg an awareness that she has a gift which can free Charles Wallace from IT. Meg and her father tesser back to Camazotz. Meg enters the main chamber of the central intelligence; she realizes that her special power is her ability to love and trust. The love inherent in her personality could only have been developed by the free and accepting nature of Aunt Beast. As in *Beauty and the Beast,* when one loves another, regardless of his outward appearance, the inner self of the one who loves is cleansed and strength of character comes forth. Once Meg realizes that she loves her brother, IT's power is destroyed. As in other fairy tales where love controls the action, all ends happily, and the Wallace family is reunited.

In *A Wrinkle in Time* the main device of credibility has been that of the fifth dimension, of tessering; in addition, other elements of the fairy tale have been introduced: the absolute triumph of love over evil, the journey–quest, and the presence of goddesses from outer space.

In pursuing the fairy tale flavor of *A Wrinkle in Time,* Meg can be seen as both a Cinderella and an ugly duckling. She is the outcast in school who becomes the heroine of the flight to combat the powers of darkness. In an early scene in the novel she is quizzed in a gossipy and malicious fashion by the school principal about the whereabouts of her father. The scene is like the taunts that the fairy tale orphan receives. This early alienation is counteracted in the last part of the plot by her loving relationship with Aunt Beast, which in a sense shows the same piety and goodness as Cinderella's tending the tree on her mother's grave. The loving kindness which saves Cinderella is like the words of Aunt Beast:

> "It is so long since my own small ones were grown and gone," the beast said. "You are so tiny and vulnerable. Now I will feed you.[14]

[13] *Ibid.,* p. 202.
[14] *Ibid.,* p. 183.

The model of love allows Meg to cast aside her vulnerability as her own powers of trusting emerge.

Science fiction, then, is a form of fantasy which relies upon the reader's acceptance of the miracles of technology and scientific investigation. The imaginary science fiction world often presents a clearer perspective of the actual world. Indeed, science fiction, in its power to inculcate awareness, is one of the most moral forms of children's literature.

The writer of science fiction fantasy almost achieves the status of prophet to an advanced technological society. *1984, The Martian Chronicles, The War of the Worlds* are uncanny in their predictions of what will be the result of continued atomic pollution, machine–mind control, and other threats to human existence which the public has only recently—and perhaps ineffectually—recognized. The smog of Los Angeles and other large cities is exactly like the cloud of blackness in *A Wrinkle in Time*. The science fiction writer has a unique way to show a technological society the pathways it is pursuing to its own doom.

Borrowings from mythology and folklore

Another means by which the writer of fantasy can create believability for his plot is by borrowing directly from mythology and folklore. Literary tradition has long accepted talking animals, heroes who perform special acts, and other worlds that exist beyond the face of the visible universe. Thus in addition to the dream fantasy and the myth of the machine, older and more deeply established conventions of mythology and folklore can be used; the individual writer of fantasy often borrows from folklore.[15]

As an example of this, there is the device of the talking animal seen in all forms of mythology and folklore. Such is the basis for the credibility of E. B. White's *Charlotte's Web*. After Wilbur the Pig has been taken to the barn of Mr. Homer L. Zuckerman, he begins to talk to various other animals: Templeton the Rat, the Geese, and finally Charlotte the Spider.

E. B. White moves slowly into the fantasy details of the talking animals. He first creates a realistic setting for the human characters, and then only in Chapter 3 enters the fantasy or secondary world. As in other examples described in this chapter, a locus or place for the plot is established. In *Charlotte's Web,* the barn, which we described in Part I, becomes the setting for the fantasy. Here the fantastical elements of talking animals and their daily world begin to emerge. It

---

[15] Consider the works of Hans Christian Andersen. Although many of his stories seem to be the work of the folklorist which must show scholarly accuracy, Andersen often goes beyond the boundaries of the folklorist's strict discipline. Stories which show the mark of his creative imagination are thus fantasy and have been borrowed from folklore and given the form of the author's own unique personality and experience. *The Ugly Duckling, The Wild Swans,* and *The Little Mermaid* are examples of Andersen's fantasy.

is also significant that the animals talk only to each other and never to human beings, who live in an alien world which is a threat to the sanctity of the barn.

The locus of the fantasy is of great importance. Alice is in a dream; Meg and Charles Wallace and Calvin are in outer space; and Wilbur and Charlotte are in the barn, which is a kind of primal paradise where it seems "nothing bad could ever happen." Without this careful building of a setting for the fantasy, the clash of improbable events with the real world destroys the illusion of actuality.

Although Wilbur is the main character of the novel, it is Charlotte who controls the action of the plot. As in the fairy tale, she is the guardian spirit who, through love, will rescue those threatened with danger. She decides to save Wilbur from becoming the Christmas ham, and finally arrives at a means of doing so by weaving a web over his crib which says SOME PIG, giving Wilbur the status of the divine child. Her web becomes the central unifying device of the plot. White builds upon the fact that a spider's web is a filament spun from within itself—a creation from within its own body. Usually, the spider uses its web only to catch prey, to move down or up a wall, and to construct a cocoon for its eggs. Charlotte, however, uses her web-making capacity to save Wilbur's life. Throughout the novel, Charlotte speaks of an approaching time when she must fulfill a task—the spinning of the egg sack. As she nears this moment, she becomes increasingly weary, as if the extra effort of giving her web to Wilbur has exhausted her life prematurely. The web, then, becomes symbolic of unselfish love—spun from within herself at her own expense and given without complaint. Charlotte never fears the death she knows is at hand: she is at peace as part of the cycles of nature and asks only that Wilbur take care of the egg sack. From the beginning of the novel she has been the figure of strength which helps the character of Wilbur to grow.

Once back home in his barn, saved from his fears of death, Wilbur nurtures the egg sack and sees the spiders emerge. It is then that he realizes Charlotte's meaning when she told him not to fear death—Wilbur sees her reborn in her children each spring. Through Charlotte's influence he becomes unselfish and secure; his growth in character is intensified by contrast with the static selfishness of Templeton the Rat, who remains at the same level of self-seeking through the novel.

Apart from the devices of credibility described above, borrowing from mythology and folklore seems to be the modern trend in fantasy. Tolkien perhaps began this trend by borrowing from Norse and Germanic mythology in *The Hobbit* and in his subsequent trilogy for adults. Dwarves, elves, goblins, and other borrowed characters abound in his plot, and he also borrows the search for the Ring of Power as seen in the Germanic myth of the Ring of the Nibelungs. *The Gammage Cup,* by Carol Kendall, likewise places itself in a mythic locale apart from the real world—a land of the River, peopled by the imaginary Minnipins. They are involved in the mythic quest for the Gammage Cup, whose owner, like the finder of the Holy Grail, will find wisdom. The characters Gummy, Muggles, and Curley, who are somewhat like mischievous elves, win the contest for the cup and also find love and marriage. *The Borrowers,* by Mary Norton, also achieves

Wilbur matures into a hero through the guidance and example of Charlotte. Illustration by Garth Williams. From Charlotte's Web *by E. B. White. Copyright, 1952, by E. B. White. Reprinted by permission of Harper & Row, Publishers.*

believability for the small creatures who live in the walls of an old house, and who live by "borrowing" from the household of adults outside, by equating them with the leprechauns of Irish legend. As in most myths and folk tales, the focus of the writer is upon the interaction of the real and imaginary world and upon the salvation of the world through love and heroism in the personagaes of the mythic and folkloristic characters portrayed.

In the bibliography at the end of the book, we describe numerous examples of fantasy. Examine them to see whether the fantasy plot is created by means of a dream, a prevalent myth, or in terms of science fiction.

The value of fantasy in children's literature lies in its extension of the possibilities of portrayal, characterization, and plot beyond the limits of the observable world. The creator of fantasy builds a world which is accessible to the imagination of the reader and lends credibility to his work through the devices of dream fantasy, the myth of the machine, science fiction, and by borrowing the devices of mythology and folklore. Fantasy also creates a Secondary World which comments on the real world. In the examples given in this chapter, even the most improbable plots and characterizations have made a statement about the nature of reality. Wonderland and Looking-Glass House reflect many of the absurdities and foibles of the real world, and science fiction often makes an almost prophetic statement on the uses of technology. Fantasy, then, is a literary genre which is a product of the probing imagination of the artist to create "a willing suspension of disbelief" for even the most unlikely events.

Ray Bradbury, in *The Martian Chronicles,* has a scene in the year 2005 in which the speaker looks back to the downfall of imagination in American culture when the Investigators of Moral Climates banished fantasy from literature:

> All the beautiful literary lies and flights of fancy must be shot in mid-air. So they lined them up against a library wall one Sunday morning 30 years ago, in 1975; they lined them up, St. Nicholas and the Headless Horseman and Snow White and Rumpelstiltskin and Mother Goose—oh, what a wailing!—and shot them down, and burned the paper castles and the fairy frogs and old kings and the people who lived happily ever after (for of course it was a fact that *nobody* lived happily ever after!), and Once Upon a Time became No More! And they spread the ashes of the Phantom Rickshaw with the rubble of the Land of Oz; they filleted the bones of Glinda the Good and Ozma and shattered Polychrome in a spectroscope and served Jack Pumpkinhead with meringue at the Biologists' Ball! The Beanstalk died in a bramble of red tape! Sleeping Beauty awoke at the kiss of a scientist and expired at the fatal puncture of his syringe. And they made Alice drink something from a bottle which reduced her to a size where she could no longer cry "Curiouser and curiouser," and they gave the Looking Glass one hammer blow to smash it and every Red King and oyster away![16]

In Bradbury's fantasy, it is significant that this death of the imagination in 1975 ends in the destruction of the earth in war at the end of the novel in the year 2026.

---

[16] Bradbury, *The Martian Chronicles,* p. 166.

4 Prose Fiction

In prose fiction—novels and short stories—the writer creates a plot, a set of characters, and events which are simulations of the real world. What we encounter in prose fiction, although sometimes bizarre and exotic, always conforms to the usual notions of the real world. That is, the main thrust of the artist's portrayal is within the confines of the commonly accepted concepts of natural human behaviour. Indeed, the subject matter of prose fiction is almost invariably the nature of man in his various periods of time, states of fortune, and relationships with other humans and with nature. The writer of prose fiction deals with the actual world in representing human nature.

The question instantly arises: "What is the real world?" For the moment let us beg this metaphysical question. Surely it is evident from our earlier examination of fantasy literature that the material in that genre does not conform to the laws of physical science and the dictates of reality. Fantasy may have direct bearing on human nature, but it does not, finally, portray actual human nature. Common sense tells us that some representations in literature are true to the real world and that others are not. Prose fiction adheres more faithfully to what most persons would call reality than fantasy literature does.

In the eighteenth century a kind of writing arose which portrayed events and characters in much the same manner as newspaper reportage. Indeed, Daniel Defoe, who is credited with being one of the originators of the novel with his *Robinson Crusoe,* was himself a journalist. A vast body of writing followed which was in the form of letters between friends or diaries meticulously documented as to time and place, both devices giving the semblance of literal truth. Novelists go to great lengths to imitate the manners and attitudes of actual persons and known events. In the history of the novel, there have also been many fictionalized accounts of famous persons or of sensational events—all attempts to give books the air of reality.

Of course it is true that the writer of fantasy also seeks to give his reader the sense of reality and credibility. Since in the real world animals do not talk, automobiles do not fly, and chewing gum does lose its taste, these improbable events are permissible in fantasy only if the proper entries into the secondary world are made. But their appearance in prose fiction destroys the picture of the real world which the novelist hopes to create.

Why is this difference between fantasy and prose fiction worth pursuing? Because the standards for judging their effectiveness are different. Both types of literature demand plot, character, and good style. But fantasy asks that we accept an improbable world while prose fiction asks us to accept a picture of the actual world. The philosophical problem is delicate at this point. Both kinds of writing spring from the imagination of the writer, but they portray different worlds.

Fantasy demands many devices of credibility to create a "willing suspension of disbelief" in the reader. This is less true of prose fiction. Stories which are compatible with one's own knowledge of the workings of the real world, as in prose fiction, ask less of the reader's acceptance of what is, after all, unreal. Any character in literature is by definition a product of the author's imagination. Unless the author is being deliberately biographical, his creations will be conjurings of his own genius and not the actual record of real human beings. By choosing to portray the real world, the prose fiction writer already has the material to achieve the semblance of truth. He does not face the task of transporting the reader to Mars or into the company of talking animals. Indeed, he is denied the option.

But if he is not to portray an unreal world as in fantasy, his representation must then be true to the real world. Here is the crux of judging a work of prose fiction: "Has the writer made a true picture of the world and of life?" The time and setting he chooses are immaterial—his plot may take place in ancient Greece or in modern Manhattan. His task is to make his characters believable as real people with understandable emotions, personalities, and appearances. The realness of the characters in prose fiction and the believability of the situations in which they find themselves allow the reader to identify with them as extensions of himself; in encountering others with problems and circumstances perhaps similar to his own, the reader enriches his experience.

Thus the plot and characters of prose fiction must create the nearest possible semblance of reality. The characters cannot rely upon magic to effect their goals, no more than you or I can. The plot cannot depend upon fairies or godmothers to resolve itself: the working out of the plot must involve the same sense of the mystery of what causes the future as life itself does. And the totality of the actions portrayed must represent a believable episode in human affairs.

This is accomplished in several ways which we will examine in this chapter. But the most important aspect of prose fiction is the presence of humans in real situations. Reality is the keynote of this kind of writing. The plot, characters, and style all serve to achieve that kind of representation. As usual, there are questions of point of view, setting, thematic development, archetype, symbolism, and structure to be considered. We must inquire into how effectively the story was told and about its internal development. But this is true of other genres of literature as well. The important consideration here is *how* the author achieves what we can accept as an accurate and believable picture of the world.

Historical Prose Fiction

Kinds of prose fiction for children

One way to give the stamp of truth to a work is to portray characters as participating in documented historical events. Actual historical personages may even figure in the action. The author need not assume the role of either the historian or the biographer, but may take for his setting and plot believable events—believable because they did indeed take place. The role of the actual historical event or personage generally will be limited to that of a backdrop for the further action of the characters and events the author is to portray. If a historical character enters the action, he usually receives a static and remote treatment; he nonetheless lends credibility to the action of the novel. If a great historical event is the background for the plot, its issues and facts—although of great importance—become subordinated to the portrayal of characters in their own part of the larger event.

Characters portrayed in the setting of a war, for example, are the focus of the action rather than the war itself. The war provides the reality within which their lives are represented. In *Across Five Aprils* by Irene Hunt, the main character is Jethro Creighton, who between the ages of nine and fourteen lives through the five Aprils of the Civil War. The book begins with a realistic setting of rural life in southern Illinois in April 1861, with its daily activities, people, their way of life, with great attention to describing details of the countryside in order to give a clear sense of a real place. The plot then changes into the continuing turmoil of a war which actually happened. But the plot involves imaginary characters and their problems within the setting of the Civil War. The Creightons are creations of the author's imagination, and as the family's problems increase—the family gradually deteriorates as one brother joins the army of the South instead of the North, and the barn is burned by nightriders—the focus remains upon the family. Although Hunt adds credibility to her narrative by naming many of the historical personages of the period—Lincoln even writes to Jethro to assure him of pardon for a deserter the boy had been sheltering—it is the characters themselves who are the central concern.

The theme of *Across Five Aprils* is inescapably the massive complications and disruptions that a civil war causes, even in a remote rural community. It states that the effects of war are brutal and shameful. But it does this obliquely through the portrayal of imaginary characters within the setting of the war. This distinguishes historical prose fiction from academic history. The academician seeks for records of actual persons; the novelist creates evidence and characters where none actually existed.

It is not essential, however, that historical fiction for children deal only with the great events and people of the past. A growing and clearly healthy trend in all areas of children's literature is toward portraying life in more contemporary settings and in presenting attitudes which are more compatible with adult interpretations of the world's problems and the circumstances of the human condition. Earlier notions that children should be shielded from tragic or seemingly sordid facts of life have given way to more believable representations of reality. This is true both in prose fiction and in historical fiction.

Certainly the past is meaningful in interpreting the present. Perhaps we can even learn from past mistakes—although, as we look back on Golden Ages crushed repeatedly into darkness, such a hope does not seem realistic. Often the best the past can do is to illuminate some of the causes of a present dilemma and provide at least the security of intellectual comprehension.

But the present has unique qualities: we are not simply products of the past— we are more, because we are new. Novelists who use the present as a historical background often achieve a power and validity denied to those who use the remote past. The present moment becomes history even while it is happening; issues which actually touch our lives can have a correspondingly greater level of interest and involvement. Two works of prose fiction for children indicate this direction of using the present as history: *The Man in the Box: A Story from Vietnam* by Mary Lois Dunn and Leon Phillips' *Split Bamboo: A Story of Espionage behind the Bamboo Curtain.* In both novels, the contemporary conflict between East and West is the historical setting for the plot.

Although the events themselves are not the novelist's major concern in historical fiction, he still will take an ethical and moral stance regarding them. The writer who chooses a Civil War background will characteristically ally himself with either the North or South. Although his aim may be to reveal the horrors of war, he usually will have to choose a side; in wars or other political issues, neutrality is virtually nonexistent. So, the author's ethical stance will be determined by his choice of material and the moral point of view he takes toward it. Art is not propaganda nor is it overt moralizing, but an ethical point of view will always emerge. That is, art by its nature makes a statement about the human condition which implicity involves a statement of how man should be.

Certainly no war is more meaningful for today's child than today's war. The conflicts between the communist world and the West have created the major political issues of the last 40 years. These have reached another peak in the last 15 years. *The Man in the Box* and *Split Bamboo* involve, then, ideas of the greatest importance to tomorrow's adult.

First, in *The Man in the Box,* we again see the pattern in historical fiction of imaginary characters in a background of a historical event or period. This novel involves two main characters: Chau Li, a North Vietnamese boy who lives in a village captured by the Cong, and David Lee, an American soldier who is brought as a Cong captive to Chau Li's village. The American is placed on public display in a box hanging from a pole in the center of the village. The box is the same one in which Chau Li's own father had earlier been tortured and killed by the Cong. The boy resolves to rescue the soldier; with the help of Ky, a Cong collaborator but Chau Li's friend nevertheless, he takes the soldier to a secret cave where the French had earlier left behind food and medical supplies. Gradually Chau Li nurses David to the point where the two can painfully make their way to a village where they will meet American soldiers. As the bond between the two grows,

David decides to take Chau Li to the United States with him, and the boy feels that he will regain the security of a family (it had been necessary for his own mother to inform on him to save her own life, thereby exiling him forever from his own village). David and Chau Li finally reach the Americans, but the helicopter which comes to rescue David is piloted by a South Vietnamese who refuses to allow a North Vietnamese into the vehicle and pushes Chau Li out the door just as he takes off. David's friends who remain behind, however, promise to take Chau Li to Da Nang where he can be reunited with the American. But a swift Cong attack wipes them all out, leaving the boy alone once again. Ky suddenly appears to take Chau Li to safety, but in his hysteria and fear, Chau Li fails to recognize him and kills him with a grenade. Once he realizes what he has done, Chau Li retreats into madness and with a vague sense of searching for David in Da Nang sets out on the river, still an outcast with little hope of ever finding his friend. The ending does not dwell on the boy's madness, but its clearly implies it.

The novel's tone is of the greatest seriousness and solemnity. Yet the author does not further darken an already tragic plot with overt statements of Chau Li's fate. The realness of the narrative of a boy caught in the completely destructive forces of the war projects its own aesthetic effect. The novel, of course, makes an ethical statement about war, but it does so through the implications of its plot and character interaction.

The style of the novel is appropriate to this kind of treatment; that is, it allows the scene itself to suggest interpretation. The writing is understated, objectively descriptive and plain. To create the effect of pain and suffering, no ornamentation is necessary beyond a flat statement of David's torture in the box, Chau Li's rejection by the helicopter pilot, and the destruction of the Americans and the village. The character of Chau Li is at first delineated by the stylistic device of dialect—his English speech contains certain syntactical peculiarities of the French language, thus associating him with the earlier French invaders; for instance, he refers to his family as *"la mère"* ("the mother"). The American soldiers, likewise, use some American slang in their speech. Another device foreshadows the plot: David Lee and Chau Li are linked by having the same second name, preparing for the possibility of David's adopting Chau Li. But because David's mouth has been injured by the Cong, he cannot pronounce Chau Li's name properly and seems to call him "Charlie," a name for the Cong, foreshadowing the eventual doom of the boy as an outcast and an enemy.

The Man in the Box is neither morbid nor macabre. The clear tone of the narrative achieves the ring of truth, and although tragic in the extreme, it presents the details of suffering as necessary elements of the plot. There is no intrusion of massacre except to project the drama of the situation. The novel achieves its effect through imaginary characters portrayed in a real historical moment, thus creating an emotional identification with the circumstances which a historical narrative of the remote past could not evoke.

The plot of Phillips' *Split Bamboo* opens with the main character, Larry Heddon, landing on the coast of Red China from an American submarine. Heddon has been transformed through plastic surgery into Richard L. Bliss, who has access to secret documents revealing the location of a Chinese spy operation in San Francisco. He has been persuaded to undertake this mission to rescue his half-Chinese son, David, who had been kidnapped several years earlier when Heddon was a newspaper correspondent in China; Larry's wife, Sue, was murdered trying to prevent her son's abduction. Although Heddon at first thought his son dead, later events suggested otherwise, and he now is committed to rescuing his son from the Red Chinese. The plot establishes two problems at the beginning: to find David and to obtain the spy documents.

Although the novel might seem like a James Bond thriller because of the plastic surgery and the spy motif, the tone is always serious not only because of the historical conflict between Red China and the United States, but further because of the father's quest to rescue his son. James Bond never has any goal other than pleasure or adventure: Heddon's quest places him on a different plane of seriousness as a hero. And the author never goes to Ian Fleming's excessive lengths of gimmickry and outrageous unreality to advance the plot. *Split Bamboo* is a statement of heroism rather than of mere and incredible daring. The fact that the focus of the plot is on the *character* of Heddon and his son David distinguishes it from Fleming's less serious *Dr. No,* although both involve the East–West conflict.

The details of Heddon's transformation into Bliss are made credible at every point. We are first told that Larry is the son of missionaries in China and that he is an authority on Chinese customs and languages—he would therefore be able to handle himself in almost any difficult situation involving the Chinese character. And he is well trained at a school for spies in realistic survival techniques, such as eating papers which might incriminate him. Further, he had been thoroughly briefed on every detail of Richard Bliss' life. His ability, then, to penetrate the spy centers of Red China is believable. His ultimate rescue of David also is realistic. No magic carpet or fairy godmother comes to save them—their own ingenuity, which is also credible, saves them. The details of their escape involve Larry's staining his skin with litchi nuts, wearing dark contact lenses to pass as Chinese, and using various dialects which both David and Larry would be expected to know.

Both plots achieve their seriousness and drama from their background, told in realistic and credible detail. No element of fantasy literature enters either plot. Whether the ending is happy as in *Split Bamboo* or tragic as in *The Man in the Box,* the basic technique of the novelist is the same: to portray imaginary characters in realistic terms within the context of a historical setting. The reader then identifies indirectly with the issues of the historical moment through these characters.

The social novel   Throughout the eighteenth and nineteenth centuries, novelists established a mode of writing that today's children's novelists rely on heavily. This can be called the *social mode*. As its name implies, this is a detailed account of the nature of man in his cultural groups. It portrays the fortunes of large, closely-knit families with many anecdotes of their doings. While the social novel abounds with the characters' troubled love affairs, rises and falls in fortune, the settings and incidents in the story are more important than the characters, who generally remain virtually unchanged from beginning to end. Such novels for adults are full of infidelities, elopements, personal and financial disasters, and other scandalous and gossipy affairs. The social customs, manners, conventions, and habits of a social class at a particular time and place are described in great detail and with great accuracy, along with how these mores exert powerful control over the actions of the characters. Galsworthy's *Forsyte Saga* and Thackeray's *Vanity Fair* come to mind as representative examples of the social novel. Such novels are often called "novels of manners." Much attention is given to landscapes, conveyances, dinners, hunts, court trials, and the customs and folkways of the characters.

The sociological novel may also be considered under this category. Such novels center on the nature, function, and effect of the society in which the characters live and on the social forces playing on them. Different from the traditional novel in the social mode, the sociological novel presents a thesis about a social issue and argues for a solution to a social problem. An example of this type of novel in children's literature is *The Empty School House* by Natalie Carlson, which deals with school desegregation in the South. The thesis of this book is that if whites can experience the shock of seeing Negro children hurt as a consequence of segregation, they will become aroused to give up their prejudices. The plot of *The Empty School House* takes this turn.

A Social Novel for Children

A novel in children's literature that conforms almost completely to the mode set by writers in the eighteenth and nineteenth centuries is that of Laura Ingalls Wilder. Wilder breaks up her narrative into seven different books.* But this is mere expediency. The seven books constitute a single novel, for each book begins where the former ends. Although the reader has no need for any special preparation for each of the succeeding books, the seven books together tell the continuing story of Laura Ingalls from about the age of three to age eighteen, when she marries. Each book describes a year or so in the life of this girl and her family on the Western frontier of America in 1860 to 1880.

---

* Some catalogers have mistakenly included Wilder's *Farmer Boy* as part of the novel. Although written in the sequence of the other books, *Farmer Boy* is not part of the Wilder novel. It appears that Wilder may have thought to develop the characters of *Farmer Boy* in depth (they later appear in the novel as minor characters) but decided against this and completed her novel around different family and thematic material.

The plot and setting of Wilder's novel are more important than her characters. Plot here means the typical narrative of the social novel, that is, the telling out of a social or familial epoch, rather than the depiction of a well developed representation of personality. *The Long Winter,* the fifth book in the series, appears to stand apart from this generalization; it has a sustained theme—the inexplicable cruelty of nature to a fragile humanity. No detail in the book acts to divert its plot from this theme. Accordingly, the structure of *The Long Winter* is more unified than that of the other volumes. The events in this section of the novel, which lead to worsening conditions of hunger, cold, and isolation brought on by a frighteningly vicious winter, move steadily forward in a chain of connected episodes toward a favorable resolution of the plot—a gallantly successful effort by brave men in the face of fierce natural odds to get the isolated community enough food to last out the winter. Also, the suspense is kept at a higher pitch, and the protagonists and antagonists are shown in steady focus. The symbolic implications of the cruel yet neutral elements of God's world pitted against His earthly creatures are apparent. As an artistic endeavor, therefore, this book is better than the remainder of the novel. Wilder's ingenuity as a writer comes to its peak here.

The characters in the book are idealized and stereotyped. They are flat characters—habitual, unchanging automatons. They enter and leave the episodes in the novel with the same set of qualities; they are not shaped by the forces that push on them. Thus, they never pause to question their actions in response to these forces. As in the typical social novel, Wilder describes her characters, praises and rebukes them in a direct fashion, allowing little or nothing for the reader to infer about their personalities and motivations. There is nothing inherently wrong with "flat" fictional characters, of course. Many people in real life react in much the same way as Wilder's characters. But these are what we call "stock" characters: the godly reverend; the shrewd storekeeper; the sadistic teacher; the righteous family. Symbolically, the main characters in her novel illustrate Christian goodness, charity, and virtue.

The rambling, meandering, slow-paced plot allows the author time and room to include a multitude of details about the family's daily life—waking, dressing, washing, eating, working, singing, and so on. While full of incident, the plot is subdued, muted, and markedly devoid of complexity or subplots. (*Little House in the Big Woods* does have some flashbacks of Pa's experiences in the form of stories told by him. This does not happen again in the novel, however.) The subject of the novel is plain, simple people, with sentimental emotions. The quiet, calm life in which they can enjoy the beauty of nature is their preference. Such characterization influences the plot, of course. A good plot cannot be only a series of happenings; it reveals and influences character. But without highly developed characters, there will not be a tightly knit plot. Nor does a geographical change of setting change the novel's atmosphere; the air the characters breathe, the world in which they live, remains the same.

The tone of the book is one of relentless optimism about life's vicissitudes. The deprivation, hardship, disappointments, and suffering are understandable only in terms of the belief the novel exudes that God hurts those he loves. This is, of course, the traditional Christian doctrine that accepts the paradox of a loving God and a cruel world. The family's psychological optimism based on its spirituality supports the hope for a better land (here and in the hereafter), and gives a buoy to their life. Seldom if ever does Wilder allow her characters to deviate into cynicism or hopelessness. A chapter heading from *A Long Winter,* "Where There's a Will," typifies the optimistic tone of the novel.

The seven-volume novel is set in the enormous Western prairie in frontier days. Despite this vastness, Wilder is able to authenticate all the minor facts of her scenes. Her observation of natural detail is impeccable. The local color, homes, manners, conversations, moral codes, customs, and fashions are fully described in lengthy passages with lavish lists of articles and items. Concentrating on setting rather than characterization, Wilder creates a panorama of visual images of events and places rather than developing characters.

Wilder adopts an omniscient point of view in her novel. She knows and tells all that happens in each character's mind and discusses in a direct fashion the meaning of their behavior and speech. As we noted was true for the social novel, the examination of intellectual motives for behavior is submerged in the mass of descriptive detail about objects and actions. Here the author's voice is loudly heard. This is reasonable enough, since a direct presentation works well with Wilder's rather flat, typical characters.

A story can be told from the viewpoint of most of its characters. If it cannot, critics maintain, there is not enough conflict of motivating forces at work to provide a reason for the story to exist. Thus, if a story will not crystallize, it may be that: (a) the dramatic qualities of the idea are weak or too anecdotal in nature, or there is too little internal conflict or protagonist–antagonist conflict; (b) the author may not have identified himself adequately with a character, or penetrated sufficiently into a character to experience his wonder, delight, or disappointments; (c) the actions of the characters may not be well enough developed to make them plausible to the reader; or (d) the plot has overpowered the character participation. With the possible exception of (b), these ideas explain why Wilder chose to adopt an omniscient viewpoint in her novel. Therefore, with Wilder we read a novel which does not allow the characters to show how they come to feel as they do.

The style of the novel is influenced by Wilder's viewpoint. A less than omniscient viewpoint would have allowed for a lighter, a more evocative style. The omniscient viewpoint does result in a style that is simple and lucid, however. Circumlocution is conspicuously absent despite the disconnected flow of incident in the novel. Too, Wilder uses descriptive words that display—without overwriting—her sensitivity to sounds, shapes, light, colors, and smells. Her style in general is physical, yet catches images like a net: "The air was soft and moist, the eaves were dripping, and the snow was slushy underfoot."[1] At other times, working

---

[1] Laura Ingalls Wilder, *These Happy Golden Years* (New York: Harper & Row, 1945), p. 106.

as explicitly as a camera, it captures the vigorous nature of the setting of the stories: "Suppertime passed quickly, and when the evening lamp was lighted and the family gathered around Uncle Tom in the sitting room, Pa still kept him speaking of the lumber camps and log drives, of roaring rivers and the wild, burly men of the logging camps."[2]

The elements of the Wilder novel cohere into no determinable form. But this is not necessary for a social novel, in which any visual act can be complete within itself. There need be little attention to new developments of the plot happening at the right point with the right emphasis. Accordingly, there is no way to authenticate whether an incident in Wilder's novel is truly necessary or pertinent. Since in the social novel there is no conception of a hero meeting a single, crucial dilemma and resolving it, one can never sense the relative importance of separate incidents in Wilder's story. That is, no critical event (except in *The Long Winter*) becomes the binding force of the work. Rather than relying on literary form for its integrity, Wilder's novel allows the activities of her family to become the fundamental force in her story. The consistency of atmosphere Wilder is able to maintain in this way serves as a unifying factor nevertheless. This atmosphere we have described as the self-reliance and persistence of the family born out of a faith in the imperceptible—yet ultimate—rationality of their God.

The major symbol in Wilder's novel has been alluded to in previous comments. It is what Rollo May calls the "central symbol" in modern Western culture. This is the supernatural order of Christianity that is formed and nourished by the family as a social system. Parents are the model and critical factor in this symbolization. But there is today a deterioration and breakdown in this central symbol; it has lost its meaning for modern man. Hence, this breakdown represents a partial explanation of today's growing generation gap, of proportions Wilder could never have dreamed. The formulation of the major symbol of Wilder's novel comes through the family's trials by God, who uses His harshest natural forces to test their faith. The characters of the novel, as we have demonstrated, can be taken to represent other meanings independent of the actions ascribed to them. The parents stand for the force of tradition and thus represent the world of moral commandments and prohibitions. That Pa is a farmer symbolizes his role as a force of regeneration and salvation, equating his bringing the crops to ripeness with raising his family; both roles are creative in the face of destructive physical nature. His is the force that joins every beginning to every end, a link that binds time together. The use of this symbol of cohesion which transcends the novel allows Wilder to write with little other unity or structure.

Pa's frequent singing and fiddle playing show his role as a mediator between heaven and earth. Singing is symbolic of the natural connection between all things, the spreading and the exaltation of the inner relationship that holds things together. It is no accident that Pa reverts to music at moments of stress or when life seems to be coming apart.

---

[2] *Ibid.*, p. 108.

The recurring storms and blizzards help form the thematic material of this novel and also have symbolic importance. Storms are a voice of a supreme diety; like everything else that occurs in heaven and descends therefrom, it has a sacred quality about it. The family must suffer it, privately regret it, but yet dutifully respect its origin. This is also true of the blindness that comes to Laura's sister as the result of scarlet fever. The blindness scourges whatever evil there was in Mary, so this apparent misfortune has positive secondary value. The violence of nature in Wilder's novel must be seen the same way. It brings to the family a sense of unity not otherwise possible.

The dramatic novel

The *dramatic* novel also emerged in the nineteenth century. The term "dramatic" rightly suggests that the novel's emphasis upon character and psychological elements is heavier than upon setting or incident. There are fewer characters than in social or sociological novels, which allows greater attention to each character. The time-lapse, rather than extending through generations as in novels such as Wilder's, is short, sometimes only days or weeks in length. The novels that represent this mode come to a strong, inevitable ending rather than ending when their epoch ends. The novel in the dramatic mode ends, then, with a feeling of deep finality as opposed to the author's simply running out of time.

The dramatic novel strongly resembles a play; its dramatic incident becomes the center of its being. As in a drama, it portrays its characters vividly in emphatic moments of crisis. The plot moves steadily through a series of minor crises as in social novels. But in contrast to the social novel, all the minor movements lead to a major crisis. At that point the minor dilemmas find their rightful perspective. In the social novel the author is apt to interrupt his narrative to express his ideas about a scene or character, or to interpret directly the feelings of the characters for the reader. In the dramatic mode, however, he presents characters much as the dramatist does, without a subjective explanation of what the character is like or is thinking. The reader learns what the characters are like as they are allowed to speak and act for themselves.

Characters in the dramatic novel are depicted in a quick succession of tense, pivotal scenes. The author's narrative is lean and concise. Since the characters themselves move the action forward, they must have more breadth and depth of personality than in other kinds of novels—they must show stronger emotions and deeper feelings and must have more significant experiences. They must consequently be more intensely realized human beings. The novels for adults of Jane Austen and the Brontë sisters and, more recently, those of Hemingway, Faulkner, and Conrad all fit this mode.

A Dramatic Novel for Children

Dorp Dead by Julia Cunningham is the story of Gilly (Gillford) Ground, who, upon the death of his grandmother (his parents are also presumably dead), finds himself thrown into an orphanage "the day before I got to be ten."[3] For a "grey and gritty year" many unsuccessful attempts are made in the orphanage to grind Gilly down. He finds sanctuary from its required mechanical, monotonous rituals by escaping to a nearby tower he discovers in his ramblings. This "very crumbly ruin of a tower . . . open to the sky" becomes to him "my kingdom and my home." In his tower Gilly meets Hunter, a "man entirely clothed in black" who carries a rifle but uses it for "protection," not killing. Gilly understands the significance of this. He can "pretend for one luxurious moment he is my father."

Upon returning to the orphanage from his tower after an overnight absence, Gilly is told he will be sent to the foster home of Mr. Kobalt, "the town eccentric," a "queer" and "fruity" man, "a man who never speaks to anyone." Kobalt is "a strange time-controlled person, lives in the lanes of time; each hour is channeled." Gilly finds Kobalt, a ladder-maker, incommunicative except to give him stern orders for work on the ladders and in the house. Gilly's one release is to visit his tower and to talk with Hunter, who gives Gilly his real name "shut away in a sealed envelope."

Later Gilly finds Mash, Kobalt's dog, slashed and bleeding from a whipping by his owner. "Mash must die," is Kobalt's excuse for his sickening cruelty. After attending to the dog's injuries, Gilly wonders if the same treatment is not intended for him. Upon spying into Kobalt's room, his worst suspicions are confirmed: Kobalt has built a cage just his size! The climax of the story comes with Gilly's flight from Kobalt's clutches to Hunter's tower. Kobalt pursues with every indication on his part that he will kill Gilly. In the nick of time Mash attacks Kobalt, which allows the boy and dog to make off to join Hunter. But not before Gilly returns and defiantly scratches "Dorp Dead" on Kobalt's shiny door. This, he proclaims, is "my last message to the false and captive world I once desired."

The two main characters of the book are fully developed. They are not at all like the stereotyped characters of the social novel, but achieve unique, distinctive identities. Equally important for the distinction between the social and dramatic novel is the way in which Cunningham develops her characters. Gilly's personality is revealed through his frequent introspections regarding his morals, motives, needs, and relationships with others. We learn in this way that he knows he is smart, which is important, because Gilly puts up a front of being dumb:

> I am ferociously intelligent for my age and at ten I hide this. It is a weapon
> for defense as comforting as a very sharp knife worn between the skin and

---

[3] Excerpts from *Dorp Dead,* by Julia Cunningham, illustration by James Spanfeller. Copyright © 1965 by Julia Cunningham. Reprinted by permission of Pantheon Books, a Division of Random House, Inc.

The threatening Kobalt. Illustration by James Spanfeller. From Dorp Dead *by Julia Cunningham. Copyright © 1965 by Julia Cunningham. Reprinted by permission of Pantheon Books, a Division of Random House, Inc.*

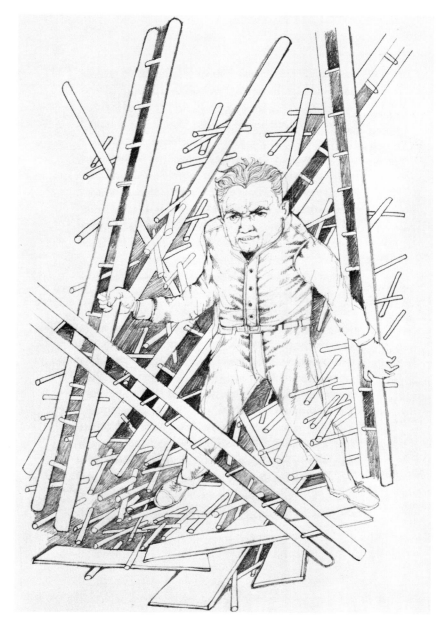

the shirt.... It's my gold, my shelter, and my pride. It's completely my possession and I save it like an old miser to spend later. I purposely never learn to spell.

We gain insight this way into why he does not get along socially:

> Anyone can see why I am never very popular or sought after: a stuffed bear in school from whom infrequent and inaccurate grunts of nonknowledge are extracted, and a true clunk at sports, besides offering nothing in the way of malice or inventiveness in between.

He considers the reasons for his apparent negativism, and

> ... all I come up with is that a person has to hold out against being the same as everyone, even if only over a few words like rabbitt. [Gilly deliberately mispells words.]
>   Maybe I'll become a nasty little squinched-up, squeezed-dry nobody, bitter as a lemon and no good to anybody.... May, but I'm still me, Gilly Ground, and I'm about to fight for my freedom even if my kind offers me nothing better than hunger cramps and colds in the head. I'm not courageous. I haven't any other choice.

Such devotion by the author to the psychology of Gilly's personality leaves little to be guessed about him. He emerges from the novel a readily recognizable individual. There may be no one else in the world exactly like him.

Gilly shows he is susceptible to the forces of his environment, nevertheless. He quavers and remains unsure of himself despite the bravado of his negativism. In the final summing up of his experiences in the novel he retreats from his commitment of no involvement: "I want no involvements, not in the orphanage and not here in the village, and that includes sparrows as well as people." Hunter's solicitude and Mash's bravery and self-sacrifice finally convince him of the folly of that outlook on life.

Certain decisions by Cunningham were helpful in her creation of the "roundness" of her characters. First, and most obvious, was her wish to keep the number of her main characters to a bare minimum, two. Second, she reduces the number of locales in her novel to the orphanage, the tower, and Kobalt's home. This allows her the time and space needed to extend the character of Gilly and Kobalt. Third, she creates a true antagonist–protagonist conflict: Kobalt finally actually intends to kill Gilly. "Come out! I order you out!" he shouts. "If I can't have you the way I want you I'll have you dead." An escalating sense of antagonism between the two is clearly demonstrated. Fourth, Gilly is the eccentric "I," the teller of the tale. The first-person subjective viewpoint is used by Cunningham, which makes the reader react vigorously to Gilly. Fifth, the plot is free of superfluous detail. No diversion or tangential incident interrupts or detracts attention from the characters.

The novel has a brisk, taut, plot with clear foreshadowings of future events. A speculative reader may sense that the tower, a symbol of refuge, will also become a place of near tragedy. We infer that Hunter's offer of sanctuary will of necessity also be taken. We foresee that Kobalt's sadistic behavior toward Mash will finally extend to physical danger for Gilly. The tension of the plot steadily moves from the relative calm of Gilly's life with his grandmother (who always gave him two well-remembered kisses at bedtime) to the impersonality and anquished, irritating tension of the orphanage, to the excruciating anxiety of living with Kobalt. The release comes, of course, with Gilly's escape to the haven offered by the Hunter. Moreover, the plot completes the standard requirement of a beginning, a middle, and an end: its development, the climax, and the denouement are clearly discernible. Cunningham also uses other devices of the traditional story: there is a journey—one to the tower and another at the close of the book to Hunter's home; there is a chase, Kobalt after Gilly; Gilly helps someone who repays in kind—Mash the dog; someone helps Gilly in his struggles—the Hunter; Gilly is heroic in that he fights against fatal odds and overcomes adversity; Gilly gains in stature as a result of his struggle—at least in his own eyes.

The book's tone closely reflects its theme. The author's attitude toward Gilly and his life, as seen through Gilly's eyes, is one of studied pessimism. This pessimism, stoic rather than panicky, so permeates Gilly's life that he finds it difficult to recognize goodness when it does appear in his life. His dialogue with Hunter reveals this:

> What do I want with your name all shut away in a sealed envelope? . . .
> You don't but you might, tomorrow or a hundred tomorrows from now. . . .
> But why give it to me?
> Because you might need it. . . . Why should I care for one-thousandth of a second what this freak of a man thinks about me and my existence? What does he know, appearing like a black spook twice in my life and assuming his ideas and opinions are the right ones?

The theme of the novel, the subject that recurs with jarring frequency, is man's inhumanity to man. This theme is demonstrated in the implications that Gilly was abandoned to his grandmother's care as well as in the scenes in the impersonal orphanage which acts as a physical custodian of children but does little to promote their emotional maturity. It appears also in the lack of anyone's concern over Gilly's being sent to a foster home run by a man notorious for his emotional instability. It surfaces in Kobalt's deadness of response to Gilly, in his outrageous demands on Gilly, and in his increasingly sadistic and threatening behavior to the boy. The novel says that the world is an evil, depraved, and absurd place to live. In this circumstance one must act to his own benefit with no commitment to others, being careful to set up many psychological defenses. Gilly expects his "existentialism" (the belief that life is essentially meaningless) to carry him through what he sees as the inconsequentiality of life.

But in terms of existentialism, Gilly achieves a self-realization at the end of the novel, a sense of brotherhood with Mash, who represents nature. As the two leave the tower, Gilly and the dog reach a mutual rejection of the vagaries and falsities of Kobalt:

> I think I must be smiling, because his tail takes up its newly learned rhythm of joy. We have troubles getting ourselves down that uneven, thickety path because when I fell under the hammer my ankle got another twist. But the pain is only pain and I have someone to help me with his love.

The path is a metaphor for life. It is by man's union with the nature around him, including the uncertainties of the future and the adversities of fortune, the blows of the hammer, that man achieves his own identity and is secure within the seemingly hostile forces of reality. It is because of his newly found self that Gilly rejects Kobalt's nonbeing by scratching "Dorp Dead!" on his door.

Cunningham's style in this novel may best be described as metaphoric; it consists of working out figures of speech which reel on and on in an almost endless chain. Cunningham can give a new twist to a common denotation; one finds a nonmetaphoric, flat passage strangely out of place. Instead of using her skill with figures as an emphasis or as a way to lighten ordinary writing, she floods each page with them. Her entire discourse is colored with a new vocabulary. Her metaphors run much beyond the need to say something in a colorful and distinct way. They are there for their own reasons; they share control of the ideas that are being professed. Through them the author is able to forge images that compress what otherwise would be a lengthy description. Mrs. Heister of the orphanage is "thunderous" and "overstuffed." Gilly himself is "a little demon." The orphanage cook is a "man as skinny as his soup." The school drags out its "long, stringy mornings." Meals are "the visual tumble of talk and squeals and skin kicking." In fashioning her analogic vocabulary, Cunningham moves words into connotations children will probably never have heard: Kobalt's shoulders "hoist," not lift; he "permits" the clock to tick off minutes; his body is not erect, but "stiffly correct." As noted, Cunningham does not reserve her metaphors to description; they enter her narrative:

> As I am slicing the breakfast bread the next morning I have no chance to rummage through my head to review what my dreaming really was, because

suddenly a thundery clatter like nightmare comes from the carpenter shop. It's as though an enormous bird with a wingspread of six feet has got trapped in that large room and is smashing itself against the walls.

Cunningham does not inevitably stick to the obvious literary level that metaphors require. She moves easily to the colloquial, even the vulgar level, when it fits the purpose of the scene. Here Gilly reacts to the Hunter's criticism:

What right have you to tell me how to run my life or to make fun of the only person in the world who would take in an orphan from a lousy institution where the noise is so crazy awful you wish you were born deaf? Who are you anyway, going around like a nut with an unloaded gun and no name, acting like the ruler of all the earth, interfering with people like me?

In terms of its ethics one might have imagined *Dorp Dead* would have raised a storm of protest, which it did! Because Gilly is presented as having a pessimistic, stoic outlook on the vagaries of an imbalanced, neurotic world, the novel has generated a host of detractors. These critics have questioned the right of an author of children's prose fiction to give his work the theme and tone Cunningham has. Some of these critics hold the novel unfit for children; they argue that the child is better off reading social novels with "healthy" philosophies. They are perturbed because the novel does not reinforce Judeo–Christian ethics. (It is true that the book, while not immoral, is often amoral.) These commentators are suspicious, too, of writers like Cunningham who value showing heterodoxical interior motives and philosophical musings of their characters rather than having manifest traditional values. They see children as not intellectually ready to be intensely concerned about the character's philosophical life. They assume that such an unrestricted and uncensored portrayal of the totality of a character's interior experience is too demanding on the inexperienced child reader, one who has limited philosophical reserves to deal with such matters.

Cunningham, as we have seen, throws a bone to these critics when she denies the novel the tragic ending it easily could have adopted. This reversal of plot in the novel comes only in the last few pages, however, and it may be that the general ethical nature of the book, its brooding pessimism, sense of social isolation, malevolence, selfishness, and neglect of any appeal for help to, or faith in, a higher force (unless Hunter is Gilly's John the Baptist) will stick with the child. The dramatic novel, which by its nature must dredge more deeply into the souls of its characters, is not likely to evoke the hopeful optimism or faith that holds Christian morality together. The mode of the dramatic novel is said to be necessary if the child is to attain levels of experience that otherwise would be closed to him. If this justification for the novel is valid—and we believe it is—heterogeneous standards of ethics in children's prose fiction will have to be expected, in spite of criticism by conservatives.

Form in the dramatic novel, as we have seen, takes on greater importance than in the social novel. The objective in the former is to compress, to distill the plot. In *Dorp Dead* this accelerates the pace of the novel, which in turn limits a writer's inclination to move into subplots or tangential incidents. In the dramatic novel, the author must be more careful to limit himself to only a few relevant incidents so their number does not exceed his control. *Dorp Dead* contains a minimum of action, not because its scope is limited but because it presents a "microscopic" view of personality—a distinguishing feature of the dramatic novel. Under such a glass, the overall view, effect, and impact of the novel is sharper, and the pattern of its structure is more obvious than in the social novel.

Usually, symbolism is used more in the dramatic novel than in the social novel. We can see this if we compare Wilder's novel (social) with Cunningham's (dramatic) . In fact, *Dorp Dead* can be interpreted as a *moral allegory*—a form of extended metaphor in which objects and persons in the narrative are equated with meaning that lies outside the narrative itself. Like symbols (which represent meaning independent of the action described in the surface story) , allegory uses representations; allegory is the mechanism of the symbol. Gilly, Kobalt, and Hunter are, then, personifications (a device that puts ideas and abstractions into human form and character) . Was Hunter furthermore intended as the symbol of Christ's goodness, which this metaphor could allow? "Maybe," said Cunningham. In any case, Hunter was in her mind a symbol of any person who passes through one's life to give it strength and meaning. Thus, in *Dorp Dead* the characters represent one thing in the guise of another. The novel tries, first, to evoke our interest in Gilly and his troubles, and secondly, to excite our speculation over the significance of this. To feel abandoned as Gilly did is essentially to feel forsaken by the god within us, that is, to lose sight of the eternal light of the human spirit. Hunter in the allegory is the force provided to relieve Gilly of this feeling. Gilly's impending journey to Hunter's home (only hinted at in the novel) could be the sign of his redemption, a sign that God has taken him up once again.

Further search for symbols in the novel is productive. The book's title itself suggests the ambiguous nature of Gilly, a boy who would not learn to spell simple words. The names of the characters also seem meaningful. Gilly's last name is "Ground"—dirt, a matter of little value. This is how he sees himself until he can be convinced differently. For his name does have more positive implications: gillyflowers are said to grow in paradise. Kobalt is like cobalt (the bomb) : a matter turned to evil and destruction. Mash is what his name implies, "inferior, and he knows it." Hunter represents the quest, the hunt, for Gilly's reunion with humanity. The black of his costume is quite naturally misinterpreted by Gilly: "For all I know he may be the devil himself!" But Hunter's "black" has another symbol: constancy, eternity, wisdom, not desolation and despair. It is the color of Good Friday, which precedes Christ's rebirth (and Gilly's?) . Mash as a dog is the commonly recognized symbol in Christian art of affection, companionship, courage, magnanimity, and devotion. Gilly's tower is also widely known to represent refuge, security, and a place of truth, but also battlement and death. Less well known is its dream significance: ambition realized, success, the universal hope for such to happen.

Gilly's return to balance means his escape from Kobalt. The ladder that Gilly uses to escape refers to the path of ascent to paradise or perfection. (In former times, a small ladder was worn as an amulet to ward off evil.) We see the significance of the ladder again, when Kobalt forces Gilly, as punishment, to sit at the top of a ladder. We know that the ladder in Christianity is one of the thirteen symbols of Christ's crucifixion. The labyrinth of ladders Gilly sets up for Kobalt as revenge for his mistreatment of Mash has an external meaning. In myth, a labyrinth typifies the infernal regions, where obviously Gilly would like to send Kobalt at this point! Kobalt's 15 clocks and 15 saws are significant as well; fifteen refers to the full moon which appears on the fifteenth day of each lunation. According to occultists, 15 is the number for evil. The fifteenth day of the month was the day of sackcloth and ashes, the day of atonement for evil in ancient Babylon. Thus, these specific symbols are sympathetic to viewing *Dorp Dead* as an extended metaphor.

From our analyses of novels in this chapter, we have established a means of approaching prose fiction. First, it is useful to establish the mode of the novel—historical, social, or dramatic. Then we can turn to how the historical or social background or the dramatic development has been achieved. Has the writer centered on the historical event to the neglect of his characters? Or do they emerge as believable personalities within the context of the historical setting? In a social novel, do the mores of the society fit with the portrayal of the characters? Do they appear to fit their time and place? Or do they clash with the social setting? In a dramatic novel, has the author sufficiently probed the motives and personalities of the characters? For example, one could examine Maia Wojciechowka's *Shadow of a Bull* to see the interaction of the main plot—of Manolo, the son of a dead bullfighter, as he resists being forced into his father's profession—with the subplot of Juan—a natural for the bullring, who dares the bulls in their pasture at night. One can examine William H. Armstrong's *Sounder* to observe the climax of the plot as the father returns, a device which is equated with the return of Odysseus from his journey to Troy. The issues of the Civil War can be seen through the character portrayal in Merritt P. Allen's *Johnny Reb*.

In Part IV of this book the reader can find numerous prose fiction titles to which he can apply the analytic techniques detailed above. His own reading undoubtedly will introduce him to many more examples. Numerous other classifications of prose fiction have been used in the past—"Adventure Books," "Mysteries," "Sports Stories"—but the same requirements prevail as in other prose fiction: the writer must achieve a believable picture of life.

The father, like Odysseus, returns home. From Sounder, *by W. H. Armstrong, illustrated by James Barkeley. Copyright © 1969 by William H. Armstrong. Reprinted by permission of Harper & Row, Publishers.*

Summary

Prose fiction is vital in the literary life of the child because of the delineation of human character it offers: the chance to share the struggles and victories of the interaction with other humans and with the forces around them—forces of history, nature, or human behavior. To become a part of the world of prose fiction is to observe the human heart as it endures, the human consciousness as it grows, and human civilization as it shapes and forms the members of cultural groups.

For additional studies of prose fiction, see *The Rise of the Novel* by Ian Watt; *The Rhetoric of Fiction* by Wayne C. Booth; *The Craft of Fiction* by Percy Lubbock.

5 Poetry

Of all the genres of literature, poetry is among the oldest and most enduring. From the earliest times of Western civilization until the present, poetry has remained a vital and major source of literary pleasure. Poetry shows a remarkable range of subject and audience. The solemn epics of the Greeks, the nonsense verse of children, the statements of mood and feeling in lyric poetry, the tales of adventures in ballads, and the good advice contained in proverbs are all called poetry. Children and adults respond equally to the pleasures of poetry, all finding in its musical pattern a distinctive and exciting language experience. Poetry forms one of the major sources of the oral tradition of literature, and has throughout Western history played a central role in the literary tradition.

Poetry as sound

The most distinctive characteristic of poetry is its use of rhythmic or metric language. Poetry makes its representation in a beat and pitch pattern which gives added interest and effect to the events and feelings described. Deeds of action and valor, as in the epic, can be orchestrated with properly grand sound devices; lighter topics can correspondingly be presented with other appropriate effects.

The oral tradition of poetry has remained strong despite the growth and dominance of written literature in modern times. When we hear Psalms from the Bible in a religious service, we react to the meter of the language which supplements the meaning of the words. The lyrics or words to songs fit the rhythmic nature of the music they are linked with. We can often take out the words from songs and call them poems. In this way, Bob Dylan and Donovan are considered poets. When we hear advertising jingles or the rope-skipping rhymes of children on the playground, language is being used in a metrical pattern which differs from ordinary speech, and which is the language use we call poetry.

Children, especially young ones, enjoy poetry as a display of rhythmic language. A lasting favorite has been this verse from *Mother Goose:*

> One misty moisty morning
> When cloudy was the weather

I chanced to meet an old man
Clothed all in leather.
He began to compliment
And I began to grin.
How do you do? And how do you do?
And how do you do again?

The story in these lines is minimal, little more than the report of an exchange of greetings between the speaker of the poem and the man in leather. But what generates interest and pleasure is the sound effect of the poem when skillfully read aloud. The alliteration, or repetition of like sounds—"*misty moisty morning*"—creates a novelty and delight in word sounds which a corresponding prose version—"foggy, damp morning"—lacks. And, of course, this is only one device —in addition to rhymes, repetitions, and the general chorus of sounds—which makes a reading of the poem a vital, special experience.

Interest in poetry can often be achieved with very young children through only this novel use of the sound system of the language. Because poetry does not sound like ordinary speech, children tend to give a special kind of attention when they hear the patterns of stress and pause which the meter of a poem exhibits. In advertising slogans, a phrase given in verse is easily remembered—the advertiser hopes, of course, that his verse will sing in the minds of potential buyers when they go shopping. Similarly, words of wisdom, such as proverbs and aphorisms, are often expressed in verse so that their message will be remembered when needed. With children, the directions for a game will often be said as they play it, as in:

Red Rover, Red Rover
Let Sammy come over!

The primary basis of poetry is the rhythmic language it uses. Poems often seem to contain no other aesthetic value than the experience they offer as sound. Nonsense verse, jingles, playground rhymes—all are examples of language as pure sound, developing beat and rhythm for their own sake. The nonsense verse of Lewis Carroll, for instance, creates only a very vague sense of meaning. The famous poem about the Jabberwock in *Through the Looking-Glass* takes place in a setting described as:

'Twas brillig, and the slithy toves
Did gyre and gimble in the wabe:
All mimsy were the borogoves,
And the mome raths outgrabe.

Only a recognizable word or two in the stanza makes us think that some sort of descriptive beginning to a tale is being offered in these lines. And we know this only because the first word, " 'Twas," echoes the archetypal beginning, "Once upon a time...."

Young children, again, are particularly appreciative of poetry as sound. The moving of heads in time to the rhythm of the poem, the swaying of bodies as the meter becomes more pronounced, all indicate that a pleasurable experience is taking place. This experience can be compared to centuries of similar such enjoyments of poetic literature.

The three-to-five year-old child is in a period of heightened sensitivity to the sounds of language, called the oral–aural period. During this time of childhood, the syntax and a great part of the vocabulary of the native language are mastered. In fact, by the age of three years, the child probably has a complete understanding of syntax. Just think how effortlessly the small child masters with great accuracy the sound system of a language. For a further appreciation of the child's greater prowess in oral language than that of the adult, consider your own efforts in college foreign language courses to master with even a passable accent the sounds of another language, one which you did not learn in childhood. Children possess a capacity for learning language sounds which is almost lacking in the adult.

The kindergarten or primary grade child enters poetry through sound. His interest in the novelty of language sounds is clearly greater even than your own. The Russian student of childhood language, Kornei Chukovsky, in his book *From Two to Five,* calls the child of that age span "a linguistic genius," capable of arriving spontaneously at

> ...word structures that were developed by the people over the centuries. His mind masters, as if miraculously, the same methods, processes, and peculiarities of word construction which were used by his very distant ancestors in building the language.[1]

Thus the experience of oral language in poetry read aloud to him will become a significant part of the linguistic experiences the child is so eager for at this time of his intellectual and linguistic development. Collections of poetry with intricate patterns of rhythm, usually called nursery rhymes or nonsense verse, are widely available for children.

In addition to those examples already mentioned from *Mother Goose* and Lewis Carroll, let's look in greater detail at the sound patterns in a verse appropriate for small children. In reading the following poem, look for the patterns of pause

---

[1] Kornei Chukovsky, *From Two to Five* (Berkeley: University of California Press, 1968), p. 5. Originally published by the University of California Press; reprinted by permission of The Regents of the University of California.

and beat which give it its unique quality, distinct from ordinary sound patterns or devices:

Timothy Tim was a very small cat
Who looked like a tiger the size of a rat.
There were little black stripes running all over him,
With just enough white on his feet for a trim
On Tiger-Cat Tim.

Timothy Tim had a little pink tongue
That was spoon, comb and washcloth all made into one.
He lapped up his milk, washed and combed all his fur,
And then he sat down in the sunshine to purr,
Full little Tim.

Timothy Tim had a quiet little way
Of always pretending at things in his play.
He caught pretend mice in the grass and the sand,
And fought pretend cats when he played with your hand,
Fierce little Tim!

He drank all his milk, and he grew and he grew.
He ate all his meat and his vegetables too.
He grew very big and he grew very fat.
And now he's a lazy old, sleepy old cat,
Timothy Tim!

—Edith H. Newlin[2]

In looking at the first line of the poem, notice that *Timothy Tim* would seem to be said as a unity with a medium beat on the first two syllables of *Timothy,* a weak stress on *-thy,* followed by an immediately stronger beat on *Tim.* Perhaps the sound could be visually represented as Ti-Mo-th*e*TIM. A slight pause occurs after *Tim;* the rest of the line builds to a similar climax of stress on *cat* at the end of the line. To describe accurately the meter of a line of verse in English, the traditional metrical markings of weak and strong stress are inadequate. The stresses heard in "Timothy Tim was a very small cat" are of at least four strengths, or intensities. Read the line over to yourself while you gently clap your hands in rhythm to it. Keep doing this until the accompaniment of claps is of the following intensities and patterns:

Tim   o   thy Tim   was   a   ver   y small cat
medium-medium-soft-hard-medium-soft-medium-soft-hard-hard

---

[2] From the book *Another Here and Now Story Book* by Lucy Sprague Mitchell. Copyright 1937 by E. P. Dutton & Co., Inc. Renewal © 1965 by Lucy Sprague Mitchell. Published by E. P. Dutton & Co., Inc. and reprinted with their permission.

Come To Think of It

I know someone who lives at the zoo.
Someone who looks a lot like you.
. . . No, not the monkey nor the kangaroo!

. . . But come to think of it, the monkey *might* do.
That's not what I had in mind, it's true . . .
But, yes, come to think of it, the monkey *would* do![4]

---

[4] "Come To Think of It" by John Ciardi from *You Know Who* by John Ciardi, with drawings by Edward Gorey. Copyright © 1964, by John Ciardi. Poem and illustration reprinted by permission of J. B. Lippincott Company.

These two illustrations and poems show a trend in modern collections of children's poetry—using a vivid drawing to accentuate the subject matter of a poem.

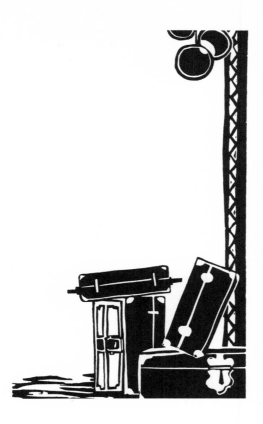

Traveling

Some days fooling back
and forth on the block,
none of us going far,
we see metal trunks stacked
outside the luggage store.
I opened one once; it was empty
but it smelled packed.
If I had one of those big black trunks,
I'd *go.*[5]

---

[5] "Traveling" by Richard J. Margolis from *Looking for a Place* by Richard J. Margolis, illustrated by Ilse Koehn. Copyright © 1969 by Richard J. Margolis. Poem and illustration reprinted by permission of J. B. Lippincott Company.

Also notice where certain small pauses can occur in the line to add variation and interest to its rhythm. There is a brief pause after *Tim,* after *very,* and after *small.* Once you feel that this sense of rhythm is discernible in the way you read the poem aloud, go on to other lines, giving them the sense of individualized meaning and expression that your own voice, manner of speaking, and feeling for the line can impart. In a short time, as your ear becomes attuned to the metrics of the poem, you will see that there are subtle nuances in stress on the strong beats. Some beats are a little stronger than the others, while some syllables are almost entirely without stress. These variations keep the verse from becoming monotonous and singsongy. Indeed the poet seems to avoid any strictly rigid pattern of beat. Each of the three lines beginning with "Timothy Tim" has the same metrical pattern. But the first line of the last verse departs from that pattern and ends in a different order of stresses and pauses.

Children very quickly hear and appreciate the rhythm of the lines. Studies of playground behavior reveal that body movements are often accompanied by verse chants or rope-skipping rhymes. Capitalize on this in the classroom by getting the children to clap their hands in time to the rhythm of the verses, and by working with them to refine the subtle differences in English stress.

The sound of the poem contributes to the esthetic effect it creates in the hearer. The quiet, musical language of the following poem makes it a beautifully expressive portrayal of a scene in the snow:

White Season

In the winter the rabbits match their pelts to the earth.
With ears laid back, they go
Blown through the silver hollow, the silver thicket,
Like puffs of snow.

—Francis M. Frost[3]

Think about the visual scene, the whiteness of the earth and of the rabbits, and how the phrase "puffs of snow" equates the graceful, effortless movement of the rabbits with the gentle blowing of the snow. Consider how the sounds are appropriate to this particular poem.

The meter of a poem is nothing more than a description of the sound which best fits the meaning to be conveyed. Anyone who reads a poem to a group of children attempts to convey with his voice what he feels the poem means. Dialects in English differ in sound patterns, but they still can give the same meanings.

Linguistics provides a way to describe the sounds of language through a

---

[3] Francis M. Frost, "White Season," in *A Pool in the Meadow* (New York: Houghton Mifflin Co.) Reprinted by permission.

description of stress (beat), pitch (tone of the voice), and juncture (pause). A combination of these three elements will convey the meaning of the words. We do not recommend that these concepts be taught to children, but rather assert that they are useful to the teacher in thinking about the metrical patterns of a poem. Reading a poem aloud is aided by understanding *what to do with the capabilities of the voice as a vehicle of communicating meaning.*

The language of poetry presents the intricate patterning of stresses, pauses, and variations in the pitch of spoken language in a unique manner. The language of poetry very often sounds quite different from that of ordinary speech because of the self-conscious effort of the poet to create a special sound effect that will highlight his meaning.

Let us consider a few descriptions of sound in language before turning to the more complex uses of sound in poetry. When we say, "He went to town," we do not hear the same rise in pitch at the end that we do when we ask, "He went to town?" The difference in sound creates a different response in the listener. The first is a statement of fact; the second is a question. Further nuances of meaning could be created by placing special emphasis or stress on a word: "HE went to town?" or "He went to TOWN!" Which sound effect we use is governed by what we want to communicate.

The emphasis we place on certain words in the sentence differentiates one meaning from another. The pitch of the various parts of the utterance also will create different meanings. Below is a set of markings which can indicate stress. Linguists indicate four stresses in English:

- ´ Primary or heaviest stress
- ^ Secondary or next heaviest stress
- ` Tertiary, or third heaviest stress
- ˇ Weak stress

An example of these stresses can be seen in the statement *bláck bîrdtràp* which indicates a birdtrap which is black in color. This utterance is different from *blâckbìrd tráp* which means a device used to catch blackbirds.

Notice also that when we are telling someone the color of the birdtrap, there is a longer pause between *black* and *birdtrap* than there is between these two words when we are saying that the trap is used to catch blackbirds; in the latter meaning, the pause would be between *bird* and *trap*. These pauses are called junctures; there are several kinds of junctures, distinguised by the length of the pause. They are indicated by slanted lines /, // (single-bar juncture, double-bar juncture), or # (double-cross juncture). The briefest pause between individual words is called a "plus juncture" and is indicated by +.

Pitch can be indicated by a line over the utterance. Look at these signs of juncture and pitch:

Whatever you want / you can get. #
You think so? #
"Yes," // Bob told me. #

Returning to the earlier line from *Timothy Tim,* we can describe its sound as follows:

Tîmŏthy̆ Tím / wàs + â + véry̆ / smáll / cát #

Again let us repeat: this description is offered here to show the variety of stresses combined with brief pauses and different pitches that creates the music of a line.

Poetry as story

Narrative poems and ballads present the story of an action or adventure in verse and figurative language. Because they present exciting, even sensational plot actions, narrative poems are of special interest to the child of six or eight who has outgrown his earlier enthusiasm for nonsense verse or nursery rhymes, that is, poems which are merely musical in effect. For the child who is not yet ready for the complex intellectual experience of poetry as symbol and image, the vivid details of ballads and narrative poems keep alive the interest in poetry generated earlier by jingles, nursery rhymes, rope-skipping rhymes, and nonsense verse.

Narrative poems and ballads achieve great appeal when read aloud. In fact most of their impact is lost if they are not heard. Ballads are essentially an oral form, deriving in large part from folk literature, and are easily adapted to music. The appeal of this kind of poetry is universal, equally strong for both children and adults. Because of this, a myriad of phonograph records of professional performances are available to present poems to best advantage in the classroom. And the history of narrative poems is as old as literature.

Sir Patrick Spens is an old English ballad which can serve as an example of the type:

Sir Patrick Spens

The king sits in Dunfermline town,
Drinking the blood-red wine:

"O where will I get a skeely skipper
  To sail this new ship of mine?"

O up and spake an eldern knight,
  Sate at the king's right knee—
"Sir Patrick Spens is the best sailor
  That ever sailed the sea."

Our king has written a broad letter,
  And sealed it with his hand,
And sent it to Sir Patrick Spens
  Was walking on the strand.

The first word that Sir Patrick read,
  So loud, loud laughed he;
The next word that Sir Patrick read,
  The tear blinded his ee.

"O who is this has done this deed,
  And told the king o' me,
To send us out, at this time of the year,
  To sail upon the sea?

"Make ready, make ready, my merry men all!
  Our good ship sails the morn."
"Now ever alack, my master dear,
  I fear a deadly storm!

"I saw the new moon, late yestreen,
  With the auld moon in her arm;
And if we gang to sea, master,
  I fear we'll come to harm."

They had not sailed a league, a league,
  A league, but barely three,
When the lift grew dark, and the wind blew loud,
  And gurly grew the sea.

"Go, fetch a web o' the silken cloth,
  Another o' the twine,
And wap them into our ship's side,
  And let not the sea come in."

O loth, loth, were our good Scotch lords
  To wet their cork-heeled shoon!
But lang ere a' the play was play'd
  They wet their hats aboon.

O long, long may the ladies sit,
  With their fans into their hand,
Before they see Sir Patrick Spens
  Come sailing to the strand!

And long, long may the maidens sit,
  Wi' the goud combs in their hair,

All waiting for their own dear loves—
For them they'ss see no mair.

Half owre, half owre to Aberdour,
'Tis fifty fathoms deep,
And there lies good Sir Patrick Spens
With the Scotch lords at his feet.

Notice the distinctive meter and stanza form, named for its mother form—the ballad stanza. Its varied regularity of beat, never singsong or monotonous, lends itself to the extended length of the narration of the adventure told in its lines. Notice the variety of sound in the first two lines:

The king / sits / in Dunfermline / Town, //
Drinking the blood / -red wine:

The sound of the ballad would become tedious if only weak and strong beats were used—the nuances of primary, secondary, tertiary, and weak beats create the full rhythmic possibilities of the ballad.

More is suggested in ballads than is overtly stated; they are typically an understatement. For example, we do not know why the king needs to send Sir Patrick out on the perilous mission. But the suggestion offered by the king's drinking "blood-red" wine might lead us to assume that some act of war threatens the kingdom, some issue involving bloodshed which we can associate with the color of the wine. We might also feel that the king is anxious and afraid, the reason he seeks the calm of the wine. Nor do we know what is in the letter to make Sir Patrick give a loud laugh. What we center upon is the honor which drives Sir Patrick to obey even though he is certain of his death.

Has someone purposely done Sir Patrick a bad turn? Or does fate control the action? Notice also the understatement of:

O loth, O loth, were our good Scotch lords
To wet their cork-heeled shoon!

We end with a portrayal of Sir Patrick's noble world as the aristocratic ladies wait patiently at home "With their fans into their hand." Notice how much of the action is carried by implication instead of overt statement.

Another favorite narrative poem is Alfred Noyes' *The Highwayman,* the first stanza of which is:

> The wind was a torrent of darkness among the
>   gusty trees,
> The moon was a ghostly galleon tossed upon
>   cloudy seas,
> The road was a ribbon of moonlight over the purple
>   moor,
> And the highwayman came riding—riding—riding—
> The highwayman came riding, up to the old inn-door.

The first lines give an ominous and appropriate setting for the poem's story of love, betrayal, and death. The entire story of the outlaw and Bess is colored by the sense of doom and death presented only by the phrases "torrent of *darkness*" and "moon was a *ghostly* galleon," and the illicit arrival of the highwayman. The mood of suspense and danger is heightened by the "white and peaked" face of the scorned Tim the Ostler, whose "eyes were hollows of madness" as he listened jealously to Bess and her lover.

One might well ask how the poet manages to evoke sympathy for the bandit and Bess—who are, after all, outlaws. Both their great, strong love, and their willingness to die for each other create the same kind of approval in the reader that a later generation felt for Bonnie and Clyde. And the fact that the steadfast bravery of Bess and the highwayman is thwarted by a sneak like Tim the Ostler and by an overpowering number of soldiers lends our sympathies to the plight of the lovers. The dramatic realism of details such as the "tlot-tlot" of the horses' hooves brings us into the story. The visual imagery and the sound make *The Highwayman* an exciting tale and experience.

Narrative poems and ballads can, through their highly dramatic quality, awaken the imagination and interest of children. The musical language and gripping adventure continue the earlier experiences of the child with poetry.

Poetry as symbol and image

Poems usually do more than create rhythmic sound. In general, poetry is the most self-consciously symbolic of the literary forms. Let's consider some examples of how poetry uses symbols.

In thinking of poetry for children, it will be helpful to arrive at a description of symbolism by considering a poem by a child in comparison with one by an adult. The first poem is by Ezra Pound:

In a Station of the Metro

The apparition of these faces in the crowd
Petals on a wet, black bough.

—Ezra Pound[6]

First let's see what is happening in this poem. Pound has been in the Paris subway, which is called the Metro. There he has seen fellow travellers coming and going, and he wishes to convey several things to the reader. First, he wants to represent what he saw there; second, he wants to evoke in the reader feelings similar to his own. He has had an experience in the subway, inspired by the sight of the faces around him.

Through his choice of language and detail he attempts to represent the scene as he might by painting with colors on canvas. Pound uses language instead of paint, however, to describe the scene. The second word of the poem, "apparition," begins to do this. Because the word means not only "ghostly" but also anything which has a particularly startling appearance, the faces must have seemed quite different from the familiar faces of friends and acquaintances in the daily routine of life; they cause an aesthetic shock rather than being an ordinary sight.

Then Pound says of the faces that they are "Petals on a wet, black bough." The second statement is so different from a description of faces in a crowd that we might at first think that Pound is talking about something entirely different from what he indicated as his topic for the poem; petals are not faces. But because the poet chooses somehow to equate the two, perhaps there is something about the petals which is *like* human faces.

Certain characteristics of a petal are similar to a human face. If the petal is delicate in texture and light pink in color, it looks like a beautifully smooth complexion. Both the hue and surface of a petal (note that we are talking only of one part of the flower, the petal, which is even more like a face in shape than the whole cluster) suggest the appearance of skin. Fine-grained, soft, with almost radiant tones, a petal reminds one of a healthy, glowing face.

And we are told also that the petals–faces are on a "wet, black bough." In this line, the emphasis is upon the contrast between the delicate coloring and softness of the petals and the dark wetness and roughness of the branch. The "wet, black" branch also seems to connote coldness and sterility in contrast to a flower's connection with a seed. Furthermore, it would seem that the petals are more vulnerable to destruction than the branch—their delicacy is seen against the background of the hard wood.

---

[6] Ezra Pound, *Personae.* Copyright 1926 by Ezra Pound. Reprinted by permission of New Directions Publishing Corporation.

Thus the faces in the Metro crowd do not look *exactly* like petals. There is rather a kind of fragile loveliness in their tones and life which is *analogical* to the image of the petals. We are not told anything, however, about the backdrop for the faces in the crowd; we have been informed that the petals are set against a wet, black bough, but nothing is said of what serves as a similar contrast with the faces. Thinking further about the poem, we know only from the title that the faces in the poem are in the Metro, but nothing explicit is said about the Metro. However, in the set of correspondences created in the poem, we can discover what Pound meant. Consider the following analogies in the poem: faces equal petals; subway walls equal black bough. The faces are like the petals, and some unknown serves as a similar background for them as a branch does for the flower. The background for the faces must be the subway station. Just as petals are like faces in both color and texture, the implication is that the subway walls are like the bough —dank (wet) and grimy with soot (black). The warm flesh tones of the passersby in the crowd are an "apparition" to Pound in their startling contrast with the walls of the Metro, just as petals form the same kind of difference in color and texture from the boughs or branch.

Not only has Pound created a visual description of the faces, he has also evoked many associations to enrich the esthetic quality of the poem. First there is the surprise which the word "apparition" indicates. The shock is of course the contrast of the faces and the walls of the subway. But further, the additional comparison of the flower with the faces extends to the warmth of the faces, the fragility of humans by comparison with the more sturdy but less beautiful surface of the subway. In addition there is the living beauty of the faces in the crowd in contrast to the grim impersonality of the subway station.

The major purpose served by this kind of comparison is to communicate the poet's perceptions and emotions to one who has not been in the Metro in Paris, and who might not have seen or felt the same things as Pound even if he had been there. We have all seen, or could easily imagine, petals on a wet, black bough; just as we can imagine the flowers on the branch, we can make the connections necessary to understand and feel what the faces in the crowd are like. Pound has used something familiar to describe his personal, unique view to the reader, which it would otherwise have been impossible for him to communicate. Instead of saying helplessly, "I cannot possibly tell you what I felt when I saw those people in the subway," Pound has communicated not only what he saw but also recreated in the reader a feeling similar to his own. His choice of comparisons recreates both scene and mood in the reader. The poet thus uses images (visual comparisons) and symbols (other analogical comparisons) to create the effect of the poem. And of course he also uses metrical language.

This poem was the work of a master, the product of maturity and genius. Does this mean that such writing is within the province of the adult alone? Let's look at a haiku by a nine-year-old, Deedee, to see if a child is capable of putting language together to equal effect:

Haiku

The trees cry sadly
Because the north wind blows cold
And brings much sorrow.

Deedee describes a common occurrence—how the wind sounds when it blows through the trees. But by saying "The trees cry sadly," she has gone a step beyond a literal description of the scene. The trees do not actually cry in the same way that humans do, but this sound is reminiscent of human weeping. By attributing human emotions to the trees, we identify this scene with human situations.

The north wind in the trees brings coldness, winter, and the death of the year. The trees feel sad about the loss of summer, leaves, and wakefulness—indeed, loss of life itself. The sadness indicated in the poem is the human sense of loss and deprivation which is likened to the dying year and earth's progression into winter. Winter is the archetype for loss, death, the dying of a hero or god, or the loss of life and energy. Here the child has brought an image from what Jung calls our "collective unconscious" to express her emotions. Identifying the seasons with feelings is so innate a human characteristic that the appearance of this archetype is not surprising. Just as Chaucer uses spring to portray the rebirth of life, Deedee has used winter to give shape and form to *her* feelings about the ebb of life.

Adversity—or sorrow of the kind which brings the same loss to men that the north wind brings to the trees—is expressed in the archetype of winter. We might recall Shakespeare's image of winter:

Upon those boughs which shake against the cold—
Bare ruin'd choirs where late the sweet birds sang.
In me thou see'st the twilight of such day
As after Sunset fadeth in the West.

—Sonnet 73

Pound, Shakespeare, and Deedee have compared something familiar—the seasons or the image of a flowered branch—with a difficult-to-express mood or emotion. It would, of course, have been entirely possible for Pound to have described his Metro scene in clinical detail, giving spectrophotometric readings of people's faces compared to those of the subway walls, with minute temperature and moisture measurements. But this would not have evoked feelings in the reader. Likewise, Deedee could simply have said what she felt in another way, but her use of image and analogy conveys the shape of her sadness.

Let us look at these poems in terms of levels of meaning. First, there is the surface, or the literal description that the poems give. In the case of Pound, this
would be the seemingly disassociated statements about faces and petals; in the
child's haiku, it is that the wind is blowing; Shakespeare is saying on the surface,
"I am at the end of the day." Left at this level, the poems do not have great significance. It is only when we look deeper that the true meaning of the statement can
be appreciated. In terms of paintings, we might say that at the surface level the
Mona Lisa is a portrait; but when the symbolic nature of the work is considered,
it becomes a statement of mood. The deeper structure of these poems is the interpretive or symbolic level. That petals are compared to faces helps the reader
reach the poet's mood. Likewise, in the child's haiku, the fact that the trees "cry"
in an archetypal setting of winter makes the deeper meaning evident. The sorrow
or loss they "feel" is like the bereavement that comes to humans, a loss which is
like the falling of the leaves.

And beyond these two levels is the third level—the reader's affective, or wholly
personal, response. On this level we find such terms as "liking" and the sense of
identification with the mood of the poem. The surface and metaphorical levels
lead to the affective response—one must understand a poem's symbolism before
one can respond to it—but for the poem to really become a work of art, all levels
of its meaning must engage the person experiencing it.

Two further examples will show how the analogies or images of a poem create
its symbolic nature as a work of art. By selecting certain visual or sensual details,
the poet evokes or stimulates a certain response in the reader. Here are two images
describing fog:

> The fog comes
> on little cat feet.
>
> It sits looking
> over harbor and city
> on silent haunches
> and then moves on.
>
> —Carl Sandburg[7]

> The yellow fog that rubs its back upon the window-
>   panes,
> The yellow smoke that rubs its muzzle on the
>   window-panes

---

[7] From *Chicago Poems by Carl Sandburg*. Copyright 1916 by Holt, Rinehart and Winston, Inc.
Copyright 1944 by Carl Sandburg. Reprinted by permission of Holt, Rinehart and Winston, Inc.

Licked its tongue into the corners of the evening,
Lingered upon the pools that stand in drains,
Let fall upon its back the soot that falls from
  chimneys,
Slipped by the terrace, made a sudden leap,
And seeing that it was a soft October night,
Curled once about the house, and fell asleep.

—T. S. Eliot[8]

In Sandburg's poem, the tentative and cautious approach of a cat portrays the slow movement of the fog into the harbor. The cat–fog does not come pouncing into the city like a cat catching a mouse; instead, "little cat" indicates a timidity and standoffishness. That the cat sits on "silent haunches" also indicates an aloofness and inscrutability. The fog, then, like the cat, remains at a distance in the harbor, not threading thickly and rapidly through the city.

In the excerpt from T. S. Eliot's *The Lovesong of J. Alfred Prufrock,* a different sort of cat is the surface image of the poem. Likewise, a different kind of fog is described in the underlying meaning of the lines. In contrast to the remoteness of Sandburg's fog, this cat–fog is very friendly; it rubs its face against the windows with a caressing greeting. Neither reluctant nor afraid, Eliot's cat moves into the scene with great enjoyment and pleasure. Like a cat rolling onto its back in sensual happiness, licking its master's hand, the fog quickly and thoroughly begins to envelop the house. First, there is a drift of haze ("rubs its back upon the window") . Next, the dampness rises higher as the cat seems to stand up and rub "its muzzle on the window-panes." Then, the farthest parts of the scene visible from the window begin to fill with vapor as the cat-fog "lick[s] its tongue into the corners of the evening." Finally, like a cat curling up to go to sleep, the fog completely cloaks the house. The fog in the verse is yellow at first, like a similarly colored cat with black stripes; then the night falls and darkens as though the house were underneath the cat.

These two fog scenes differ in their degree of haze and obscurity. Likewise, different cat images are used. The surface image is the face of the symbol behind it.

In exploring a poem, think about the symbols and imagery of the poet's language. Almost all language in a poem will be an indicator of its deeper structure. But the first and most helpful step in arriving at the full experience of a poem is to describe its surface meaning before moving to the deeper level. Usually the poem's first surface indication is its title. Consider this poem:

---

[8] T. S. Eliot, "The Lovesong of J. Alfred Prufrock," in *Collected Poems, 1909–1962* (New York: Harcourt Brace Jovanovich, 1963) . Reprinted by permission.

The Eagle

He clasps the crag with crooked hands;
Close to the sun in lonely lands,
Ringed with the azure world, he stands.

The wrinkled sea beneath him crawls;
He watches from his mountain walls,
And like a thunderbolt he falls.

—Alfred Tennyson

From the title we assume that the poem is on the surface about an eagle; the remainder of the lines support this assumption. Several words in the poem, however, seem to indicate that the eagle is a metaphor for human qualities—the eagle is called "he," and his talons are referred to as "hands." In fact, the heavy use of the pronouns "he" and "him" diverts one's attention from the literal surface, the eagle. The sole mention that the poem is about an *eagle,* as only a bird, is in the title.

The qualities of the eagle described on the surface, then, seem to make a statement about human existence. A kind of human is described who is *like* the eagle. What facts are indicated? He is "close to the sun"; the sea is far, far beneath him so that the waves look like wrinkles. And in the height and splendor of his aerie, he is in "lonely lands." Correspondingly, a man like the eagle who has the same strength and bravery—in other words, a hero—must dwell apart from the crowd, spiritually alone in his greatness. The eagle seems to own the mountain, it is in "*his* mountain walls" that his vigilance takes place. The mountain is close to energy, the sun, and the entire world is held in his view, "ringed" around him. This heroic eagle–man is capable of great force, even of destruction, when he falls like a thunderbolt—like Zeus, whose emblem, significantly, is the eagle. These associations underscore the swift and powerful action the bird is capable of, and point to the similar strength of the heroic nature symbolized by the eagle.

The steps to reach the second level of a poem are: (1) describe its surface; (2) carefully recreate its details of setting and images; (3) notice in the poem's language entries to the second level, in this case the use of the words "he" and "hands" to indicate that the surface leads to a metaphor showing human personality or being.

Let us consider another poem, this popular one by Robert Frost:

Stopping by Woods on a Snowy Evening

Whose woods these are I think I know.
His house is in the village though;
He will not see me stopping here
To watch his woods fill up with snow.

My little horse must think it queer
To stop without a farmhouse near
Between the woods and frozen lake
The darkest evening of the year.

He gives his harness bells a shake
To ask if there is some mistake.
The only other sound's the sweep
Of easy wind and downy flake.

The woods are lovely, dark and deep
But I have promises to keep,
And miles to go before I sleep,
And miles to go before I sleep.

—Robert Frost[9]

The first thing to consider is the setting for the poem. The title tells us that it is a "snowy evening," initially setting a certain tone for the poem. This is a different setting from summer, spring, or daytime. Use of the archetype of winter suggests the serious mood the poem will convey. The woods, if they represent a place of enchantment, magic, imagination, danger, and possibly all the fears of the human race, present a singular image of beauty mixed with awe. Woods in literature represent places of unknown, unknowable mysteries.

The surface of the poem, then, presents a man's inner thoughts as he sits looking at the scene of snow falling into the dark forest, hearing his horse shake his harness bells to indicate his impatience to be on the way, and the man's awareness of the miles to go before he is in out of the night's cold.

That is the surface of the poem. But several other parts of the poem support the interpretation that these woods may represent more than merely a stand of trees. The time of the poem is "the darkest evening of the year" during winter, the death of the year. The man is thus contemplating the lowest ebb of life. Nothing is to be heard but "easy wind and downy flake," both cold and impersonal, and the lake is frozen. No one is near; he is totally alone except for the horse as he looks into the woods. The horse is clearly no companion to the man, because the horse completely fails to comprehend any of the scene's significance —indeed the horse's nature is destructive in many ways of the man's mood of wonder.

It seems clear that the man wants to remain, but the horse seems insistent that stopping is a mistake. The man's longing to remain near the woods is a desire to cease the journey, which can most likely be taken as a desire not to have to go on

[9] From *The Poetry of Robert Frost,* edited by Edward Connery Lathem. Copyright 1923 by Holt, Rinehart and Winston, Inc. Copyright 1951 by Robert Frost. Reprinted by permission of Holt, Rinehart and Winston, Inc.

"Snap the Whip," by Winslow Homer. Oil on canvas, reproduced by permission of the Metropolitan Museum of Art, gift of Christian A. Zabriskie, 1950.

to the village. In effect, the man muses upon dying. Not to complete the journey is to die.

The speaker, however, returns to an awareness of his responsibilities and duties in life, his "promises to keep," and continues his journey. The last two lines, in their repetition, underscore the awareness that the journey ahead is not only the miles remaining to the village but the remaining years of the speaker's life. The differences between the horse and the man in the poem are that they do not share either the sense of beauty of the wood, the longing for or knowledge of death, or the sense of duty or responsibility. Neither the pleasure nor the pain is known to the horse. Frost presents the complexity of the human situation, our sense of beauty, and our awareness of mortality.

The poem which follows has been directly inspired by a painting. Examining the poem and the painting at the same time, a further sense of surface and metaphor emerges.

Winslow Homer
"Snap the Whip"
Oil on canvas, 1872

Eight boys in a rocky meadow,
sired just before the drums rolled at Shiloh,
their pants turned up above their ankles—
one, larger than the rest, has outgrown his.
Some are patched at the knees.
They all wear suspenders.

Their shirts—long-sleeved, or hidden under their coats—
were made at home by their mothers or
sisters sitting by coal-oil lamps.
They have hats or caps just shading their eyes.
Five are barefoot; three are wearing shoes.

We see by this that it is an indefinite season.
Spring has put forth the grass
and brought the sun down upon them,
but there are clouds, they are dark under—
it may just have rained. There are flowers,
indistinguishable bits of blue and yellow.

They play in a clearing, the woods behind them,
and in the foreground the tangle
of flowers and red leaves—the new leaves of sumac?
The wood is encroaching—two small trees
threaten the turf where they are playing.

The building behind them—a square
too small for a house. Around it
the grass is packed into ground. Outside each window
shutters stand open on the red wall. The sash
is partly lifted to the new spring air.

Why are they here, so far from the village?
You can see the white steeple off in the distance,
a few white buildings all but hidden in trees.
In between, a ploughed field and two barns
or a house and a barn. Where are their fathers?

The boys play hard. The pivot leans backward
holding the center while the others run past
and the boy at the end tumbles on hands and knees.
Their faces are serious. The third boy is shouting.
No one listens. They are rousing boys,
school is out for the day, the trees are green, summer is
    coming.

—Ann Stanford[10]

---

[10] From *The Descent* by Ann Stanford. Copyright © 1970 by Ann Stanford. All Rights Reserved. Reprinted by permission of the Viking Press, Inc.

The surface of this poem is a description of Winslow Homer's painting. In reading the poem carefully, notice how many of the painting's details the poet has noticed and commented on, which otherwise might go unnoticed. In the sixth stanza, she asks "Why are they here, so far from the village?" This brings up a brooding and ominous mood from the painting, one which suggests that the boys' play is symbolic of the transitoriness of youthful pleasures, one moment of freedom from school and chores, which will be replaced by work and responsibility in adulthood just as the rural calm of their games in the clearing will soon be replaced by work on the farms in the background. Explore the interrelationship of painting and poem to see the further connections between its surface and its interpretation.

It might seem that detailed examinations of poems destroy their aesthetic value. Archibald MacLeish expresses a prevalent idea about the nature of poetry when he says:

> A poem should not mean
> But be.

This does not mean, however, that understanding of the images and symbols in a poem ruins it. For a poem to "be," in MacLeish's terms, it is not the literal subject matter that is all-important—instead, it is the combination of all levels of meaning in a poem which will capture the mind of the reader or listener. Unless we know what the images and symbols of the poem mean, the work remains unknown. Unless we know what poems really say, we do not hear them speaking. If we are not aware of the odor of a flower, the scent is wasted. If we do not understand the meaning of words, communication cannot occur. If a poem's language is heard uncomprehendingly, it is like a lost sound escaping into ether. Here is one suggestion on how to experience poetry:

How To Eat a Poem

Don't be polite.
Bite in.
Pick it up with your fingers and lick the juice
    that may run down your chin.
It is ready and ripe now, whenever you are.

You do not need a knife or fork or spoon
ór plate or napkin or tablecloth.
            For there is no core
            or stem
            or rind
            or pit

or seed
or skin
to throw away.

—Eve Merriam[11]

Children experience a poem

In this chapter, it seems valuable to bring up the question of teaching a poem to children. In the other chapters we have left that matter for the third section of the book, Teaching Literature to Children. But teaching poetry has special problems which are best considered while in proximity to the poems themselves.

Experiencing a poem often involves talking and thinking about it. A certain kind of thinking, moreover, is called for—pliant and flexible.

As an example of how a teacher can help children understand a poem, we have recreated an actual lesson with third and fourth graders in a demonstration school at San Fernando Valley State College. The poem we chose is admittedly a difficult one, Blake's *To the Evening Star*. But we thought this choice could point to some new directions for children and poetry; we wanted to see what level of perception children could reach when led by a teacher.

A Teacher Prepares

First, the teacher should explore the text of poem on his own:

To the Evening Star

Thou fair-hair'd angel of the evening,
Now, whilst the sun rests on the mountains, light
Thy bright torch of love; thy radiant crown
Put on, and smile upon our evening bed!
Smile on our loves, and, while thou drawest the
Blue curtains of the sky, scatter thy silver dew
On every flower that shuts its sweet eyes
In timely sleep. Let thy west wind sleep on
The lake; speak silence with thy glimmering eyes,
And wash the dusk with silver. Soon, full soon,
Dost thou withdraw; then the wolf rages wide,
And the lion glares thro' the dun forest:
The fleeces of our flocks are cover'd with
Thy sacred dew: protect them with thine influence.

—William Blake

The first striking feature of the poem is its quality as a hymn to the evening star, who is called a "fair-hair'd angel." This seems to mean that this first star which appears is the patroness of the evening, its guardian angel. The star is further urged to put on her crown; this suggests that the star is as much a queen or goddess as an angel, which is supported by the implication that the evening star is Venus, the Roman goddess of love, because she is asked to light her "torch of *love*" and to "smile on our *loves*."

As the star-goddess first appears each night in the evening sky, she is the only star visible, and thus is apparently the ruler of the star world.

As the star first appears, it is twilight, just at the end of the day, when the sun would be touching the horizon, when it "rests on the mountain." Visually the star would be less bright because of the twilight than later when the sky is darker. Thus she is "fair-hair'd" when first seen, but will light a torch or grow to full radiance. In these first two lines, the surface of the poem addresses the still dim star to grow brighter. The metaphoric meaning of the poem here suggests that as the star becomes brighter, the aura or power of love which Venus brings will become more and more powerful.

The time of day, evening, is of great importance to the meaning Venus will have. Evening is just at the balance of day (sunlight, heat, and energy) and night (when lions and wolves are on the prowl). This quiet and beautiful moment is characterized by the gentle wind on the lake, the sun going to sleep behind the mountain, the ascendancy of Venus, the flowing of love in the form of starlight from heaven to earth, the shutting of the flowers into gentle rest, and the protection of the sheep from harm. All is tranquility, security, and peace symbolized by the love of Venus who holds the world in safety and in harmony for the brief time she is visible in the early evening.

Later, of course, she will withdraw into the crowd of stars, and her power will be diminished. The speaker in the poem who addresses Venus is aware that her beneficial force will vanish, that the starlight from the sky will be replaced by the glaring eyes of the lion in the forest, that the safety of this moment of love will disappear. The archetype of the forest is like that of night—early evening will end and so will the balance of star and sun, of wind and lake, of lion and lamb, of day and night. For the moment, however, the rule of love is complete, and the speaker prays it will at least partially remain.

The sounds of the poem reinforce the symbolism—the first lines are filled with delicate vowel sounds which match the quiet "s" sounds of the second line. In lines 11 and 12 the sound shifts abruptly to a description of the night, which is filled with raging wolves.

Creating a Setting for the Poem

We learn or perceive what our experience has prepared us to understand. Sometimes the connection between literature and actual experience may not be readily apparent to the person looking at it. Thus, in presenting a poem to children, we must relate it to the life and perceptions of the child by finding some event or scene in his life which is similar to the surface level of the poem; this prepares him to see what is implicit in the images. Obviously the sensitivity of the teacher, librarian, or parent to the life-style of the child will help determine which events lead meaningfully into the poem.

The scene in the lives of the children in the San Fernando Valley of California which led into *To the Evening Star* was evening on the beach at Santa Monica. This is a place all the children enthusiastically agreed they had seen, liked—indeed, completely enjoyed—and where they wished they could be at that very instant. The teacher brought this up because he had felt an emotion similar to that described in the poem one evening on the beach. The class discussed how it feels when evening comes, when day hangs longingly in the sky, lingering before the fall of dark night—the visual scene on the beach. The scene began to develop along somewhat these lines. First, a picture of the beach at evening began to emerge. When evening falls on the beach, the group decided, the waves seem to become calmer. A gull or two, earlier squawking and almost vicious, will now glide effortlessly close to the water, coming low over the still sheen with no movement of its wings. The sun will begin to turn bright orange, at first, and then will shade into purple mist as a haze drifts up from the sea to enclose the brightness in its veils. And then the first star will appear.

Earlier the beach scene has been filled with heat, lots of running around, children scattering sand and throwing beach balls. The air is likely to echo rock and roll music from portable radios. When evening comes, however, families have quietly started putting their belongings together to go home. The noisy people leave. Only a few others remain as the air becomes too cool to stay any longer. What was as energetic a place of play as a bull ring or a crowd at a ball game has become almost as hushed as a cathedral; the brilliantly sunlit beach has been transformed by the colors of the sunset; the earlier heat has changed to chilliness.

Almost word for word, these details emerged from the discussion period; the children felt involved because they offered their own ideas to the group. None of the children, however, had remained near the beach after dark, so the teacher supplied a few descriptions to stimulate the children to imagine the scene. He told them about some enormous machines with teeth on the front of them which are used to rake up the beer cans and trash left in the sand during the afternoon. No one is allowed to camp out on the beach at night because of these big tractor-like devices, which seem to maul the sand for the debris left in it. These machines, of course, are similar to the danger and threat of the lions and the wolves to the lambs.

After this discussion, the children agreed that they had a clear picture of this scene, the energy of the day, the calm of the first moments of evening, and they were properly respectful of the danger of the machines. Indeed they were led to say that the best moment of all was after the heat of the day, when the cool of the evening began.

The teacher then said that poets often make pictures out of language to recall scenes they have been a part of. Teacher and students then agreed that they knew about a particular scene, the one described earlier of the beach at evening. The group had a sense of common awareness. It then seemed a challenge to see if the poet had also been in on the same sort of experience.

The poem was printed on a large poster board and hung on the board for all to see. Then began an examination of whether the poet had been aware of the same sort of experience that the group had recreated from an actual scene. Could Blake have guessed what the group felt, when he lived so long ago and lacked the adventure of going to Santa Monica Beach?

The class then approached the text of the poem. The evidence was examined. Once this interest in Blake's ability to describe the scene was generated, the appreciation of the poem's language began. The teacher had also prepared for this experience by discussing a story about Venus on the previous day. The poem was read together by the group, with some perplexity, and then the teacher asked if anyone knew the name of the evening star. No answer. The information was provided, and then a light dawned. The teacher asked what Venus is the goddess of. "Love" was the answer, and then the question was asked, "Does love have anything to do with this poem?" With the text in front of them, the children pointed out the references to love.

The group then began to consider how the scene described in the poem compared with the beach at Santa Monica. Several students pointed out that the sun was resting, that the wind was quiet, that it was still. Then the talk turned to the visual imagery of the "fair-hair'd angel." The teacher asked the students to direct him in drawing how the star looked. He was told to draw a dim star, one with light shining in a glow around it, in fact in a nimbus which resembled flowing hair. The next step was the idea that lighting the torch of love meant that the star became brighter and that the goddess also became more and more powerful and in command of the evening.

The students easily saw that the teethed machine which churned up the sand was potentially dangerous, like the lions and wolves raging and glaring at the sheep. At this point the teacher slowly read the poem aloud as the children followed the text on the board; then the poem was left without probing further into its meaning.

Children Write about the Poem

Some days after the experience with *To the Evening Star,* two students asked to do something different from the others, who had been busy for an hour with dramatic play, imitating rather obstreperous beasts in the jungle in preparation for a story about monsters. The teacher invited the two to write about the poem if they liked, and they readily agreed to do so. They were given a copy of the text of the poem, with no other instructions than to say what they felt and not to worry about spelling or punctuation. They wrote for 30 minutes; here is what they had to say.

Pamela, aged 9, writing about Blake's
To the Evening Star.

To THE Evening Star

Angel star or goddess of
love who rules the star
world in the evening.
Just as the sun is
slipping from the sky,
light yourself with
star-light; put on your
crown of glimmering light and
shine brightly while you can.
Shine on the people we
love, and make the sky close
to blackness. Keep you shining,
silver star-light upon the earth.
flowers, houses as they drift off
to sleep. Let the world have
a time of peace.
Then as the earth drifts
into timeless sleep talk peace
with fellow stars and shine
britely guiding travellers home.
— When you fade into
the night then the time of
peace is ended. The animals
of woods and forests wake and
run speedily after prey but
while you watch invisibly, guard
our flocks with your love.

From the sky

Susan, aged 9, writing about Blake's
To the Evening Star.

1 how fairhaired angel of the evening, what does that mean?
Well faired angel of the evning could fit both Venus the god of Love because she is rather fairhaired & beutifull, plus Venus the star is indeed beutiful in light.

Now, while the sun rests on the mountains mean's, when the sun goes down it looks like its setting on the mountains Because it moves so slowly. also its going behind the mountains.

Thy Bright torch of love means it shines apon you in the evning & it makes you feel warm & needed, thy Radiant crown, put in & shine apon our evening beds means when the star shines it kind of looks like a crown & also it means put on your light & shine apon our beds. Smile on our loves, means shine over us & into the love of our hearts.

And while thou drawest the blue curtains of the sky, means the Blue of the sky is kind of pulled back while darkness closes in.

Scatter thy silver dew on every flower that shuts + sweet eyes. Silver dew grows on every flower the plant & some flowers close up at night.

In timely sleep let the west wind sleep on the lake speak silence, with its glimmening eyes. means the wind like settles on the lake. And the lake shines at night when the moon shines on it

and wash the dusk with silver. means when dusk comes shine apon it with your silver light. Soon full soon does thou withdraw, (it goes away.) & leaves everything in darkness.
Then the wolf rages wide

Both girls have repeated many of the lines from the poem in their own words, but they have not merely parroted what is in the text. In each case, the statements go beyond the literal surface of the poem, and the following concepts are apparent:

1. The poem symbolizes love and tranquility in the image of the star-goddess Venus;
2. The time of peace contained in the metaphor of evening as balance between night and day will not be everlasting;
3. The poem is an invocation or prayer to the star to continue her influence of beneficence and protection.

We can see these concepts implicit in such statements as: "let the world have a time of peace"; "guide travellers safely home"; "it makes you feel warm and needed"; "shine over us and into our hearts."

Without the teacher's guidance and help in experiencing the poem, the children could not have been expected to discover spontaneously the meaning of the images. The discovery method does not mean that we will simply wait patiently until—like Athena's birth, full-grown, from the forehead of Zeus—some meaning pops startlingly into the child's mind. A teacher is a guide, not a disinterested observer. We can say that classroom discovery of poetry means, first, that the teacher understands the poem himself; second, it means that he constructs a context in which he can help the child find the cognitive elements of the poem. After this, the obviously strong affective responses seen in Susan and Pamela's writing can emerge.

Summary   That Americans care little for poetry should be obvious to even the most casual observer; we are almost as indifferent to poetry as stones are to music. Too often, books on children's literature and language arts tend to obscure the real issue—children and adults not only are indifferent to poetry, but dislike it when they encounter it.

One reason for this neglect has seldom been articulated—we do not like poetry because we do not understand it. What is meaningless can become threatening and a chore to sit through. But when its beauty and richness become clear, it is pleasurable and welcome. Because of poetry's complex, compressed meaning, the full uses of language emerge to challenge the intellect. To the uninitiated mind, the layers and resonances of meaning in poetry can seem to be a deliberate and tedious obscurity. To an intellect active and attuned to the fullness of language expression, poetry is a most delightful, meaningful, and compelling form of expression. We have failed to interest generation after generation of students in poetry because we have made a rainy-day activity of it, a simple-minded pastime pursued when there is nothing better to do in the classroom. This is a tragic loss and a waste of meaningful experience.

We can correct it. We can in the course of the early years of childhood acquaint children with the treasures of poetry. This is clearly possible even with very young children because language and intellectual ability for early cognition of symbol are present even in the first-grade student. Children never care for what they do not understand. The task then is to lead them to understand poetry, to get them interested in "biting into it."

This is done by the teacher who is himself sensitive to poetry's dimensions and pleasures, who is aware of the life-experiences of the children in the class, and who can find in the myriad images in our daily lives the significant ones which lend shape and understanding to what we see in poetry. The teacher who can create the atmosphere in which the child can see his own life will open the doors of perception to this unique art form which creates a fusion of the known and unknown, the felt and the seen, the imagined and the experienced. Poetry thus enters the body of awareness which is the child's literary life.

For further studies of symbolism in poetry see *Understanding Poetry* and *The Well Wrought Urn* by Cleanth Brooks and Robert Penn Warren and *Sound and Sense* by Laurence Perrine. On the subject of teaching poetry, see *Time for Poetry* by May Hill Arbuthnot and Sheldon Root and *Poetry in the Elementary Classroom* by Flora Arnstein.

For collections of poetry for children, consult the bibliography in Part IV of this book.

6 Picture Books and Picture Storybooks

Pictures in books have a special attraction for the modern child, whose visual senses are deeply sensitized by extensive television viewing. He has come to expect all books to be amply supplemented with highly colorful and detailed illustrations. The programs children see during their many hours of watching television (which exceed the number of hours they spend in school) are made to seem very real. Television corresponds to the imagined real world of prose fiction and the created world of fantasy, where magic is accepted. The pictures a child sees on television are selected to excite him quickly rather than to present a deep treatment of real life.

Television has conditioned children to think of stories in visual terms. But pictures in books seldom approach the excitement of television's moving pictures. Picture books can, however, give a visual representation of life with greater aesthetic appeal and stimulus than television customarily does. To be convinced of this one need only compare the pictures in books that have won the Caldecott Medal (or have been runners-up) for the best illustrated book each year with the general run of television programming for children. At present, television for children is only beginning to realize its potential, and for the time being seems inferior to what children's books offer.

The picture book, in the first place, provides a greater diversity of illustrative style than most television shows. And the book's pictures have greater significance. A variety of important ideas and concepts—serious, touching as well as humorous —are seen in contrast to either the simple tomfoolery of the television cartoon offering or the overtly didactic quality of "Sesame Street" and "Misterogers Neighborhood." The illustrations in books and the text accompanying them go beyond themselves in ways pictures on television do not. That is, they are specifically designed to help children to grasp and appreciate the book's meaning. And finally, the stylized drawings in books serve up impressionistic form and color instead of television's highly representational pictures. Pictures in books often act on the child metaphorically, subtly intriguing his sense of proportion, color, and form through the use of analogy to life rather than giving him an imitation of the real world. These pictures in books become synonyms of life, not simple declarations of it. They resist descending to the apocryphal nature of cartoons on television by avoiding the burlesque and bathos of the television productions. And while good books teach, they do not preach. They create, instead, a literary image of life and not merely a pleasant context for learning the sound of a letter or some other piece of useful information.

Despite all we want to say of the superiority of picture storybook literature over television cartoons, we must admit that there seems little doubt that those children who are not yet committed to the values of literature can easily become possessed by television. Picture storybooks take energy to read, while watching television requires little energy. Verbal material in comparison to television programs is clumsy, delayed in its message, and easily forgotten. Television is dynamic, immediate, vast, and easily retained. It permits the child's mind to get and to hold a great number of images in an extremely short time. Enthusiastic advocates go further to insist, "The handwriting is on the celluloid walls of Hollywood; the Age of Writing has passed. We must invent a new metaphor, restructure our thoughts and feelings. The new [electronic] media are not bridges between man and nature; they are nature."[1]

Picture storybook literature obviously cannot compete successfully with television in a contest to see which can provide the most raw experience for children. "Television children have lived several liftetimes by the time they enter grade 1, just as they have travelled farther by the age of seven than their grandparents ever travelled."[2] Television presents so complete a range of titillation that one might question literature's chance for success as a competitor. At present, however, television belongs either to the modern-day Mr. Gradgrinds (who want to program certain beloved concepts into children—early toilet training, reading before age six) or to the snake-oil salesmen (with their tinsel wonders of the world).

But literature shall always decline to enter into such a race. It has never been said that one reading a poem by Wordsworth would receive the same number of raw or unrefined images he would get from walking through a woods. So, picture storybook literature is not to be judged by the number of random, indiscriminate images it feeds the child's mind but by how well it engages his intellect.

One may think that the television cartoon is like picture storybook literature in that neither will survive without being entertaining. We note, too, that both can leave a great deal of expansion of their content for the viewer/reader to do on his own. But this seemingly fair comparison is superficial. As even a strong advocate of television readily admits: "Cartoons—though true to children because they are wholly based on make-believe and action—display stereotypes that are soon so predictable that viewing becomes a game of beating the author of the cartoon in unfolding of the story, rather than an extension of a power offered the author by his viewers."[3] In short, while we would agree that to live is to exchange this time (given man by life) for as much experience as it can buy, as defenders of literature we assert that we need a high quality of experience rather than simply a large quantity of it; this claims a place for picture storybooks in our

---

[1] Marshall McLuhan, *Counterblast* (New York: Harcourt Brace Jovanovich, 1969), p. 140.
[2] *Ibid.,* p. 28.
[3] Caleb Gattegno, *Toward a Visual Culture* (New York: Outerbridge & Dienstfrey, 1969), p. 34.

visual culture. At the same moment we must admit that the combination of television and literature will result in "an alchemy of the media," as McLuhan puts it:

> But why should it be doubted that radio and TV will transform prose and verse styles? Or how could anybody, in view of the history of such transformations, wish that they would cease to affect language and expression? The difference between the artist and the organization man in these matters would seem to be that the artist senses at once the creative possibilities in new media even when they are alien to his own medium, whereas the bureaucrat of arts and letters moans and bristles whenever his museum of exhibits is threatened by invasion or desertion. The artist is the historian of the future because he uses the unnoticed possibilities of the present.[4]

Identifying illustrated books   We have said that today there really are no nonpicture books for children. How, then, can we differentiate a true picture book from the remainder of illustrated books? This will be the major effort of this chapter. We can immediately note that many books especially written for pre-school and primary grade children have large—often full-page—pictures which occur frequently along with a relatively short written text. Quite obviously in books of this kind, the pictures carry a much greater proportion of the message of the book than the text.

Other books for children contain no written story content whatsoever. Here the illustrations carry the complete load of the book. Whatever "language" the book speaks must be given by the pictures. A well-known example of one kind of these "nonliterary" books is alphabet and counting picture books. Almost all of us recall the ABC books of our early childhood. We call these "nonliterary" books since they contain virtually none of the forms we have described for prose fiction, fantasy, and poetry. Included in this nonliterary category are the numerous "counting" picture books. These are like the ABC books in that they are intended to teach something specific to children, in this instance to recognize numerals and how to count objects. As with the great majority of ABC books, the counting books, while replete with pictures, contain no literary forms and serve no literary functions. We should identify one other type of nonliterary picture book. This is a very elementary form of the information books we will discuss in Chapter 8. In these so-called concept or idea books, pictures and a bare minimum of written text are used to help the child understand the concepts of roundness, weight, speed, shape, size, time, and so on.

---

[4] Marshall McLuhan, *Verbi-Voce-Visual Explorations* (New York: Something Else Press, 1967), pp. 16–17.

These picture books can be contrasted with illustrated prose fiction for older children where pictures occur here and there to bring some character or prime event to clearer focus. The better of these are related to the written text in a free, loose, subtle way. They do not act as a screen between the author and the reader, nor in any other way inhibit the reader's freedom to interpret the writing. Our discussion here will pass over this category of *books with pictures* as well as those books which consist primarily of pictures or illustrations serving as marginal drawings or decorations. These latter pictures are not book illustrations in the finest sense of the term. They serve primarily to attract the reader's eye, to give some visual relief to unbounded stretches of print, to help delineate the beginning and end of literary forms, as in poetry, rather than to help explicate the text.

Intermediate between the *picture book* (a book in which the pictures carry almost all the content the volume contains) and the *book with pictures* (where pictures are included only whenever the author and/or writer thinks it convenient, or for the sake of emphasis) there is another type of illustrated book, the *picture storybook,* to borrow Arbuthnot's term.[5] This category has a fairly well-developed story—that is, one that will stand on its own in literary terms. It also passes the test of being enjoyed by children as a story if read to them without showing the pictures. (Some suggest that this be the standard procedure for reading picture storybooks to children—the literary text first, then a display of the pictures.)

We call this a picture storybook, nonetheless, since it is usually created through the joint efforts of author and illustrator, often from the moment of the book's conception (it is convenient, of course, when one person is both author and illustrator) . The picture storybook, although having a large number of pictures but fewer than the picture book, is less of a visual production and more of a linguistic one. The critical distinction between picture books and picture storybooks, therefore, is that the latter is enough of a self-contained linguistic creation to function without pictures, which undoubtedly add to its character but are separable from it. The picture book, on the other hand, has fused pictures and text, and as Cianciolo rightly says, presents for the child "numerous pictures which enable him to comprehend the story independently of the text."[6]

This distinction is important in analyzing the illustrated book as a piece of literature. We feel it to be critical that the teacher keep these distinctions among the three kinds of illustrated books clearly in mind; any illustrated book that cannot stand on its own in the sense of story quality (that is, one which depends mostly on its pictures for the story) is semiliterary at best, if not nonliterary. If so, it is essential to the success of a literature program or curriculum that the teacher be careful to provide more picture storybooks than picture books for his pupils.

But one should not assume that all picture storybooks are of high literary

---

[5] May Hill Arbuthnot, *Children and Books* (Chicago: Scott, Foresman & Co., 1964) , p. 52.
[6] Patricia Cianciolo, *Illustrations in Children's Books* (Dubuque: William C. Brown, 1970) , p. 4.

merit. An example of a generally mediocre picture storybook is the easy-to-read, or beginning-to-read book, a trade book written with a restricted vocabulary for the young child. This book again depends on the pictures to convey the greater share of the book's content. This narrow limitation of vocabulary and syntax makes it hard for the writer to use the most effective style for his subject.

Patricia Cianciolo seems right, then, in saying that:

> Traditionally, educators and publishers do have some specific elements in mind when they speak of a picture book. Typically, the picture book is addressed primarily to the young child. The picture book usually contains a simple plot developed by way of a brief text which the youngster enjoys having read to him, and numerous pictures which enable him to comprehend the story independently of the text. Hopefully, the text is an important part of the book and worthy of the pictures that accompany it. The text alone is not the 'heart' of the story and neither are the illustrations. The two must be together.[7]

Picture books thoroughly fuse pictures and words. Thus, the illustrator's graphic art forms function to interpret the significant aspects of the story and to extend the text's depth.

We are not convinced, on the other hand, as is Cianciolo, that "the picture book is simply a special form of the illustrated book,"[8] and, therefore, that it poses no more threat to teaching literature than other illustrated books. This disagreement seems to us the heart of the problem of identifying picture books and should stimulate us to carefully examine what are the best uses of picture books with children. Picture books, as we discuss them here, cannot be seen simply as special forms of the illustrated book because, first, they exhibit a complexity of form and structure, an intensity of total design so different from other books that they require a commitment from readers, one that is not demanded by other illustrated books. The illustrations in books with pictures, for example, are used mainly to emphasize and clarify some isolated, special event. Deciding where to put a picture appears to be a very subjective matter at best and many times formal and mechanistic—some think pictures are required at the beginning of each chapter. They seldom seem to have, in any case, the purpose of influencing the pace or structure of the book. Accordingly, the book with pictures appears as two entities, text and pictures, along with an obviously forced attempt at their harmony. The picture book's written text and pictures, on the contrary, are fused from the beginning of the book into a close partnership, an organic unity.

Second, the pictures in the book with pictures tend to reiterate the written story; the pictures in the picture book are essential to the story; they are not after-

---

[7] *Ibid.*, p. 4.
[8] *Ibid.*

thoughts. The picture book must act out a role of narrative action that one would normally assume is possible only with prose narrative. But this does *not* mean, as Georgiou contends, that "A child's initial approach to a picture book is primarily a literary one."[9] Nor can we agree with another of his statements about the child and picture books: "if the pictures in his first books capture his interest and arouse his curiosity, he will then become absorbed in the art of reading."[10] As we shall demonstrate, picture books as highly attractive visual stimuli are not literary, and may work against the development of verbal imagination and appreciation for linguistic art. Picture books are neither purely literary or purely visual: they are an inseparable mix of the two. And the development of interest in graphic art in children is not the same as the growth of their interest in linguistic art.

Third, special attention must be given in the picture book to the page format. These pages must be individually devised to provide reasonable breaks in the written discourse. They must be designed, as well, to relate to each other in a continuing way, much as one paragraph should refer to another in written language. The focus of attention in these pictures, whether they will be well-spaced or crowded, depends as much on the relationship of page to picture as it does on the actual content the pictures depict.

Fourth, taken as whole the picture book and picture storybook give an astonishingly greater sensation of experimentation and diversity on the part of writer, ilustrator, and editor than is true in the book with pictures. Moreover, this diversity stems from a well-disciplined economic judgment of picture book merchandising, which assumes that potential buyers evaluate picture books on the basis of their appearance rather than text. New, inventive, and fresh-looking picture books generally find a hospitable buying audience. There even seems little doubt that picture storybooks with mediocre writing can effectively hide this fault with splendidly illustrated pages by directing the reader away from the weak writing. In fact, as James Steele Smith rightly notes, "the pictures can completely knock out even a well told story or fine poem."[11] Smith seems to agree, in effect, that illustrations should not overly dominate a book to rob it of its vitality. Pictures that merely decorate the book or repeat the text are also wasteful. One must be careful in judging this form of children's literature not to see it through "wishcolored" glasses. That is, what one might hope would be the case may not, in practice, be followed. Therefore, we reiterate: the illustrations in a picture book (and to a lesser sense in a picture storybook) seem to be the major reason for its success.

Fifth, picture book and picture storybook artists, as opposed to those who illustrate books with pictures, tend to eliminate more of the representational art, the

---

[9] Constantine Georgiou, *Children and Their Literature* (Englewood Cliffs, N.J.: Prentice-Hall, 1969), p. 63.

[10] *Ibid.*

[11] James Steele Smith, *A Critical Approach to Children's Literature* (New York: McGraw-Hill Book Co., 1967), p. 329.

traditional art, the figurative art, from their pages. Picture book artists, especially, are inclined to demonstrate their belief that representation of a subject is not what matters most in illustrations for children. Historically, the painters who led painting to nonrepresentational art also brought new conceptions to book illustration. Children's literature interested them since it enabled them to display their imaginative graphic ideas. A well-known artist of both picture books and picture storybooks, Roger Duvoisin, explains it:

> In eliminating the representational from painting painters were better able to examine what painting was. All the graphic arts profited from the discoveries the painters made.
>
> Illustrators were able to learn the importance of the design which holds the narrative elements together in a page and gives order and visual qualities to that page. They could reflect over the conception that what makes a painting beautiful is not what it represents, a conception which to some extent is applicable to illustration. *What makes an illustration beautiful is not its descriptive qualities but its underlying graphic inventions. Even in children's book illustrations it is worthwhile to think of the narrative elements as materials with which to build a beautiful page instead of concentrating on them for their own sake.* (Italics added.) [12]

(The relationship of the italicized part of Duvoisin's statement to the subsurface or metaphorical nature of literature is obvious. There seems little doubt that the creative artist, whether he works in graphics or words, has much the same point of view.)

Sixth, the picture book is different in kind from the book with pictures in its effect on the child's imagination. Picture books, largely because of their very nature, act to screen out the child's use of his verbal imagination. The child's ability to use this area of his imagination is minimized by striking, compelling visual stimuli; picture storybooks are often so finely formulated and designed that children remember only the visual part. As a simple test, teachers have asked children after a picture storybook presentation to recall one or the other: its pictures or words. Invariably, the ideas so reconstituted come in significantly large numbers from the pictures. Furthermore, it can be said that these pictures tend to restrict the child's verbal imagination in a deeper sense. For example, when children are asked to draw pictures about a picture storybook from either a simple, nonpictorial reading or a telling of the story, as distinct from a reading of its pictures, greater diversity is found in the pictures drawn by children responding to the verbal situation than to the visual. This suggests, of course, that a picture in a picture storybook conditions the child's imagination and thereby limits his ability to think of the story in other terms than the illustrations. In books with pictures,

---

[12] Roger Duvoisin, "Children's Book Illustration: The Pleasures and Problems," in *Only Connect,* Sheila Egoff, ed. (New York: Oxford University Press, 1969), p. 371.

because of the relatively fewer number of pictures, this is much less likely to happen.

Seventh, one may say that the picture book is nonliterary. Seldom is this true of the book with pictures. To understand this one should remember that *A New Look at Children's Literature* strongly supports the notion that literature is an aesthetic experience with language. So we would argue that the picture book as it handicaps the child's ability or will to respond to a word story becomes a nonliterary commodity. If it acts to limit a child's interest in linguistic art, we must deem it a threat to the realization of the purposes of literature as we have described them in this book.

We are concerned, in addition, that the picture storybook may be viewed by the child as an extension of television. If so, this vision ties the child still closer to the visual media, which, we have argued, does little to enlarge the child's appreciation of and sensibilities to literature. It is one thing, then, to hope as Cianciolo does that picture books "should enlarge upon the story elements that were hinted at in the text and should include details that will awaken and strengthen the imagination of the reader and permit him to interpret the words and pictures in a manner that is unique to him."[13] It is quite another to admit that this may not happen. One can concede that the liberal use of picture books in schools will serve the functions described for it: a source of pleasure, fun, and laughter; a mirror to oneself as a functioning, growing individual; a builder and extender of vocabulary, concepts, and experience; and a developer of appreciation and understanding of the graphic arts. One can continue to worry, nonetheless, about whether the essentially visual experiences of the picture book do not consistently act to remove the child, or at least keep him at an unnecessary distance, from both written literature and the oral tradition of storytelling. We must argue, therefore, that the gross statement, "the more picture book experience for children the better," is a dangerously unbalanced position for teachers to take if they have serious hopes of developing appreciation and understanding of literature.

One can see from this critical description of the nature of picture books that we believe they have a dual nature: heightened attractiveness and potential undesirability. They are by nature neither all good for, nor absolutely antithetical to, literary study. Our discussions of picture books throughout this chapter should be seen as reflected through this critical filter.

The rise of modern picture books and picture storybooks

The first illustrated book especially done for children, and in movable type, is said to be the *Orbis Pictus* of the German John Cominius, written in the seventeenth century. Chapbooks, small illustrated booklets of high adventure and

---

[13] Cianciolo, *Illustrations in Children's Books,* p. 19.

vigorous action, were also read by children in this century. But it was not until the eighteenth century that a book publisher, John Newbery,[14] contracted with reputable artists to illustrate books for children. Accordingly, for almost the first time, "artists of established reputations began to sign their pictures for children's books."[15] In the same century, however, scholars ruefully admit that the most well-used illustrated book in America was the *New England Primer,* a religious tract for children that emphasized the gloomy side of Christianity—sin, punishment, and death.

By the middle of the nineteenth century in England, the number of masters of children's book illustration had grown prodigiously. In this half-century, and the fifty years that followed, the work of an impressive list of artists found its way into children's books. Richard Doyle, Palmer Cox, Howard Pyle, Leslie Brooks, George Cruikshank, John Tenniel, Arthur Hughes, Walter Crane, Kate Greenaway, and Richard Caldecott (after whom the "most distinguished American picture book for children" is named by the American Library Association annually) all did much during this century to establish trends in illustrations for children which have continued to the present: treating high humor with fine drawings; harmonizing written text and picture pages; creating diversity in spite of realism; emphasizing beauty and fun over piety, tribulation, and repentance; satirizing human foibles; creating great clarity and realism of picturization; developing delicacy in colors instead of an earlier gaudiness; depicting graceful, natural appearing, vigorous figures; and creating sophisticated cartoon-like techniques. Unfortunately, to a great extent in the nineteenth century, American children's illustrators, like most of our culture, were a weak imitation of those of the Europeans. (Howard Pyle is the only American in the above list, and his greatest efforts came in the twentieth century.)

It was not until the twentieth century that large publishers in America set up children's departments which attracted outstanding illustrators; this century became the heyday of American illustrators for children. Their books finally lost their limiting imitative qualities, and are now ranked among the world's first. Especially helpful in this direction was the publishers' decision to move away from didactic purposes and somber designs and toward colorful, amusing, pleasant attractions for children. These publishers also made special efforts to try out books with children and consider children's evaluations rather than publish only what they deemed children *ought* to like.

We should also remember that illustrated books did not always have the irresistible features of color and three-dimensionality that they now possess. Until after World War I, pictures were necessarily reproduced in black and white and could not have had the same influence as modern highly colored illustrations. Also, before this time, most illustrations were line drawings. After World War I,

---

[14] This is the John Newbery after whom the Newbery Award is named: The American Library Association gives this award each year for the "most distinguished contribution in American literature for children."

[15] Arbuthnot, *Children and Books,* p. 55.

illustrations could be reproduced in many shades and hues of color and thus be given infinitely great dimension. Because of this advance, pictures came to be considered an integral part of children's books. Consequently, interest in the appearance of the book was heightened as never before.

Parallelling the advances in techniques for color reproduction in books were increased job opportunities for book artists. Many exceptionally good illustrators from other fields of the graphic arts were attracted to children's books from the 1920s on, as were many accomplished artists from foreign countries. Jean P. Colby believed there were two reasons for this:

> *"The human one*—the majority of children's books are lots more fun to illustrate than an advertisement for a bar of soap or a glass of beer. Most artists love children and are generous in contributing to their pleasure, and they themselves realize that they get a spiritual reward and satisfaction from so doing. *The material one*—if royalties are allotted an artist, even though they be small, they are apt to mount up handsomely over the years, because good juvenile [books] are long-lived."[16]

A well-known artist of children's books, Edward Ardizzone, suggests why many who would like to illustrate children's books have not been successful:

> Now to make drawings which tell a story clearly and in which characters are portrayed convincingly and subtleties of mood are conveyed is difficult. It demands some professional ability, more ability even than the writing of the text. There is an idea that the work of an amateur or inexperienced artist is suitable for books for little children, provided they have a certain spurious brightness of colour. Though there may be exceptions, I think this idea a bad one. Little children should have the best possible pictures to look at, and I think, too, that good or bright colour alone is not sufficient to make a good picture. Drawing is of paramount importance.[17]

Doubtless a *third* element attracts true artists to children's books. This would be their chance to realize their enthusiasm or inspiration, in one artist's words, "to work for images of the highest quality—full, rich, and provocative images that carry the imagination to new heights that will be launching pads for new and always more daring discoveries."[18] These qualities of inspiration are hard to describe. They have something to do with innate ability, of course, but probably

---

[16] Jean P. Colby, *Writing, Illustrating and Editing Children's Books* (New York: Hastings, 1967), p. 94.

[17] Edward Ardizzone, "Creation of a Picture Book," in Egoff, *Only Connect*, p. 349.

[18] Colby, *Writing, Illustrating, and Editing Children's Books*, p. 110.

depend as much on an educated imagination, enthusiasm, and an eye for color. Inspiration also appears to depend largely on the peculiar temperament of the individual artist. For Maurice Sendak it comes from music:

> All of my pictures are created against a background of music. More often than not, my instinctive choice of composer or musical form for the day has the galvanizing effect of making me conscious of my direction. I find something uncanny in the way a musical phrase, a sensuous vocal line, or a patch of Wagnerian color will clarify an entire approach or style for a new work. A favorite occupation of mine is sitting in front of the record player as though obsessed by a dybbuk and allowing the magic to provoke an automatic, stream-of-consciousness kind of drawing.[19]

Types of picture books   We have described a picture book as a publication for young children that is designed and written for special purposes. The many large pictures carry the majority of the book's content, so the child who has not yet learned to read may grasp its central theme and the author or illustrator's intention. Accordingly, the written text is relatively meager. Five different types of picture books are readily noticeable:

1. *ABC or alphabet books.* In the ABC picture book each letter of the alphabet is usually given a name and a full page or two of pictures. Ordinarily, some minor comment is also included, like "S is for Swan." Because so many ABC books have been written over the years, illustrators contemplating new editions must come up with a striking, distinctive, new motif. An example of an ABC picture book of an original nature is *Adam's Book of Odd Creatures,* verse and pictures by Joseph Low (New York: Atheneum, 1962). To organize his ABC picture book, Low concocts the idea that Adam named every living creature (as Genesis reports) except a leftover twenty-six, which he proceeds "To place in order alphabetical; Anything less would be heretical." The book is made up of full-page graphic depictions and inventive couplets that give the "leftovers" their names.

2. *Counting picture books.* Generally these books have a format similar to the ABC picture books. That is, they present a number, a picture to go along with it, and then a short written text: "3 is three swallows up in the sky." This book is obviously intended to help a child learn his numbers, just as the ABC book helps him learn letters. And, again, the authors of such books strive to find some unique way to put together the simple content they purvey. Sometimes this is done indirectly, as in *3 × 3—Three by Three* by James Kruss, illustrated by Johanna

---

[19] Maurice Sendak, "The Shape of Music," *New York Herald Tribune, Book Week Fall Children's Issue,* Nov. 1, 1964, pp. 1, 4–5.

*B, basilisk; if looks can kill,
I'm bound to say I think yours will.*

*G goes to gnome who's never neat,
And yet his mother thinks he's sweet.*

*O.K. Okapi here's the O,
Up with your heels and away you go!*

Rubin. (New York: Macmillan, 1963). This is "a picture book for all children who can count to three." In a series of verse triplets, the author points out many "threes" shown in the illustrations: roosters, hens, cats, foxes, mice, dogs, and men. The book's light plot consists of three roosters awakening three hunters and their three dogs. The dogs unsuccessfully chase three foxes who are a threat to the three hens. The chase scatters three cats and three mice.

3. *Picture books that portray basic concepts.* These books contain a relatively easy written text and make no pretense, ordinarily, at any narrative or storytelling effect. They try to relate the phenomena of the physical, biological, or chemical world to the average child's everyday experiences. Accordingly, the objective of these books is to sharpen the young child's powers of observation of and sensitivity to these phenomena. Of course, one must be careful lest the preoperational child not understand such offerings. A typical example is *On the Beach There Are Many Pebbles,* written and illustrated by Leo Lionni (New York: Ivan Oblensky, 1961). Lionni draws for the young child a showcase of a great number of pebbles in all sizes, shapes, and similarities to living things. Depicted are the "ordinary," the "strange," and the "wonderful" pebbles, as well as those shaped like fish and geese. "Number" pebbles have holes or marks one can count. "Peo-

From Mother Goose (*New York: Franklin Watts, Inc., 1964*) *by Brian Wildsmith. Reprinted by permission.*

Jack Spratt could eat no fat,
His wife could eat no lean:
And so betwixt them both, you see,
They licked the platter clean.

ple" pebbles resemble faces, "letter" pebbles, letters. After this museum tour of sizes, shapes, and markings, the child is asked, "Why don't you go out on my beach and look for other pebbles?"

4. *Mother Goose or Nursery Rhyme picture books.* These often comprise a child's first experience with books, even before ABC and counting books. There are several reasons why we remember the appeal our own early experiences with these books. Young children are lured to strong rhyme and rhythm in verse, and Mother Goose keeps the young child glued to such language patterns. Strong language is no infrequent occurrence in Mother Goose. Above all else, they abound with masculine rhymes, even accents, logical stresses, many refrains and chanting qualities, abundant alliteration, closed couplets, functional metaphor

(when used at all), homey onomatopoeia, vibrant aural values (texture), and witty reasoning. This particular language pattern or style invites the child to participate in its reading by chanting, joining in refrains, and voluntarily memorizing parts. Too, the antics of the vigorous, likeable, true-to-life characters (at least analogically) in these little verses come to peculiarly satisfying conclusions. After the verses set up some quandary (along came a spider) or some unusual act (he put in his thumb), these are resolved in reasonable ways. In short, the humorous, childlike, linguistically strong nature of much of Mother Goose's content holds a great appeal for the picture book–age child.

A qualified representative of modern Mother Goose is the *Mother Goose* collected and illustrated by Brian Wildsmith (New York: Franklin Watts, 1964). Wildsmith often puts only a part of well-known verse—Humpty Dumpty, Georgie Porgie, or Tom, Tom the Piper's son—on a page, which leaves at least three-fourths to be covered with his watercolor washes. A more intense use of nursery rhymes for picture books is seen in *Old Mother Hubbard and Her Dog,* illustrated by Paul Galdone (New York: McGraw-Hill, 1960). Each page of this book is devoted to little more than a single line from this nursery rhyme.

5. *Nonsense humor.* In this final category of picture books, some relatively slight joke can be told to the accompaniment of large full-page pictures. Sometimes these books are little more than a simple riddle, or the depiction of a series of slapstick occurrences. In all cases the text is subdued and unimpressive in contrast to the pictures that accompany it. There are distinct differences between this picture book and the *humor picture storybook,* which we will describe below. An example of a nonsense humor picture book is Neil Appelbaum's *Is There a Hole in Your Head?* (New York: Ivan Obolensky, 1963). This book is organized into a question–answer sequence (one to a page), something like "Twenty Questions," a children's game. About some unknown thing the questioning begins: "Is there a hole in your head?" "Yes." "Are you a flowerpot?" "No." And so on, until: "Do you have a tail?" "Yes." "Are you a whale?" "I thought you would never guess."

Types of picture storybooks

Picture storybooks, we have shown, are different from picture books in their storytelling qualities and conventions. They are intended for the slightly older child who can enjoy and appreciate having literary elements—rather than visual elements, as is the case with picture books—carry the book.

We can identify eight different types of picture storybooks:

1. *Real-life animal stories.* As Arbuthnot notes, animal stories "fall into three distinct groups—talking beasts, animals true to their species but with the power of speech, and animals objectively reported." Picture storybooks of real-life animals ordinarily portray animals in the second category—that is, they act as other members of their species do but can speak to themselves or other animals, al-

though not to human beings. (These imaginary talking beasts are best described under fantasy picture storybooks. Objective reports of animals fit best under informational picture books.) A real-life animal picture storybook is typified by *Red Bantam,* by Louise Fatio, illustrated by Roger Duvoisin (Whittlesey, 1963). Big Rooster, king of the farmyard, chases Red Bantam rooster away from the hens and derides his crowing. "So Red Bantam spent his days at the duck pond behind the stable." Pig and Cow try without success to bolster his courage. Monsieur Dumollet also notices his weakness and therefore decides to sell him. Just then Fox attacks and captures Nanette, Red Bantam's favorite hen. Red Bantam, forgetting his fears, "fell furiously upon Fox to save Nanette." Everyone is impressed with Red Bantam now, even Red Rooster, who swears to be his friend.

2. *Humor and nonsense.* Such books always attract children. They contain many of the aspects of physical and situation humor: odd experiences; inappropriate or incongrous situations; the unexpected or surprising; things that do not occur according to plan; boisterous departures from normal happenings; incongruous appearances, like contrasts in size and behavior; the ironic; physical mishaps of an irrelevant nature; grotesque physical appearance and weird dress; rough-and-tumble goings on. Humor is also imparted in the text of the picture storybook by borrowed, made-up words, fanciful slang, nonsensical or abnormal doubletalk, puns, jests, dialects, and switches in the levels of usage (very polite language in informal scenes and vice versa).

The overlap between the categories of humor and nonsense picture storybooks and fantasy picture storybooks, our next category, is immediately apparent; a humorous, fantastic animal story would fit both classes.

Thus, we must say that there seems no truly separate or distinct category for humor picture storybooks. Since the majority of picture storybooks of all categories have *some* elements of humor, the discrete nature of this category of illustrated books is less obvious than the other categories we describe. About as close as one can get to a *total* humor picture storybook would be an animal fantasy such as *Curious George Gets a Medal,* written and illustrated by H. A. Rey (New York: Houghton Mifflin, 1957), or a story with a folk literature flavor such as *Too Much Noise* by Ann McGovery, illustrated by Simms Taback (New York: Houghton Mifflin, 1967).

In the former book, George is a very curious, mischievous monkey. In trying to write a letter, he spills a big puddle of ink; in attempting to clean it up, he fills the room with water. He finds a pump to get the water out, but since he cannot pull it himself, hooks it up to a cow. This distresses the farmers, who chase him until George hitches a ride on a truck which stops at a museum, where George gets into further trouble. "Lock that naughty monkey up right away," says the man in charge, Professor Wiseman. At this moment George's friend, the man in the yellow hat, bursts in with a letter from the same Professor Wiseman in which George has been invited to participate in a space flight. George flies off in the rocket and parachutes down to receive a medal that reads: To George, the first space monkey.

In *Too Much Noise,* fussy old Peter thinks his house is too noisy—the bed and floor squeak, the tea kettle hisses, the leaves fall on the roof. "What can I do?" he asks the wise man. "Get a cow," says the wise man. But the cow simply adds to the noise with its mooing. So back goes Peter with the same complaint. "Get a donkey," is the advice now. Repeated trips to the wise man result in Peter's house becoming noisy beyond belief, filled with the sounds of a cow, donkey, sheep, hen, cat, and dog. "I'm going crazy," says Peter. "Let them all go," is now the wise man's advice. Which Peter does. "Ah. Oh," says Peter. "How quiet my house is."

3. *Fantasy.* By the time children are able to enjoy and appreciate picture storybooks, they begin to respond favorably to fantasy picture storybooks. This is a highly improbable world, yet one with a logical, nonmagical development. Fan-

Reprinted with the permission of McGraw-Hill Book Company from Red Bantam *by Louise Fatio. Copyright 1963.*

tasy depicts improbable, adverse animals, natural phenomena, machines, or travels. In addition, young children see books set in the distant past (all of the past is vague for this age group) as fantasy—*Drummer Hoff,* by Barbara Emberly, illustrated by Ed Emberly (Englewood Cliffs, N.J.: Prentice-Hall, 1967), is an example of this kind of book. Although the older reader senses the authenticity of the military uniforms of the eighteenth-century soldiers who help Drummer Hoff fire the cannon, a young child would not.

A typical fantasy picture storybook is *Otto at Sea,* written and illustrated by William Pène du Bois (New York: Viking, 1958). Otto is a "world-famous giant dog" who has a series of heroic adventures and receives medals. In this particular story, Otto and his master leave on a good-will trip from France to America. There is room for only two other passengers on the ship since Otto is so heavy. His size pays off during a storm, at least for awhile. Otto keeps the ship upright simply by shifting his weight from one side to the other of the deck area. He blows the waves so hard that they calm down. The ship is swamped, nevertheless, and goes down. Otto tows the lifeboats along to New York, a deed for which New Yorkers give him their typical hero's welcome and a medal for his valor.

4. *Minority subculture picture storybooks.* A fast growing type of picture storybook which narrates the life of children in foreign countries or in a minority subculture of the United States is called a picture storybook of the *culturally different.* Beyond their literary function, these books also aim to explore the life of children of other cultural patterns within and outside our country. *Nine Days to Christmas,* by Marie Hall Ets and Aurora Labastida, illustrated by Ets (New York: Viking, 1959), is such a book. It tells the story of a culturally different celebration of the birth of Christ—that of the Mexicans. The heroine of the story, Ceci, wonders if she will have a piñata at the posada, the special Christmas party held at this time of the year. Her apprehensions are calmed as she and her mother shop for one in the old marketplace. Ceci imagines that all the piñatas plead with her to be the chosen one. After choosing a star-shaped piñata, Ceci helps stuff it with good things to eat and watches it being hung in the patio. Finally, the posada begins and the piñata is broken to everyone's delight—except Ceci's. But a real star "talks" to her: "Don't cry, Ceci. Look! Because a little girl chose me for her first posada, I'm a real star now!" The story incidentally treats several more aspects of Mexican life, its culture and values, which should make an impression on the young child. The subcultures of American life are seen in such books as *Moy Moy,* by Leo Politi (New York: Scribners, 1960), and *Salt Boy,* by Mary Perrine, illustrated by Leonard Weisgard (Boston: Houghton Mifflin, 1968), that depict the life of urban Chinese–Americans and rural Southwest Indian–Americans respectively.

5. *Traditional folk literature.* Many picture storybooks are fables, folktales, fairy tales, myths, and legends that have been revised, abridged, and rewritten as picture storybooks. Traditional folk literature is a natural hunting ground for story material since practically all the elements and conventions of modern prose fiction are derived from this earlier genre. One can also notice that many of the fantasy picture storybooks described above also rely for their essential structure

and actions on the traditional folktale. The danger inherent in retelling or adapting the folktale is that its simplicity and straightforwardness become distorted into something slick, overly sophisticated, precious, or excessively embellished. We can also see that sometimes the charm of the language of the original folk literature disappears, to be replaced with charmingly attractive illustrations, which are a joy to behold, but which wreak havoc with the linguistic art on which they are based.

From Otto at Sea *by William Pène du Bois. Copyright 1936, copyright © renewed 1964 by William Pène du Bois. Reprinted by permission of The Viking Press, Inc.*

Traditional literature is damaged least in picture storybooks that adapt simple or short pieces of folk literature, such as seen in *The Gunniwolf,* adapted by Wilhelmina Harper and illustrated by William Wiesner (New York: Dutton, 1967) . This traditional tale, retold in a modern style, recounts a widely-used folktale convention—the threatened maiden. Little Girl is cautioned, "NEVER ever go NEAR the jungle." Little Girl disobeys, of course, and goes picking flowers in

From The Gunniwolf *retold by Wilhelmina Harper. Copyright ©️ 1967 by William Weisner. Published by E. P. Dutton & Co., Inc. and used with their permission.*

the jungle, singing happily as she wanders deeper and deeper into it. "SUD-DENLY up rose the Gunniwolf!" He said, "Little Girl, why for you move?" "I no move." "Then you sing that guten sweeten song again." Which she did, lulling the wolf to sleep. She escapes for only a short distance before he wakes and re-captures her, however, and requests the song again. This sequence is repeated until the girl gets to the edge of the jungle and the safety of her own door.

An *original* story based on the folk literature tradition is *Zeralda's Ogre,* written and illustrated by Tomi Ungerer (New York: Harper and Row, Publishers, 1967). The story includes an ogre, often found in folktales, and an unsuspecting girl who does not know he likes to eat children. After the girl finds him lying un-conscious after an accidental fall, she hears him moan, "I'm so hungry." Putting her cooking skills to good use, she makes a sumptuous meal on the spot. The ogre likes this so much that he persuades her to be his full-time cook at his castle. Her meals are so scrumptious that the ogre and his friends are overwhelmed and lose their taste for children. Such a fantastical tale depends directly and obviously on folktale conventions.

6. *Adventures away from home.* Borrowing the folklore device of the journey, the distinguishing characteristic of this category is its setting. The main character always takes a journey or a quest. The book is up to date in its adventures, but these adventures are acted out away from the home ground of the hero. These journeys are not the same as those in fantasy picture storybooks because they are probable.

The picture storybooks by Edward Ardizzone are distinctive examples of this category. In *Tim and Lucy Go to Sea,* written and illustrated by Ardizzone (New York: Walck, 1958), the reader is introduced to seven-year-old Tim, walking down a road with a rucksack over his shoulder. He meets Lucy, whom he tells that he is a shipwrecked sailor. Mr. Grimes, her guardian, takes up the children's idea of buying a steam yacht so they all can go to sea, and away they sail—all happy except Mrs. Smawley, the housekeeper, who immediately becomes seasick. A storm hits, in the middle of which they rescue some castaways on a raft. They prove to be a villainous lot whom Tim and Lucy overhear plotting to take over the ship. Through quick thinking and nimble action the mutineers are locked below. All this excitement makes Mrs. Smawley quite forget about being sick. A warship answers their SOS and takes the mutineers off for their just deserts. Now Mr. Grimes thinks it time to go home. Mrs. Smawley pleads. "Oh please, sir, don't go home for my sake. I like the sea now and don't feel sick any more." "Hurrah!" shout Tim and Lucy. "Bravo!" says Mr. Grimes. "MAKE FOR THE OPEN SEA!"

7. *Familiar everyday experiences.* This category of picture storybooks describes adventures set in and around the home, neighborhood, or community of the child characters of the story. These books generally involve slighter adventures than those in the adventures-away-from-home category since they do not involve the hero venturing into unfamiliar geographical areas: they include everyday experiences with animals; situations involving family relations and home life; re-lations with friends and neighbors; events requiring moral judgments; and some-

From Zeralda's Ogre *by Tomi Ungerer. Copyright © 1967 by Tomi Ungerer. Reprinted by permission of Harper & Row, Publishers.*

times a slight mystery or unresolved complication of events. These books usually are emotionally reassuring in that they contain little of the unexpected, the fantastic, or the unknown. Some small attempts at humor are by and large not intended to evoke laughter. They tend, instead, to be basically serious depictions of mainstream America and its middle-class morality.

An example of this type of picture storybook is *One Morning in Maine,* written and illustrated by Robert McCloskey (New York: Viking, 1952). This homey tale covers the time between Sal's waking and lunchtime. Brushing her teeth before breakfast, Sal discovers a loose tooth. Her mother consoles her that this is quite natural. Sal rushes out to help her father dig clams and tells him about it. She is still concerned about her discovery, since she asks lots of questions about what creatures have teeth. Gulls? Big clams? Loons? Hawks? Sometime during this discussion the tooth falls out and is lost in the sand, much to her dismay. She seems somewhat relieved, however, to learn that a gull's feather she has found can be replaced by the bird. But now it is time to go by boat to Buck's Harbor for supplies. Her father must row when the motor breaks down. Upon arriving, Sal eagerly tells everyone about the lost tooth. She finds that her secret wish—which one makes upon losing a tooth—actually comes true as the grocery man gives her a chocolate ice cream cone. And then back home in the repaired boat for "CLAM CHOWDER FOR LUNCH." A simple portrayal of daily life characterizes this type of book.

8. *Easy-to-read beginners' books.* These books contain restricted vocabularies designed for the child with a better than second-grade reading level. Publication of this category has accelerated greatly in the past few years, spurred on by recent criticisms by advocates of individualized reading of the group reading procedures of the typical basal reader. At present, hundreds of these easy-to-read tradebooks (nontextbooks) are available. Many of them have storytelling qualities and carry the major weight of their story in the text. But the vocabulary constraints often cripple the author's powers of imaginative creation. The easy-to-read picture storybook is in general the least well done, in the sense of literary excellence, of any category of picture storybook, although its critical advantage—that it can be read by the individual child on his own—makes it significant. Almost all other picture storybooks require reading skills that are beyond the attainment of average primary grade children.

Representing some of the best in the easy-to-read category is *Little Bear's Friends,* written by Else Minarik and illustrated by Maurice Sendak (New York: Harper and Row, Publishers, 1960). This book tells three incidents in the life of Little Bear. First, he meets a new friend, Emily, by showing her the way home. Later Emily, Little Bear, and Emily's doll, on their way to Owl's party, meet Duck, who is baby-sitting. After a lost duckling is found, they meet Cat and Hen, who have already arrived at the party. They have all put on party hats and have just begun to eat when Lucy, the doll, falls out of the tree where she had insisted on sitting. Lucy's broken arm is mended and the party fun goes on. Finally, Emily comes by Little Bear's house to say goodbye since it is now time for her to go back to school. She gives Little Bear a pen as a going-away present and he

reciprocates with a toy boat. His tears at the farewell are stemmed when his mother reminds him that he will learn in school how to write to Emily, which he later proves he can do.

Books of another type with frequent, full-size pictures do not fit any of the above eight categories, but should receive some comment since they are so numerous. These we will call *picture information books.* They are different from the *basic concept picture book* we described above in that their written texts outweigh their pictures in providing information and ideas. Books of this kind are on science, nature, the seasons, weather, history, occupations, and many other scientific or sociological subjects. Their pictures are much the same size, color, and frequency as those in the picture storybook. The style of illustrations used for them obviously tends to be highly representational. These books properly belong in the category of information books, but it is worthwhile to mention here that their similarity to true picture storybooks is only a superficial one. We should not be confused by their surface appearance into believing they have literary qualities. This warning seems necessary since many teachers make little distinction between these two categories, resulting in a bad balance between fiction and nonfiction reading.

Most illustrators of children's books are more concerned with creating a visual artistic experience for the child than with either teaching him a lesson through pictures or providing an equivalent of the text action. Instead of giving a photographic likeness of the story line, the illustrator hopes to lead the reader of the book into areas of imagination that transcend the explicit verbal nature of the book. Through pictures, the illustrator wants the reader to go beyond the text, to enlarge upon the story elements, to sharpen his recall of the plot—in short, to breathe his own life into the book. The artist wants to enrich, not merely duplicate, the narrative. Color, form, line are his media for complementing and extending, visually, the limits of the verbal plot.

Style and media in illustrated books

Modern art is largely nonrepresentational, not bound to a literal or actual depiction of reality. The twentieth-century painter feels that his work surmounts reality: like the literary fantasist, he creates "another nature." But as with the demands of credibility in literature, the modern artist, with his predilection for the nonrepresentational and abstract, must often modify these tendencies in his pictures if they are to be usable with children. An artist must remember his audience's likes and dislikes in pictures—for example, children's fondness for reality, or life-likeness, in illustrations. He must remain aware of children's capacities to understand and judge his pictures. As the noted children's artist Roger Duvoisin puts it:

The making of children's picture books is indeed like playing with children. The game is on even when the author–illustrator sits alone at his drawing table. For he is really not as lonely as he seems to be. He has his abstract public with him as have artists in every field. In his case it is a public made up of two kinds of children. First, there is the child *he* was, a child who is very much present and who inspires him and helps him understand the other children. Second, there are the abstract children who are watching over his shoulder.

From his own childhood, he remembers the things, impressions, attitudes which impressed him most. He remembers his childhood conceptions of people, of animals, of scenes, and of books which were part of his world.

From the abstract children watching over his shoulder, he will have the fresh, unexpected, imaginative conceptions which they have expressed during games or conversations. In this give-and-take with his abstract public of children, the illustrator will learn to let his imagination flow more freely.[20]

By such watchfulness, the modern artist avoids the coy or condescending picture, or that which is overly-demanding in graphic perception and vision. Especially in picture books, each picture must have storytelling quality; the picture ideas are of paramount importance here. This rule is not applicable to picture storybooks, of course, of which we demand that their written text have the genuine literary merit not demanded in picture books.

Modern picture books and picture storybooks come in two styles. First, there is the representational style, with true-to-life, authentic pictures. This is the style of most picture books and picture storybooks.

But representational art can, by its very nature, restrict the viewer's freedom to interpret the picture by strongly suggesting certain reactions rather than subtly evoking any of a wide range of possible responses; the child must interpret the picture in precise or expected ways. The literalism and realism of representational illustrations prevent distorting the surface appearance or features of its objects. Thus, the nonrepresentational artist is much more free to point up mood or feeling by exaggeration or distortion of reality; he can alter shapes, relationships, colors, or other parts of a visual scene to create his effect.

Again, children do like realistic art. Research shows that for young people, "whether a picture is colored or not is less important than the success of the picture in making the content appear real or life-like." "Realism tends to be a more important factor in illustrations than color" (and colored illustrations are definitely preferred by children over black-and-white ones).[21]

The obvious problem for editors concerned with providing children with a variety of styles in illustrated books is to decide how much nonrepresentational art they can allow. As publishers have been known to say, "Art work should not be published for its own sake." And, "It is hard to sell the creative and original unless it is by a well-known author." One book publisher accused librarians of practices which could account for the preponderance of traditional art: "It has been my experience that libraries are deeply and profoundly committed to research and scholarship; to teaching; to adult education; to self-help; to reference service, in ways that make them one of our finest and most indispensable institutions. But it has also been my experience that, with a few notable exceptions, they feel no such commitment to the processes of creative literature."[22]

On the other hand, it seems only logical to agree with Cianciolo that "The younger the child, the more representational the art style should be. To some ex-

---

[20] Duvoisin in Egoff, *Only Connect*, p. 358.

[21] Ethel M. King, "Critical Appraisal of Research on Children's Reading Interests, Preferences, and Habits," *Canadian Education and Research Digest*, December 1967, p. 312.

[22] Dan Lacy, "Federal Foundations for Arts and Humanities," *Publisher's Weekly*, March 29, 1965, p. 16.

tent, the younger the child, the more conservative the artist will have to be in his use of space, in his use of the combinations and color relations, in the dramatic use of forms and lines, and in his treatment of surfaces."[23] However, if one chooses only books with representational art, he can limit children's development of taste and appreciation for other styles of illustration. We know that this taste and appreciation will develop slowly, only through repeated exposure to nonrepresentational art which the child can accept and understand at his present level of development, and which slightly raises this level. Such exposure means that children's level of appreciation of various art styles is growing and expanding rather than stultifying into a narrow frame of reference. Achieving such a balance is difficult. A highly questionable practice, one we do not recommend, is to use the literature program's time to study contrasting styles and media of illustrations or to compare "mediocre" and "beautiful" illustrations. This does not appear to be a legitimate part of the literature program.

What is there about *nonrepresentational* art in picture books and picture storybooks that makes appreciation for this style so difficult to develop in children? First, nonrepresentational illustrations often use, to varying degrees, symbols, unfamiliar illustrations, and unrealistic imagery. Second, this style employs many more different designs, shapes, sizes, and forms than does representational art. Often these elements (along with various color elements and graphic techniques) are combined in unexpected, uninhibited, nontraditional ways. Third, these artists concentrate in their pictures on what they believe to be the essential or most striking qualities of their subjects. Sometimes this results in primitivism, which looks like childhood drawings. This oversimplification results, as one artist put it, from the decision to draw as if he were a child who had years of advanced technical art training behind him. Thus, many details are missing in these pictures. Many parts are purposely distorted. The nonrepresentational modern artist obviously is less concerned with perspective and proportion than his representational colleague.

Fourth, the nonrepresentational artist's point of view toward his subject makes it difficult for children to understand and accept such art. The artist appears to be more detached from his image, or at least not as emotionally moved by it, as is the representational artist. What appears to be an offhand approach to his pictures shows up as he paints his objects as if they would not stand still long enough for him to catch them in any more than a fleeting way. These subjects, seen as "passing" figures, often do not project their emotions clearly. Their intentions and attitudes toward life are therefore more ambiguous to the viewer. Their postures, often stiff, awkward, or oblique, reflect a lack of overt emotionality, the feeling that representational art for children tends to imitate explicitly. Fifth, the medium used is another difference between the two styles. The representational artist is inclined to fix boldly the outlines of boundaries of his pictures with saturated or relatively heavy lines. The nonrepresentational artist, on the contrary, is less concerned with fixed boundaries and will often use washes that give his

---

[23] Cianciolo, *Illustrations in Children's Books*, p. 23.

painting an overall fuzzy or indistinct watercolorist effect. The latter artist has no reluctance to paste common "nonart" materials together into collage forms, and then even to draw his pictures on top of these collages. He is more likely to combine media than to stick with a single one. The nonrepresentational artist may make a picture that involves a number of different media, whether these be pen and ink, casein, watercolor, washes, acrylics, gouache, crayon, or tempera, or utilize more than one of the graphic techniques of collage, cutouts, scratchboard, linoleum block printing, wood cuts, or stone lithography. Finally, it appears that color in nonrepresentational art is more exaggerated, uninhibited, exuberant, forceful, and outgoing than that seen in representational art. The concept of color in and for itself or as a visual stimulus as worthy as form obviously is held more frequently in the modern movement in art than with those who do the traditional representations. Color combinations which in traditional art circles are thought of as clashing or garish are also more commonly accepted in these modern illustrations.

Of the illustrated books surveyed here, the picture storybook is the most effective combination of visual and linguistic art. The plot, the illustrations, and the story line must work harmoniously together to create a work which is genuinely literature.

For a truly critical analysis of picture books, see Selma G. Lanes, *Down the Rabbit Hole* (New York: Atheneum, 1971).

7 Biography

the lives of great men have historically served as models of human conduct. In Plato's *The Republic,* Socrates concludes that

> ...You must be quite sure that we can admit into our commonwealth only the poetry which celebrates the praises of the gods and of good men. If you go further and admit the honeyed muse in epic or in lyric verse, then pleasure and pain will usurp the sovereignty of law and of the principles always recognized by common consent as the best.

Ever since, and even before, the literary artist has been fascinated by biography. Implicit in Socrates' remarks is the need to balance reason and imagination in portraying a man's life. Avoiding the "honeyed muse" is the strict task of the biographer, who, although not exactly a historian, is not a novelist either. A literary artist in the sense of selecting details from reality and coloring them with his own thought, the biographer must remain within the limits of the subject's actual life. The biographer is not as free to range within the "zodiac of his own wit" as is the fantasy writer.

Numerous biographical approaches can be used to represent a life. These range from slavish reconstructions of a man's itinerary from letters, diaries, and other personal documents to the almost complete freedom which the historical fiction writer assumes in attributing all kinds of statements, feelings, and actions to someone he probably has never met.

Some biographers feel a librarian's classification of biography under history is inaccurate. Instead, they see biography as a genuine province of literature:. "The essential nature of life-writing ... becomes obscured if it is classed as a branch of history. Both explore the remains of yesterday, as arts, interpret those remains; and there ends the similarity.... Biography ... is not a branch of history; for history is not a mosaic of lives, that is, a vast accumulation of biographical sketches, but a generalized narrative concerning events, movements, institutions."[1] The weight of traditional literary precedent, however, runs against such protests, and many biographers believe that an accurate definition of biography is "the record

---

[1] Paul Murray Kendall, *The Art of Biography* (New York: W. W. Nortion & Co., 1965), p. 4.

of a human life." Bernard De Voto believed that "biography is different from imaginative literature in that readers come to it primarily in search of information."[2] In fact, he concluded, "literary people should not be permitted to write biography."

While the arguments over biography's place in literature rage on, unqualified differences between it and prose fiction exist in terms of how the two genres use imagination and illusion. We have seen that the prose fiction writer creates an imagined world to which he gives the illusion of reality. The biographer works in reverse: he recreates a real world, one that actually happened, to which he attempts to give something of the charm of illusion. The prose fiction writer may luxuriate in language and in a proliferation of character types—anything goes. The novelist may create either a very complicated character or an uncomplicated one, as he wishes, but the biographer has both more and less to deal with. He has more because he cannot set the limits of the real life of his character; he has less because he never knows all he would wish about his character. The critical task of the prose fiction writer is to convince his readers of the "realness" of his characters. The biographer, it would seem at first, need not concern himself with this. We can say that the fiction writer *imagines* his characters into their "realness." But the biographer, too, must do something similar. He also must use insight, a form of creative thought, to define his character. Biography concerns itself, then, with a kind of imagination that academic historians do not use. Biographers' subjects are characters they would have liked to create had they been novelists.

There are restrictions on whom one can write about. It is plain that some figures could not be vividly described: the complacent, respectable, mild, reticent, and unglamorous. There are others about whom it would be almost impossible to write a dull biography. About some figures there are abundant data, both of a public and private nature. Others have left virtually nothing for the biographer to use. And while a biography might be written for adults about someone like Frank Harris, an eminent editor and writer, his faults would exclude him from biographies for children: "Boor, lecher, liar, blackmailer, traducer, braggart, fraud, Harris was one of the worst men of his time; the sheer versatility of his wickedness, the variety of reasons why people itched to horsewhip him, commands admiration."[3]

Biography must be content to shine with a dimmer light than prose fiction because it must be true. Modern dramatic novels have generated new devices to tell old stories, can manipulate time as they choose, can use several different view-

Differences between biography and prose fiction

---

[2] Bernard De Voto, "Skeptical Biographer," *Harper's,* January 1933, pp. 181–192.
[3] Richard D. Altick, *Lives and Letters* (New York: Alfred A. Knopf, 1965) , p. 355.

points to tell their stories, and can manufacture other variations that will enrich and enliven their narrative. Biography is confined within the limits of its vow to tell the truth. Whether biographers do limit themselves to the truth has been hotly debated. In modern times, the critics have asked, "Is psychoanalysis by the biographer a way to tell the truth? Is probing into the dark corners of the subject's motives and desires and describing the symbolism of the subject's life (as interpreted through his actions and words) fair game for the biographer?" The extent to which this is justified is controversial. While most critics hold that a biographer should know as much as he can about the development of modern psychology, he should not write a psychological sketch or case study and call it a biography. Critics contend the biographer is not fulfilling his role unless he tells what the man *did* as well as what kind of person he "really" was.

Biography varies in emphasis on action and personality. Like other genres of literature, it has passed through identifiable stages: (1) historical biography, from the eighteenth century to about 1900; (2) romantic biography, from about 1900 to 1930; and (3) contemporary biography, from about 1930 to the present. We shall see how each period has affected biographies for children.

Historical biography

Historical biography emerged into English letters in the eighteenth century as a recognizable and clearly defined genre. Alexander Pope's precept in this century, "the proper study of mankind is man" exemplifies the interest in writing about personalities that flourished at the time.

Some say that modern biography began at the end of this century with James Boswell's *Life of Samuel Johnson,* which is an example of the best kind of biographical writing. Before Boswell's time, a well written life was almost as rare as a well-spent one, to use Carlyle's words.

Boswell brought together the main elements of modern biography. He worshipped truthfulness, had a passion for accuracy and completeness, and arranged a great deal of diverse information into a clear and fascinating story. In spite of this, Boswell's work did not presage a continuing growth toward what we will call contemporary biography, for the intimacy and personal comment that characterized the Boswell biography was forestalled when Victorianism, with its tedious studiousness and prudishness, blurred the picture. Religious orthodoxy, piety, and moral judgments dominated the form, overturning Boswell's model. An unwillingness to tell everything of the foibles and transgressions of great men—an anti-Boswell position—became the general practice of historical biography in the nineteenth century.

Aiding the decline of the quality of biography during the 1830–1900 period were the many unqualified biographers whose writing weakened this genre's overall effectiveness and quality. Even more devasting was their gratuitous preoccupation with minute, trivial external circumstances and the imposing stores of unassorted information and undistinguished subjects. This "journalistic" infection raged to a feverish depiction of small and meaningless details of ordinary life—the antithesis of art, which it smothers. Adding to its discredit, this "social history" veiled as biography was pretentious. These biographers looked upon their elaborate trumpetings of the trivial as heroic object lessons:

> Hence, obviously, the usefulness of biography, which could be interpreted as parable, not only for the guidance of men in society but for inspiration in their private lives. Their consciences troubled by the grimy compromise and capitulations seemingly required by the mounting fierceness of commercial rivalry, the people of the time needed moral guidance of the kind the Bible and its ministers seemed no longer able to supply.[4]

Biography in the Victorian age acted as a powerful propaganda machine for the middle-class principles of industry, thrift, shrewd financial investments, and a compromised social conscience.

Historical biography was undistinguished indeed for several reasons. The cultural and social forces of the era beginning in the nineteenth century stressed moral earnestness, a deep belief in a personal deity, prudent middle-class respectability and sanctimoniousness, and the image of man as a decorous animal. Accordingly, innocuousness over candor, simulation over imagination, devotion over cynicism, officialdom over personality, and eulogy over truth were the watchwords for the biographer of this time. "Biography became a neohagiography, a return to the biographical conditions of the Middle Ages."[5]

Historical biography reverted primarily to a commemorative purpose—hero worship, the idealization of the great man. It was supposed to satisfy readers' native desire for an idol on which to project their admiration, wonder, and reverence. As Carlyle believed: "We cannot look, however imperfectly, upon a great man without gaining something by him." Historical biography became a glorifying of a great man's life—a eulogy or panegyric—so the reader could reflect upon his lofty example.

Historical biography then took on a strong second purpose, that of ethical instruction. As Izaac Walton put it, biography should be "an honor due the virtuous dead and a lesson in magnanimity to those who shall succeed them." Biography was thought to serve the function of the study of philosophy by example, a sort of agreeable relearning of Sunday School lessons. Biographers of this period were sure, as Carlyle explained, that the rise of a hero to meet a crisis results from God's grand design, not from chance. Such belief discouraged the study of the individual and stressed the ethical nature of his endeavors. Biographical characters were described almost entirely from external details of their lives, the well-

---

[4] *Ibid.*, p. 85.
[5] Kendall, *The Art of Biography*, p. 106.

authenticated anecdotes of their behavior. When conjectures were made, they were clearly stamped as such, with a great parade of evidence given to justify them. Thus, the biographer's intuition about his subject was held firmly in check. Jared Sparks in 1830 set the tone: "Biography admits of no embellishments that would give it the air of fiction." Until the twentieth century, these traditions were closely followed in the United States; a biography here was "with few exceptions ... campaign lives, hero portraits of Civil War figures, and pious accounts of clergymen and their erring flocks."[6] In retrospect, historical biography has been described as dull, verbose, clumsy in its rhetoric, uncritical, and devoid of insight. The books of this type were marked by poor literary quality and chaotic organization, and cluttered with odds and ends of every meaningless detail obtainable. As Stephen Vincent Benét said of the type: "A three-story gingerbread monument to a defunct reputation."

Romantic biography   To move away from the style of historical biography, a dramatically enlarged viewpoint of life and a substantial change in man's perception of himself was needed. Lytton Strachey, André Maurois, Emil Ludwig, Gamaliel Bradford, and others led the way to a more humanized concept of character in biography with a highly fashionable selection of biographical detail, an overall ironic or cynical tone, an air of apparent novelty, and of a psychological approach to their subjects. (Freud and his emphasis on the individual's inner life cleared the path for the last of these changes.)

The official, socially imposed view of man destroyed by Strachey and the other revolutionaries in this field made all degrees of explanation of life possible, from despair to euphoria. The field of biography had revolted from its previous stance and was now wide open.

Almost every tenet so dearly held in historical biography was now denounced as faulty or worthless. Instead of a carefully weighted, ponderous succession of facts, the romantic biographers selected and omitted evidence almost as if by whim. An ounce of interpretation was considered worth a pound of fact. The romantic biographer admitted no limits on the quality of information he would accept. He invented and transposed data almost at will, compounding fact and fancy. No such writer worth his salt, so the notion seemed to go, should be overly concerned with the accuracy of detail in a subject's life if the detail did not happen to suit the writer's purposes. Biography was no longer supposed to be laudatory portraiture. Instead, the revolutionaries sought only those details which they felt were essential to or characteristic of their interpretation of their subject.

---

[6] Mark Longaker, *Contemporary Biography* (Philadelphia: University of Pennsylvania Press, 1934), p. 221.

These biographers made little if any attempt to make a scholarly or bibliographic contribution to the existing knowledge about their man. Their purpose seemed to be to make biography readable, if not academically respectable.

Strachey and his contemporaries represented a condemnation of the polite historical biography of the nineteenth century. A continuation of hero worship had become increasingly difficult, in any event, since the publication of Freud's psychology, which suggested to romantic biographers that they take a prying, almost scandalous curiosity about the inner drives and motives of their subjects. They felt it was necessary to strip away the trappings or exterior appearances of the great man's honors or offices, all the better to see the real living being and answer the question, "What is he *really* like?" Thus, the off-the-record face and mannerisms of the man were sought. As Freud said, one knows another person only by an analysis of the symbolic nature of the small, seemingly petty details of his life: chance expressions, casual mannerisms, oddities of behavior. This type of biographical analysis was a direct contrast to the hero worship of the previous period; in fact, it was seen by many to be "debunkery biography." Just as hardly any serious biography in the nineteenth century gave a psychological treatment of the inhibitions and aberrations of its subject, so hardly any prominent biographers of the period 1900–1930 completely denied the debunking approach.

The romantic biographers were also more concerned with the form of their work, its style, than of the substance of its facts. They substituted wit and use of irony, innuendo, and an epigrammatic flair for incident in place of the ponderous detail of the multi-volume work of the nineteenth century. Now, for a change, the biographers were willing to use words which had broad implications and double meanings. Their emphasis upon the psychological interpretation of their subjects affected their style to a remarkable degree, because emphasis upon a great man's inner desires, frailty, or regret reads more easily than an account of his sober-sided public activities and pronouncements.

We have seen in our discussion of dramatic novels for children how an author can delineate character through a series of cunningly selected episodes and with a searching, often introspective, view of his inner nature. The romantic biographer attempted to do the same for his real-life hero. In this process, the "intuition" of the author came into full play. He arrogantly related what went on in the mind of his subject. Balancing evidence and factual, ample documentation was discarded as clumsy and unliterary. In its place was substituted a sprightly product, the result of what Strachey called "a becoming brevity." This is the crafty use of the principles of biographical selection and omission to achieve an enjoyable exposure of the inner forces of the great man's life and nature against which the reader can contrast his own nature and struggles. Any literary device was allowed as a tool to thrust aside source material about the subject whenever recorded facts about the subject did not confirm the general psychological truth that the author had intuited about his character.

Modern psychology, especially the psychology of abnormal people, suggested strongly to the romantic biographer that most people, including great men, exhibit unusual behavior. They asked, "Are 'great' men normal? Isn't genius itself a manifestation of abnormality or neurosis?" And accordingly, "Isn't it the same curiosity about self that leads man to the psychiatrist and to read biography?" If the romantic biographers were accused of being the "vice squad" of biography, they would retort that their major objective in writing was to demonstrate the unhappy but true thesis that all men are human and that humanity is weak. To the charge that they neglected the ethical function of biography, they would explain that their subjects' inner conflicts could be regarded as a mirror in which the reader could clearly and profitably view his own struggles. Yet this ethical influence was so indirect that it affected the reader almost unconsciously and incidentally.

Purely outward manifestations of historical achievement simply do not establish a sympathetic point of view in readers, without which biography has little popular appeal or influence. The romantic biographers turned, then, from history or God's design as the maker of men to the hypothesis that it is man who makes history; they rejected the determinism that the historical biography had propounded, just as they rejected eulogies or didactic biographies.

If in this quest to define the man—who is the cherished element of biography—a disassociation of the man from his time came about, portraying him without great regard for his milieu, so be it. Since the life of a person was not supposed to be a clue to the tone and temper of his age, the reader was expected to assimiliate the necessary historical atmosphere in some other way.

Some of the romantic biographers went even further. That they contributed little if anything to historical knowledge did not bother them. In fact, they went so far as to fictionalize: to manufacture dialogue, invent evidence, describe actions as they might have occurred, and abandon the exactitude of dates. Defending their practice of making up stories that "illustrated" typical traits of their subject, they contended that if the overall impression that they left of the man had been accurate, then these spurious "details" did not matter. If a biographer selects certain facts anyway, why not go farther and make up evidence? To capture the key to the man's nature, not necessarily the details about him, was at the core of their biography. An intuition about the man's essential nature, the motif to his life, was sought; when found, all the subject's actions—real or imaginary—were supposed to fall into a clearly reasonable pattern. Goethe was thus seen as "a struggle between the poet's genius and his demon"; Bismark: "the conflict between pride and ambition"; Thoreau: "a recognition of the world's sickness and a search for her doctor"; Luther: "an Oedipus complex"; and Poe: "the forces that wrecked his life were those which wrote his books." Imagined conversations or anecdotes, for example, were supposed to be more "real" than the subject's actual words.

Sometime after 1930, a counteroffensive against the worst excesses of romantic *Contemporary* biography was mounted by more conservative historians and biographers. "In *biography* their search for fat royalty checks and vivid characterization, the fictionizers, the Freudians, the intuitive writers, and the debunkers forgot that biographies were supposed to describe what a man *did* as well as what he was like personally, and that, essentially, biography was a form of nonfiction, subject to the restraints imposed by fact and reliable records."[7] By 1940 the biggest guns of the conservative critics of romantic biography were trained on the psychological biographers and on those who took exceptional liberties with their biographical source material. "Psychology," wrote one, "is about as useful in the hands of an ordinary biographer as a stick of dynamite." Other critics asked them to combine research and scholarly integrity with their imaginative literary qualities and the readability of their books. They pointed out the romantic biographers' tendencies to substitute cleverness for profundity, distort subjects through oversimplification, dismiss scholarship to disguise their ignorance of history, be excessively iconoclastic for purposes of self-aggrandizement, and substitute a little psychological jargon for equally valid older expressions.

After about 1940 the worst of the radical forms of romantic biography were distinctly out of fashion. To replace it, a new school of thought we shall call contemporary biography emerged. Attempts were made to synthesize, not destroy, the radical methods of the romantic biographers to meld the best they had to offer with the extensive research and scholarly methods that had traditionally been associated with this art of writing. This contemporary method did allow made-up quotations but insisted that they be used sparingly and be based on fact, protecting the reader, with solid evidence supporting each imagined scene and conversation. In this way, contemporary biography avoided the charge put to romantic biography, that it was hastily thrown together or merely clever. The popularity of the contemporary style reflected the growing demand of science-minded readers for true evidence in biography, not the romantic biographers' frequent flirtations with truth:

> The excesses of the "age of Strachey" were a reaction against the extreme objectivity of the scientific historians and the pomposity and restraint of the Victorians. While scholarly biographers could never accept the sloppy research and cynical sensationalism of the "new" biographers, they learned from them the value of liveliness, concern for character, frankly confessed interpretation, and artistic organization. Many scholars who had disparaged biography early in the century and who were contemptuous of the methods of the popularizers, eventually altered their views about biography and then borrowed from the techniques that the popularizers had invented."[8]

While it is convenient to describe biography as moving through three stages— the historical, the romantic, and the contemporary—seldom does one find "pure"

---

[7] John A. Garraty, *The Nature of Biography* (New York: Alfred A. Knopf, 1957), p. 138.
[8] *Ibid.,* p. 148.

examples of each stage. This is especially true with biography for children, because an author must keep in mind children's unenlightened mentality, their immature emotionality, their general lack of experience, their ignorance of adulthood, and, more specifically, their relative lack of ability to read. But, above all, it is true because of stringent cultural taboos, as we shall see.

However, these three stages are useful in describing biography for children. The author's treatment of the separate aspects of biography—why the subject was selected, the biographer's point of view, his selection of detail, the style of the piece, the integration of detail, the theme or key to the subject, and the book's scholarship or authenticity of detail—may vary from historical to romantic to contemporary. A biography for children which moves through all three categories is *George Washington,* by Clara Ingram Judson. It is a commemorative work, a hero worship of Washington. The theme or key to her subject chosen by Judson was "Washington as superman"—"probably no man in the thirteen colonies equalled him at twenty-seven years of age." Washington is portrayed, therefore, as an almost godly figure, intelligent, honest, trustworthy, obedient as a child, brave, courteous, humble, dedicated, sensitive to human needs, reasonable, and logical. The only reflection of his ordinary humanity is that he was a shrewd businessman and military general. Unwittingly, Judson's story also describes the great deal of influence peddling among Virginia's dominant families which brought them political power, military offices, and much affluence. At the same time, this inevitably added to the perpetuation of slavery, the forced evacuation of the Indians from their lawful properties, and a social class structure which limited upward economic movement by the lower classes, especially the tenant farmers on whom Washington's social class depended.

Judson flees from such thoughts; their treatment, while inescapable to the sophisticated reader, is so slight as never to catch the child's attention. Thus her repression of ugly facts about Washington's milieu is almost complete. Not that she does not seek to assume the mantle of scholarship we associate with contemporary biography. "It has been a challenge," she remarks self-effacingly in her foreword, "to separate truth from fancy and to write with fidelity." This should read, of course, "It has been a challenge to separate the truth and fancy I found convenient for my theme from the truth and fancy that did not fit." She is right in noting that "modern scholarly research [makes it] possible, now, to get a real understanding of our first president." Nevertheless, Judson's did not present one.

Her "scholarship" suffers especially as she interprets the role of Indians versus Virginia's landed gentry of the time. She sees the red man's eviction in favor of the white families as quite normal. Thus Washington views the Indians' reactive violence with "horror." "Those in greatest danger were the settlers," Washington supposedly said with deep feeling. "Indians massacre and terrorize." . . . "Someone needs to rescue the poor settlers from the Indians," Washington's brother says. Replies George: "There will be no living settler if they are not stopped soon." The Indians' violence is assumed to be due to the inferior intelligence whites attribute to them. (Being as "stupid as an Indian" is considered the ultimate insult from one white to another.)

Why the subject was selected. One reason Judson selected this subject is apparently that she believed she could balance the picture of Washington between the hero worship of historical biography and the debunking accounts given in romantic biography.

Point of view. But Judson's personal affection for the Father of Our Country intrudes too plainly into her judgment. Writing about Washington obviously represents to her a chance to display her stated beliefs that he was a sensitive man untouched by war and the acquisition of wealth, easily moved by the beauty of nature, the simple pleasures, folksy ruralism, and the nurture of growing things. Washington is, then, a neighborly, humble, kind, and generous man, one

From George Washington, Leader of the People *by Clara Ingram Judson. Copyright 1951 by Clara Ingram Judson. Used by permission of Follett Publishing Company.*

who always sees the needs of others as more important than his own. Judson requires her subject to be more than a political and military genius, a political potentate, and a war-god—he must also have the personality trait expected of any American folk-hero, namely humility.

Selection of detail. The historical mode of biography requires a plethora of sequential details about Washington's life placed alongside, as if equal to, those actions for which he was so long remembered. For example, Washington's presence at the First Continental Congress is described mostly by trivia: "Shops in the big city were enticing. Before Washington left for home he bought a pocketbook for Martha and a cloak for his mother." The chapters on Washington's domesticity—apparently meant to convince her child readers that somehow public life, military power, and wealth were only sidelines with him—are crowded with meaningless and forgettable details, although the greater portion of the book is, in fact, devoted to Washington's wartime conduct. Judson borrows from the historical tradition to string out little-remembered dates, names, actions, and other mundane matters.

Style. The style of *George Washington* can be characterized as restrained, flat, unemotional, without flair, plodding—it lacks verve or quick movement. Judson cannot infuse the most dramatic of biographical material, a battle, with anything more than stiff and inhibited details:

> The terrible bombardment lasted for days; it riddled the British defenses and the little town nearby. Washington was ever in the midst of the battle; one day he dismounted, handed the bridle to a sergeant and joined General Lincoln and General Greene at a battery. The risk of a British shot worried his aide.
> "This situation is very exposed sir," he ventured.
> "If you think so," the commander said," you are at liberty to step back." Neither man moved. Soon a shot did strike close by. General Greene took Washington's arm and pulled him back as the ball rolled at their feet.
> "We can't spare you yet, General," he explained.
> "It is only a spent ball," Washington answered.[9]

This style serves well to justify Judson's theme of icy bravery but does little to promote a nonchalant or reluctant reader's interest in the excitement of battle.

Integration of detail. Typical of the historical tradition, no liberties are taken with time and sequence, as in romantic biography. Judson moves slowly and methodically through Washington's life from his eighth year to his death regardless of the relative importance, pivotal character, or imperativeness of events. The first four (of 19) chapters bring Washington to age 16. Contrast this with just three chapters on his activities in the Revolutionary War. Typical, too, of

---

[9] Clara Ingram Judson, *George Washington* (Chicago: Follett, 1951) , p. 188.

the historical tradition is using events as the frame of reference for the movement of the biography; Washington did not make history, history made him.

Theme or key to the subject. Consequently, no key to Washington's personality emerges in Judson's treatment. Instead, the evolution of her chapters depends mainly on the predetermined dictates of history. Where history cannot give this direction—that is, in the early chapters and years of Washington's life—there is no apparent organizational scheme to the book at all. Washington's personality determines little of the organization or integration of the detail of the book. Adding to the jarring, plotless nature of the generally brusque organization of the book is Judson's habit of trying to contain sequences of time in consecutive paragraphs, and unexpectedly scattering trivial, irrelevant details into the narrative. These create an unnecessarily difficult thicket for readers to get through, and thereby remarkably enlarge the reading difficulty of the book.

Scholarship or authenticity of detail. Romantic biography allows the biographer to invent dialogue and describe dramatic scenes which logically could have happened, but actually did not. *George Washington* abounds with examples of this. Judson would have us believe, however, that she has moved beyond the romantic mode of such excesses to the cautious contemporary mode of ensuring the general truthfulness of a scene. Hence, she contends that what she imagines is "historically accurate." The highly apocryphal sound of some of these makes one wonder at her scholarly judgment, nonetheless. Finally, she adopts another device of romantic biography, the omniscient viewpoint. Seldom, then, does she allow Washington's personality to develop through anything other than her direct comments about his emotions, thoughts, motives, and reactions to others. This gives Judson an immense power over the explication of the theme of her subject since she is in no way required to "prove" his personality by anything besides her own comments. It leaves little opportunity for the reader to judge Washington's character on his own or even to be sure he has read a valid interpretation of his character.

A biography for children in the romantic mode is *Daniel Boone* by James Daugherty. Written in 1939 at the end of a disastrous economic depression in our country, one would expect *Daniel Boone* to take a different thematic approach to its subject than *Washington* by Judson. Boone represents the disgruntled farmers who did not stay to make the landed gentry of Washington's Virginia rich and powerful. For there was little doubt "the great landlords were demanding costly land titles and bringing in slave labor so that it was a disgrace for a white man to work with his hands." The theme of Daugherty's biography is how Boone's "whole life and the blood of his sons had been spent opening up a promised land of untold wealth—for others." (Boone, as Daugherty tells it,

A romantic biography for children

chronically forgot to sign the legal papers that would have assured him his share of the wilderness land he helped wrest from the Indians.) This theme is "the American dream," "the path for history," "the curious mind to see and know about America." It is "the gateway to a new America, a fabulous western world with a destiny of glory like the towering storm clouds in a fiery sunset." Boone seemed destined to lead "God's chosen people," and so at any time in his life "it was as plain as the nose on your face that [he was] soon going to need more elbow room and plenty of it." Boone's personality is, then, a symbol of the "manifest destiny" of the settler. Boone becomes the metaphor for the nerve, strength, audacity, the relentlessness—and, in current terms, the illegality—of the settler. While Daugherty does not debunk Boone nor desert, for that matter, the commemorative purposes of historical biography, Boone is not the superhero to him that Washington was to Judson. For, if Boone by analogy is "pioneer family," his life is also "a comic-tragic drama of struggle and violence." Daugherty proclaims the life of the settler to be "a rough and violent saga full of lights and shadows, sweet and bitter as the wild persimmon, rough and tough as the shag-barked hickories, fierce and tender as the tall waving corn of the valleys." These are hardly saint-like qualities. ". . . Boone's story was the story of a whole people. It had all their griefs and tragedies and restless longings and rich half-fulfilled dreams, all their ranging freedom and moral bondages."

In defense of the *selection of his subject* of Boone as settler, not a superman, Daugherty believes Boone to be "a free singing rider in a lost dream," not the walking stone monument Judson makes of Washington. Boone, as personality and as biography, rests as the vengeful battler of resentful Indians whose lands were systematically and voraciously stolen from them. The modern sophisticate can read *Daniel Boone* as a consummate piece of irony, with the Indians, protecting their homelands by the means they understood best, becoming the heroes, and the settlers—avaricious for land, callously destructive of nature, reprobate in their land deals, and offensive to the Indian culture—becoming the antagonists. But for child readers of *Daniel Boone,* Daugherty says Indians had no more right to contest a settler's advances than did those who objected to Abraham's movement into the land of Canaan. For Indians were "raiders"—murderous, violent, terrorist, "red varmints,"—who "surround the cabins just before dawn, terrible in the ghastly white and black war paint, fearsome images of violent death that haunted the dreams of every border family." "Bloody tales of massacre, torture, and desperate escapes" abounded. "A doomed race," the Indians were best dealt with when settlers set to "burning their towns and destroying whole tribes." The chilling account by Davy Crockett tells of the settlers' vengeance:

> We now shot them like dogs; and then set the house on fire, and burned it up with forty-six warriers in it. I recollect seeing a boy who was shot down near the house. His arm and thigh were broken, and he was so near the burning house that the grease was stewing out of him. In this situation he was

still trying to crawl along; but not a murmer escaped him though he was only about twelve years old.[10]

Daugherty claims the settler needed such emotional release, which clearly illustrates his adoption of the techniques of romantic biography.

---

[10] James Daugherty, *Daniel Boone* (New York: Viking Press, 1939), p. 25.

Moreover, Daugherty's *selection of detail* and the *integration of this detail* further place his biography in the romantic mode. While the biography is organized somewhat according to the chronology of Boone's life, such a structure is as inconspicuous as the ebb and flow of daily frontier life. Thus, the chronological details of Boone's life are merged whenever needed, to create the higher order of the book, Boone as a metaphor of the settler. Daugherty sensed that a careful, deliberate exposition of time was unneeded, that in fact, for the purposes of his romantic biography, this would stand in the way of its development.

It is, therefore, freed from contemptuous detail, or a nagging dependence on "necessary" fact, or binding time, that Daugherty's *style of writing* rests. His style can emerge with an excited energy, as shown in this slick picture of Boone in his old age:

> To the new generations sweeping on he was like a page out of the past, a patriarchal figure around whom hung fantastic legends and romance. He was pointed out to strangers when he rode into the ragged streets of a sprawling boom town. Being a curiosity annoyed him, and he grew more and more uncomfortable in the raw, new undergrowth of humanity sprouting up so rankly on the old hunting and battle grounds that were full of memories.[11]

Never does Daugherty use standard statements if more elaborate, ornamented figures of speech can be found. An example of his almost over-ripe style is:

> The next day the clear-shining sun rode over the vast land like high-calling trumpets of glory. The splendor and the brightness came upon his spirit like the rushing of mighty wings, and the voice of mighty thunderings: "Enter into a promised land such as no man has known, a newborn creation all your own; drink deep, O Daniel, of the mysterious wine of the wilderness."[12]

The *point of view* chosen by Daugherty for his biography is a complex of past and present tense. Tenses in his narrative switch from paragraph to paragraph; this shifting of tenses, so regular that it must have been calculated, leaves the reader with a confused point of view. Nor does Daugherty choose a single vision to view Boone's life. Boone is seen through his own thoughts and words and also in the third person, generally in documents. But usually Boone is described by the omniscient biographer. For example, whatever runs through the minds of both sides in a settler–Indian skirmish is always given in full detail.

This multi-dimensional point of view makes a startling impression on the

---

[11] *Ibid.*, p. 84.
[12] *Ibid.*, p. 34.

reader. It mixes up the narrative's sense of direction and stability. This could be particularly annoying to the child reader, of course, who benefits from a narrative with a constant viewpoint. With Daugherty, the child must weave back and forth in time and then skip to the more remote future. Daugherty apparently chose his multiviewpoint to depart from the straightforward, precise, caution of viewpoints in historical biography. In doing so, he exposed one difficulty in writing romantic biography for children.

The uses of *scholarship* in *Daniel Boone* are reflected by Daugherty's hyperbolic style, by his tendency to transmogrify the absurdities of *Settler* to virtuous acts, and by the array of simplistic motives he gives to Boone. His florid style depends on the exaggeration of fact and the free mixing of truth and fancy. One often senses that the biographer ran out of verification for his theme. Moreover, the settler is controversial among modern students of Indian history. That any country, invaded by a technologically superior enemy, would produce any less violent forms of guerilla warfare by its natives is unlikely. Hence the atrocities the Indians commit, the "unprovoked" assassinations particularly, have been partly fictionalized, as this story strongly implies. There is little doubt of the life-and-death nature of the conflict, however.

Finally, one wonders at the artless disingenuity which Daugherty attributes to Boone when he desires to sentimentalize him, as opposed to the shrewd, hard-bitten expediency he otherwise marks for Boone's life. The *single* motive attributed to Boone (his dedication to opening up promised lands) is at once too clever and too grand an idealization for this unlettered frontiersman. At times, Boone's love of killing, either men or lower animals, escapes from Daugherty's pages and we have a taste of what it would be like to learn of more than the single-sided Boone.

Before 1900, there was little worthwhile biography for children.

How should biography for children be written?

Considering the long recognized interest of young people in personality and accomplishment, their tendency toward hero-worship and their aptitude for inspiration by example, it is strange that biography took so long a time to establish itself in the field of children's literature.... It is curious that the years at the turn of the century, which saw so clearly the beauty and significance of epic material, and which produced such fine retellings of epics, did not have equal vision as to the similar significance and importance of biography in children's reading.[13]

---

[13] Cornelia Meigs. *A Critical History of Children's Literature* (London: Macmillan Co., 1969), p. 365.

Arbuthnot believes that excellent biographies for children, those "not stereo-typed, stuffy, and unpopular," did not appear until the 1930s.[14] From what we have learned of the depressing characteristics of historical biography, we should be thankful for an absence of biography for children during that period. During our period of romantic biography, much of the biography for children was, in reality, biographical fiction, a type written to help children understand politics and sociology. The latter has only small literary qualifications. Whether we believe with Arbuthnot that biography "is flooding the market and threatening to capture young readers so completely that they will have no time or taste for any other kind of reading,"[15] it is rather certain that little good biography for children is being written. The Center for Children's Books at the University of Chicago lists less than 1 percent of their 1400 "good books" of the years 1950–1966 as biography.[16]

One group of biographers for children has seemed to exemplify its generally nonliterary approach. This is the "rewrite" school of children's biography. The members of this confraternity go to prior accounts of the lives of great men for their major source of information and inspiration. They do not treat biography from new and fresh viewpoints and interpretation. Instead, they retouch earlier portraits with the brush of fashionable thought. These biographers go to full-length, heavily documented accounts of a man's life—treatments children could not read—and rewrite them in a brief, popularized, and understandable narrative.

The rewrite biographer does not make a committed search for truth and new information. His job is merely to simplify, often disastrously, the style of the original to make it suitable for children. Instead of a skillful recombining of prior elements, the rewrite biographer chooses a few characteristic incidents in the subject's life and combines them chronologically, losing whatever sense of continuity and transition the original work contained.

The traditional advice for teachers regarding biography—that it should be interesting as well as authentic—strikes at the two aspects of biography which have created the greatest dispute. Of course, if a book cannot be made interesting for the child reader, it should not have been written. Yet, if we are to accept the conditions that follow this demand, we must be prepared to accept fictionalized biography. Children cannot be provided a biography which is in essence a "fast-moving narrative" or a continuous story unless the biographer is allowed much literary license. The writer often cannot satisfy the child's wish for action, deeds, conversation, and the character's thoughts unless the writer, himself, creates many of these incidents. What, then, is meant by the insistence that "authenticity is the hallmark of good biographical writing, whether it is for adults or for children?" Can this be interpreted to mean that the author should lessen the pleasure of his story to achieve "a true and accurate picture of a human being?"

---

[14] May Hill Arbuthnot, *Children and Books* (Chicago: Scott, Foresman and Co., 1964), p. 518.
[15] *Ibid.*
[16] Mary K. Eakin, *Good Books for Children* (Chicago: University of Chicago Press, 1966).

Taboos

Before we answer this question, let us look at an influential factor, taboos. We have seen that the synthesis of the historical tradition—with its verbose but factual data—and the romantic tradition—with its fictional details, which, critics claimed, extraordinarily influenced readers' opinions—resulted in contemporary biography, which seeks to be factual but includes many apocryphal and fictional details. It would seem, then, that the contemporary biography could be both as accurate and as readable as we require for children. But the taboos of our society prevent this. They demand that a biography about a great man seldom reveal anything of the dark, unsavory, or undistinguished side of his life, further limiting the already narrow range of material the biographer can draw on to enhance his work's interest. Such censorship is not a liberty the writer takes, as some critics claim. It is more often a matter that is fiercely debated by the respectable biographer and his editor, who believes he faces the unpleasant consequences of taboo violation and so usually upholds this kind of censorship. These taboos are based on the argument that children do not have the comprehension and judgment necessary to deal with depictions of evil or inhumane acts, or that reading about trickery and deceit or, above all, brutality and terror will encourage such responses in a child's behavior. While there is no convincing evidence of this, it is a widely and persistently shared belief. Logically, of course, one could argue that reading about the dire consequences that generally result from inhumane behavior would act as a moral lesson in reverse and would illustrate the appropriateness of the golden rule and other moral precepts. The strength of the taboo against writing about infamous people continues unabated, however, and these negative lessons continue to be prohibited. Reinforcing this particular taboo is an equally strong notion held by many that if a child reads stories of "good" men's lives, he will model his life after their deeds, and thereby grow up to be a respectable, generous, and responsible member of the adult society. This supposition, which has no scientific evidence either, again shows our remarkable faith in bibliotherapy.

It is wrong for teachers to expect, therefore, that biographical characterization for children will be true to life. A treatment of the shortcomings versus the virtues of the great man is seldom to be found. And while describing the unseemly, improper, even illicit activities of a supposedly great man might make him come alive for the child, the teacher should realize that taboos prevent such characterization for children.

The well-known writer of children's novels in England, Geoffrey Trease, argues that this inevitable selection of sympathetic and admirable protagonists for children's biography is necessary for another reason: children's limited understanding of history. He insists that "children cannot normally be expected to have this historical approach"—the capacity to make critical judgments about historical evidence or to entertain alternative hypotheses about historical events.

In his words, children "need not biography, but story-biography."[17] The latter is described by Trease as truth in "an attractive and digestible form." Story-biography demands that its writers make their issues clear and concrete, and give a plain black-and-white conflict situation which is resolved with a moral victory by the hero. The lives of infamous men, with this notion in mind, must be displayed only as antagonistic to sympathetic, heroic figures in biography. Full length, complete lives of most great men are impossible, then, because of the taboo aspects.

Nevertheless, the influence of taboos does more to make biography for children difficult to write than do the problems of determining some biographical detail's accuracy or importance. For example, as a biographer searches for a subject, he must find the "key" to his subject, an insight into the man's essential nature. Before he finds this key, the biographer must consult all the facts at his command. He cannot let contradictions in the mass of this evidence dispirit his search for the vital nature of his man. But what if this theme turns out to be pessimistic or morbid? At this point, whether the writer continues to write the biography as dictated by his discovery depends on his integrity as an artist. Some biographers have devised respectable ways to escape this dilemma: they write an innocuous story of the subject's childhood, or they write just up to the point of the subject's transgressions or scandalous behavior and then quietly stop telling the story. Other less honorable alternatives include: (a) disregarding any transgressions of a subject whose essential character is tainted or repugnant to our taboos—in short, effectively deleting anything at all bad about the man; or (b) changing the negative key to the man—which the author believes is the true key—by stacking up all his positive behavior as a counterforce to what is the actual meaning of the subject's behavior. These are indeed insidious ways to avoid offending society's taboos. That many biographers for children have chosen the latter course helps explain the faults that still weaken much biography for children: an incomplete recreation of the subject, a panegyric or commemorative tone to the work, and the presentation of a flaccid goody-goody, one whom children infer never could really have existed in his times, let alone have succeeded there.

Beyond the restraints of taboos, the biographer for children is likely to struggle with other factors in his attempt to balance the axes of interest and authenticity. A thoroughgoing search by Garraty on how biographers develop their work shows the complexity of the task.

> . . . a search of the records discloses no fully acceptable pattern for the writing of biography, but shows that many contradictory theories and practices have been applied by all sorts of writers. Some of these precepts have been silly, some ambiguous; most have been advanced by their protagonists with a dogmatic assertiveness indicating, to take the most charitable view, that the writers have not troubled to study the history of the biographical form very

---

[17] Geoffrey Trease, *Tales Out of School* (London: Heinemann, 1964), p. 58.

closely. That biography is by its very nature a subject attractive to individualists may explain its bewildering variety of form and theory.[18]

Only two general rules emerged from Garraty's comprehensive study. First, the would-be biographer should know his subject by reading all he can about him and by taking copious notes which he then thoroughly analyzes and logically organizes. Second, he should be concerned with the basic chronology of his book:

> Every effective biographer has had to combine materials topically in order to reduce the complexities of existence to understandable form. . . . Within these general rules, there is room for endless variety as long as the biographer honestly tries to describe his subject's career and character and does not encumber his work with what very long experience has proved to be extraneous and essentially unworthy motives.[19]

This by no means explains the "almost impossible act of synthesis" the biographer makes as he creates a full and unified picture of his subject out of diverse and often seemingly unrelated facts. To do this he must exercise logic, controlled imagination, and impartiality. We have noted the forces working on biographers for children that resist this.

In short, we see biography for children at present to work under exceptionally restraining influences, restrictions that shape its essential nature. As much as we might wish otherwise, it is generally accurate to say that with rare exceptions, biography for children:

1. Cannot be written as a scrupulously truthful account of a man's life.
2. Cannot be written with every event in its proper chronological order.
3. Cannot avoid a fictionalization of its subject's life.
4. Cannot consider the whole man in the total of his various moods, behaviors, eccentricities, achievements, and so on.
5. Cannot deal directly with infamous men or their deeds.
6. Cannot be rigorously documented accounts, with verifying footnotes, and so on.
7. Cannot be written with the assumption that children perceive adult life properly.

---

[18] Garraty, *The Nature of Biography,* p. 256.
[19] *Ibid.,* p. 257.

Children's Perception of Adult Life

This last point is especially pertinent. The biographer confronts a difficult task since he seldom knows as much about his subject as he would like. Even if he does, the writer must still choose and arrange his material. Furthermore, he must package this in a readable, enticing way to attract his readers.

The problems that challenge the biographer's ability to produce a comprehensible narrative result also from who his readers are. He must write skillfully enough so readers can comprehend the meaning, intent, and style of the biography. Writing biography of adults for children is further complicated because it in no way allows for the kind of empathizing that can be generated in a piece of prose fiction about children for children. Since children have had no personal experience in being adults, their view of this stage of life is necessarily filtered through an immature, unsophisticated, inexperienced, and untrained vision.

In our attempts to study how children read biography, we should ask how children visualize the world of adulthood, how they perceive adult life, how well they understand the behavior, social relations, occupations, appearances, and so on, of this older group.

The answer would seem to be readily available since so much of what school children are expected to learn in history and related subjects deals with a portrayal of adults. Thousands of biographies about adults have been written for children. But, sad to say, it does not appear that these questions have been considered. Unfortunately, the child's awareness of the adult world is one of the least understood aspects of his nature.

What little information we can apply to how children read biography generally comes from studies of child-parent relationships. While many child psychology theorists agree that the child will generalize his attitude toward his parents to many other individuals, this is far from conclusive. A correlation of only about .40 (about 16 percent of common elements between two factors) is found between the ratings of children's attitudes toward parent figures and the children's social status.[20] Studies suggest that the child soon learns he is different from the authoritarian adults in his world. This is partly due to the young child's observable attempts to understand the adult world *before* he concerns himself with a comprehension of the world of peer relationships. In any event, the child soon learns he is living in an alien world, a world of adults hostile to his age group, a world from which he must shield himself. The overwhelming evidence that children feel adults do not understand them is evidence of this. In spite of this, children still identify (view themselves as another person without absorbing the other's image totally) with adults or parents more than with their child peers. But all the actions of an adult tell children they are different from him. The child learns to expect different and unequal treatment from that which adults give each other, and he develops concepts of himself that tend to reinforce this feeling. School

---

[20] F. N. Cox, "An Assessment of Children's Attitudes toward Parent Figures," *Child Development,* December 1962, pp. 821–830.

children, for example, are well aware of the overt means by which teachers can threaten their self-esteem.

Children are not mistaken on all adult matters. They clearly differentiate the male from the female adult. For example, father-type adults are seen as authoritative and punitive, as well as the economic provider—the hunter—of the family. (This is true except with lower-class black children, where the father often is a fleeting figure.) Although Western industrial society in general can be epitomized as mother-centered, at least in the eyes of some sociologists, children, especially boys, do idealize their fathers. In spite of all this, however, who the parent actually is or what he does may be less important than the extra-familial influences which provide an interpretation of parental behavior.

While this provides us with only scant evidence on the matter of how children read biographies, it is all we have. In summary, we must speculate from this evidence and add our own personal experiences with children. From this we can conclude that as children read biography, the following factors are operative:[21]

First, an exaggerated biographical figure of the same sex as the reader will be more emotionally acceptable than one of the opposite sex.

Second, children will undoubtedly incorrectly interpret many of the adult subject's activities. The question remains, then, as to how much of the complex or sophisticated behavior of adults as depicted in biographies can children understand? As there seems no answer to this question available yet, the teacher must resort to his common sense or rely on his personal experiences with children to guide him.

Third, children see adults as authority figures who play decision-making roles. They are more likely to interpret such behavior in a biography correctly than they are to interpret indecisive or tentative behavior correctly.

Fourth, if biography is to have the bibliotherapeutic effect that some claim it has, it must portray adults dealing with children in ways that indicate an understanding, sympathy, and acceptance of the child. Since this very rarely happens in biography of adults for children, the generally accepted idea that children can easily take adult biographical subjects as moral exemplars is probably wrong. Since children probably have a great deal of difficulty interpreting adult behavior in biography, if the child is to perceive a character as an ethical or moral model, it will take more on the writer's part than a mere description of an adult doing valiant deeds. It will require the biographer to decide what part of the adult's behavior a child can properly interpret. Moreover, if the American culture is as matriarchal as some claim, the biography of a vigorously overbearing male might be just the right figure for the child for whom excessive mothering or maternal overprotection has created some psychosexual problems.

Fifth, to assume that a child who apparently has had good relationships with his parents will understand the motivation, behavior, or code of conduct of the adult world is stepping beyond the bounds of any current evidence. While our instinctual impulse would be to say, "Yes, this will happen!" no evidence supports this.

---

[21] Patrick Groff, "How Do Children Read Biography about Adults?" *Reading Teacher*, April 1971, p. 609–615.

Sixth, biographical figures seen through the eyes of children in the biographies may be an effective model for more biographers for children to follow. This approach would require a writer to consider the issues we have raised here. This viewpoint would require a constant interpretation and review of the appropriateness of the adult subject's activities. It might even deter those writers who have no understanding of the mentality and life-experiences of children from working in this genre.

American Heroes

American culture also determines what is "proper" for today's child. The romantic form of biography fits our culture with remarkable ease for several reasons. First, Americans have worshipped their heroes more for their human likeability than for their distinguished achievements, rank, or prestige. Rather, American heroes have been very human. Any greatness they may have gained on the traditional bases of family stock, nobility of spirit, or exclusive effort is less well respected than that gained through energetic struggle. Thus an inventor of a gadget useful to our comfort, or an explorer, athlete or other adventurer who displays his muscle, is more highly regarded than a brilliant cabinet officer or a saintly bishop.

History in the United States has never exercised the force on national culture that it has in Europe. Social mobility tells Americans that their historical origins are of little concern. Our almost divine notion of equality dispels any exceptional reverence for traditional social class structure or traditional offices of power. Accordingly, the psychological study of the inner man, the essence of romantic biography, rather than the account of the man's shaping by history and environment, is well accepted as the core of good biography.

America is a fast-moving society; this is reflected in its biographies. Many traditional scholars once contended that a biography could not be written in fewer than several volumes. Strachey and his peers proved it could, however, and the scope and the pace of their models was well accepted in American biographical circles. Americans seem to believe that intimate companionship is not necessarily the result of a long acquaintanceship. Accordingly, crucial, revealing experiences occur among Americans within brief periods of friendship. So Americans do not require a full, detailed biography to feel they know a great man well.

And the American searches for vicarious experience in biography. The battles and political crises of historical biography were not satisfying in this respect, but romantic biography was. A man with a denied career could find solace in the accomplishments of a great man in his field. Someone with an unsatisfied libido could find excitement in the account of a libertine artist or actor. A man out of tune with his times could find an easy acquaintanceship with a general or potentate of the past. But romantic biography also served to justify and to pardon human foibles and errors of judgment. A great man portrayed in his biography as scurrilous, unlucky, opportunistic, or as a weakling or a rake, allowed the reader to gloat over his own relative virtue and strength of character. If notable men can be shown to have dark sides, lesser men can feel a little more comparable to them.

In conclusion, literary trends affect all aspects of literature. The historical tradition told us biographies must be factual; the romantic biographers told us they must be short and moving; the contemporary tradition tells us to combine the best of the other two. Although biography for children has been written with special restrictions, none of the overall developments of the genre have failed to affect it.

8 Information Books

today's elementary school offers more information about the world around us than ever before. The miraculous advances in technology of 25 years ago have become common knowledge to the young. The great push to improve science instruction after Sputnik in 1957 resulted in elementary school children learning subject matter which not even college students a decade earlier had learned. Instruction in mathematics, physics, and biology reached a high level of sophistication, accompanied by a great increase in books designed to teach children as many aspects of these and other factual subjects as possible. Such books can be called information books.

Information books aim for a clear and immediate presentation of knowledge to a child. Although most of them are about scientific matters, they treat virtually every topic imaginable. This wide range of subject matter enables the teacher to satisfy the curiosity of any student on any topic. Furthermore, information books are available at various levels of reading difficulty. Therefore, these works serve the valuable function in individualizing instruction—allowing each child to suit his own needs and abilities in reading on his own.

Information books are extra-literary Information books are not drawn from the imagination of the writer, nor do they deal in illusion. Their subjects come directly and absolutely from reality. This demands a strong sense of style in the writer. First, he must be sure he can express himself clearly without resorting to lengthy technical terms that children will not understand. Though his range of expression is limited, the knowledge he presents must be completely true to the subject. However, the best information books are not distinguished by their style but by how well they serve their purpose —introducing the child to some subject or state of affairs. Such books discuss the phenomena of the scientifically ascertainable world, for example, the operation of the post office, the functioning of jet engines, and the duties and daily routines of persons in various professions such as nursing, law enforcement, or journalism.

In the past, information books often involved a character and some kind of plot in presenting the subject. A train ride from New York to Chicago, for example, might be described in terms of child characters and their parents who visit a relative. As these youngsters roam around the train, friendly adults tell them how the locomotive functions, how the food is prepared in the galley, or how the luggage is handled. Although presented in a somewhat imaginative narrative, the information about trains is true and instructional.

Making information books attractive to children

Some modern information books for children still follow this pattern. The characters and their actions are not designed to forward a plot but instead as a device to catch children's attention by making the book look like fiction since they know that children prefer it to nonfiction. Some writers of information books for children disapprove of this imitation of prose fiction. They contend that clearly presented information has enough inherent interest to attract the child. Yet with some subjects and some children, this does not seem true. Including personalities in information books can be harmless if done with subtlety and invention. This works especially well with primary grade children, who then are as interested in this type of book as they are in fiction. Information books for older elementary school children make little use of this practice, perhaps because authors for this age group wish to devote maximum attention to the information itself.

In addition to a prose effect, colorful, highly detailed pictures, photographs, diagrams, charts, cartoons, and other pictorial guides and their captions can make the book more attractive to a child. Yet these devices must suit the purpose for which they were designed. For example, the author should be able to defend his use of a drawing instead of a photograph. Drawings are often more useful in portraying internal aspects of an object, while photographs are often more appropriate for outer appearances. The degree to which pictures dominate books of fact is also important. Media can overpower the print so much that a child looks at the pictures and does not read the text. The relative size of designs, diagrams, and pictures can be confusing to children. Accordingly, some point of reference, some scale or model, is usually provided for the child to help him make judgments of size where unknown figures are presented.

The readability of information books is very important. Many teachers have experienced the frustration of selecting books for their students only to find they were beyond the children's reading abilities. In assessing the reading difficulty of information books, numerous variables are involved. The first of these is the language difficulty and readability. Next, the nature of the concepts presented will largely determine readability. Technological and scientific data often deal with abstractions such as the conservation of matter, molecular speed, or wave length theory. These notions cannot be grasped by a child unless they are translated into concrete images; also, concepts must be given at a rate compatible with the child's ability to assimilate them. Difficult material must be repeated and retold in various ways so that the reader has more than one opportunity to learn it. Concepts must be developed in a sequence beginning with the most general and proceeding to the more specific. One means of determining how effectively the writer of an information book has organized his material is to examine the paragraphs, which should begin with a strong topic sentence that signals what will be developed in the sentences to follow. The topic sentence gives the abstract form of a concept; succeeding sentences give varied details and examples which bring the concept within the range of the child's own experience.

The successful reader must be able to process the concepts presented him; he must be able to figure out words from their context. This means the child must recognize that unknown words can be explained by the remainder of the sentence, that he can come up with a reasonable meaning for the unknown word. Authors can write with this in mind: they may repeat an uncommon word or show it in apposition to a common word; sometimes a new word becomes a summary of something previously explained in great detail.

Another factor which affects a child's ability to read a book is his interest in and attitude toward its content. A child must be very curious about a topic before he will read difficult material about it. In fact, controlled experiments show that an interested child is somehow able to read over his head. His comprehension of reading he likes exceeds his score on standardized reading tests.[1] This curious phenomenon makes the readability factor highly unpredictable. One can never be sure which book will appeal to an individual.

In the past, young children, especially, were assumed to be interested in and able to understand only what they directly experienced in their immediate environment—their family, home, yard, pets, street, and school. Social studies textbooks assumed this for years.[2] They began in a child's family environment, and grade by grade expanded their content to include the city, state, country, hemisphere, world, and finally the universe. Today's children have much broader experiences than children did twenty-five years ago. Hence these guidelines no longer apply. Television programs—which succeed in attracting children's avid attention—have never been based on these guidelines.

The consequence of this newer argument about the effect of a child's interest on his ability to understand information books has been to recommend reading many subjects at all grade levels, projecting the child beyond his immediate life experiences. One proviso is demanded: a child must be able to relate the beginning of an information book to his own life experiences. When this base is established, the child feels secure in venturing vicariously into new areas of information.

The interest of information books is also greatly enhanced if the teacher can provide a previous warm-up experience that closely relates to or parallels the content of the material. Experiencing scientific phenomena firsthand and then reading about them increases reading comprehension by creating interest.

But making an attractive book is not to be confused with using pseudoscientific or watered-down terminology, or avoiding scientific terms altogether. In the past,

[1] Shnayer, Sidney, *Some Relationships between Reading Interests and Reading Comprehension,* unpublished Ed. D. dissertation, University of California, Berkeley, 1967.
[2] Taba, Hilda, *Curriculum Development; Theory and Practice* (New York: Harcourt, Brace and World, 1962) .

"science was often disguised by insipid stories of personified raindrops and stars."[3] Children correctly interpret this as condescending. An authentic approach to scientific writing must be attempted regardless of the vocabulary problems inherent in such an effort. In his work the author must realize, however, that children of elementary school age are passing through certain definite stages of intellectual or cognitive development. To gain the child's attention, the author must focus on aspects of scientific phenomena that the age-group for whom he writes can understand.

Suppose a science writer discussed a pendulum as an object suspended from a string. How should he describe how frequently the pendulum will complete a full swing? He knows that the length of the string, the weight of the object, and the initial swing are variables. The writer wants the child to understand that the shorter the string, the faster the swing. If the writer knows his readers are in the "concrete operations" stage of mental development, he can predict that they will think the weight of the object is what makes it swing faster or slower. The author should write with this in mind, leading the child to demonstrate for himself that string length is the significant variable. The writer must not conclude from this, however, that the child's thinking has progressed to the stage of formal operations, as Piaget calls it. Such conclusions depend on "faculty" psychology, which states that one can train a certain kind of thinking which will transfer to all situations. This has been thoroughly discredited. In each case, the writer must remember what level of thinking his reader will use and write to that level of development.

Most children in elementary school are at the *"concrete operations"* stage. The child of this age can think of a whole as being made up of the sum of its parts and can put these parts together to form a class of objects. The child can also combine subclasses into a supraclass and then reverse the process, separating them into the original subparts. For example, he can roll a ball of clay into a long, thin string and answer correctly that the long string does not contain any more clay than the ball did. In addition, the child can put data together in various ways to solve a problem. He realizes that there are different ways of putting parts of things together and that the result of such different operations remains the same. When comparing two objects or events, the child can establish their identity by adding up the properties of each one. Then, he can do the same for the second set of objects. Finally, he can make a one-to-one comparison between them. In contrast to that stage of intellectual development, the child at the level of *formal thinking operations* can form hypotheses and deduce possible consequences from them. The child at this level of thinking is usually in adolescence and might say, "I wonder if it is the length of the string that makes the object go faster or slower." The child at the formal stage of operations can be

> ... given a candle, a projection screen, and a series of rings of different
> diameters; each ring is on a stick which can be stuck into a board with evenly

---

[3] Arbuthnot, May Hill, *Children and Books* (Chicago: Scott, Foresman and Co., 1964), p. 580.

spaced holes. The instructions are to place all the rings between the candle and the screen in such a way that they will produce only a single "unbroken" shadow on the screen—the shadow of "a ring." Gradually, the adolescent discovers that "there must be some relationship," and he tries to find out what relationship it is by systematic attempts, until finally he becomes aware that it is a matter of proportionality. As one bright fifteen-year old said, "The thing is to keep the same proportion between the size of the ring and the distance from the candle; the absolute distance doesn't matter."[4]

The child in elementary school, at the concrete level of operations, does not identify his variables in this manner nor state them in terms of propositions, proceeding to each new point systematically, holding the others constant, and finally stating his finding abstractly as a generalization. The implications of this are clear to a writer; if he writes in such a fashion, he makes his book unreadable for his audience. He must find other ways to induce the child of this age to make such generalizations.

This is a much more involved problem than some have admitted. Arbuthnot believes that "the author must be able to begin within the framework of the child's limited world."[5] As we can see from our example of the pendulum, it was not the limited nature of the child's world that would prevent him from discovering the generalization about the swing of a pendulum. What matters here is not that the child does not recognize string, an object, a push on the object, and the result, but whether the child can cognitively process this matter to reach the generalization desired. It is not the question of whether the author "must expand the world *step by step* at a pace which the child can follow" that is of importance.[6] If a child is not at the logical stage required to process certain information, the author may go very slowly and not miss any "steps," and the child will still not comprehend the concept involved. Therefore, it is quite naive to imagine that merely slowing down (giving more explanatory detail or making each step involved more explicit) will insure a child's understanding. A more direct reference to the child's level of mental functioning is imperative.

Equally unrealistic is the assumption that a chronological exposition of scientific phenomena, say evolution or social history, is necessarily appropriate for children. One wonders at the validity of statements such as, "If we step into the timeline elsewhere [except at the beginning]—say at the age of reptiles or at the beginning of man—we run the risk of causing confusion about the chronology of developments. If we start at the beginning, however, we can build the world anew in the order that science tells us it happened."[7] There is very little, if any, evidence from the studies of children's thinking that would support such an iron rule for authors to follow. As a matter of fact, the time element in the logical deductions of children is so different from that implied in the above advice that this

---

[4] Furth, Hans G., *Piaget and Knowledge* (Englewood Cliffs, N.J.: Prentice-Hall, 1967), p. 32.
[5] Arbuthnot, *Children and Books*, p. 580.
[6] *Ibid.*
[7] *Ibid.*, p. 590.

advice might well work against the development of a child's understanding of time sequence.

Part of the process of a child's mental development also is his ability to accept things in a tentative way. In our illustration of the adolescent who discovered how to form the ring shadow we saw that he needed to be tentative. A different form of tentativeness creeps into the language of the child long before adolescence. Logan found that children make tentative statements fairly early in elementary school.[8] He also found, however, that cultural and environmental influences bear heavily on the development of such language. Any scientific writing is likely to use qualifications for what it reports. Scientists are noted for their extrapolations of evidence as they come to conclusions about the significance of the phenomena with which they deal. Evolution, for example, cannot be proved, if by this we mean there are first-hand reports of what happened. From the evidence on this matter, however, a scientist would say, "I believe from the evidence," or, "This strongly suggests to me." To comprehend information books, the child will find it necessary to keep what is demonstrably true, as found through controlled laboratory examinations and reexaminations, separate from what we infer to be true from the persistence of historical evidence that leads us to have faith in an assumption. Only a careful reading by the child will bring to his awareness the qualifying terminology that scientists use.

To attract children to information books, writers also personalize the discourse to help the child pretend he is an eyewitness to its events. Simulating some of the aspects of prose fiction accomplishes this purpose. There are several other ways the author sensitive to children's need to internalize their experiences can create empathy or identification in the child. He can compare the reader's life with his subject or induce the child to do so. Some authors describe the scientist in their books as a detective out to unfold a mystery. (This leaves the impression that the scientist is an imaginative, creative person.) A description of the lives and techniques of scholars and scientists, as well as their findings, helps in this effort. Some authors describe to the child, either directly or by implication, how they researched their book. Many authors of science books are actually scientists, which makes their account take on an autobiographical form. Also, from such a discussion, children learn scientists use more carefully defined methods in their work than the ordinary man on the street does. They learn in this way how scientists decide what questions are important to study, how to gather data in a representative way, how data are verified by reexperimentation and reexamination, how data are analyzed and interpreted, and how conclusions about them are drawn.

In social studies information books, the author can help personalize his book by describing the lives of boys and girls rather than of adults, especially their daily activities. He can make cross-cultural references—discuss a historical period by showing how people in different geographical regions lived during that period. Putting the common man into focus in the information book and discuss-

[8] Logan, Walter D., *The Language of Elementary School Children* (Champaign, Ill.: National Council of Teachers of Education, 1963).

ing the effect of inventions, discoveries, and historical events on his way of life brings a more personal tone to the book. Being frank and objective about historical events, their causes, and the strengths and weaknesses of historical figures also helps in its way. (We will see below how taboos restrict this practice.) Books of information that deal frankly with racism, poverty, war, overpopulation, violence, and environmental pollution obviously can present data that has a feeling of freshness without window dressing or sugar coating. For example, Robert Mc-Clung's *Possum* (New York: William Morrow, 1963) reveals in no uncertain terms the harshness of nature and the survival of the fittest. McClung explains without mincing words that all animals born cannot survive, and the balance of nature depends on this arrangement. This kind of realism rarely shows the condescending tone children dislike.

Such writers can also personalize their work by developing a "doing" book. Material the child should learn is presented as a laboratory or exploratory exercise. This information book can make observations that lead to stimulating questions that, in turn, can be answered by simple experiments. Here children are led to make their own discoveries through an inductive approach to the topic. The book leads the child through an activity and then gives him data from which he can infer generalizations. In this way the child comes to realize the relationship between fact and principle, but in his own way and on his own terms. Herman and Nina Schneider's *Now Try This* (New York: W. R. Scott, 1947) and Athelstan Spilhaus's *Weathercraft* (New York: Viking Press, 1951) are excellent examples of this special kind of book.

Some information book authors attract children by putting an emphasis on the *why* of human endeavor, conflict, and change as well as on the *how* and the *what* of these phenomena. Such books do not merely ask children to believe the often fantastic facts that they present; they also explain them. We recognize that young children are mercilessly persistent in their inquiries as to why things are as they are. The writers of good information books try to keep this curiosity alive during the later years in the elementary school.

Information books that *document* what they say bring the child into the author's scholarship. This process sometimes is augmented by linking phenomena together in a certain way. For example, if things are explained only in terms of their purpose, children are not encouraged to ask why there are such purposes. If the scientist–writer stops with the description of the apparent purposes of things, he will never encourage the child to question whether these purposes are real, best, logical, beautiful, moral, useful, or have fundamental causes. Developing a questioning attitude toward natural and social phenomena will inevitably involve them in the philosophy of these matters although it is not discussed as such in elementary school.

Children like information books that tell how to predict probable future events or explain observed or invented information. That his book of information may be outdated almost before it is published is probably the writer's recurring nightmare. Thus many authors turn to the still theoretical speculations of their field for leads as to what may be forthcoming.

Sometimes an author uses Socratic dialogue, asking questions that require the reader to examine his own experience and to relate it to the subject at hand. This is more than mechanical exercise of intelligence; the child must see analogies between the subject and his own life experience. Since children's lives vary and the author does not have any immediate feedback, many books fail in this respect. A modern example is a programmed learning book, which presents its information in small pieces or frames, each one leading to the next. A child's answer in one frame leads him to understand the question in the next frame, and so on. But children usually find such information books so dull that only those with remarkable persistence can stick with them for any length of time. Also, many of these books, especially in the past, have been criticized because they often have a condescending and prissy, overly formal tone. But any kind of dialogue is useful because it creates a sense of involvement on the child's part—a feeling that the book is glad to be read by him and shows its appreciation. This is quite the reverse of information books that seem to defy us to understand what they are about.

Children readily accept authors who can humbly admit they do not know everything and that science does have unanswered questions. Children become frustrated when they search for solutions to problems which have none. Authors can lessen this frustration by imagining which questions children will ask and admitting that they are not answerable yet. They can also encourage the child to speculate by showing that answers may be discovered or invented in the future.

Many pleasurable information books for children have been planned and prepared through the collaboration of a scientist, a teacher, a professional writer, and a professional artist. Each collaborator has strengths and influences that can contribute to an especially accurate, responsible, and yet moving presentation. Sometimes a professional writer or artist who is not familiar with the subject is an asset because he must simplify the subject so he can understand it. This process, in a way, duplicates what the child reader must do. As he discovers what was difficult for him to understand, the writer can try to overcome such difficulties in his own writing.

Another form of information book that has proved fulfilling to children has been the general book on science. These books attempt a panoramic view of science. Although such books suffer from a lack of in-depth coverage, they do demonstrate that the separation of knowledge into the traditional categories we study is contrived and unnatural. Such an overview of science is especially important in view of our increasing awareness of the problems of ecology.

In summary, the scope of an information book remains a serious problem for the writer. So-called "all about" books generally exhibit a serious weakness if they attempt to cover too large a subject. For example, all about horses or even mammals is possible. But "all about" animals probably is too much to get under a single cover. A better approach than the "all about" technique (which sometimes becomes a catalog of items) is to begin the information book for children with an idea that interests children, or one that the writer believes can be made interesting. The writer is bound to lead into different subject matter areas as he explains his idea. Need these ideas be narrow and simple? Some successful writers of information books for children say no. Adler, for example, claims that the broader, more theoretical ideas can be described. To him, scientific ideas at this level are basically simple because nature is simple. Thus, "a science book is most easily comprehended if based on the most advanced scientific ideas." "Chemistry becomes simple and understandable if these [separate] reactions are shown to be the consequences of the properties of the atom as postulated in modern atomic theory."[9]

We believe that understanding how well children comprehend subject matter rests on a careful examination of the cognitive processes that are involved. This can and must be substituted for the intelligent guesses so often made about this relationship. If atomic theory, or any other broad idea of science, can be explained at the level of concrete operations, all to the good. But merely to say that such information can be made understandable for children does little to reduce the confusion surrounding this matter.

Another way to encourage children to read information books is to organize them so the child uses the information he learns, perhaps by making it a "doing" book. Or leisure-time follow-up activities could be suggested to the child: using inexpensive or home-made equipment; duplicating experiments the book describes; making collections; recording observations; or questioning members of his community.

Still another type of information book which appeals to children tells how and why common machines, gadgets, and toys work. John Lewellen's *True Book of Toys that Work* (Chicago: Children's, 1953) is an example. Explanations of the very familiar objects and toys in a child's life break down any feeling he may have that science is something "out there" that does not really touch ordinary peoples' lives in a direct way.

Information books can also become more closely allied to a child's interests if they are related to the prose fiction he reads. The meaning of a novel about a foreign land, for example, is heightened by his understanding of the cultural, social, and political forms of life of that area. The teacher should compile bibliographies that help children find fiction reading that has some of the aspects of the information book; a natural correlation can be made between science fiction and science information books in this way. Information books often include additional titles on their subject to help and encourage children to continue their reading in the field.

The technical aspects of information books

Information books use many strategies to invite, compel, and capture their child audience. Since children's interest is so important, all other considerations

---

[9] Adler, Irving, "On Writing Science Books for Children," *Horn Book*, Vol. 41, October 1965, pp. 524–529.

seem to pale in comparison to the readability, comprehensibilty, and general attractiveness of the book. Nevertheless, as a professional publication—intended to be authoritative, rational, unbiased, balanced, truthful, modern, and adequate for the purposes for which it was written—an information book has other important considerations.

These more technical aspects of information books have a rough hierarchy of consequence. The leading principle is *accuracy,* because these books are essentially compilations of purported facts arranged in a readable order. Surprisingly, perhaps, accuracy is not easy to come by. The accuracy we want in children's books obviously cannot be the accuracy that the scientist or the adult reader requires. Instead, the accuracy of children's books must meet or slightly exceed the needs of the child reader. This is an unsettling and complicated matter for the writer to resolve. If by omitting some detail the writer can make a less ambigious comment, he will probably do so. If a comment about a generalization that should emerge from the discussion is out of the cognitive range of the child, the writer will ask, "Is this statement of this generalization functional to the effect I wish to create?" If the answer is no, he will give up such a generalization in favor of a less abstract, more personal conclusion.

To accurately present facts, the writer must fight his own biases and prejudices about his subject, especially if it is controversial in any way, as all social subjects are. Also, he must realize his responsibility to balance his presentation of facts. Because the first impressions children have of a subject are often lasting, they are therefore difficult to change at a later date; so, it is critical to give all sides in a controversial issue, to leave no false impressions by either commission of error or by omission of truth, to avoid emphasis disproportional with the importance of stated events or functions. Omitting evidence sometimes can result in quite the same degree of misinformation, stereotyping, or underinforming as the deliberate presentation of wrong evidence. To hide the unattractive side of life in a foreign country or to present pictorial material that displays only certain classes of people in a country or culture is an example of the error of omission. Although showing attractive, prosperous aspects of a country is valid, an author who fails to balance this with other, less attractive aspects leads a child to an incorrect impression. The writer should seek, then, in describing a society, to balance his presentation of the young and old, the men and women, the rich and poor, the country and the city, the capitalist and the socialist, the worker and the manager, and so on.

Young children who cannot make critical comparisons of information typically accept what they read in an unquestioning fashion. It is useless for the teacher to ask them to attempt to do otherwise, since critical reading is a mature skill, beyond the range of most young children's cognitive development. Consequently, the teacher must protect children from unbalanced presentations in their information books. This can be done in part by referring children to additional sources of information so that their coverage of a subject is more complete. Or, if a book is tremendously biased, the teacher may reject the book from his classroom library.

Another consideration, how current is an information book, concerns the adult selecting books for children. Oppenheimer, the father of the atomic bomb, reportedly said that the physics of his generation was so changed by later discoveries as to be practically unrecognizable as truth a generation later. The seething social, political, economic, and cultural changes of our day also cause information books about these areas to become misleading. The copyright or revision dates are important guideposts to a book's usefulness.

To be accurate, the writer must also show the relationship of scientific facts to humanity, describing the social consequences they may have. We are lately coming to agree that it is important for the objective scientist to consider ethics in his work. The day when scientists can explain away or escape their responsibilities for the consequences of their inventions or discoveries of radically dangerous substances or mechanics is quickly passing. The child should learn about these ethical responsibilities.

An information book's accuracy is also related to how adequately the writer treats his subject, or what information he chooses to explain and what he discards or suppresses. How much detail to present is indeed a ticklish matter to resolve in a precise and exact way. As we have seen, it involves a decision as to which details a child can process cognitively at his given stage of development. Really vast amounts of detail can be given children if we make it possible for them to process it. A book with even a small number of details, if it stands beyond the child's cognitive level, will quickly turn him away from the subject in question. The degree of detail the author presents is related, as well, to the type of information book he writes. Books that present only a single aspect can, of course, be more detailed than books with a broader scope. In short, one cannot generalize that much detail in a book confuses a child or vice versa, or that any certain number of details is called for; it all depends on the child's development and the scope of the book.

The modern children's science book writer avoids the cloying anthropomorphism that so often characterized nature stories of the nineteenth century. In these earlier books, animals and other aspects of nature—wind, rain, or plants—were given human emotions and even the ability to talk to their own kind and to other animals and humans. These older stories often involved wild animals whose family life and habits closely resembled those of reputable middle-class families. Such anthropomorphism is no longer considered necessary or cute. It is recognized as distortion of the animal's life history, used to cover up ignorance of how the animal really lives. Such books do exist today, but they are rapidly falling out of favor. A talking animal is quite legitimate as a character in fantasy books but not as a character who explains true conditions in the animal world.

The heavy-handed didacticism of early nature books was particularly offensive. Obviously, all information books are by definition didactic, or intended to teach. In the older books, however, the condescending, maudlin illusion of animals sincerely caring for the needs of others—often their natural enemies—was unpleasant enough in its own right. But when coupled with moral preachment, as it often was, these books become insufferable. Such attempts to interest children in the scientific message of an information book have been widely rejected by modern writers. They have adopted other, more satisfactory ways of personalizing information books—as we have seen—to increase a child's sense of involvement or identification with the books without attempting to create in the child a false sentimentality about science and its natural processes. Some writers are careful to qualify what might be interpreted as anthropomorphism in their books by using restrictive structures such as "It *looked like* the birds were saying . . ." or "The birds were singing together *as if. . . .*" Also, as we have seen, some writers of information books do give their works the mock appearance of human characterization. This is not literal anthropomorphism, however, but is intended as a way to personalize the book by encouraging a child reader to identify with a character.

A word of caution: in avoiding anthropomorphism, we should not reject all forms of metaphoric science writing. For example, referring to nature as an active agent—as in "nature is ruthless"—is metaphoric, not anthropomorphic. As we have said elsewhere, factual material presented in a completely literal way can become oppressively boring. Information books occasionally need some lyrical or metaphorical diversion. One should not be overly critical of this stylistic device, then. Metaphor creates a vocabulary of emotion and sensory imagery which cannot otherwise be depicted in straightforward accounts of the phenomena this involves. In fact, clever writers can in this way involve more of the child's sensibility to help him relate the familiar and concrete aspects of his existence with unfamiliar or abstract aspects. This seems the critical task of all successful writers of this material.

Style is also important. While information books must be written in an interesting way, their authors are restricted in what style they can use. An ornamental, poetic, or abstract style would be ineffective. Although sometimes a mixture of the fantasy of language and the strange analogies we see in metaphor can lessen the heaviness or the didactic tone of an information book, the substantive style of the information book should be mechanical, straightforward, and concrete, not fanciful.

Equally important to consider in selecting information books for children are *taboos*. Which of our culture's taboos affect the authenticity, scope, or coverage? Some say information books that show American culture as the ideal one for all peoples should not be acceptable for children. This is unrealistic in view of the taboos that operate in our country. Such statements sound grandly neutral, and therefore objective, but they are quaintly naive. Since education in the United States is a local matter, taboos exert a powerful force on the selection of information books for school use. For example, reactions to information books on the Soviet Union from local boards who select school books are so taboo-ridden that publishers are frankly reluctant to issue them. Apparently, such a book must cast the Soviet Union in a bad light. Any favorable description must be cancelled out by several unfavorable descriptions of other aspects. Certain groups in our country actually make counts and calculations of this matter. From all accounts, this same taboo operates in reverse in communist countries. In any event, the injection of a cold war psychology by adults, who have proved themselves unequal to the task of resolving ideological differences on an international scale, into the children of the coming generation is an example of the practical consequences of a dominant taboo.

Taboos have affected books for children in ways contradictory to our national ideals, especially regarding national adventures that we now consider shameful: the Indian wars, the Mexican War, the Spanish–American War, and doubtless the Vietnam War. The taboo against depicting these wars in any terms besides defense of national interests illustrates our apparent unwillingness to admit to children that our federal government can make mistakes, although as adults, we are clearly aware of this. We noted before that most information books for children are on scientific topics. This is partly because social studies perennially inflame people's passions and arouse their prejudices, while science is generally interpreted as a psychologically neutral subject which has few philosophical implications. Of course, this is not true; increasingly, modern scientists realize the relationship of psychology and philosophy to their own disciplines. But many people consider science "safer" for children since it uses supposedly clear-cut, definitely verifiable data to arrive at precise answers to questions we all agree are important. To see this, contrast the relatively shorter debate in Congress over space agency appropriations with those over appropriations for social welfare and you will see how little science is subject to taboo in our culture.

Another taboo in our society relevant to information books for children is the Judeo–Christian ethic that says nature as a force of God is benevolent, in spite of its manifestly observable malevolence. To suggest that books for children depict nature as basically unfriendly challenges a deeply-held faith that somehow it is not. Thus, discussions of the balance of nature are meant to leave the impression that there is some great, grand design of benevolence and charity to balance any pain and suffering. In several states, evolution in information books for children is still controversial.

The censorship of information books about sex also reflects society's taboos. Many schools rigorously withhold sex information books from children although many well-written, unemotional treatments of this subject are available. It is paradoxical that with the advent of children's literature after 1890 writers have felt increasing pressures to omit any reference to reproduction in either prose fiction or in information books. In the pre-children's-book era, accounts of these matters appeared in materials written for adults that children read widely, for example, *Gulliver's Travels*. We are just now emerging from almost four centuries of righteous prudery and intolerance of revealing sexual matters to children. Little wonder, then, that even today books on the life cycle are bowdlerized, or purged of any indelicate references to procreation.

Discussion of economic ideologies which compete with capitalism is also governed by highly regarded taboos. The Calvinist ethic of individual effort and its personal reward is translatable into taboos on children's reading favorable treatments of communism or socialism or criticisms of the production and marketing systems of free enterprise. Efforts of critics like Ralph Nader, whose exposés of unsafe automobiles, for example, largely responsible for federal legislation regarding this condition, are seldom, if ever, found in children's information books. The controversy that the work of such social reformers arouses effectively seems to put them off-limits for children.

Teachers who use information books should neither reject nor accept taboos but rather try to understand them. Taboo is closely related to myth, and therefore should not be dismissed as the effect of depraved, irresponsible, or nonfunctional thinking. On the contrary, man lives by his myths. Mythology, and often taboo as well, works to maintain man's emotional homeostasis. But myths must change as the culture demands it.

The teacher or librarian must judge which information books his students can handle. Often, those who select information books to use in schools are poorly equipped for this function since they are not familiar enough with the subject matter to detect its inadequacies. Teachers rarely have time. Also, librarians necessarily take an expedient outlook: while they are careful to disqualify a shoddy, undistinguished addition to an already well represented area, they are much less inclined to reject a poorly written book on a new or unusual subject on which the library lacks material. They feel that half a loaf is better than none. Once acquired, ineptly written, inaccurate, inadequate material may remain in use long after its contents have been discredited. The book initially rejected because of taboos never gets a chance to compete with these leftovers, of course.

Selecting good information books

All this illustrates the great difficulty of identifying good information books for children. Potential frailties of these books are numerous: inaccuracy, mediocre style, obsolete content, and concepts described in a manner that is incomprehensible to children. Making the matter more difficult are self-serving reviews of these materials, generally produced by book publishers or their associations, that find virtually no information unacceptable, and the taboos which give certain topics a blanket rejection. That a central source of disinterested, professionally qualified reviewers is urgently needed for this purpose is an understatement. But the teacher or librarian has some help. Bibliographical sources built out of the critical reviews of information books are available. The appendix to this book is one of them. Considering how complicated the identification of good information books is, consulting such lists is imperative.

In summary, the selector of information books should be alert to several general approaches to this art. He should:

1. Resist pretentious books, those with lavish illustrations or lush layouts, glossy exteriors whose brightly written promotional blurbs also exaggerate their intrinsic merit as a written discourse on the subject.

2. Beware of the series book, a set of volumes on different countries or cultures using the same format, identical organization, limited perspective, and usually pedestrian style.

3. Seek references to the book by specialists in the book's subject area.

4. Get the reactions of a pilot group of children before deciding to purchase the book in sizable quantities. Children can quickly relate any vocabulary and conceptual problems they have.

5. Try to develop a system to review books. Often a small school district can observe larger districts noted for their book selection practices and follow their example.

6. Be continuously sensitive to the needs of children at different reading ability levels. There are always a few very bright or otherwise exceptional children in school whose special abilities and problems must be recognized.

7. Make regular evaluations of the classroom book collection, involving pupils in this. Substitute new books for those that seem no longer useful.

Information books versus literature   The information book should not be used to the exclusion of the literature we have discussed in other parts of this book. Sometimes this happens, posing a genuine threat for prose fiction and other genres. A survey of the typical elementary school library is proof that past budget allocations for nonfiction books were much larger than for fiction, resulting in many more information books than good prose fiction, poetry, or traditional folktales and myths in the library. Is this so because information books are more attractive to children than genuine literature? We believe not; rather, it is because teachers in the past have assigned greater importance to other aspects of the curriculum than literature, with distressing consequences. Some classrooms have no literature programs. Perhaps children are allowed to read independently, but then they often read information books rather than literature. Any discussion of information books, therefore, should be viewed with this past imbalance in mind.

Continuing pressures act to perpetuate this imbalance. Great bursts of new information, particularly in the sciences, have occurred in each decade since World War II. Literature, on the other hand, has not shown such spectacular recent development. What new device or genre, for example, has appeared in the last 50-years? One can point only to the anti-hero, and nonnovel, which we have seen are inappropriate for children. The forms of the genres have been set for ages. But the discoveries of literature come in other ways. They appear through the forces of its creativity, its power to recombine the customary forms of life into ever-renewed, redirected, and reborn forms. In this dimension we can say that literature is not dead but as vital as when its genres first evolved their essential characteristics. The prose fiction writer creates a host of real worlds in his imagination, and the poet, through metaphor and other inventive language forms, creates new terms for the emotions which we ordinarily cannot express. In any event, the vast amounts of new knowledge developing can never be assimilated by the coming generation of elementary school graduates. The idea of a modern Renaissance man, one who knew about all fields, is a tarnished if not completely corroded notion. So, since we can never again really know enough of all things to claim such complete, symmetrical development, the teacher is unwise to emphasize information books in the vain attempt to foster this goal.

Instead, we should pursue another Renaissance ideal—the richly knowledgeable, aware human being who is equally fulfilled in his imagination and his reason. Literature and information books can complement each other in reaching that goal.

Part Three
Teaching Literature to Children

9 Teaching Literature to Children

1iterature has always been of germinal influence in culture, particularly for the young. The extent of representation which literature contains should now be evident. From that foundation we can proceed to the question: "How should literature be presented to children?" The teacher's own sensitivity and perception are necessary prerequisites to any approach. Building upon such critical awareness, we will try to describe how to help children develop literary understanding. But first, let us review concepts developed earlier. Returning to our first notions about literature, we recall that literature is both language and art.

Literature as language

Because literature is always built of language, it is first a collection of linguistic symbols which are sounds or marks. In a study so complex as language and literature, it is usually helpful to return again and again to these most fundamental facts about the subject when faced with the difficulties of communicating literature to children.

Equally important in linguistic communication is that both parties understand the meaning of language. A term which indicates this kind of mutual agreement about the meaning of words is *cognition,* the recognition that a word stands for a given mental concept. Cognition allows us to agree, within general terms, that words have specific meanings.

As we learn our language in childhood, we learn to recognize the common lexical meanings of words as well as the basic syntax, or sentence structure, of the language. We thus learn to achieve cognition of the language's symbol system. The growth of a child's language usage is a remarkable process, the most amazing development of his early years. By the time a child has reached his fifth year, for example, he has already mastered the essential fundamentals of the symbol system which we call his native language. The child comes to school, then, with relatively sophisticated syntactical, lexical, and phonetic abilities. He understands and uses all parts of language with a high degree of accuracy. Of course, the child is unaware of his cognition of his language; talking and listening are part of the capabilities of the young child, but thinking about his thinking has not yet developed as a skill.

We can assume a certain language ability in the primary school child even if he cannot verbalize just what his mental or cognitive processes may be. Therefore, if a child understands language when he hears it, he can understand the fundamental part of literature. And this, of course, is the beginning of the entire literary experience.

But even though we might agree that a picture for a word is a fair representation of its cognitive meaning, we will doubtless all have individual and personal feelings about a word. Perhaps merely hearing the word will conjure special feelings and memories. For instance, when we hear or see a word, a highly personalized, unique daydream may start which quickly departs from the meaning of the word. Such reactions are called *affective responses,* or reactions which are separate from, although probably derived through, cognitive responses to the word. It is apparent that affective responses have more to do with emotionality, with the uniqueness of an individual's feelings, and with his highly subjective responses to stimuli than do the cognitive responses. Nevertheless, it is almost impossible to dissociate the one from the other in discussing a specific reaction to an event, either linguistic or otherwise. Still, for the sake of discussion, it is essential to recognize the broad differences between the two kinds of responses and how each one leads to the other. For example, we want to know how feelings influence the recognition of symbolic meaning and how the understanding of language values can lead to affective responses in literature. The interrelatedness of these two responses cannot be overstressed. One response will trigger the other, and a mutually supportive resonance between the two can occur. The more directly a cognitive response is linked to the affective, the more meaningful the linguistic communication will become. The more our feelings are stirred by a clear cognitive apprehension of a word, the more we can have true feelings about it. Naturally we can expect to have strong feelings which have little connection with the meaning of a word. When this happens, we are not responding to the cognitive value of a word but to some obscure, subtle, or different meaning it holds for us. Language demands, therefore, that we come to it, embrace it, accept it, and adapt our emotions to its structure and style. The reward, of course, for doing so is the joy and richness to be found in communication or linguistic art. As we will see next, this is true in literature. We must grasp both its cognitive and affective identity and force before a really meaningful experience with literature can move us to say, "I like that—it speaks to me."

Literature as art

The second basic quality of literature is that it is *art,* a term as large and variable as language. The vital qualities of a few examples of what we call art should provide a framework for thinking about literature as art. Perhaps if we think about what happens when we look at a painting we can see some further characteristics of literature as art by pointing out the common elements. Looking at a painting of a woman's face, for example, we see a face that stands for the actual face of the model just as a word is the symbol of a mental impulse. The painting stands as a visual representation of the view the artist had of the actual face. In da Vinci's *Mona Lisa* we see painting as the representation or symbol of the face of the model.

But this particular painting, through its symbolic nature, has come to stand not only for the face of the one model da Vinci used, but also for all faces with a similar expression, which we call a "Mona Lisa smile." Indeed, the symbol of this painting has gone even further than this; the *Mona Lisa* has become a symbol for the mood of tranquility and enigmatic calm which its features suggest.

We can see, then, that art represents many associated meanings or symbols which may at first appear to be hidden in the surface of a painting or statue, symphony or literary work, but which actually can spring forth once one looks for other dimensions of meaning in the object. These other units of meaning are as essential to art as the surface object or symbol.

Painting, like language, also possesses cognitive and affective elements. As an initial cognition of the *Mona Lisa,* it is necessary to recognize it as the face of a woman. The next step in cognition is the perception of the mood it portrays. If one were not to see that the *Mona Lisa* represents a face, he could not recognize that the expression on the face is important as an indicator of a mood, and thus of the symbolic statement which the painting makes. Of course, there are certain clues in the painting to the cognitive basis of interpretation. The position of the hands in repose on each other repeats the tranquility of the smile. The fact that the smile is not wide and toothy but in a gentle arc, the eyebrows lowered, helps us make cognitive statements about the painting. The colors used by the painter also make us think about the face in certain ways. The point is that there are definite indications in the painting which point to its symbolic nature. We are not involved in a mystical process when we talk about art; rather we can derive meaning from technique, form, and visual imagery.

Inextricably linked to the cognitive aspects of a painting are one's affective responses to it. Through the use of images which have almost as clear a symbolic meaning as words, the painter creates an object which may strike a chord in our own emotions similar to the mood the face portrays. The viewer in this way can identify with the painting's symbolism. For the affective response to be closely joined with the cognitive, the painting should engender in the viewer the same mood it represents. The painter thus evokes or calls forth through his choice of symbol a response in the viewer.

Of course, it is possible to recognize a painting's symbolism without having much affective response. Our reaction to a work of art may be almost wholly cognitive. If so, the painter or other artist has not been able to reach into our affective domain. This may be partly because our cognitive reactions to the art object were incomplete. An inaccurate or incomplete affective response may result from inaccurate cognition.

Literature shares with art the common grounds of symbolic representation. The clear parallel between painting and literature is the portrayal of the visual in painting and the presentation of character and action in literature. Just as the *Mona Lisa* extends its meaning beyond the mere surface image of the painting, the characters in a work of literature take on dimensions which make them representations of universals in human experience. A story does more than simply report events. And the portrayal of character is within the same symbolic context as the carving of a statue, which can be called a symbol for a mood or other abstraction.

In summary, art is the second parent of literature: literature is language transformed into art. Literature is the art form of language.

Art   Language

Literature

The common ground of language and art is that both are symbolic in nature and function. Both employ symbols to create communication; both develop a set of symbols which stand for mental images. Literature, then, is itself inherently symbolic and a representation deeper in meaning than its apparent surface. Just as we cannot stop by saying that *Mona Lisa* is a portrait of a woman and nothing more, just as we cannot say "She is copper-headed" means only "She is red-haired," neither can we say that a piece of literature is merely a literal story and nothing more.

Literature is language transformed into art. Paintings and language are both bodies of symbols, language of course being more systematic in total design than paintings. Both, however, communicate through symbols—language in words and paintings in images. Literature has the symbol system of language as a basic fundamental from which the writer builds portrayals of character, action, scene, or mood which are in the same vein of representation as a painting or a statue. Literature is a kind of representation of experience larger than that contained in the surface alone. The writer relies upon language's expressive potential to create a picture of experience. Just as the painter creates his effect with paints, the writer draws character, plot, and mood with words.

Like paintings and language, literature has cognitive and affective dimensions. In language it is necessary to recognize the cognitive value of a word before a related and therefore meaningful affective response can occur. In painting we must recognize the visual nature of the painting. Likewise, in literature it is essential to achieve a cognition of the story and its symbolic meaning for a communication between author and reader to take place. When we look into literature, we do not enter exactly into the experience which inspired the literary artist; nor can we ever know exactly what the author intended the effect to be. What we can be more certain about, however, is the symbolism or depth of meaning *which is contained in the language and structure of the literary work itself.*

Childhood intellectual development and literature

Equally important, those who teach children about literature must know about children's cognitive and affective domains. No matter how successful an adult might consider a piece of literature, its value will be lost for the child who lacks the intellectual capacity to grasp the cognitive or affective elements of the work. Again, if one cannot see that the *Mona Lisa* is a woman's face, he cannot be expected to interpret the mood it represents; no matter how good a novel *Bonjour Tristesse* is, it is lost on a person who cannot reach French unless he can find a translation. Offering the child the right book demands knowing both books and children. Books must be known in critical terms; children are understood through psychology and one's experience with them.

The Swiss psychologist Jean Piaget is an authority on how children learn and develop intellectually. Piaget's observations of children form a schema of how the human intellect develops from infancy to maturity. His theories of developmental psychology help us understand what learning experiences are most effective and valuable at various stages of a child's mental growth. The following conclusions are basic to Piaget's description of intellectual development:

1. The human mind is dynamic and always growing in its attempt to give meaning and order to experience;
2. The growth of the intellect from infancy to maturity is characterized by an ever increasing ability to manipulate symbols;
3. Although there are several clear phases or periods of intellectual development, the whole forms a continuum with interrelated points of definition;
4. Learning is related not only to development but also to experience, so that what we can learn at one point is influenced by prior learning experiences.

The general implications of Piaget's psychology are that children can learn—assimilate and accommodate—only what they have the experience and maturity to absorb. Furthermore, what children learn now will determine what their future learning will be. Because what they can learn today depends not only upon their maturity but upon their prior learning, we can see that learning in a school situation should be a development of concepts, allowing for growth at the individual's own pace.

Piaget describes three stages of interrelated development which will occur along the continuum from infancy to maturity:

Sensory–motor intelligence (0–2 years). This early period is characterized by learning practical and perceptual adaptations to the environment such as learning to walk or learning to use the hands when they cannot be seen; this period shows almost no symbolic or intellectual manipulation of reality.

Preoperational representations (2–7 years). This stage shows the gradual development of symbolic representations or an ability to organize symbols.

During this time language is learned. The last part of this period of intellectual development Piaget calls *Concrete Operations* (7–11 years.). By this time the child has largely developed a stable picture of "how things are" by which he approaches new experiences in meaningful terms.

Formal operations (11–15 years). The child is now able to think in abstract, logical terms, to speculate on "what if" questions, and has a highly developed sense of logic.[1]

Piaget's descriptions can be taken as a basic guideline to thinking about children's mental development and therefore about what in literature concerns them. It must, however, be remembered that the ages Piaget gives are stages of development and not norms or absolute ages at which the periods of development will invariably appear. The states of intellectual development for individual children may appear earlier or later. Regardless of when they occur, however, the stages will appear in the order given and show the characteristics indicated.

This view of the intellectual development of childhood has numerous implications for literature in the elementary school. The first of these is that the child is capable of some degree of symbolic manipulation by the time he enters first grade. The second most important implication is that the elementary school covers the crucial period of development from concrete operations to formal operations. This transition from infantile thought to adult intellectual abilities is governed by the conceptual framework which we develop during the transition period of childhood. This is really when much of our identity is formed.

Literature has a vital role to play in the emergence of this identity. Only one of the many concerns of literature, for example, is with the portrayal of a hero. A hero is a standard by which we measure our own lives, through which we discover the model of what a man might become. Bringing the child into contact with the picture of man presented in literature as a hero will provide him with images of experience to give him added facets to his own world view.

The elementary school period of a child's life is when the cognitive grasp of literature can be started and developed. The child comes to the first grade in the later stages of the preoperational period and is thus capable of some kinds of symbolic manipulation by this time. The child of five or six already possesses considerable cognitive skills. Although his affective responses at this time will predominate over cognitive responses, many of these logical abilities are nonetheless emerging.

The greatest cognitive development the child has made by the time he enters school is his high degreee of control of most of the structures of one language. In fact, language is of such large and governing importance in a child's life that its value in the classroom cannot be overstressed. Strickland says of this:

---

[1] John H. Flavell, *The Developmental Psychology of Jean Piaget* (New York: D. Van Nostrand Company, Inc., 1963), p. 86.

> Growth in oral language is one of the most important elements in the entire program of the primary school. It is not a matter of course of study and lessons but of rich and varied experiences and constant practice in the use of language.[2]

Literature is part of this experience in language. As language and art, literature is a perfect source of talk, pleasure, meaning, and identity to the elementary school child. Creating literary experiences which will develop cognitive and affective responses helps the child appreciate both literature and his response to the world.

Implementing the literature curriculum

Teaching literature to children is a multidimensional task as complicated as literature itself. How, then, should a teacher set up guidelines for selecting the literature curriculum? We will discuss this in the remainder of the chapter and give some practical answers, always keeping in mind the nature of intellectual growth in children.

The decision on what the literature curriculum shall be depends on what the teacher considers to be the primary reasons for including literature in the elementary school. We feel that the most helpful description of literature's importance to the young is its capacity to serve as a mirror of life, a source of contact with the intellect of the author, and a model of linguistic excellence. Of these capacities, the most important one is the reflection of one's own life that literature provides—the insights into identity and existence which emerge from literary portrayal.

Logically, the best program, then, would be one in which the individual is allowed to explore various kinds of literature until he finds those types of writing which speak directly and forcefully to his own experience with life and which gratify him because they answer an otherwise unsatisfied need. In such a concept of literature in the classroom, a prescribed curriculum with the goal of "covering the material" seems petty and even destructive. We propose that the nonstructured approach to literature will provide the most effective atmosphere for individual growth. The nonstructured approach rejects the idea of rigid content; the pupil's experiences should govern his choice of books. The nonstructured curriculum generally takes the form of the teacher making available in the classroom a variety of good and enjoyable literary experiences for the children.

---

[2] Ruth Strickland, *The Language Arts in the Elementary School* (Boston: D. C. Heath & Co., 1957) , p. 152.

These areas of enjoyable literary experience correspond to areas of experience he sees as important. For example:

> Having friends.
> Doing things you are told not to do.
> Helping or protecting your friends.
> Finding something that is lost or hidden.
> Being scared and resisting this feeling.
> Knowing something others don't.
> Tricking someone.
> Deciding on what you want to do.
> Going away from home for adventure.
> Having something special that allows you to do things others can't.
> Fighting those you don't like.
> Straightening out problems.
> Helping people in trouble.
> Escaping from someone who is after you.
> Proving you are strong or smart.
> Having people know you are good.
> Getting a reward.

The nonstructured approach can offer only the most general objectives, never grade-level expectations. Although the teacher may keep general objectives in mind, he should be patient about reaching them. As teachers we should remember how long it takes to respond even to some literature of our own choice, how often we are unaware of important aspects of the literature we encounter. Often a teacher must give up trying to elicit enthusiasm for pet subjects and be deliberately nondirective in order to discover what children think about literature when they are free to show their real feelings.

If we consider curriculum this way, a child's reading becomes an encounter, not an assignment. The child's discussion of literature with other children becomes his description of his own experience rather than whether he has satisfactorily fulfilled an assignment. In this way literature becomes internalized by the child. He grows to trust it and his responses to it. Thus, if curriculum guides are to be used in the nonstructured approach to children's literature, they should have the effect of reminding the teacher what pupils may discover in literature. This he will know from his own adult awareness of literary meaning. The curriculum is not a package of knowledge arranged to be dispensed to the child, but rather a healthy atmosphere in which literary enjoyment is possible.

The primary reasons for literature in the elementary school using the nonstructured approach are:

1. To show the relationship of actual life to its representation in literature. We always long for vicarious experience; literature can provide this. The

child's exclamation, "That's me!" confirms the affective impact, which depends, of course, on the child's own experiences.

2. To help the child make his own decisions and interpretations about literature, trust his own responses. If children accept the teacher's analysis of a work of literature—without seeing this as an extension of their own experience—literary appreciation is denied. Such rigid curricula often scare and confuse children about literature, shattering their confidence that they can make sense of it. Attempts to transplant adult models of literature into children's heads fail; all the child learns are words or slogans that he memorizes for tests.

3. To help the child realize that being a spectator in literature is much the same as being a spectator of life through films, television, or spoken narrative. The child learns to accept or reject emotional values in the narrative of literature as he does in other narrative. Thus his imagination as a spectator becomes educated.

4. To help the child experience the oral tradition of literature. The teacher often will read children's literature aloud and tell stories. Starting in the early grades, he will steep the pupils in authentic folklore, fairy tales, drama, myth, fable, and romantic and comic literature. The class might attempt to discover the conventions or structures of these genres, not for their own sake but to help achieve other goals of the approach. Since multiple copies of the same text often are not available, the teacher using the nonstructured approach will continue to read aloud long after the pupils have learned to read. Or the teacher my find it necessary to duplicate materials, especially for such activities as choral reading.

5. To help children realize that literature is closely related to other aspects of the English curriculum. For example, the pupils' own writing can be used as literature whenever it shows a shrewdness of observation, fidelity to the writer's experience, and a truthfulness that comes from his interest and personal involvement. After a child writes a story or poem, he can be given the opportunity to see how an adult author handled the same topic. The choice in literature is important here. If the child is to write imaginatively about the mysteries, wonders, and even terrors of his inner life he must have literature which reconstructs and gives shape to these areas of his experience. In the nonstructured approach to children's literature the pupil will also come to realize the close relationship of drama and literature as he becomes both creator and actor; he will compare what he composes with the works of others and interpret roles he acts based on the nonliterary reality he has experienced.

6. To widen the scope of the child's imagination. In the nonstructured approach, the child can respond to the rich world of literature as an addition to his real experiences. This teaches him to think and to imagine. It becomes one of the important experiences the child will have to expand his imagination. If literature represents experience, it expands that experience by improvising unpredictably upon that representation. The child "who delights to think that all the earth might be paper and all the sea might be ink" will also be delighted to find similar imaginativeness in literature. In this way the nonstructured approach capitalizes on the experiences in creative thinking or play activities the child brings to school. By respecting his responses to literature as being worthwhile it attends to, encourages, and reinforces this preschool imagination.

7. To help the child understand the literal meaning of literature. Without understanding the surface quality of literature—what it says in its least

artistic and complicated terms—the child can never sense the underlying or subsurface nature of literature, or those qualities that give it its unique place in written discourse.

8. To help the child make intelligent guesses and rational judgments about the choice and arrangement of words and why certain modes of expression, structures, and conventions were used in the literature he reads. In behavioristic terms, this means the child will react to literature, notice its forms, interpret its parts, and evaluate its importance. This comes from discussing literature, exploring the child's encounter with it. Such discussion should arise naturally, otherwise it has no place. This avoids the danger of explication of literature becoming an end in itself. The pupil will move from the personal and literal level of his response to its literary level *inductively*—not through definitions given by the teacher but through his own experience with it. The teacher helps the child to detect certain literary elements by suggesting he think about the work in other ways than he would have on his own. The discussion questions typical of the nonstructured approach given later are examples of such help. Such questions help the child to recognize the value of the critical approach to literature; he sees that the more he knows about literature, the more he enjoys it. Familiarity with its craft helps the child to approach literature with confidence, sympathy, and appreciation. This, in turn, adds to the child's enjoyment of literature.

An overly formal approach to literature is dangerous. In emphasizing formalistic criticism to the exclusion of human and personal significance is misguided. The spirit of literature as it speaks to the individual is a more vital force than the numerous techniques of analysis. As valuable as criticism is, it cannot replace the personal experience with literature.

The scope of the nonstructured approach does not appear different from that of most structured approaches. That is, objectives such as developing understanding and favorable attitudes about literature can emerge with either approach. Nor could it be said that the nonstructured approach neglects sequence or continuity of literary experience. The nonstructured approach differs from structured approaches by not deriving its sequential curriculum from any set of concepts of structure in the literature. Rather than insisting that plot, hero, or archetype be introduced in a certain order (as we see in structured curricula), the nonstructured approach leaves these concepts to emerge as they are most relevant to immediate experience. Rather than programming learning, the nonstructured approach strives for establishing relationships between life and literature. Because each life is unique, no preconceived structure can fit individual needs.

The origin and momentum of the nonstructured approach develops mainly from outside the school situation and is intimately related to the individual's whole intellectual, emotional, social, and spiritual growth. This means that the teacher's most effective guide to select literature is the children's individual and

Scope and sequence in the nonstructured approach

group life experiences, especially those gained out of school. The teacher will ask himself what a book will have to say to the student's own experiences. The nonstructured approach sees no topic as intrinsically more worthwhile than another; no topic is either a guarantee of, or a bar to, the objectives we listed earlier.

Of immediate concern in teaching literature is whether a child's cognitive and affective structures can be changed more quickly to more closely resemble those of the adult. Scant empirical research evidence prevents a definitive answer but suggests that the child who lives in a richly developed, intellectually challenging environment seems to change his immature cognitive and affective structures more quickly than does the child from a culturally underdeveloped environment. This suggests, in turn, that experience with literature, because of its nature, can act as a stimulant to cognitive and affective development.

In the nonstructured approach to literature, the life experiences of the child determine the sequence or continuity of the literature curriculum. This means that a piece of literature is presented at any given point in the program when the teacher feels that it will order, extend, enrich, and, above all, approach the experience of the child. So the inner life of the child holds precedence over the best presentation of each book's content. Because of this relationship of human needs to the nature of literature, it is legitimate to consider literature as teaching the whole child rather than just teaching him a certain subject. Fortunately, there are no standardized tests in children's literature to cripple the implementation of this ideal.

Also, the nonstructured approach requires the teacher of children's literature to be familiar with the forms and conventions of the literary materials about which he asks questions. Questions like those which follow later are designed to lead the child to discover such forms and conventions as he reads. They should be formulated so that the child can respond to them in his own vernacular.

A further concern in the nonstructured approach is the problem of readability, or children's reading abilities. Quite obviously, before children have learned to read well enough to handle many good books of prose fiction (perhaps the third or fourth grade for many children), the teacher must read aloud stories which will meet the objectives of the nonstructured approach. As soon as possible, however, the teacher will involve the pupils in choosing what they want to read from prose fiction provided by the teacher. No pupil is pressed to read books he finds uncomfortably difficult. Since no grade level requirements are imposed, any book is valid reading material; book lists can be adjusted to children rather than the other way around. The teacher sets up with the pupils certain ways of sharing or discussing their reading. These can be visual (graphic art), dramatic, written, and spoken. The discussion can deal with the surface structures or obvious meanings of the books initially, and then will proceed to the literary aspects of the reading (characterizations, plot, uses of language, conventions and inventions in literary content and style, and the recognition of aspects of the different genres involved).

The general method is inductive. That is, the child discovers, as he realizes the relationship of the content of his reading to his own psychological and sociological existence, that certain literary generalizations can be deduced. From this point he can be led to realize that these generalizations are useful in discussing literature in general; that is, he will note how a piece of literature fits into his total field of experience with literature. The objective of growing in ability to make abstract generalizations about literature is not an intellectual exercise, but is aimed at accomplishing the goals of the nonstructured approach—to see the relationship of personal and literary life, to develop decision-making power about literature, to develop powers of selectivity in literature, to revisit the oral tradition of literature, to use the understanding of literature to reinforce other language skills, to develop the imagination, and to find pleasure in reading.

The problems of readability will require that the teacher include in the selection of books offered children those of as wide a range of reading difficulty as the reading abilities of the class exhibits. A common practice is to estimate each child's reading level and determine his present interests and experiences and then decide what books to offer him. This is a complicated process, obviously, and requires the assistance of a children's librarian.

Readability problems are reduced when pupils can recognize elements of their own experience, either actual or vicarious, in their reading. Then a child is said to be interested in a book. We discussed earlier the effect this has in increasing a child's ability to read difficult material.

Discussion questions for the nonstructured approach

Classroom motivation is important in encouraging children to read. Instead of asking children to read so they can answer questions like, "What is the book about?" or, "Who are the characters?" or, "Where did this story take place?" or, "What did you learn from the book?" try asking questions that depend on the affective response:

1. What has happened in the story or poem that has happened to me? Is my life like the one in the book? How?
2. How did I feel when it happened to me?
3. How did I feel when it happened in the book?
4. Have I known people like those in the book?
5. What funny thing in the book have I seen before?
6. Did anything happen in the book that I would like to happen to me?
7. What did a character do that I could do?
8. What did a character do that I would not/could not do?
9. What did a character do that I would like to do?
10. What did a character do that I am afraid to do?
11. How is this book more/less interesting than television?
12. What kind of person would you have to be to like this book?

13. How did this book make me feel? Why?
14. How would I have changed this story?
15. Did the author like the characters in the book more than I did? Why?
16. What can I guess about the characters that is not told about them?
17. Why did I/didn't I feel I was right alongside some character in the book?
18. Have I read another book like this one?
19. Was there something in the book I couldn't understand?
20. If the author were telling the story aloud, how would he act? How would his audience react?
21. What character in the book was like another? Which two were more different than alike?
22. What happened in the book that angered, disturbed, or startled me?
23. Was the book happy or gloomy? Why?
24. Did the book move fast or slowly?
25. What was the author trying to do to me in the book?
26. What kind of experiences did the author need to have to write this book? What kind of life does he live?
27. In what part of the book were you told what it was going to be all about?
28. Is the book trying to teach me a lesson?
29. Did I like the book? Why?
    a. Did it do what I think books should do?
    b. Was it exciting enough?
    c. Did one event lead to another?
    d. Were interesting words used?
    e. Was it better than most books?
    f. Was it different from most books?
    g. Did the author accomplish what he wanted to do?
    h. Will other children like it?
    i. Was it like my life?
    j. Was it too much like everyday happenings? Too different?
    k. Was it about things I know are important?
    l. Was the author honest and sincere?
    m. Did it describe things as they really are?

After questions such as these have been discussed, the teacher can proceed to help the child discover how certain aspects of the writing can influence one's feelings about a piece of literature.

At this point the child is encouraged to read or reread to discuss questions like the following ones, which depend mainly on cognitive instead of affective reader response.

1. When some people like or don't like a book they say, "it hits me hard," "it towers over others," "its story carried me along," or "it made me sick." Can I use language like this about my book? (Metaphor)
2. Did any words or sentences the author used make me think of some other thing than what he was telling about? (Implied action)

3. What can I say, either good or bad, about the book in one sentence? (Critical summary)

4. If I were to help someone get ready to read this book, what would I say? (Critical summary)

5. What can I say about how long the book is and how it is divided into parts? Can I describe the beginning, middle, and end of the book? (Structure)

6. Is the book easy to read? Why? (Readability)

7. Did I notice whether the author used long or short sentences? Did certain parts of the book have shorter sentences than other parts? Did the chapters begin and end the same way or differently? (Style)

8. Does the author know everything that everyone does or is thinking about in the book? Or does he only know what a real person would know about another person? Did the author ever talk to me directly as a reader? (Point of view)

9. Did any character act like he didn't belong in the story?

10. Sometimes it is fun to not know the reason everything is happening in the book. Did I ever get lost in reading the story, not knowing how everything would turn out? Or did each chapter of the book always get me ready for the next? (Structure)

11. Did any of the characters in the story not seem to know what was going on? Would it have been better if they had known? (Dramatic irony)

12. Did anyone in the book speak in a different way from the way I do or my family does? (Style)

13. Was there a lot of exaggeration in the story? (Hyperbole)

14. Did the author of the book compare his characters with famous people? How were they like famous people? (Analogy)

15. Crown = king. Love = peace. Fox = clever. Roller skates = freedom. Did the author ever use words in this way? (Symbols)

16. How did I learn what each character in the book was like?

17. Is the place where this story happens like anyplace I know? Would the story be better if it happened somewhere else? (Setting)

18. Sometimes animals in stories act like humans, but in regular ways: a rabbit is always fast, a fox is always clever, a lion is always strong, and so on. Did this happen in the book? Sometimes bad weather, winter, being poor, or being alone means something bad will happen later in the book. Did this happen in this book? (Symbols and archetypes)

19. Is there anything in my book like a myth, a fable, an epic, a folk tale, a comedy? (Elements in these generic classifications will have to be discovered previously by children largely through the teacher's reading aloud and through group discussions.)

20. Is the book a fantasy or a real-life fiction? How did I decide this?

21. What kind of actions were in the story?

22. Which of these actions did the good guy do? The bad guy?
    a. Tried to find something to eat or drink.
    b. Tried to keep himself or others from harm.
    c. Tried to make friends or win the affection of others.
    d. Worked or fought for his country or was loyal to it.
    e. Tried to get some money, goods, or property.
    f. Tried to become someone important.

g. Worked to uphold justice or to punish law breakers.
h. Tried to defeat his opponent.
i. Tried to learn something or to be smarter.
j. Tried to be very good or god-like.
k. Tried to be boss or someone in charge who tells others what to do.
l. Fought against tyranny or someone who was very bossy or a dictator.
m. Saved someone from harm by sacrificing his own safety.
n. Tried to get back at someone or take revenge on him.
o. Did something good to make up for acting bad or making a mistake.
p. Tried to solve a puzzle or a problem or to do a feat no one else had done.
q. Tried to kidnap someone.
r. Had some bad thing happen through an accident or from poor thinking.

Success in using the questions on the list that involve the effect of the book either on the child's sensibilities and/or on his cognitive powers will require that the teacher ask these same questions about material he reads to the class. Very few questions should be asked about any one piece of literature so each question can be treated intensively. This sets the stage for individuals to begin reading the books they chose, asking themselves some of these questions and sharing their reading with others in these terms. In this way the child chooses his own questions and finds his own answers with a minimum of teacher supervision.

This is essentially different from the structured approach: literature is read, questions are asked, and answers judged to be proper or correct are given from a source outside the child's life experience—and, unhappily, often outside that of the teacher's when a teacher's guide in a standard reading textbook or a prearranged curriculum guide is used. In short, in the nonstructured approach the teacher introduces affective questions first, then cognitive questions. Preparation for individual work is given in group sessions. Reporting or sharing can be verbal or nonverbal. Children self-select from available material what they wish to read and read it at their own pace. Using or enjoying literature branches off subtly into *learning about literature*.

Organizing the classroom for teaching literature   The teacher should remember several important considerations about classroom organization. A cheerful, inviting, and exciting room atmosphere should let children know that the reading will be an important part of each day's activities.

Large numbers of books and other literary materials are needed in the nonstructured approach if a child is to be able to select books he actually can read. Jeannette Veatch suggests several ways the teacher can enlarge the classroom collection of reading materials for a ready availability of books.[3] The teacher should consult with the school librarian to see if literature is available in a good balance with information books and ask for his help in attending to children's reading interests. The teacher can inquire how to obtain boxes of books on loan as well as how to purchase library throwaways. The availability of bookmobile service should be investigated and requests made for its expansion. Each child should learn how to obtain a library card. Libraries usually allow each card holder to check out five books. Thirty children times five books could mean the instant addition of 150 books to the temporary classroom collection. Establishing a school library should be a recurring topic at teacher and parent meetings. Many influential parents are unaware of the importance of these collections but can bring much pressure to bear when they understand how vitally they are needed. There are other ways to augment the classroom library. Book fairs are organized to publicize and distribute books; teachers could take advantage of them to select new or used books. Teacher representation on school budget committees is useful if library appropriations need to be increased. Ubiquitous paperbacks, newspapers, and magazines in children's own homes can be used as additional classroom reading materials. Current basal readers offer good literary selections. The teacher may be able to obtain one copy of many different series of basal readers for his classroom rather than many copies of a single series. These suggestions, among others, will help the teacher fulfill the vital need for children's literature in their classrooms.

The teacher should be ready to help children find books they can read comfortably and with interest, with a vocabulary level that matches their reading ability. There are several ways to determine reading difficulty. By briefly reading a few paragraphs at random, a child can feel whether the book is overly difficult; very easy, beginning-to-read books are so marked. Librarians and publishers provide rough estimates of the readability of books, usually given in grade levels.

Since the nonstructured approach means children select only books they want to read, no titles should be required. Nor should children be asked to read books for extraliterary, utilitarian reasons—learning moral lessons, improving their personalities, improving reading skills, or preparing for some future job. We reject the notion of some authorities, notably Arbuthnot,[4] that the major purposes of reading literature are to add to a child's life by satisfying his need to know, his need to love and be loved, his need to belong, and his need for change. These are secondary to the major purpose of literature, which is to provide him an artistic or esthetic experience not found elsewhere in life. The only requirement is that children should be willing to discuss and share their literary encounters in groups set up for this purpose.

Literature discussion groups should be organized so there is group activity for

---

[3] Jeannette Veatch, *Reading in the Elementary School* (New York: Ronald Press, 1966).
[4] May Hill Arbuthnot, *Children and Books* (Chicago: Scott, Foresman & Co., 1964).

all children, with a definite purpose for each group. (Group size will depend on the number of groups the teacher finds it convenient to handle; eight to ten children is not too large for our purpose here.) A typical group of children coming to a meeting to discuss their encounters with literature may each be reading a different genre of literature; the teacher must use discussion techniques which are not antagonistic to the pattern of self-selection, and yet which include each child in a discussion, telling the group about the book he read. We suggest that for this purpose the teacher always begin a discussion activity with questions before leading the children to an involvement with the cognitive nature of literature. Furthermore, many children will want to share with the group the effects of their encounters with literature nonverbally, perhaps through art and drama activities.

Part of the group session should also deal with book selection, the availability of interesting reading materials, and the readability of books. Through the group processes, the teacher will find that children can productively discuss each of these questions. Children's recommendations of good books generally have a positive effect on their peers, improving their success in selecting books they like. The availability of books can also be enlarged through group planning. Children can think up ways to improve classroom holdings and to introduce additional materials from home or the public library.

Poetry discussions especially need careful planning. Because of the particular nature of poetry, the teacher has the responsibility for helping children to interpret it. In the chapter on poetry we described techniques used with one group of children.

Poetry sets the stage for choral reading of poetry or verse choir, which for children is an especially effective way to approach literature. Some poems lend themselves to a refrain arrangement; the teacher reads most of the poem and children read the repeated element of the poem. Other poems have emphatic lines or couplets that can be read aloud by individual children in turn. Antiphonal verse choirs speak back and forth to each other. Poems with questions and answers, dialogue, or those with obvious contrasts are all suitable for this arrangement. Finally, the most difficult arrangement of all may be tried: reading in unison. Coordinating a group—whether adults or children—to make their voices into a pleasant chorus is a task that perplexes even experienced teachers. Generally, brief poems with short lines that depict vigorous, fast-paced action are best for this arrangement.

A special activity that lends itself especially well to coordination in the group meeting on literature is creative drama. Through creative drama children can display their understanding of action, plot, characterization, and other elements of prose fiction and poetry. Experts realize the importance of imaginative play to children. It gives them a chance to explore the roles of the adult world as a foreshadowing of maturity; to play a role is partially to experience this reality. So, too, in the classroom, creative drama stimulates deeper perceptions of oneself.

To prepare for creative drama the teacher often encourages youngsters to express their ideas and feelings about literature through rhythmic activities: galloping, hopping, jumping, leaping, skipping, running, and walking in certain ways. Children are shown that rhymes and jingles like "Jack and Jill went up the hill" can be dramatized. This can be done with dialogue or in pantomime. Then a funny, exciting, or suspenseful dramatic event in a story book can be acted out spontaneously by children using their own dialogue or in pantomime. A favorite activity is for children to pantomime certain impressive points in stories the entire group has read and then ask others to guess the scene and the book. Children also enjoy making puppets to act out these scenes.

The traditional folktales or fairy tales are especially useful as source material for creative drama because in this genre, scenes, actions, characters, and other aspects are quite explicit, open, and obvious and were originally oral in intention. After listening to a folktale, children are asked to act it out after they have decided which characters were involved (what they looked like, how they walked or moved, what they wore, their ages, how their voices sounded, and so on) and the setting and the number of scenes in the story and their sequence. Each child can decide which character in which scene he will play. Someone should announce the setting for each scene and return to the stage to make a final comment after the actors leave. The departure of the announcer signals the beginning of the next scene. Children should realize that in creative drama they are allowed to proceed in an uninterrupted way. There is no dialogue to memorize, but this means that each actor must make it his responsibility to keep the talk flowing. When nothing more occurs to anyone to say on stage, the scene is at an end; the actors should leave the stage. Making costumes and scenery is time-consuming at the expense of time for the actual drama. Sometimes, however, simple settings and costumes are appropriate. These can be constructed or collected ahead of time. One ingenious teacher kept a large cardboard box in his classroom into which children put old clothing and other articles they brought from home; these articles were often used during creative drama sessions.

Should creative drama lead to formal plays with learned lines and long hours of rehearsal? We think the fewer of these formal productions in the elementary school the better. For one thing, there actually is very little valuable formal drama available for children. Moreover, the time and organization required to assign roles, memorize lines, and practice is far too demanding in view of the importance of other activities. Creative drama is more acceptable to children and more in keeping with their talents.

Certain stagecraft ideas borrowed from formal drama can be useful in creative drama. For example, when children learn to speak more slowly, loudly, and clearly, they are applying fundamental crafts of the actor. They will find their audience more appreciative if they stand still and face the actor speaking on stage and then turn to face the audience when they speak their own lines. They can realize that keeping a distance between groups of actors on stage makes for better theatrics than having everyone spread about evenly. These ideas need not be forced on children. They are such fundamental principles of drama that children will easily discover them if given the opportunity to discuss their creative drama productions.

Another activity that should be included in the group processes of literature teaching is storytelling. We have noted that one of the basic objectives of the nonstructured approach to the teaching of literature is for the child to experience the oral tradition of literature. Storytelling succeeds with stories that appeal to teller and listener alike. The successful storyteller is aware of the parts of his story, the actions and scenes, from the point of the exposition of the problem through to the climax of the tale, and on to its conclusion. He is conscious of his characters' personalities in the story, in which parts of the tale characters appear and why, as well as the extent of their dialogue in each part. He understands the power of certain words to excite his listeners' sense of touch, taste, smell, vision, and hearing. He uses the tone and timbre of his voice to act out the story while using body and face for expression. He knows that the arrangement for the physical setting for his story and what time of day it will be told are important considerations. For example, he must stand close to his listeners as he talks. They must be seated comfortably, without distractions. A storyteller must be able to react to danger signals of unrest or lack of interest from individual listeners. Talking directly to a listener, "And then, John, . . ." or asking rhetorical questions, "Jack was getting scared, wasn't he?" sometimes helps. The story's length will depend on the mood and the need of the audience; the storyteller must be prepared to condense his story. Children are usually unable to do this.

The complex planning that must precede successful storytelling suggests children must hear a great deal of storytelling before they, themselves, can actively explore this form of literature. All the necessary steps in planning a story can be recognized by children after they have heard several good stories told by the teacher. Children will grow in their ability to tell stories through hearing them.

The nonstructured approach to elementary school literature stresses individualized use of literature. Accordingly, the purpose of group work is to offer each reader a chance to discuss his readings. Part of the time allotted for other subjects, say art, can be used to construct graphic examples of ideas and feelings that children can display in the literature group activities. Other kinds of sharing, including drama, storytelling, introducing others to books, reading favorite parts aloud, and responding to open-ended questions from the teacher, make up some of the activities of this group work. Book reports of the traditional kind are neither necessary nor recommended in this approach since their format and requirements usually deny the child his right to choose reading materials.

It is not against the principles of the nonstructured approach to conduct discussions of single pieces of literature with an entire group of children. This is appropriate with poetry, creative drama, and storytelling. It is also appropriate after several children have read the same book to discuss with them their affective and cognitive responses to it. Such a talk period might include questions similar to these:

What makes the book fiction instead of nonfiction?
What makes the book prose rather than poetry?
What genre of literature does the piece fall into?
What is the structure of the plot?
What were characters like and how were they developed?
What is the theme of the story?
Where is the story set?
What is the author's style?
What is the author's point of view?
What was the author's purpose?
What other books are like this one?

Using children's reading interest in teaching literature

The nonstructured approach to literature depends on helping the child find the right book for himself and, most important, maintaining strong motivation in children to read.

Some research information on children's reading interests is useful for this purpose. Generally speaking, primary grade children seem to like animal stories, humor, fairy tales, adventure stories, how-to-do-it books, and nature stories. Intermediate grade children like these too, but also like action–adventure stories, books about children in other lands, biography, and hero worship stories, books on hobbies, sports, mysteries, and those involving mild romance and family life (girls especially like these). Rewritten myths, legends, and folk tales replace fairy tales for this age group. It has also been found that in the middle grades, boys do not like description, moralism, didacticism, fairy tales, romantic love, sentimentalism, physical weakness in males, or females as the leading characters in stories. Girls avoid violent action, description, didacticism, slightly younger children, and threatening animals. Remember that these choices reflect what books are generally available; obviously children can like or dislike only what they have read. In addition, in any category, some books are better than others; a child may think he dislikes an entire category of books simply because he has read only mediocre or inferior examples of it.

In the middle grades, differences in reading interests of boys and girls become more visible. Boys actively reject "girls' books," those with heroines instead of heroes. And boys read more information books than girls; girls voluntarily read more poetry. Boys prefer stories with vigorous action; girls prefer home and school stories and sentimentalized prose fiction. Boys seem to have a wider range of reading interests than do girls. The patterns of reading interest for bright and slow children of the same age, surprisingly, are very similar. It seems that the process of growing up determines interests more effectively than differences in intelligence.

Reading interests of children in the elementary school change rapidly, especially when compared to such changes in children of secondary school age. Apparently children in the lower grades in school are attracted to many new experiences. They readily exchange their current interests for other newer interests. This is reflected in their reading. Thus, the teacher need not be as concerned or worried as some teachers tend to be at "streaks" of reading one type of book exclusively. Children's natural tendency to change to new things will act to divert them to other content.

In this book we have examined and explored many kinds of writing for children. The most important point, however, is to apply these concepts and techniques of close reading to other works by the student of children's literature. We have described a process of evaluation, not merely presented a package of facts to be memorized. We hope our method is transferable to all books.

But the most important person in the advancement of children's literature is the adult who wants to acquaint children with good books. Children do not have a natural proclivity for discovering books by themselves—if they did, we would have a nation of great readers and no need for teachers of literature. Such errors in thinking have in the past led to many destructive practices: no analyzing literature to discover if there is any substance to it; conducting classes in literature in the elementary school as if they were either circus romps or morality lessons instead of a serious part of the intellectual development of the child. Hopefully we can reassess the intellectual vacuity of those who continually stress the mere "wonder" of children and stand at a distance from the inquiring intellect of the child, which probes not for saccharine and nebulous adult cooing but for significant mental stimuli.

Many books helpfully discuss the problems of presenting literature to children. Some of them have already been mentioned: May Hill Arbuthnot's *Children and Books* (Chicago: Scott, Foresman & Co., 1964) ; Charlotte Huck and Doris Young Kuhn's *Children's Literature in the Elementary School* (New York: Holt, Rinehart & Winston, 1968) ; *Curriculum for English* of the Nebraska Curriculum Materials Center at the Univesity of Nebraska. In addition to these, we feel that real innovation is described in Herbert Kohl's *The Open Classroom* and James Moffett's *The Student Centered Language Arts Curriculum K–13* (Boston: Houghton Mifflin Co., 1968) . On the uses of theatre in the classroom no more valuable book exists than Viola Spolin's *Improvisation for the Theatre* (Evanston, Ill.: Northwestern University Press, 1963) .

Part Four
Books for Children

Annotated Bibliography

Mythology, folklore, and related forms

Arnott, Kathleen. *African Myths and Legends*. Illustrated by Joan Kiddell-Monroe. New York: Henry Z. Walck, 1963.

The Hausa, Fulani, Bantu, Ibibio, Xhosa, Zulu and twelve other African tribes are represented in this collection of 34 tales: how-and-why stories to explain natural phenomena, familiar folk themes of good rewarded and evil punished, and stories that contrast wisdom and folly using human and animal protagonists. A fine resource for the story-teller and an introduction to West Indian, Haitian, and Southern Negro folklore. An A.L.A. Notable Book. Ages 10–12.

Asbjornsen, P. C. *East of the Sun and West of the Moon*. Translated by George W. Dasent. Illustrated by Edgar and Ingri D'Aulaire. New York: Viking Press, 1969.

Twenty-one Norwegian folktales in the classic Dasent translation with appropriately strong, simple illustrations. This collection includes such popular childhood favorites as "The Three Dauntless Billy-goats," "The Princess on the Glass Hill," the great white bear of the title story and many others. The tone varies from sheer nonsense to the heroic and romantic. A matchless collection in a matchless reprint. Ages 6–adult.

d'Aulaire, Ingri, and Edgar Parin d'Aulaire. *Norse Gods and Giants*. Illustrated by the authors. New York: Doubleday & Co., 1967.

Drawing from the two great Icelandic Eddas and scattered folklore and songs, this book presents the beliefs of the ancient Norsemen. Their nine worlds, from the realms of fire and the underworld to Asgard and High Heaven, with the gnomes, giants, elves, men, and gods who inhabited them, are recreated in vigorous prose. The virtue that the Norsemen prized above all others—unflinching courage in battle—is reflected in the numerous conflicts between gods and giants, leading to the end of both in the final upheaval of Ragnarok, "the destiny of the gods." An outstanding portrayal of the vanished beliefs that shaped the Vikings. Dramatic, stark, roughhewn lithographs, many in vibrant color, accompany the text. Ages 11–14.

Belting, Natalia. *The Sun Is a Golden Earring*. Illustrated by Bernarda Bryson. New York: Holt, Rinehart and Winston, 1962.

Here is a collection of folk sayings and proverbs from around the world, all dealing with the sun and the sky, storms and thunder, wind and rain. Only sky-colors are used in the book—the yellow of the sun, the blue of the night, and the gray of the storm. The source for each saying is given, and the delicate, ethereal drawings reflect the mystery and awe primitive man felt in the presence of nature. A Caldecott Award runner-up. Ages 6–9.

Bertol, Roland. *Sundiata: The Epic of the Lion King*. Illustrated by Gregorio Prestopino. New York: Thomas Y Crowell, 1970.

A masterful retelling of an African epic that has been handed down orally for seven hundred years. A blend of myth and history, it is the story of a great medieval warrior-hero who set up an empire in what is now the Republic of Mali. The eleventh child, ugly, crippled, and mute, Sundiata, during years of exile, changed into a handsome, fierce champion of his people and led them to victory over the demonic Sumanguru. Written in the cadenced style appropriate to an epic with dramatic black and white drawings. An A.L.A. Notable Book. Ages 10–adult.

Brown, Marcia. *Backbone of the King.* Illustrated by Marcia Brown. New York: Charles Scribner's, 1966.
A distinguished version of an epic Hawaiian tale. The noble Paka'a is the friend, the advisor, the "backbone" of the king. Two jealous courtiers discredit him and he sails away to exile. His son, Ku-a-Paka'a, born in exile, with his father's training and his own strength and ingenuity, journeys to the court, convinces the king of his father's loyalty and sees him reinstated in his former place. This book offers a wealth of information about ancient Hawaiian life and customs. It includes numerous chants and a useful pronouncing glossary. The handsome olive green linoleum block cuts match the quiet strength of the narrative. An A.L.A. Notable Book. Ages 11–14.

Bryson, Bernarda. *Gilgamesh, Man's First Story.* Illustrated by the author. New York: Holt, Rinehart and Winston, 1967.
An ancient legend (B.C. 3000) retold with devotion to the spirit of the Babylonian original; the author's explanatory note details her deep interest in this tale and its several versions whose texts she has read and reread many times. This version, with its occasional use of blank verse, has the flavor of a direct translation from the original cuneiform tablets. Gilgamesh, a Sumerian king, makes friends with Enkidu, the half-beast, half-man sent by the gods to destroy him. Together they perform feats of valor, but Enkidu is eventually slain. The anguished Gilgamesh seeks the aid of his immortal ancestor, Utnapishtim, the Babylonian Noah, to bring Enkidu back to life. When Utnapishtim refuses, Gilgamesh wills himself to die so that he may rejoin his friend. The illustrations in blue, green, ocher, and red are based on archaeological discoveries of figures contemporary with the epic. An A.L.A. Notable Book. Ages 12–adult.

Carlson, Dale. *Warlord of the Genji.* Illustrated by John Gretzer. New York: Atheneum, 1970.
History and legend combine in the story of the Japanese warrior hero Yoshitsune, who led his deposed clan, the Genji, against the rival Heike clan. How he escapes from prison, how he wins the help of the giant warrior-monk Benkei, his elder brother's jealousy, his battles, marriage, and ceremonial suicide are familiar stories to all Japanese children and the source of many Noh and Kabuki dramas. The political and religious background of twelfth century Japan is unobtrusively woven into the narrative, together with details of custom and dress. Ages 12–14.
Some of Yoshitsune's adventures are found in Marion M. Dilts' *Pageant of Japanese History* (New York: Longmans, Green, 1961) and Helen McAlpine's *Japanese Tales and Legends* (New York: Henry Z. Walck, 1959).

Chase, Richard. *Grandfather Tales.* Illustrated by Berkeley Williams, Jr. Boston: Houghton Mifflin Co., 1948.
Twenty-five stories set in the framework of a Southern mountain celebration of Old Christmas, January 6. Variants of "Molly Whuppie," "Three Billy Goats Gruff," "Three Little Pigs," "Cinderella," and other regional and tall tales are included. There is a mummers' play and songs with music such as "Froggy Went A'Courtin'," and "The Babe of Bethlehem." Interesting Americana, though the dialect may hinder some readers.

But as with the author's *Jack Tales,* the vigor and irrepressible humor make this an inviting source for the storyteller. Ages 14–adult.

Church, Alfred J. *The Iliad and the Odyssey of Homer.* Illustrated by Eugene Karlin. New York: Macmillan Co., 1967.
An attractive one-volume edition of two standard works previously issued separately. The author's retelling follows Homer's sequence of events and retains the classic spirit. There is an afterword by Clifton Fadiman, and new, heroically simple and beautiful line drawings replace the familiar Flaxman illustrations of the earlier editions. A superior version of the immortal Greek epics. Ages 11–adult.

Coolidge, Olivia E. *The Trojan War.* Illustrated by Edouard Sandoz. Boston: Houghton Mifflin Co., 1952.
The complete story of the most famous war in epic literature. It begins when the goddess Discord throws the golden apple marked "For the Fairest" among the Olympians present at the wedding feast of Thetis and Peleus and ends with the return of Odysseus to Ithaca. The account of the heroes, Trojan and Greek, the gods and goddesses, the incomparable Helen, and the fall of Troy are based on the original Greek sources. A masterful and vivid blending of the *Iliad* and *Odyssey,* rounded out with background and aftermath. A helpful list of characters and places is included. Ages 12–14.

Courlander, Harold. *The King's Drum and Other African Stories.* Illustrated by Enrico Arno. New York: Harcourt Brace Jovanovich, 1962.
Twenty-nine brief tales: perceptive observations of human behavior, filled with wit and humor. From Africa south of the Sahara, they deal chiefly with human and animal tricksters, heroes and pseudo-heroes, conflicts and dilemmas. Legends, myths, and creation stories are omitted. Excellent notes at the end of the book list the sources, variants, and moral of each tale. Rich with information on African customs and philosophy, these stories have their counterparts in Europe, Arabia, and India, but their African origin gives them a flavor all their own. They are not duplicated in the author's other collections of African lore: *Cow Tale Switch* (New York: Holt, Rinehart and Winston, 1947), *The Fire on the Mountain* (New York: Holt, Rinehart and Winston, 1950), *The Hat-Shaking Dance* (New York: Holt, Rinehart and Winston, 1957) and *Olode the Hunter* (New York: Harcourt Brace Jovanovich, 1968). An A.L.A. Notable Book. Ages 10–12.

Dayrell, Elphinstone. *Why the Sun and the Moon Live in the Sky.* Illustrated by Blair Lent. Boston: Houghton Mifflin Co., 1968.
When the hospitable Sun, who lived on earth, urged his friend Water to come visit him, Water demurred, saying that his followers were too numerous; but Sun insisted. As Water and his cortege entered Sun's house, Sun and his wife, Moon, were floated higher and higher until they finally had to take refuge in the sky. A Nigerian folktale with distinctive, stylized illustrations. The Sun, Moon, Water and Water's people appear as African tribesmen wearing colored masks representing their characters—shades of gold and white for the Sun, blue-grey for the Moon, and blue-green for Water. Runner-up for the Caldecott Award. Ages 5–8.

Feagles, Anita. *He Who Saw Everything.* Illustrated by Xavier Gonzalez. Chicago: Scott, Foresman and Co., 1966.
Though shorter than the Bryson retelling and intended for younger readers, this version of the Gilgamesh legend, is outstanding for its unique paper-sculpture illustrations. An afterword establishes time, geographical setting, and the enduring impact of the epic. Ages 10–12.

Gaer, Joseph. *Adventures of Rama.* Illustrated by Randy Monk. Boston: Little, Brown and Co., 1954.

An attractive, short version of the great Indian epic the Ramayana. Prince Rama, with his beautiful wife Sita and faithful brother Lakshman, is exiled to the forest for fourteen years. There his wife is abducted by the demon king Ravan, and Rama, with an army of monkeys, pursues them. Battle after battle follows, and at last Ravan is killed and Sita freed. The bravery and prowess of Rama, the fidelity of Lakshman, the beauty, purity, and constancy of Sita have made them the epitome of all desirable qualities to Hindus through the ages. A dramatic and simple retelling. Ages 9–13.

Garfield, Leon, and Edward Blishen. *The God beneath the Sea.* Illustrated by Zevi Blum. New York: Pantheon Books, 1971.

Thrown from Olympus by his mother Hera, who resents her deformed son, Hephaestus is rescued by the nymph Thetis and raised in her home beneath the sea. Later his skill as a creator of beauty wins him admission to the society of the gods. Interwoven with the life of Hephaestus are stories of the creation of the world, the gods, and man. The authors' rich, image-laden prose creates distinct and memorable characters, from lustful, cruel Zeus, anguished Demeter, and lame Hephaestus to the first pitiful man, who lives only a moment and goes down to Hades bewildered, asking "why?" A brilliant recreation. The sensual passages may offend some readers, others will find them appropriate in context. This is not an introductory mythology; it resembles Robert Graves' *Greek Gods and Heroes* (New York: Doubleday & Co., 1960) in tone, though it is meant for older readers. The distorted black and white illustrations are powerful, but some readers may find them merely grotesque. Ages 14–adult.

Garner, Alan, editor. *A Cavalcade of Goblins.* Illustrated by Krystyna Turska. New York: Henry Z. Walck, 1969.

An engrossing anthology of excerpts, poems, and stories about goblins and other eerie creatures. Drawn from the folklore of the American Indians and of the Asian and European peoples, it provides a rich source for storytellers. Folklorists will be pleased by the Notes and Sources. There is good material here for reading aloud, though the difficult names and unusual colloquial expressions may daunt some storytellers. An A.L.A. Notable Book. Ages 10–13.

Goldston, Robert C. *The Legend of the Cid.* Illustrated by Stephane. New York: Bobbs–Merrill Co., 1963.

A fast-paced retelling of the legends about the Spanish hero Rodrigo de Vivar, whose valiant deeds on the battlefield and whose loyal and magnanimous nature won him the title *El Cid Campeador,* or Lord Champion, from his enemies the Moors. Ages 12–14.

Merriam Sherwood's *Tale of the Warrior Lord: The Cid* (New York: David McKay Co., 1957) is a prose translation of the famous epic poem *"El Cantar de Mio Cid."* It retains the Spanish idiom and period flavor of the original, but Goldston covers the Cid's youth, courtship, and heroic victory after death, which are not found in the epic poem. Goldston's version is more readable, but Sherwood's glows with the unbending, unflinching pride of the Spaniard. Ages 12–14.

Green, Roger Lancelyn. *Tales of Ancient Egypt.* Illustrated by Elaine Raphael. New York: Henry Z. Walck, 1968.

A fascinating collection of some of the oldest stories in the world. Divided into "Tales of the Gods," "Tales of Magic," and "Tales of Adventure," it tells of the creation of the gods and man, the murder of Osiris, the wanderings of Isis, a journey to the land of the dead, and the remarkable exploits of 12-year-old Se-Osiris, the greatest magician in Egypt. It includes the earliest version of the Cinderella story ("The girl with the Rose-red Slippers") and a surprising account of Helen of Troy. The text and illustrations are distinguished. Sources for each tale and a time chart. Ages 11–adult.

Habte-Mariam, Mesfin. *The Rich Man and the Singer*. Edited and illustrated by Christine Price. New York: E. P. Dutton & Co., 1971.

A collection of thirty-one tales told by the various peoples of Ethiopia: the Amhara, the Gurage, the Gallas, and those who live in the Tigre and Sidamo areas, especially the Amhara. Familiar themes of kindness rewarded, evil punished, and the clever triumphing over the powerful are found here. Several tales are reminiscent of Aesop. "The Faithful Servant" has a Dick Whittington touch; "Mammo the Fool" is the Ethiopian "Epaminondas"; excellent marital advice is given in "The Hair of the Lion"; and "The Man Who Wanted to Mind the House" speaks for itself. Variants of two of the tales are found in Harold Courlander's *Fire on the Mountain* (New York: Holt, Rinehart and Winston, 1950), and five in Russell Davis's *The Lion's Whiskers* (New York: Little, Brown and Co., 1959). The present version, which is more like Courlander's, includes an excellent foreword, "The World of the Stories," which sets the scene. It is adequately illustrated with small spot drawings in black and white. Ages 10–12.

Haley, Gail E. *A Story, a Story*. Illustrated by the author. New York: Atheneum, 1970.

A folk tale from the Caribbean, traced back to its birthplace in Africa and illustrated with patterned woodcuts, strikingly colored and boldly designed. The origin of the spider tale, a favorite form in African folklore, is explained in rhythmic, repetitive prose. Ananse, the "spider man," wanting to obtain the Sky God's stories, is set three seemingly impossible tasks: to bring Osebo, the leopard-of-the-terrible-teeth, Mmboro, the hornet who-stings-like-fire, and Mmoatia, the fairy-whom-men-never-see, to the Sky God. Though small and defenseless, Ananse succeeds through his cleverness and wins the golden box of stories, which he takes back to earth. Caldecott Award 1971. Ages 5–9.

Hamilton, Edith. *Mythology*. Illustrated by Steele Savage. Boston: Little, Brown and Co., 1942.

A clear, penetrating presentation of Greek and Roman mythology. The author, a classical scholar, draws on the earliest sources as well as on classical dramatists and poets to preserve as much of the original flavor as possible. In this way the reader learns not only the myth, but also something about Homer, Hesiod, Pindar, Aeschylus, Sophocles, Euripides, Ovid, and Vergil. A brief but clear explanation of Norse mythology derived from the Elder Edda is also included. Not as comprehensive in scope as Bulfinch, who includes chivalric literature and information on Eastern mythologies, but written with greater empathy. Outstanding! Ages 12–adult.

Harris, Christie. *Once upon a Totem*. Illustrated by John Frazer Mills. New York: Atheneum, 1963.

Five legends from the Indian tribes of the North Pacific Coast give insight into Indian customs, ethics, and ideals. The theme of the unity of man and nature is expressed through taboos and totems. The tales are dramatic and elaborate in structure, though the writing does not always convey their basic strength. Prefatory notes provide sociological and cultural background information. The black and white woodcuts appropriately primitive. Ages 10–12.

Haviland, Virginia. *Favorite Fairy Tales Told in Spain*. Illustrated by Barbara Cooney. Boston: Little, Brown and Co., 1963.

The familiar story of Half-Chick and five other stories dealing respectively with an enormous flea, four brothers, an enchanted mule, Juan Cigarron, and a wicked ogre are told with simplicity and ease. Barbara Cooney's illustrations in warm yellow, red, and olive convey the Spanish feeling. In this, as in the other Haviland adaptations—all published in New York by Little, Brown and Co.: *Favorite Fairy Tales Told in France*, 1959; *Ireland*, 1961; *Norway*, 1961; *Poland*, 1963; *Scotland*, 1965; *Czechoslovakia*, 1966; *Sweden*, 1966; *Japan*, 1967; and *Greece*, 1970—the stories are skilfully retold; Haviland simplifies without losing the spirit of the original. The large print and the handsome illustrations by such notable artists as Ness, Bettina, Duvoisin, Weisgard, and Hoffman add to the attractiveness of the series. Children who are not yet ready for the length and fine print of the Lang fairy books and those beginning to read independently will find Haviland an excellent introduction to folklore. Ages 9–10.

Hazeltine, Alice I., editor. *Hero Tales from Many Lands.* Illustrated by Gordon Laite. New York: Abingdon Press, 1961.

Thirty tales chosen from classic retellings of the world's heroic literature, gathered by an outstanding anthologist. Many are from out-of-print sources. Famous heroes include Hector, Odysseus, Beowulf, Arthur, Tristram, Cuchulain, Roland, Siegfried, and El Cid. Other, lesser-known warriors are the Welsh Manawyddan, Iceland's Grettir and Njal, the Finnish Wainawoinen, Arabia's Antar, India's Rama and the five Pandavan brothers, Japan's Yoshitsune, and a Blackfoot Indian named Scarface. Since the hero tale is strongly national in its presentation of human character, this collection will afford insight into the peoples from whom they sprang. Alfred Church, James Baldwin, Padraic Colum, Sir Thomas Mallory, Howard Pyle, Kenneth Morris, Ella Young, Merriam Sherwood, Allen French, and Dorothy Hosford are some of the authors represented. Their writing styles give the variety and depth needed to describe the different times and locales in which the hero lived and which would be difficult for one author to achieve. These excerpts may lead the reader to each author's longer accounts. A list for further reading, a glossary, and index. Ages 10–12.

Heady, Eleanor B. *When The Stones Were Soft: East African Fireside Tales.* Illustrated by Tom Feelings. New York: Funk & Wagnalls, 1968.

Sixteen East African folktales based on material from Kenya, Tanzania, and Uganda. Each tale is told by Mama Semamingi, whose introductions evoke the African setting. Animals, nature spirits, witchcraft, and people are involved in these short, simple how-and-why stories. Sensitive, soft, black and white illustrations match the quiet fireside quality of the narrative. Ages 9–11.

Hope-Simpson, Jacynth. *A Cavalcade of Witches.* Illustrated by Krystyna Turska. New York: Henry Z. Walck, 1967.

An engaging literary collection of witchlore drawn from many sources. Excerpts from the Bible, medieval authors, Shakespeare, and Milton and such modern authors as Mary Norton, Ian Serraillier, Arthur Ransome, and Walter de la Mare carry out the book's stated aim, to show how diverse descriptions of witches have been. Though some of the selections may be found elsewhere, much of the material is either out of print, not easily available, or has never before been anthologized. Its atractive format, with atmospheric black and white drawings, underscores the horror, humor, and magic of witches. Ages 10–12.

Keats, Ezra Jack. *John Henry.* Illustrated by the author. New York: Pantheon Books, 1965.

The legendary career of John Henry, who was born with a hammer in his hand and beat a steam drill machine through a mountain, is retold with vigor in an outstanding picture book. The illustrations are superb, with bold vibrant double spreads in color touched here and there with collage. Certain to entice the poor reader and a natural for picture book storytelling. Ages 5–9.

Kelsey, Alice G. *Once the Mullah.* Illustrated by Kurt Werth. New York: David McKay Co., 1954.

A collection of 26 Persian folk tales centered around the Mullah, who was the teacher, judge, and priest of his small village. Like his Turkish counterpart, the Hodja, the Mullah is constantly getting in and out of scrapes and readily appreciates a practical joke even when turned on himself. His solving of his neighbors' troubles often results in disaster. He has the simplicity of Simon combined at times with the wisdom of Solomon, at times with the foolishness of a noodlehead. Short, sometimes subtle, with a down-to-earth humor, the stories are universally appealing and excellent choices for storytelling. Ages 10–adult.

King, Cynthia, *In the Morning of Time*. Illustrated by Charles Mikolaycak. New York: Four Winds Press, 1970.

Balder, the innocent god, the good, is troubled with dreams. In them he sees the creation of the world and its destruction following his own death. The foreknowledge of doom spurs the gods to resist, though they know Ragnarok is inevitable. By making Balder the central figure, the author gives a dramatic unity to the familiar stories of Thor, Odin, Loki, and other gods and heroes of Asgard. Quotations from the Eddas appear at the beginning of each chapter and at appropriate places in the text. The black and white illustrations are vigorous. There is a pronouncing glossary of names and terms and an afterword on Iceland and its myths. For older readers than the D'Aulaire *Norse Gods and Giants* (New York: Doubleday & Co., 1967) and worthy to stand beside Padraic Colum's longer, more detailed *Children of Odin* (New York: Macmillan Co., 1962). Ages. 12–14.

Krueger, Kermit. *The Serpent Prince: Folktales from Northeastern Thailand*. Illustrated by Yoko Mitsuhashi. Cleveland: World Publishing Co., 1969.

Nineteen folktales collected by a Peace Corps volunteer blend Thai history, mythology (a unique mixture of Hinduism, Buddhism, and older faiths), and changeless village life in a smooth, dignified rendition. The stories are varied in theme. "The Girl Who Wore Too Much" shows the fatal results of vanity; "The Black Pool" has a Romeo and Juliet plot; "Pen and Four Foolish Ministers" is an inspiring tale of a Buddhist princess who voluntarily gives up her life to end a war. Much of the background mood is caught in the stylized, serene illustrations. Ages 10–12.

Leach, Maria. *The Rainbow Book of American Folktales and Legends*. Illustrated by Marc Simont. Cleveland: World Publishing Co., 1958.

A broad sampling of American folklore, this book includes tall tales and legends, ghost– and supernatural stories, noodle stories and jokes, Indian tales from North, South and Central America, and folk– and regional lore for every state, including state nicknames, birds, and flowers. All of the tales are brief, but their vigor begs for telling aloud. Notes and sources of material are given and an index is included. A large, handsome book with color illustrations matching the text in vigor and directness. Ages 10–adult.

Other collections by Maria Leach, a noted folklorist, are: *The Thing at the Foot of the Bed* (Cleveland: World Publishing Co., 1959), ghost folklore; *Noodles, Nitwits, and Numskulls* (Cleveland: World Publishing Co., 1961), noodle tales; *The Luck Book* (Cleveland: World Publishing Co., 1964), proverbs, tales, and superstitions about luck, and *How the People Sang the Mountains Up* (New York: Viking Press, 1967), how-and-why creation stories.

McLeod, Mary. *King Arthur and His Knights*. Illustrated by Herschel Levit. New York: Macmillan Co., 1963.

First published in 1949, this is a distinguished retelling of Sir Thomas Malory's *Le Morte D'Arthur*. Though faithful to Malory in spirit, it is easier reading than the original, or than either the classic retelling by Sidney Lanier or the magnificent monumental four-volume version by Howard Pyle. The language is clear, flavorful, and only slightly modernized for the reader's better understanding. When necessary to preserve the true essence of the book, the author will explain original words like Siege (seat) Perilous. Mary McLeod deals principally with King Arthur, Sir Lancelot, Sir Gareth, Sir Tristram, Sir Galahad, with the quest for the Holy Grail, and the death of Arthur. An afterword by

Clifton Fadiman gives a brief but fine explanation of the appeal of the Arthurian legend. Ages 10–13.

Jay Williams' *Sword of King Arthur* (New York: Thomas Y Crowell, 1968) —based on Malory but retold in simple, direct language which still conveys the excitement, romance, and tragedy of the original—is by far the easiest version of the legends of Arthur. Separate stories by Ian Serraillier—*The Challenge of the Green Knight* (New York: Henry Z. Walck, 1966) —and Constance Hieatt—*Sir Gawain and the Green Knight* (New York: Thomas Y Crowell, 1967), *The Joy of the Court* (New York: Thomas Y Crowell, 1971), *The Knight of the Cart* (New York: Thomas Y Crowell, 1969), and *The Knight of the Lion* (New York: Thomas Y Crowell, 1968) —introduce readers unready for the longer versions to all that Camelot signifies.

MacManus, Seumas. *Hibernian Nights*. Illustrated by Paul Kennedy. New York: Macmillan Co., 1963.

An outstanding storyteller's own selection of the 22 tales he considered best and most representative of his art. These tall tales and traditional fairytales about foolish kings, youngest sons, cruel stepmothers, and the little people are full of Irish charm. The introduction by Padraic Colum, himself no mean teller of tales, introduces Seumas MacManus to the readers and storytellers of today. Handsomely printed and illustrated, this book lends itself equally to reading aloud or reading alone. Ages 10–12.

Manning-Sanders, Ruth, editor. *A Book of Magical Beasts*. Illustrated by Raymond Briggs. Camden, N.J.: Thomas Nelson, 1970.

Thirty-seven selections from such familiar authors as Dasent, Jacobs, Lang, and Andersen, as well as from lesser-known writers and anonymous balladeers. Some of the animals are bewitched princes and princesses, but most are magical in their own nature. There is the Tibetan tale of the stone lion who coughs gold into a poor man's bucket but wreaks vengeance on his greedy brother. The Scandinavian counterpart of Puss in Boots appears in "Lord Peter." A note before each tale gives its source and biographical information on the author. Fifteen of the stories are out of print. The remaining twenty-two are scattered throughout various anthologies; but the reader interested in fairytale animals will find it helpful to have them all together in this handsome book. Ages 10–12.

Other similar collections (all published in New York by E. P. Dutton & Co.), by this author are: *A Book of Dragons* (1964), *A Book of Dwarfs* (1963), *A Book of Ghosts and Goblins* (1968), *A Book of Giants* (1962), *A Book of Mermaids* (1967), *A Book of Princes and Princesses* (1969), *A Book of Witches* (1965), and *A Book of Wizards* (1966).

Matsutani, Miyoko. *The Crane Maiden*. Translated by Alvin Tresselt. Illustrated by Chihiro Iwasaki. New York: Parents' Magazine Press, 1968.

An old Japanese tale about a grateful crane who, released from a trap by an old woodcutter, takes human form and comes to live with him and his wife as their daughter. (In some versions she appears as his wife. This theme—a grateful creature who takes human form—is found in many cultures.) Hoping to relieve their poverty, the loving and devoted maiden weaves a magnificent brocade for the foster parents to sell. Unfortunately, the old wife disobeys the girl's injunction never to watch her work, and the crane must leave forever. Lovely double-page watercolors enhance the Oriental quality of the story. Ages 5–8.

Mehdevi, Alexander. *Bungling Pedro and Other Majorcan Tales*. Illustrated by Isabel Bodor. New York: Alfred A. Knopf, 1970.

Ten tales whose robust humor is based on common folklore themes. "The Count and the Little Shepherd" has the familiar motif of three riddles to be solved; "Bungling Pedro" is the universal simpleton. Other well known folk tale characters are the master thief, the greedy giant, and the princess with golden hair. The lively writing is well matched by the sprightly line drawings. Ages 9–11.

Mosel, Arlene. *Tikki Tikki Tembo*. Illustrated by Blair Lent. New York: Holt, Rinehart and Winston, 1968.
     When Tikki Tikki 'Tembo-no Sa Rembo-chari Bari Ruchi-pip Peri Pembo, eldest son of a widow, falls into a well, it takes so long for his little brother to tell what happened that he almost drowns. Based on a Chinese legend explaining why short names are preferable to long. Stylized drawings in color reflect the Chinese setting. An excellent book to use for storytelling, with or without the pictures. An A.L.A. Notable Book. Ages 4–9.

Nic Leodhas, Sorche. *Kellyburn Braes*. Illustrated by Eveline Ness. New York: Holt, Rinehart and Winston, 1968.
     The old folk theme of the shrewish wife. Even the devil refuses to keep her, returning her to her husband because, says he, "The worst of my torments cannot beat your wife." A rollicking picture story. Vigorous woodcuts in gray and brown project the ironic humor of the old Scottish ballad. The music is appended. An A.L.A. Notable Book. Ages 6–8.

Nic Leodhas, Sorche. *Thistle and Thyme*. Illustrated by Eveline Ness. New York: Holt, Rinehart and Winston, 1962.
     Magic, mystery, wonder, and humor characterize these ten Scottish stories whose cadence suggests the rhythm and lilt of the original Gaelic. Mothers who boast of their child's beauty receive a warning in "The Changeling and the Fond Young Mother." The steadfast love of a mother for her child is reflected in the tender "The Stolen Bairn and the Sidhe." Humor abounds in "The Bride Who Out Talked the Water Kelpie," and the price of stinginess is the theme of "St. Cuddy and the Gray Geese." The author's introduction gives the background of each tale and tells a little about the storyteller's place in the lives of the people. A storyteller with an ear for the Scottish language and the tongue to reproduce it would find a wealth of material in this and other collections by the same author. An A.L.A. Notable Book. Ages 9–11.
     Other titles by this author (all published in New York by Holt, Rinehart and Winston) are: *Heather and Broom* (1960), *Gaelic Ghosts* (1963), *Ghosts Go Haunting* (1965), *Claymore and Kilt* (1967), *Sea Spell and Moor Magic* (1968), and *By Loch and Lin* (1969).

Nye, Robert. *Beowulf: A New Telling*. Illustrated by Alan E. Cober. New York: Hill & Wang, 1968.
     Another retelling of Beowulf's epic struggle with the fearsome Grendel and his mother, and his fatal though victorious encounter with the Firedrake. Not as literal a retelling as Serrailler's *Beowulf the Warrior*, which adheres to the verse pattern of the original, and more detailed than either Hosford's *By His Own Might* or Sutcliff's *Beowulf*, both prose versions that reflect the stark grimness of this ancient Anglo-Saxon poem. Nye's interpretation adds some humor, gives Beowulf's character real depth, and offers by far the grisliest monsters. Ages 10–13.

Picard, Barbara Leonie. *Tales of the British People*. Illustrated by Eric Fraser. New York: Criterion Books, 1961.
     From the different peoples—Celts, Romans, Saxons, Danes, and Normans—who settled the British Isles, nine traditional tales are retold in chronological order. Written

with strength and dignity, from the Celtic "Quest of the Sons of Turenn" to the Middle English "Marriage of Sir Gawaine," the stories serve as a stepping-stone to more complete versions and to other hero tales. Each selection is preceded by a brief historical note giving the origin of the legend. Ages 10–12.

A companion volume, *Hero Tales from the British Isles* (New York: Criterion Books, 1963), includes eleven tales of such heroes as Pwyll, Finn MacCool, Tam Lin and Cuchulain, as well as a helpful guide to the pronunciation of names. *Celtic Tales* (New York: Criterion Books, 1964) adds nine more fine retellings of Irish, Welsh, and Scottish legends. Ages 10–12.

Polland, Madeleine. *Deirdre*. Illustrated by Sean Morrison. New York: Doubleday & Co., 1967.

The story of Deirdre, the "Helen of the Gael," is haunting and timeless, with its theme of tragic, foredoomed love. At her birth it was predicted that her beauty would bring death and sorrow to Ulster. To forestall the ominous prophecy Deirdre is reared in seclusion as the bride-to-be of the aging King Conor. But when Naoise, the young champion of the Red Branch Knights of Ulster, inadvertently stumbles on her hiding place, it is love at first sight. The pair, accompanied by Naoise's brothers, flee to Scotland for fear of Conor's jealousy. But lured back by false promises of forgiveness and friendship, the brothers are killed and Deirdre dies of a broken heart. A slightly different version of the Deirdre legend is found in Pilkington's *The Three Sorrowful Tales of Erin* (New York: Henry Z. Walck, 1966). Both versions retain the poetic quality of the Celtic original. But both sadly lack a guide to the pronunciation of Irish names. How does one pronounce Naoise? An A.L.A. Notable Book. Ages 11–13.

Ransome, Arthur. *The Fool of the World and the Flying Ship*. Illustrated by Uri Shulevitz. New York: Farrar, Straus & Giroux, 1968.

A Russian story about a kindhearted, simpleminded peasant lad who, though scorned by his parents and two older brothers, wins the hand of the Tzar's daughter. His rise to eminence is brought about by seven men of unique abilities who reward his kindness to them by helping him fulfill the impossible demands of the Tzar. An extravagant, exuberant, classic folktale, brimming with vitality. The illustrations perfectly match the text, with their panoramic sweep and larger-than-life feeling, intensified by glowing colors and skilful use of white space. Excellent for storytelling. Caldecott award winner, 1969. Ages 6–9.

Rudolph, Marguerita. *I Am Your Misfortune*. Illustrated by Imero Gobbato. New York: Seabury Press, 1968.

The familiar folklore theme of conflict between rich and poor, greedy and generous is expertly handled in the humorous retelling of a Lithuanian folk tale. A poor man meets a monster named Misfortune who has been following him and manages to trick it into his snuffbox, which he throws into a deep millpond. His greedy, rich brother, envious of his sudden prosperity, finds out what happened and sets Misfortune free. It turns out to be his own undoing, for the grateful monster says, "I am *your* misfortune now." Droll illustrations in color. Excellent for storytelling or reading aloud. Ages 6–9.

Schiller, Barbara. *The Kitchen Knight*. Illustrated by Nonny Hogrogrian. New York: Holt, Rinehart and Winston, 1965.

Malory's story of Sir Gareth of Orkney in a simplified retelling. Refusing to identify himself, young Gareth appears at King Arthur's court and begs three boons: a year's food and lodging, then knighthood and a quest. After working in the kitchen for a year he sets out on his quest in the company of a lady who scorns him as a "kitchen knight." But he valiantly performs many heroic deeds and fulfills his quest by rescuing a lady in distress—the mistress of his disdainful companion—and weds her. An attractive introduction to the King Arthur cycle for children too young to cope with the ornate, complicated narratives of Howard Pyle and Sidney Lanier. Ages 9–10.

Seeger, Elizabeth. *The Five Sons of King Pandu*. Illustrated by Gordon Laite. Chicago: Scott, Foresman and Co., 1967.
Condensed from the monumental Sanskrit classic, the *Mahabharata,* this is a masterful retelling of the adventures of five heroes, whose rivalry with their cousins, the sons of Kuru, results in an epic struggle to the death. The battles, exiles, and wanderings of the five Pandavas and their joint wife, the beautiful and virtuous Draupadi, are set against philosophy, customs, and traditions that survive in India to this day. The nineteen full-page jewel-toned illustrations, reminiscent of Indian minatures, are a striking complement to the text. Ages 12–adult.

Seeger, Ruth Crawford. *American Folk Songs for Children*. Illustrated by Barbara Cooney. New York: Doubleday & Co., 1948.
An attractive collection of ninety-five American folk songs within the singing capacity of practically everyone, even small children. Simple piano accompaniments and guitar chords are included, as well as suggestions for singing and using the songs. In addition to the conventional indexing by title and first line, there are extremely useful indices by Subject (e.g. Airplanes and Automobiles to Zoo), Type of Rhythm (e.g. Clapping and Rhythm Band, Galloping and on to Walking and Marching) Tone Play, Name Play, Games, Finger Play, Small Dramas, and Quiet Songs. Charming black and white illustrations frisk through the text. Ages 6–adult.

Serraillier, Ian. *The Challenge of the Green Knight*. Illustrated by Victor S. Ambrus. New York: Henry Z. Walck, 1967.
Accepting the challenge of a giant green knight to strike him if he will submit to an exchange blow twelve months later, Sir Gawain decapitates the stranger, who then picks up his head and rides away. A year later Sir Gawain seeks him out for the return blow. A great medieval classic is retold in vigorous verse that recreates in vivid detail the court life and character of the chivalric period. The test of Gawain's courage, intregrity, and purity involves not only the Green Knight but a hospitable nobleman and his beautiful and over-hospitable wife. Spirited illustrations, some in glowing color, enhance the text. Ages 12–14.
Constance Hieatt's *Sir Gawain and the Green Knight* (New York: Thomas Y Crowell, 1967), is a simply written prose version for ages 9–11.

Singer, Isaac Bashevis. *Zlateh the Goat*. Illustrated by Maurice Sendak. New York: Harper & Row, Publishers, 1966.
Seven tales, translated from the Yiddish by the author and Elizabeth Shub, give insight into the vanished world of Eastern European Jewry. Devils and everyday people, the foolish inhabitants of Chelm with their zany antics, a boy and a goat who survive a blizzard and the butcher, all reflect the wisdom, humor, and pathos of a past that is almost extinct. The illustrations are in complete harmony with the text and remind the reader of the world of Sholom Aleichem. All Ages.
Singer draws on the same rich vein of Jewish folklore for *Fearsome Inn* (New York: Harper & Row, Publishers, 1967), a Newbery Award runner-up, *Mazel and Shlimazel* (New York: Harper & Row, Publishers, 1967), and A.L.A. Notable Book, and *When Shlemiel Went to Warsaw* (New York: Harper & Row, Publishers, 1968), a Newbery Award runner-up.

Stoutenberg, Adrien. *American Tall-Tale Animals*. Illustrated by Glen Rounds. New York: Viking Press, 1968.

A captivating collection of weird, impossible creatures culled from newspaper accounts, folklore, journals, storytellers and well-known American legends. Squonks, Wifflepoofles, Gillygaloos, furbearing trout, talented rattlesnakes and others are described in a folksy, entertaining style and sketched in backwoodsy fashion. Great chucklebait for storytellers. Ages 9–12.

Sutcliff, Rosemary. *The High Deeds of Finn MacCool.* Illustrated by Michael Charlton. New York: E. P. Dutton & Co., 1967.

A detailed, poetic retelling of the deeds of the legendary Fianna, Ireland's warrior band, led by the proud and daring Finn MacCool. There is enchantment and heartbreak in Finn's marriage to a lovely fairy woman who is forced from him by a cruel magician; there is tragedy when the much older Finn takes revenge on the friend who ran away with Grania, his betrothed. The return of Finn's son, Oisin, from the Land of Youth 300 years after his father's death ends the cycle. More famous than Cuchulain, Finn is known not only in Ireland but in Scotland and the Isle of Man. Other accounts of Finn appear in Eileen O'Faolin's *Irish Sagas and Folk Tales* (New York: Henry Z. Walck, 1954) and Barbara L. Picard's *Celtic Tales* (New York: Criterion Books, 1965) and *Hero Tales from the British Isles* (New York: Criterion Books, 1963). All three ably retain the Celtic flavor, but none equals the poetic imagery of Ella Young's *Tangle-coated Horse* (New York: David McKay Co., 1968), which is nearest to the original Irish sources. Many readers will prefer the more straightforward Sutcliff version. Ages 11–13.

Sutcliff, Rosemary. *The Hound of Ulster.* Illustrated by Victor Ambrus. New York: E. P. Dutton & Co., 1963.

The exploits of Cuchulain from his early boyhood to the death brought on him by evil magic are retold in strong, poetic prose that conveys the beauty, heroism, and tragedy of the epic Champion of All the Heroes of Ireland. Like Achilles, he died young but he won enduring fame; like Rustem, he unwittingly slew his only son in combat; and like Iseult, beloved of Tristram, Eimer his beloved died beside him. Folklorist Rosemary Sutcliff has made an outstanding contribution to the literature of the hero tale. An A.L.A. Notable Book. Ages 12–14.

Tashjian, Virginia. *Once There Was and Was Not.* Illustrated by Nonny Hogrogrian. Boston: Little, Brown and Co., 1966.

Seven Armenian folktales with universal themes—kindness rewarded, stupidity mistaken for wisdom, evil thwarted, and greediness punished—based on the stories of folklorist Hovhannes Tounanian. The colorful Armenian setting is perfectly reflected in the watercolor illustrations with their folk art flavor. An A.L.A. Notable Book. Ages 9–10.

Titus, Eve. *The Two Stonecutters.* Illustrated by Yoko Mitsuhashi. New York: Doubleday & Co., 1967.

Two brothers assist an old crone who turns into a supernatural being, the Goddess of the Forest. As a reward she offers them seven wishes. The younger brother, content with his lot, keeps only one. The elder brother, seeking happiness through power, changes from rich man to prince, to wind, to the sun, to cloud, and finally to a stone with his last wish. It is the unselfish younger brother who rescues him. Similar in theme to the Grimms' tale "The Fisherman and His Wife." Stylized pictures in muted colors reflect the Japanese setting. Ages 5–9.

Treece, Henry. *The Burning of Njal.* Illustrated by Bernard Blatch. New York: Criterion Books, 1964.

A retelling of the renowned medieval Icelandic epic, *Njal's Saga.* A story of feuds and revenge reflecting the rude code of justice of eleventh century Iceland. Old, wise, peaceloving Njal's friendship with the brave warrior Gunnar leads to a blood feud that results in the death of Gunnar, Njal, and all his family. Only Kari, Njal's son-in-law, remains to carry on the feud and avenge his father-in-law's death. The author succeeds superbly in catching the strength and stark beauty of the saga. His affinity for the Northman is apparent here as well as in his excellent Viking stories: *Horned Helmet* (New York: Criterion Books, 1963), *Viking's Dawn* (New York: S. G. Phillips, 1956), *The Road to Miklagard* (New York: S. G. Phillips, 1957), *Viking's Sunset* (New York: Criterion Books, 1961) and others. Ages 12–17.

Untermeyer, Louis, editor. *Aesop's Fables*. Illustrated by A. and M. Provensen. New York: Golden Press, 1965.

Forty fables selected and adapted by Louis Untermeyer appear in an oversize book with a trim, concise text and original illustrations. The fifteen double-page color spreads invite browsing, though their cartoon-like captions may be too light and amusing for purists accustomed to a less dashing approach. The didactic core of the fables is still present, but the humor has never been so apparent as it is in this outstanding version. Children will take it to their hearts. Ages 6–9.

Vo-Dinh. *The Toad Is the Emperor's Uncle: Animal Folktales from Viet-Nam*. Illustrated by the author. New York: Doubleday & Co., 1970.

Eighteen sharp, lively folktales that reflect the influence of Buddhism, Confucianism, and Taoism on the Vietnamese character. We learn how the toad won the right to be called "uncle," a respectful form of address, by the Emperor, and how he summons rain from heaven by his croaking. Elsewhere, a usurer is outwitted by a peasant boy, and in "The Fourth Leg of the Dog" the reason why the dog lifts his leg is not at all the one a Western reader might expect. There is extensive information on the background and significance of the stories. Vigorous ink drawings accompany the text. Gail B. Graham's *The Beggar in the Blanket and Other Vietnamese Tales* (New York: Dial Press, 1970) is shorter—only eight selections. It deals with romance, patience in adversity, and a Vietnamese Cinderella who wins love by her cooking ability. Pleasing, delicate, black and white drawings catch the exotic background of the tales. Ages 10–12.

Whitney, Thomas, translator. *The Story of Prince Ivan, the Firebird, and the Gray Wolf*. Illustrated by Nonny Hogrogian. New York: Charles Scribner's, 1968.

Three brothers go in search of the Firebird at their father's request. The youngest, Prince Ivan, receives aid from a gray wolf, captures the Firebird, and wins a beautiful princess for his wife. A classic Russian fairytale with language retaining the oral folktale shadowy, not-quite-real, old Russia. Ages 9–10.

essence. Soft toned water colors and simple linear drawings capture the aura of a

Fantasy   Andersen, Hans Christian. *The Little Match Girl*. Illustrated by Clair Lent. Boston: Houghton Mifflin Co., 1968.

The familiar, touching story of a freezing child who dares not go home because she has not sold any matches, starkly depicted in illustrations that convey the loneliness and chill of her surroundings, with towering grey buildings and driving snow. Even the warmth and comfort of the dying girl's visions are in muted tones. A distinguished visual interpretation. Ages 6–adult.

————. *The Nightingale*. Translated by Eva Le Gallienne. Illustrated by Nancy Burkert. New York: Harper & Row, Publishers, 1965.

Eva Le Gallienne's affinity for Andersen is apparent in this admirable translation of a favorite tale. In keeping with the Chinese setting, the double-page color illustrations glow with a quiet serenity reminiscent of a Chinese screen. Marginal decorations embellish the text and lead the eye from one picture to the next. An unusually beautiful book. An A.L.A. Notable Book. Ages 8–10.

Seven Tales (New York: Harper & Row, Publishers, 1959) include "The Fir Tree," "The Princess and the Pea," "The Ugly Duckling," "The Steadfast Tin Soldier," and three other Andersen tales translated by Eva Le Gallienne with illustrations by Maurice Sendak.

————. *The Snow Queen*. Translated by R. P. Keigwin. Illustrated by June Atkin Corwin. New York: Atheneum, 1968.

The classic tale of Gerda's search for her beloved friend Kay in the Snow Queen's country, newly illustrated by June Atkin Corwin, whose black and white drawings have an eerie, fantastic quality in keeping with the story. R. P. Keigwin's translation is memorable. Danish scholars consider him without peer in his ability to catch the grace, cheer, freshness, and simplicity of Andersen's language. Ages 9–11.

————. *Thumbelina*. Translated by R. P. Keigwin. Illustrated by Adrienne Adams. New York: Charles Scribner's, 1961.

One of Andersen's most popular tales. The diminutive heroine, born in a tulip bud, escapes an unwelcome marriage to become queen of the flowers. Adrienne Adams' exquisitely detailed pictures in soft bright colors follow the story so accurately that the book is ideal for picture book storytelling. Her illustrations for *The Ugly Duckling* (New York: Charles Scribner's, 1965) are equally good. Ages 6–10.

Alexander, Lloyd. *The Book of Three*. New York: Holt, Rinehart and Winston, 1964.

Dissatisfied with his role as Assistant Pig Keeper and longing to be a hero, young Taran joins the famous warrior Prince Gwydion of Prydain in his fight against the evil forces of Arawn Death-Lord. He acquires as companions the hairy, grotesque Gurgi, who is neither human nor animal, the minstrel Fflewddur Flam, whose harp strings break whenever he stretches the truth, and the tomboy princess Eilonwy, who rescues Taran from a dungeon. Inspired by Welsh mythology, Lloyd Alexander has created a mythical land and peopled it with memorable characters. An A.L.A. Notable Book. Ages 10–14.

In *The Black Cauldron* (New York: Holt, Rinehart and Winston, 1965) Taran destroys the monstrous vessel in which Arawn Death-Lord brings back the dead to a bleak and mute existence as slave warriors. An A.L.A. Notable Book. In *The Castle of Llyr* (New York: Holt, Rinehart, and Winston, 1966) the trio rescue Eilonwy from an enchantress. An A.L.A. Notable Book. In *Taran Wanderer* (New York: Holt, Rinehart and Winston, 1967) he learns to accept the fact that whatever his parentage may be, it is unimportant compared with knowing himself and his capabilities.

————. *The High King*. New York: Holt, Rinehart and Winston. 1969.

In the fifth and last book of The Chronicles of Prydain, Taran and his companions take part in the final struggle between good and evil under the banner of Prince Gwydion. The Death-Lord and his creatures are vanquished, and Taran is offered everlasting youth and joy with the lovely princess Eilonwy in an enchanted realm where there is no death. Though sorely tempted, he chooses to remain in Prydain and help its people. His decision brings him the position and burden of the High Kingship. Through the entire series courage and self-sacrifice give depth to the adventures, while humor and nonsense are provided by Fflewddur Flam, the fiercely loyal Gurgi, and others. An A.L.A. Notable Book. Newbery Award 1969. Ages 10–14.

————. *The Marvelous Adventures of Sebastian*. New York: E. P. Dutton & Co., 1970.

A naive young fiddler loses his position in a baronial household and sets out to find a new one. He becomes involved in a series of dangerous exploits, among them rescuing a spirited princess, whose language is extremely formal, from a hateful marriage. He aids a rebellion against the obnoxious and tyrannical Regent and acquires a strange fiddle that produces music of unearthly power and beauty. The picaresque tale is set in an imaginary eighteenth-century principality; the author's style reflects the era in its mannered elegance, enlivened with wit and irony, and a touch of caricature in the characterizations. An A.L.A. Notable Book. Ages 10–12.

Babbitt, Natalie. *Kneeknock Rise*. Illustrated by Natalie Babbitt. New York: Farrar, Straus & Giroux, 1970.

The villagers of Instep take shivery pride in their proximity to Kneeknock Rise, a high hill on whose summit lives the dreadful Megrimum. This unseen but fearsome creature's moans on stormy nights make the Instepians shudder deliciously. When a visiting lad, Egan, climbs the hill and discovers the natural cause of the sounds, his hopes of being hailed as a hero are dashed by the town's refusal to give up its belief in the Megrimum. An unusual story with folk tale flavor, satiric wit, and piquant imagery. Newbery Award runner-up. Ages 9–11.

————. *The Search for Delicious*. New York: Farrar, Straus & Giroux, 1969.

Young Gaylen, the king's messenger, set out to poll the kingdom. A definition for "delicious" is needed for the new dictionary, but no two people can agree on one, and civil war seems imminent. It is only through Ardis, a lonely mermaid, that a satisfactory definition is found and war averted. Humor, suspense, and a perceptive look at human foibles blend into a light-hearted but sensitive tale. Ages 9–13.

Bomans, Godfried. *The Wily Wizard and the Wicked Witch*. Illustrated by Robert Bartlet. New York: Franklin Watts, 1969.

A most unusual collection of tales. All the familiar ingredients of folklore—witches, wizards, dragons, and spells—are mingled in a potpourri of the unconventional, the wry, the unexpected, the humorous, and the touching. The witch in the title story is safe from the law because she tells her victims exactly what she means to do to them, and when they enter her house willingly because they think she is joking, the mayor is powerless. Death grants "The King Who Did Not Want to Die" his dearest wish—to see his mother—in the only way possible. When the lost children in "The Toys" escape the wicked witch and return home, there is a sentence reminiscent of Andersen: "And the father filled his pipe, which he was not usually allowed to do because it made the curtains black." Lovers of the traditional fairytale may look askance at first at Bomans' treatment of familiar folk tale themes. But his originality and vitality have no counterpart, except perhaps in James Thurber. Ages 11–adult.

Boston, Lucy. *An Enemy at Green Knowe*. Illustrated by Peter Boston. New York: Harcourt Brace Jovanovich, 1964.

Mrs. Oldknow tells her grandson Tolly and his Chinese friend Ping about a mad alchemist who lived at Green Knowe in 1630 and came to a mysterious end. Then an oddly unattractive woman, Miss Melanie D. Powers, calls on Mrs. Oldknow, seeking the alchemist's books. The boys and the old lady find themselves fighting an evil and malignant adversary who plagues Green Knowe with maggots, bird-killing cats, vipers, and finally a dreadful phantom hand. The harmonious atmosphere of the other Green Knowe books, *The Children of Green Knowe* (New York: Harcourt Brace Jovanovich, 1954) and *Treasure of Green Knowe* (New York: Harcourt Brace Jovanovich, 1958) is altered and dominated by conflict in this title. Even the imperturbable Mrs. Oldknow almost concedes defeat. Only the boys' discovery of the sinister Miss Powers' true name ends the siege. Neither a caricature nor a fairy tale witch, Melanie D. Powers is a chilling portrait of evil, throwing into bright contrast the goodness and wisdom of Mrs. Oldknow and the sturdy innocence of the boys. A thoroughly eerie, engrossing, and suspenseful tale. Ages 10–11.

Butterworth, Oliver. *The Enormous Egg*. Illustrated by Louis Darling. Boston: Little, Brown and Co., 1956.

When one of the Twitchell hens laid an enormous, leathery egg, Nate Twitchell had to turn it for her every few hours. To everyone's surprise and amazement, a Triceratops hatched out. Nate's unique pet grew so large he finally gave it to the National Zoological Park in Washington, D.C. Here, "Uncle Beazley" became a national issue when an economy-minded senator wished to save the taxpayers the expense of feeding a useless creature like a dinosaur. An utterly fantastic tale told with deadpan seriousness. Ages 10–11.

Cameron, Eleanor. *The Wonderful Flight to the Mushroom Planet*. Illustrated by Robert Henneberger. Boston: Little, Brown and Co., 1954.

A newspaper want ad asking for one or two boys to construct a space ship out of materials at hand, without adult help, sends David Topman and his friend Chuck Masterson to meet the mysterious Mr. Tyco Bass, inventor, astronomer, and artist. A voyage through space to the planet Basidium follows. Scientific fact skilfully combined with fantasy and fiction. Ages 9–11.

There are four popular sequels: *Stowaway to the Mushroom Planet* (Boston: Little, Brown and Co., 1956), *Mr. Bass's Planetoid* (Boston: Little, Brown and Co., 1958), *Mystery for Mr. Bass* (Boston: Little, Brown and Co., 1960), and *Time and Mr. Bass* (Boston: Little, Brown and Co., 1967).

Christopher, John. *The White Mountains*. New York: Macmillan Co., 1967.

This is earth of the future, dominated by mysterious entities called Tripods, who keep mankind under control by implanting steel caps in the skulls of all 14-year-olds, who then become obedient and docile. To escape the capping, Will, Henry, and Beanpole decide to flee to the white mountains, called Switzerland by the "ancients," where a colony of free men live. Before they reach their goal, they encounter hunger, fear, pursuit by the Tripods, and, hardest to resist, temptation to give in to the safe but mindless life of the capped. Ages 11–14.

The sequels carry on the nightmarish adventures of the trio. In *The City of Gold and Lead* (New York: Macmillan Co., 1967), Will and Henry enter the domed city of the Tripods to learn what their enemies are like and how to combat them. In *The Pool of Fire* (New York: Macmillan Co., 1968), the Tripods are vanquished just as they are about to exterminate all earth life. A chilling and absorbing trilogy by an author who also writes for adults.

Cleary, Beverly. *The Mouse and the Motorcycle*. Illustrated by Louis Darling. New York: William Morrow & Co., 1965.
Ralph, a young mouse living behind the baseboard of Room 215 in The Mountain View Inn, is irresistibly drawn to a toy motorcycle belonging to one of the guests, a boy named Keith. Appreciating a fellow enthusiast, Keith shows Ralph how to ride the motorcycle and Ralph Mouse, speed demon, is born. A delightful humorous fantasy. An A.L.A. Notable Book. Ages 8–9.
The sequel, *Runaway Ralph* (New York: William Morrow & Co., 1970), sees Ralph cycling off to summer camp, where he learns to appreciate the home he left behind him.

Curry, Jane Louise. *The Change-Child*. Illustrated by Gareth Floyd. New York: Harcourt Brace Jovanovich, 1969.
Lame, sensitive, poetic Eilian is called a fairy changeling by the country folk because her fair coloring is so unlike that of her parents. To escape an unwelcome bridegroom she is sent to stay with her grandmother's people in the Dark Wood, and there she meets the Fair Folk, one of whom chooses mortality for love of her. A fantasy set in seventeenth-century Wales. Smells, colors, sounds, tastes are evoked by skilful writing, and the use of Welsh words throughout adds to the "faery" quality of the story. An A.L.A. Notable Book. Ages 10–12.

Dahl, Roald. *Charlie and the Chocolate Factory*. Illustrated by Joseph Schindelman. New York: Alfred A. Knopf, 1964.
A contest, with a candy factory as the prize. Among the contestants are a gluttonous boy, a spoiled girl, a vulgar, gum-chewing girl, a boy addicted to TV, and poor but honest Charlie. Their progression through the factory becomes a process of elimination for the four nasty youngsters, who bring upon themselves well-deserved and suitable fates, leaving our humble, obedient hero to inherit the prize. A highly humorous moral tale with characters exaggerated to the point of caricature. Ages 9–11.

Du Bois, William Pene. *The Alligator Case*. Illustrated by the author. New York: Harper & Row, Publishers, 1965.
Three thieves using a small-town circus as cover for their nefarious activities are shadowed and brought to justice by a boy detective, who employs various disguises—one of them an alligator suit—to track down the villainous trio. The humor is lively and articulate with bright and equally lively illustrations. Ages 9–11.

Eager, Edward. *Half Magic*. Illustrated by N. B. Bodecker. New York: Harcourt Brace Jovanovich, 1954.
When four children find a talisman that looks like a nickel but is not, strange things begin to happen. Their wishes come true, but only half true. Jane, in boredom, wishes for a fire and a spoiled girl's playhouse burns down. Martha wishes that Carrie the cat could talk, but the resulting gibberish is only half intelligible. As one surprising and amusing adventure follows another, the children learn how to adjust their wishes to get the desired results. Ages 9–11.
The author, influenced by the Nesbit books, and cheerfully admitting it, has followed *Half Magic* with *Knight's Castle* (1956), *Magic by the Lake* (1957), *Magic or Not* (1959), *The Well Wishers* (1960), and *Seven Day Magic* (1962), all published in New York by Harcourt Brace Jovanovich. Though the sequels vary in quality as the author's power of invention flags, they are popular and may lead the reader to the rich vein of

Victorian fantasy in Edith Nesbit's *Five Children and It* (New York: Random House, 1959), *The Phoenix and the Carpet* (New York: Random House, 1960), *The Story of the Amulet* (New York: Random House, 1960), and *The Enchanted Castle* (New York: E. P. Dutton & Co., 1964).

Enghdahl, Sylvia L. *Enchantress from the Stars*. Illustrated by Rodney Shackell. New York: Atheneum, 1970.

The people of the planet Andrecia, whose culture is primitive, are terrified by a large dragon that is ravaging their land. Their king has offered a great reward to the man who can slay the creature, and young Georyn is approached by an "enchantress from the stars" who urges him to try. Three worlds at different levels of advancement are represented in this intriguing science fantasy. Georyn's world, the most primitive, is threatened by another whose people have mastered space travel and consider "inferior" worlds fair prey; if necessary they will exterminate the people of Andrecia. Georyn's "dragon" is one of their bulldozers. The heroine Elana's culture is far more advanced. She is a member of the Anthropological Service of the Federation of Planets; with her father and betrothed she has been sent to Andrecia to save it without letting either the Andrecians or the invaders learn that the Federation exists. Nor must the natural cultural progression of either people be interfered with. Told from the viewpoints of Elana, the "enchantress from the stars," Georyn, and Jarel, a medic with the invaders, the three interwoven narratives build up slowly but strongly to a suspenseful and exciting finale. Newbery Award runner-up. Ages 12–16.

Heroines of science fiction and fantasy are rare. Similar in plot but less complex is Andre Norton's *Ice Crown* (New York: Viking Press, 1970), whose protagonist is a girl. Other girl-dominated science fiction novels are Sylvia Engdahl's *Journey between Worlds* (New York: Atheneum, 1970), Madeleine L'Engle's *Wrinkle in Time* (New York: Farrar, Straus & Giroux, 1962), and Robert Heinlein's *Podkayne of Mars* (New York: G. P. Putnam's, 1963).

Enright, Elizabeth. *Tatsinda*. Illustrated by Irene Haas. New York: Harcourt Brace Jovanovich, 1963.

In the mountain kingdom of Tatrajan all the people have "glittering white hair" and cool, ice-blue eyes—all except the foundling Tatsinda, who is golden-haired and brown-eyed. This makes her an object of pity to most of the Tatrajanni, but the king's youngest son falls in love with her. When an invading giant captures Tatsinda, the prince rides to her rescue. The careful descriptions of the Tatrjanni, their homes, their customs, their animals—all of whose names begin with "ta"—give depth to this charming fairy tale, and the glowing pictures by Irene Haas perfectly complement the text. 1963 Spring Book Festival Honor Book. Ages 9–11.

Farmer, Penelope. *The Summer Birds*. Illustrated by James J. Spanfeller. New York: Harcourt Brace Jovanovich, 1962.

Life in a staid English village becomes filled with adventure when a strange, Peter Pan-like boy teaches two sisters, Emma and Charlotte, and their classmates to fly. Not until the end of the summer does the boy disclose his true identity and his fantastic mission. The highly descriptive writing creates a remarkable feeling for the ecstasy of flight and the haunting atmosphere of strangeness that surrounds the boy. The sequels, *Emma in Winter* (New York: Harcourt Brace Jovanovich, 1966), and *Charlotte Sometimes* (New York: Harcourt Brace Jovanovich, 1969), are equally imaginative. Ages 9–10.

Fleming, Ian. *Chitty-Chitty-Bang-Bang*. Illustrated by John Burningham. New York: Random House, 1964.

To the stolid, sensible, practical, "life is real and life is earnest" person, a car is only a machine. To the Potts family, a car was something special and their car, rescued from the scrap heap, was as super-special as her license plate, GEN II, indicated. She flew her way out of bumper-to-bumper traffic, became a hovercraft to rescue her owners from a rising tide, and foiled the dastardly plans of Joe the Monster and his gang. Described with an enthusiasm that carries the reader over the occasional didactic asides, Chitty-Chitty-Bang-Bang is a car any family would be privileged to own. Most readers will devour the book in one sitting. An A.L.A. Notable Book. Ages 10–12.

Garner, Alan. *The Owl Service*. New York: Henry Z. Walck, 1968.

Teen-ager Alison, her step-brother Roger, and Gwyn, a Welsh boy, are caught up in a reenactment of an ancient Welsh legend. The story of the flower-maiden Blodeuwedd, who became an owl when her infidelity brought death to her husband and her lover, springs into new life when Alison and Gwyn find the "owl service," a set of supernatural dishes. A complex, errie story whose blend of realism and fantasy will prove obscure and baffling to some readers and deeply engrossing to others. Winner of the English Carnegie Medal in 1967. An A.L.A. Notable Book. Ages 11–13.

Goudge, Elizabeth. *The Little White Horse*. Illustrated by C. Walter Hodges. New York: Coward-McCann, 1947.

Orphaned Maria Merryweather travels to her cousin's home in the West Country of England, where she finds herself entangled in a feud. With the help of Wrolf—dog or lion?—Robin the shepherd boy, and the little white horse—a unicorn elusive as moonlight—she heals the breach between the Merryweathers and the Black Men. Fantasy and reality blend in wonderfully descriptive writing with clear, vivid characterizations of humans and animals alike. Winner of the Carnegie Medal. Ages 10–12.

Harris, Rosemary. *The Moon in the Cloud*. New York: Macmillan Co., 1970.

To win passage on Noah's ark for himself and his beloved wife, Reuben, an animal tamer and musician, sets out to find a pair of lions and a cat to make up Noah's quota. Accompanied by his pet cat, dog, and camel, he journeys to Egypt, where he is captured and imprisoned. To nobody's surprise, he wins his freedom and fulfills his mission. The writing is sprightly with humorous overtones, and the characterization is excellent. Cefalu, Reuben's cat, given to caustic comment, is outstanding. An irresistible fantasy combining Egyptian myth and history with Biblical elements. Winner of the 1969 Carnegie Medal. An A.L.A. Notable Book. Ages 10–14.

The sequel, *Shadow of the Sun* (New York: Macmillan Co., 1970), brings Reuben and his wife and pets to Egypt after the flood but, like many sequels, is not quite as effortless as its predecessor.

Heinlein, Robert. *Red Planet*. New York: Charles Scribner's, 1949.

Jim Marlowe and Frank Sutton, teen-age colonists on Mars, have a series of incredible adventures on their two-thousand-mile, runaway trek from school back to the earth colony at Mars' equator. Their flight is triggered by Willis, a Martian roundhead, who is Jim's pet. Willis, who resembles a fur-covered basketball with retractable features, is capable of reproducing anything he hears. His playback of a nefarious conversation between the school's headmaster and a company bigwig sends Jim and Frank on their mad dash for home to insure the safety of the colonists and end Earth's domination. Robert Heinlein's science fiction is based on the most accurate scientific data available. His speculations, rooted in realism, are both convincing and suspenseful. Ages 12–adult.

An outstanding author in the genre, Heinlein has also written: *Space Cadet* (New York: Charles Scribner's, 1948), *The Star Beast* (New York: Charles Scribner's, 1954), *Podkayne of Mars* (New York: G. P. Putnam's, 1963), *Have Space Suit, Will Travel* (New York: Charles Scribner's, 1958), and many other books.

Horwitz, Elinor Lander. *The Strange Story of the Frog Who Became a Prince*. Illustrated by John Heinly. New York: Delacorte Press, 1971.

A handsome frog living contentedly in a pond encounters a skin-diving witch who changes him into a prince. Much distressed, he begs her to reverse the spell, but she has forgotten how. "Anyone would rather be a prince than a frog," she insists. The prince-who-was-a-frog keeps pleading with her, and so she tries to please him. From prince to princess to centaur to merman he goes before he finally regains his true form. An entertaining switch on Grimm's *Frog Prince*. Sophisticated black and white line drawings point up the humor of the tale. Ages 5–7.

Jarrell, Randall. *The Animal Family*. Illustrated by Maurice Sendak. New York: Pantheon Books, 1965.
A hunter, alone and lonely on an uninhabited coast, finds himself a family consisting of a mermaid, a bear cub, a lynx kitten, and finally a boy. The writing is poetic and tender, full of imagery that glows. The concept of interdependence and family closeness is made clear, though the family's members are startlingly diverse. A unique allegory fittingly embellished with Maurice Sendak's decorative landscape drawings. Newbery Award runner-up. Ages 9–adult.

Juster, Norton. *The Phantom Tollbooth*. Illustrated by Jules Feiffer. New York: Random House, 1961.
An amazing and amusing set of fantastic adventures begin when lazy Milo enters a fantastic world through the Phantom Tollbooth. With Tock, a watchdog who ticks, he is sent on a quest for the lost princesses, Rhyme and Reason. The story is full of plays on words and liberally sprinkled with puns. Pen and ink sketches complement the humor of the text. Ages 10–14.

Key, Alexander. *Escape to Witch Mountain*. Illustrated by Leon B. Wisdom, Jr. Philadelphia: Westminster Press, 1968.
Tony and his sister Tia, who is mute, cannot remember who they are or where they came from. Their strange abilities to communicate in ultrasonic speech, open locked doors without keys, and move objects without touching them place them in peril from sinister figures who wish to exploit their talents. A slender clue, a piecing together of vague memories, leads them in a desperate flight to a mountain community where others like themselves have found sanctuary. Here, as in *Forgotten Door* (Philadelphia: Westminster Press, 1965) , the author's ability to sustain a high degree of suspense, action, and characterization never flags. Ages 10–12.

Knight, Damon, editor. *Toward Infinity*. New York: Simon and Schuster, 1968.
A varied collection of nine suspenseful science fiction stories by well known authors in the genre. Outstanding among the selections are Ray Bradbury's "The Earth Men," in which the first men to reach Mars are clapped into an insane asylum because the Martians consider them crazy; Don Stuart's "Who Goes There," a classic tale of creeping horror in which an Arctic research team revives a perfectly preserved alien from outer space; and Wilmar Shiras' "In Hiding," a touching story of a lonely boy who must hide his intelligence from those around him. Ages 12–adult.
Other anthologies by Knight are *Worlds to Come* (New York: Harper & Row, Publishers, 1967) which includes "The Sentinel," a short story later expanded into *2001: A Space Odyssey*, and *Dimension X* (New York: Simon and Schuster, 1970) with the heartbreaking Asimov tale of "The Ugly Little Boy."

Lawson, John. *The Spring Rider*. New York: Thomas Y Crowell, 1968.
Steeped in tales of the battle fought long ago where his farm lies, Jacob encounters, without surprise, a soldier of the Union Army, whose bugle summons the dead of both sides to a tenuous, but tenacious, existence. Jacob and his sister Gary are enmeshed in that existence and drift farther and farther from reality until President Lincoln, the Spring Rider, comes to compel a separation. Plot lines are vague and elusive, but the mood is marvelously sustained in keeping with the action. Another unusual fantasy from the author of *You Better Come Home with Me*. Ages 11–14.

Le Guin, Ursula. *A Wizard of Earthsea*. Illustrated by Ruth Robbins. Berkeley: Parnassus Press, 1968.

In Earthsea, a world of many islands, a gifted boy becomes a student of magic. While studying at the Wizards' School, Ged is taunted by a jealous rival and misuses his power: inadvertently he calls up a dreadful, malignant shadow that threatens his life and the world of Earthsea. Fleeing the shadow from island to island, Ged finally turns on it and destroys it in a dramatic confrontation. The setting of Earthsea is drawn with realistic detail and lends conviction to a world where wizards have place and power and magic is natural. A superb fantasy dealing with man's essential nature, this book may be read as an unusual allegory or simply as a tale of an exciting quest. Ages 11–13.

L'Engle, Madeleine. *A Wrinkle in Time*. New York: Farrar, Straus & Giroux, 1962.

Meg Murray, her younger brother Charles Wallace, and Calvin, an older boy, set out on a dangerous search for Meg's father, a missing scientist. With the help of three entities from outer space, they travel by means of a "tesseract" or "wrinkle in time" to the dark planet of Camazotz, where Meg's father is a prisoner of the monstrous "It," a disembodied brain. The theme is an old one—good versus evil, love against hate. But although there are overtones of C. S. Lewis, H. G. Wells, and George Orwell, *Wrinkle in Time* emerges as a fresh story, and one that is impossible to put down. Monster fanciers will thoroughly enjoy the dreadful "It," who attempts to reduce all life to puppet-like subservience. Newberry Award 1963. Ages 12–14.

Lewis, C. S. *The Silver Chair*. Illustrated by Pauline Baynes. New York: Macmillan Co., 1953.

In the fourth book of the Narnia series, Aslan, the great lion, summons Eustace Scrubb of *The Voyage of the Dawn Treader* and a classmate, Jill Pole, into Narnia to search for the lost Prince Rillian. Accompanied by Puddleglum, a Marshwiggle, they find the prince after many strange adventures. Lewis's characters are, as always, memorable. But in the pessimistic Puddleglum, a tall, angular creature something like a man with frog and spider touches, he reaches new heights. The Marshwiggle's shrewd common sense saves the children time and again, and he voices the author's own view of reality in his defiant speech to the witch who has enchanted Prince Rillian. The entire Narnia series is outstanding fantasy to be read and enjoyed by readers who have progressed from Baum to Grahame and Tolkien. Ages 10–adult.

Lifton, Betty Jean. *The Dwarf Pine Tree*. Illustrated by Fuku Akino. New York: Atheneum, 1963.

A lovely Japanese princess is fading away of an unknown malady. Only a dwarf pine tree "as pure of heart as it is of beauty" can heal her. A tiny pine tree, scorned by the other trees in the forest, offers shelter to the goblin king Sojobo. Given a wish, he asks to be made into a dwarf tree to be given to the princess. Warned that he will suffer great pain in the process and live only six months after attaining his goal the little pine remains resolute and his wish is granted. Love, courage, and sacrifice win back the princess' health. Soft, dreamlike, imaginative illustrations, Japanese in style, accompany a gentle story with the flavor of a Japanese legend. Ages 9–10.

————. *The Many Lives of Chio and Goro*. Illustrated by Yasuro Sagawa. New York: W. W. Norton & Co., 1968.

Old farmer Goro and his wife Chio plan to become foxes in their next life, but absent-minded Chio forgets and becomes a chicken instead. When fox Goro raids the hen coop, Chio is in deadly peril, but Goro cannot bring himself to harm her and dies of shame. He has denied his vulpine instincts. Reborn as a rooster, he is united with Chio, and in a further rebirth they become human once more. The Japanese countryside is the background for this humorous introduction to the doctrine of the transmigration of souls. Ages 5–8.

Lindgren, Astrid. *Pippi Longstocking*. Illustrated by Louis S. Glanzman. New York: Viking Press, 1950.

Pippi Longstocking has the life every child dreams of. She lives alone with no parents to tell her what to do; her companions are a monkey and a horse. Pippi has a lively imagination, and having spent most of her life at sea rather than in polite society, is completely uninhibited in carrying out her outlandish whims. Furthermore, she is the strongest child in the world. If someone tries to stop her, she merely picks him up and sets him in a tree until he is ready to behave. Her two little neighbors, Tommy and Annika, are awed, shocked, and delighted to see her poke fun at the solemn adult world and get away with it. The unpredictable Pippi carries on in *Pippi Goes on Board* and *Pippi in the South Seas*. Ages 9–11.

Lovett, Margaret. *The Great and Terrible Quest*. New York: Holt, Rinehart and Winston, 1967.

Ten-year-old Trad befriends a wounded knight who has lost his memory. Escaping from his cruel grandfather, he joins the knight on a quest for the rightful heir of the dying king. Flight and pursuit, good versus evil, and suspense are the ingredients of this fantasy, where cryptic clues obscure Trad's true identity until the last page. Despite overmuch soliloquizing and dependence on coincidence, there is enough action to carry the reader on to the breathless, triumphant ending. Ages 10–12.

MacGregor, Ellen. *Miss Pickerell Goes to Mars*. Illustrated by Paul Galdone. New York: McGraw-Hill Book Co., 1951.

An elderly spinster finds a rocket ship in her cow pasture. Indignantly she orders its crew to take it away, and they do—with her in it. Adapting rapidly to outer space, the spunky Miss Pickerell shows a remarkable ability to cope with unusual situations, rescues a crewman on Mars, and returns to earth a heroine. Ages 9–10.

Other titles in this series are *Miss Pickerell Goes Undersea* (New York: McGraw-Hill Book Co., 1953), *Miss Pickerell and the Geiger Counter* (New York: McGraw-Hill Book Co., 1953), and *Miss Pickerell Goes to the Arctic* (New York: McGraw-Hill Book Co., 1954). Contagious fun, unusual adventures, and adroitly integrated scientific information make these books popular with reluctant readers and science fiction fans alike.

Mayne, William. *Earthfasts*. New York: E. P. Dutton & Co., 1967.

An eighteenth-century drummer boy emerging from a crack in the earth into present-day England sets off a series of strange and terrifying events which end only when the inextinguishable candle he has left behind is restored to its proper place in King Arthur's hall. After a slow beginning this becomes a gripping, spine-tingling tale of time out of joint. An A.L.A. Notable Book. Ages 11–14.

There is another excursion through time in Mayne's *The Hill Road* (New York: E. P. Dutton & Co., 1969), when two young people from Roman Britain exchange places with three modern English children. Very skilfully done, but without the impact of *Earthfasts*.

Nichols, Ruth. *A Walk Out of the World*. Illustrated by Trina Schart Hyman. New York: Harcourt Brace Jovanovich, 1969.

Judith and Tobit, brother and sister, follow a light into the magical world once reigned over by their ancestors but now ruled by the harsh and hated usurper Hagerrak. To overthrow Hagerrak and restore the house of the true king becomes Judith and Tobit's goal. The age-old theme of good versus evil is always gripping when handled with conviction and skill. The author, eighteen at the time, has written an engrossing and credible fantasy. The style is smooth, the imagery beautiful, the action peopled with unusual beings—the centuries-old but lovely Lady Iorwen, the glimmering Water Folk, vicious gray Kobalds, and cats with glass claws. To be read along with C. S. Lewis, Lloyd Alexander, and J. R. R. Tolkien. An A.L.A. Notable Book. Ages 10–11.

Norton, Andre. *The Zero Stone*. New York: Viking Press, 1968.

Searching for the origin of the mysterious and alien stone left him by his father. Murdoc Jern finds himself hunted by both the powerful Thieves Guild and the Patrol. His only friend is a feline mutant, Eet, who is gifted with ESP. Brought to bay on a remote planet, they make their final bid for life and freedom. A prolific writer in the science fiction field, Andre Norton displays a certain repetitiveness: the intelligent animal mutant is one of his favorite characters. But however familiar in plot and action, his work is never dull. His skill in writing credible, engrossing fantasy is unsurpassed. Ages 12–adult.

Norton, Mary. *The Borrowers Aloft*. Illustrated by Beth and Joe Krush. New York: Harcourt Brace Jovanovich, 1961.
The fourth in the ingenious series about a tiny family whose adventures lead them from their home under a clock to the world outdoors, where they are carried off in a spring freshet. The first three, also published in New York by Harcourt Brace Jovanovich, are: *The Borrowers* (1953), *The Borrowers Afield* (1955), *and The Borrowers Afloat* (1959). This time they must take to the air to escape imprisonment in an attic, where a mercenary "human bean" plans to build a glass house to exhibit them in. The characterization remains excellent, and the tiny people's survival techniques in the world of the huge—always a fascinating subject—are described once more in realistic detail. Ages 10–12.

Nye, Robert. *Taliesin*. Illustrated by Dorothy Maas. New York: Hill & Wang, 1967.
Gwion, a peasant boy, is forced to stir the magic cauldron of the witch Caridwen. When he accidentally drinks the three drops of inspiration, he becomes a master poet and magician. Pursued by Caridwen, he shifts from form to form to escape her. As a grain of wheat, he is swallowed by the witch and is reborn as Taliesin (Radiant Brow). Though Taliesin the Welsh bard really lived, his life has been obscured by legend. Nye invests the legend with humor, and his portrait of Taliesin has the power of true poetry. Ages 10–11.

O'Brien, Robert. *Mrs. Frisby and the Rats of NIMH*. Illustrated by Zena Berstein. New York: Atheneum, 1971.
Mrs. Frisby, a widowed fieldmouse, is worried: her son Timothy is ill. In desperation she seeks the owl's advice; he sends her to the rats of NIMH for help. Escapees from the National Institute of Mental Health, where various injections have made them long-lived, inventive, and literate, the rats aid Mrs. Frisby. Later she is able to warn them that the farm family is planning to exterminate them. The rats move away to form a colony far from civilization where they can live without fear. Earnest, industrious, loyal, courageous, and trustworthy, they are certain to succeed. Well written, with excellent characterization throughout. Ages 9–11.

Orgel, Doris, and R. E. Raspe, *Baron Munchausen: Fifteen Truly Tall Tales*. Illustrated by Willi Baum. Cambridge, Mass.: Addison-Wesley Publishing Co., 1971.
An affadavit signed by such notable personages as Gulliver, Sinbad, and Aladdin attests to the truth of the adventures recounted by Baron Munchausen, a narrator "admired as much for my modesty and truthfulness as for my feats of bravery." A series of hilarious extravaganzas follows. The Baron visits the moon by climbing a Turkish bean stalk, flies around the world on an eagle's back, and, anticipating Jules Verne, goes down a volcano (Mt. Etna) to the center of the earth, emerging in the South Seas. Retold with an exuberance that is matched by the vivid illustrations. Ages 7–adult.

Ormondroyd, Edward. *Broderick*. Illustrated by John Larrecq. Berkeley: Parnassus Press, 1969.
Inspired by library books detailing the exploits of famous mice, though regrettably guilty of chewing them, Broderick takes up surfing at his lakeside home. Intent on be-

coming the first and foremost surfing mouse, he is able, in time to hang eleven by using his tail. He travels to the ocean, escapes from a seagull, and is retrieved by a boy surfer. They team up for worldwide surfing exhibitions, and Broderick retires a celebrity and an inspiration to other young mice. Irresistible whimsy buoyantly illustrated in soft colors. A bibliography (Broderick's reading list) is included. Ages 4–8.

Selden, George. *Tucker's Countryside*. Illustrated by Garth Williams. New York: Farrar, Straus & Giroux, 1969.

Tucker Mouse and Harry Cat receive an urgent summons from Chester Cricket to join him in the country. There they find the local animals in despair over a projected housing development that will ruin their meadow. The city pair, with the unwitting aid of several humans, finds a masterly solution to their problem. This book resembles *Rabbit Hill* (New York: Viking Press, 1944) in its depiction of the countryside and the small creatures that live in it. Pompous, excitable, clever Tucker; tough, resourceful Harry, who temporarily abandons his independence for life as pampered pet, and conscientious, earnest Chester are a memorable trio. Their personalities shine forth in the text and in the wonderfully expressive illustrations. A worthy sequel to *The Cricket in Times Square* (New York: Farrar, Straus & Giroux, 1960). Ages 9–11.

Sharp, Marjorie. *The Rescuers*. Illustrated by Garth Williams. Boston: Little, Brown and Co., 1959.

The Prisoners' Aid Society—an organization of mice—seeks volunteers for a dangerous mission to rescue an imprisoned Norwegian poet. It finds them in humble but hard-working Bernard Nils, a rough sailor whose knowledge of Norwegian is indispensable to the rescue, and the delicately nurtured white mouse, Miss Bianca. The latter abandons her luxurious life as the pampered pet of the ambassador's son to help in the venture. The story is imbued with humor and a delicate satire adults will find irresistible. ("There is nothing like breeding to give one confidence: she was descended in direct line from the senior of the Three Blind Mice.") Children and adults alike will enjoy the humor, pace and, above all, the characterizations of the protagonists—as distinctive and individual as Kenneth Grahame's immortal "people in fur." Garth Williams' illustrations are matchless! Ages 9–adult.

The sequels, also published in New York by Little, Brown and Co.—*Miss Bianca* (1962), *The Turret* (1963), and *Miss Bianca in the Salt Mines* (1966)—are equally beguiling and retain the Williams artistry. *Miss Bianca in the Orient* (1970), alas, does not. Erik Blegvad's imitation Williams is imitation.

Smith, Dodie. *The Hundred and One Dalmations*. Illustrated by Janet and Anne Grahame-Johnstone. New York: Viking Press, 1957.

An English fantasy about a pair of Dalmatians, Pongo and Missis, whose fifteen puppies, dognapped by the sinister Cruella DeVil, are fated to be made into fur coats along with eighty-two other Dalmations. By means of the "twilight barking" message relay, Pongo and Missis trace their puppies to Cruella's country house, rescue *all* the imprisoned dogs and bring them home to their human "pets," Mr. and Mrs. Dearly. In the course of events two more Dalmations, Perdita and Prince, join the others and one hundred and one Dalmations live happily ever after. Engrossing, humorous animal fantasy where the animals speak to each other but never to humans. Ages 10–13.

In the sequel, *The Starlight Barking* (New York: Simon and Schuster, 1968), Sirius, Lord of the Dog Star, invites the Dalmations to live in his realm.

Snyder, Zilpha. *Eyes in the Fishbowl*. Illustrated by Alton Raible. New York: Atheneum, 1968.

The elegance and order of a luxurious department store were 14-year-old Dion James' refuge from the clutter and insecurity of home life with an improvident, though charming and talented, father. When a series of eerie events finally cause the store to close, Dion learns that he has unknowingly been the medium through which the spirits of children whose lives were shattered by war relive their lost childhood in this store's glamorous confines. A completely believable blend of reality and fantasy. The characterizations are superb. Ages 10–12.

Stahl, Ben. *Blackbeard's Ghost*. Illustrated by Ben Stahl. Boston: Houghton Mifflin Co., 1965.
Two 14-year-old boys hold a seance, not at all expecting to make contact with the spirit world. But they do! The ghost of the infamous pirate Blackbeard arrives and is outraged to learn that his old Boar's Head Tavern is to be razed and replaced with a gas station. Visible only to the boys, Blackbeard launches a campaign of harassment to save the tavern. One inexplicable event follows another. In the end, a museum of pirate lore is established in the old building. The crude, grubby, harmlessly lecherous, belching, scratching pirate is the life of this well-written fast-paced tale. Ages 11–13.

Steele, Mary Q. *Journey Outside*. Illustrated by Rocco Negri. New York: Viking Press, 1969.
Weary of the endless search for the Better Place, Dilar, whose people live on rafts floating on an underground river, breaks away and discovers the outer world of light, space and freedom. He also encounters hunger, thirst, sunburn, and danger as he tries to find his way back to the caves to introduce his people to the outside world and all it has to offer. An absorbing study of a boy's growth and awakening maturity as he is forced into situations he has never dreamed of in his life. Newbery Award runner-up. Ages 10–11.

Stockton, Frank. *The Griffin and the Minor Canon*. Illustrated by Maurice Sendak. New York: Holt, Rinehart and Winston, 1963.
The people of a small town are terrified when the last of the griffins comes to look at his stone likeness over the church door. Only the canon is brave enough to make friends with the formidable creature. The self-centered townspeople exile the canon, thinking the griffin will follow him. But he stays—and carries on the canon's duties, teaching school and visiting the sick with remarkable results. Eventually the griffin carries off his image, and the canon returns to a position of prominence in the chastened town. There is subtle humor in this fanciful tale that all children may not fully appreciate, but the illustrations—some of the best that Maurice Sendak has ever done—are completely beguiling and complement the text to perfection. Ages 8–11.
Stockton's *The Bee-Man of Orn* (New York: Holt, Rinehart and Winston, 1964) and *Old Pipes and the Dryad* (New York: Franklin Watts, 1969) display the same fanciful, satirical humor couched in the fairy tale form. And the former has the additional advantage of more superb Sendak illustrations.

Tudor, Tasha, editor. *Take Joy!* Illustrated by the editor. Cleveland: World Publishing Co., 1966.
An appealing, attractive omnibus of Christmas material in which carols (each framed in a garland of holly), poems, legends, stories by authors from Dickens to Dylan Thomas, and mouth-watering recipes combine to form a family browsing book redolent of the spirit of the season. The section on the Tudors' own observance of Christmas concentrates on family traditions and homely, old-fashioned pleasures. The tender sentiment and old fashioned costumes in Tasha Tudor's many illustrations are particularly appropriate. A jewel for all ages.

Uttley, Alison. *A Traveler in Time*. Illustrated by Christine Price. New York: Viking Press, 1964.

Sent to visit the old manor house where one of her ancestors once served the Babington family, Penelope Cameron goes back in time to the reign of Elizabeth I. Unable to control her excursions back and forth, she becomes involved in Anthony Babington's plot to rescue Mary, Queen of Scots. Although achingly aware of the futility of the plot and the tragic end of the participants, she is unable to change what has been. A dreamlike work with strong characterizations. The author's deftness in handling the transitions between present and past lends conviction to the absorbing plot. Ages 11–13.

White, E. B. *The Trumpet of the Swan*. Illustrated by Edward Frascino. New York: Harper & Row, Publishers, 1970.

Louis, a trumpeter swan cygnet, is born voiceless; his parents consider him fearfully handicapped. Doomed to lifelong bachelorhood because he cannot make the proper sounds of courtship, Louis is helped by his father, who steals a trumpet for him. An intelligent swan (he has already learned to read and write), Louis soon becomes a proficient performer. The soul of honor, he uses his talent to earn enough money to pay for his instrument and then woos and wins the lovely Serena. The pathos of *Charlotte's Web* (New York: Harper & Row, Publishers, 1952) is lacking in this book, but it offers the same masterly blend of the real and the fantastic—a blend suffused with humor. A natural for reading aloud. Ages 8–11.

Williams, Jay. *The Practical Princess*. Illustrated by Friso Henstra. New York: Parents' Magazine Press, 1969.

Besides the conventional christening gifts of beauty and grace, Princess Bedelia is given common sense. When the expected fire-breathing dragon comes to eat her, Bedelia offers him a dummy royally attired but stuffed with straw and gunpowder. He explodes! Imprisoned in a tower, Bedelia discovers a sleeping prince, rouses him, and climbs down his beard to safety. Then, after a haircut and shave, they marry and live happily ever after. A humorous reversal of the traditional fairytale princess role. The illustrations— elaborately stylized Pop art with Victorian undertones—complement the anti-traditional story and may repel some readers. Most will find the book good fun. Ages 7–9.

————. *Stupid Marco*. Illustrated by Friso Henstra. New York: Parents' Magazine Press, 1970.

Amiable, attractive Prince Marco can whistle loudly through his fingers and has an infallible cure for hiccups, but he's not very bright. Unable to tell his right hand from his left, he takes the wrong turn when sent out to rescue a princess. He does encounter one, however, who joins him—and with her wit and his two talents all ends well. A light-hearted, brisk story that engagingly spoofs traditional folk tale motifs. The illustrations are both mod and oddly formal, with some of the sturdy humor of old-fashioned wooden toys. Ages 6–9.

Yolen, Jane. *Greyling: A Picture Story from the Islands of Shetland*. Illustrated by William Stobbs. Cleveland: World Publishing Co., 1968.

A grave and poignant story based on the haunting legend of the "selchies." A fisherman and his wife long vainly for a child. One day the husband finds an abandoned seal pup, wraps it in his shirt, and brings it home, where it turns out to be a grey-eyed baby boy. The "selchie" is raised with care and devotion but never permitted to enter the water until one day the fisherman is in danger of foundering in a stormy sea. He is rescued by the boy, now a youth, who then turns back into a seal. Stark illustrations in glowing colors capture the sweep of the sea and the dignity and aloofness of the island people. Ages 8–10.

Prose fiction   Almedingen, E. M. *Young Mark*. Illustrated by Victor Ambrus. New York: Farrar, Straus & Giroux, 1968.

From her great-great grandfather's journal the author has reconstructed his early life and arduous journey from the heart of the Ukraine to St. Petersburg, where he became a singer. Mark feared his harsh father, and when told he was to marry a shrewish girl he ran away. His beautiful voice, which could "charm pennies from a stone," earned him his bread during his two-year trek to the city. An indomitable boy's odyssey through eighteenth-century Russia, though slow-moving at first, offers a realistic picture of the times. The fairytale ending (which is true) comes when Mark sings for the Empress Elizabeth and joins the Emperial Chapel Choir. Explanatory notes and a glossary. An A.L.A. Notable Book. Ages 12–14.

Armer, Laura Adams. *Waterless Mountain*. Illustrated by the author and Sidney Armer. New York: Longmans, Green, 1931.

Steeped in the lore of his people, the Navajos, Younger Brother learns the songs of the medicine men and makes up his own. Deeply responsive to the religious beliefs of his tribe, he longs to follow the trail of the Turquoise Woman, a greatly revered Navajo deity, to her home in the wide water of the West. With the help of a kindly white trader he travels to California and for the first time in his life encounters the crowds, the confusion, and the noise of a large city. Thrown into a panic by his first movie, he almost forgets his quest, but before returning to his desert home, he sees the "great water" and the island of the Turquoise Woman. Long acquainted with the Navajo country, its myths, legends, and people, the author shares her insight and appreciation in this somewhat introspective but revealing book. Newbery Award, 1932. Ages 11–13.

Armstrong, William H. *Sounder*. Illustrated by James Barkley. New York: Harper & Row, Publishers, 1969.

A poor black sharecropper steals food for his hungry family. He is carried away in chains, and his dog Sounder loses an eye and is lamed in his defense. When his son takes a cake to him in jail, a prison guard wantonly plunges his hand into it, and "police brutality" becomes more than just an academic term. The boy fills the years of his father's absence learning to read, working, and thinking. Then one day Sounder scents his master returning, sheds his lameness, and races toward him, barking again after years of silence—a poignant climax. Based on an old Negro school teacher's own story, told to the author as a child, *Sounder* is written with an almost Biblical simplicity and restraint that leaves the reader shaken to the core. Newbery Award, 1970. Ages 11–adult.

Atwater, Richard and Florence. *Mr. Popper's Penguins*. Illustrated by Robert Lawson. Boston: Little, Brown and Co., 1938.

Though Mr. Popper, a mild little house painter, had never been outside the town of Stillwater, he was an authority on Arctic and Antarctic exploration, having avidly read everything he could find on the subject. The gift of a penguin from Admiral Drake, the famous Antarctic explorer, and the arrival of another from a zoo, changes the lives of the Popper family overnight. Nesting in the refrigerator, the penguins increase from two to 12. To support them Mr. Popper goes on stage, and Popper's Performing Penguins become a smash hit. The implausible plot is narrated in a serious style that heightens the humor. Newbery Award runner-up. A favorite funny book for ages 8–10.

Baker, Betty. *Walk the World's Rim*. New York: Harper & Row, Publishers, 1965.
Wanting to learn more of the ways of the white man, an Indian boy, Chakoh, joins Cabeza de Vaca and his companions to "walk the world's rim" to Mexico and back. The friendship that springs up between Chakoh and the Negro slave Esteban is threatened by Chakoh's feeling that "slave" and "coward" are synonymous. But before he returns to his people, his exposure to Spanish civilization changes his views, and he develops an enduring respect and admiration for Esteban. Historical fiction based on fact (Chakoh is the only fictional character). The underlying theme of freedom and human dignity gives added dimension to a well written adventure story. An A.L.A. Notable Book. Ages 10–14.

Balderson, Margaret. *When Jays Fly to Barbmo*. Illustrated by Victor G. Ambrus. Cleveland: World Publishing Co., 1969.
Teen-age Ingeborg, living with her father and her aunt during the German occupation of Norway, is forced to choose between two ways of life after the adults die. Should she remain with her mother's people, the Lapps, where she has gone for refuge, or return to rebuild her island home after the war? Her wise Lapp grandfather believes she will be content with Lapp ways "when jays fly to Barbmo." Barbmo has two meanings: "the place where migratory birds live in winter" or "a place of fictitious delights." Since jays do not migrate, Ingeborg's final decision to go back home is no surprise to her Lapp kin. The cold and the dark of the arctic world, the struggle for survival, and the girl's mental turmoil are revealed in a gripping, first-person narrative. Ages 12–14.

Beatty, Patricia. *Hail Columbia*. Illustrated by Liz Dauber. New York: William Morrow & Co., 1970
When Columbia Baines returned to Astoria, Oregon, in 1893, after 19 years' absence, her brother's staid family was shocked. Aunt Columbia was a suffragette who retained her maiden name, though married and a mother. She began to enlist the ladies of the town in a series of much-needed reforms that finally won the men's approval, grudging at first, and their support. Her 13-year-old niece, Louisa narrates the tale, which is full of zest and humor. Here, as in *Bonanza Girl* (New York: William Morrow & Co., 1962) and *Nickel-Plated Beauty* (New York: William Morrow & Co., 1964), the author recreates a past that is lively and entertaining as well as authentic. Ages 10–12.

Behn, Harry. *The Faraway Lurs*. Cleveland: World Publishing Co., 1963.
When the Lurs, warlike Sun people with bronze weapons and great bronze trumpets, invade the home of the peaceful stone-age Forest people, Heather, girl of the forest, falls in love with Wolf Stone of the Sun people, who seeks her for his wife. But superstition, jealousy, ambition, and treachery are too strong for this Bronze-Age pair of "star-crossed lovers." Death comes to Wolf Stone at the hands of Heather's rejected suitor, Blue Wing. And Heather dies willingly to bring life back to the sacred spring of her people, "for she thought of Wolf Stone waiting for her in the glade only a little distance away." Triggered by the discovery of a 3000-year-old "wet grave" containing the

perfectly preserved body of an 18-year-old-girl, Mr. Behn wrote his own version of what might have happened, and a hauntingly beautiful version it is. Ages: 11–13.

Benchley, Nathaniel. *Gone and Back*. New York: Harper & Row, Publishers, 1971.

Sixteen-year-old Obed looks back on his life from 1882, when he and his parents left depression-struck Nantucket, to his return with his mother nine years later. On their way West calamity strikes the family again and again—in the form of a swindler, a blizzard, Indians, horse thieves, and a rattlesnake—but Obed's father, eternally optimistic, keeps going on. His son gradually realizes that given two choices his father will always make the wrong one, and he becomes the head of the family when his father is shot in a ridiculous fight during the Oklahoma Land Rush. The theme of failure, almost nonexistent in pioneer stories, makes this pioneer story different. Another difference is contained in a short passage where 13-year-old Obed is seduced by a girl named Leni; his surge of adolescent curiosity is wholly believable. Ages 14–17.

Bonham, Frank. *Durango Street*. New York: E. P. Dutton & Co., 1965.

Rufus Henry, a 17-year-old Negro parolee from a forestry detention camp, breaks the condition of his parole by joining a gang in order to survive in the violent, lawless neighborhood of Durango Street. A timely, realistic, and powerful picture of juvenile gang life in the ghetto, with characterization neither overdrawn nor sugar-coated. The ending, while avoiding a pat solution, does leave the reader with the impression that there may be some hope for the Rufus Henrys of our society. An A.L.A. Notable Book. Ages 12–15.

Bragdon, Elspeth. *There Is a Tide*. Illustrated by Lilian Obligado. New York: Viking Press, 1964.

A lonely, motherless boy, shunted from school to school and expelled from all of them, goes to an island off the coast of Maine with his father. Almost strangers to one another, the two search for a better relationship. Told in first person, this strong story presents the boy's self-discovery in a powerfully evoked setting. His growing realization of his father's loneliness is developed without sentimentality. Hitherto unable to make friends, he develops a friendship with two boys and a rather mysterious girl that evolves naturally as the summer progresses. An illuminating story of a teen-ager's maturation. Ages 11–13.

Burch, Robert. *Queenie Peavy*. Illustrated by Jerry Lazare. New York: Viking Press, 1966.

Taunted by her schoolmates because her father is in jail, 13-year-old Queenie becomes a tough, scrappy girl who can best the boys at rock-throwing and tobacco-spitting. Her resentment and misery make her rebellious and quarrelsome and keep her in constant hot water. When her father is paroled, his lack of interest in her forces Queenie to realize that he wasn't worth fighting for. Excellent characterization and dialogue, fine atmosphere of small town life in depression-ridden Georgia, and Queenie herself is impossible to forget. An A.L.A. Notable Book. Ages 11–13.

Burnford, Sheila. *Incredible Journey*. Illustrated by Carl Burger. Boston: Little, Brown and Co., 1961.

A Siamese cat, an old bull terrier, and a young Labrador retriever leave the temporary home where their vacationing family has left them to travel through 250 miles of Canadian wilderness. The trek is arduous and full of danger for the three pets, but their survival and joyful reunion with their family is believable and deeply moving.

The three animals, each a unique personality, are portrayed without sentimentality or humanization. Ages 11–adult.

Byars, Betsy. *The Summer of the Swans*. Illustrated by Ted CoConis. New York: Viking Press, 1970.

Fourteen-year-old Sara Godfrey's moods bounce from elation to tears, but when her brain-damaged little brother is lost, she is shaken out of her pitying self-absorption. A warm, perceptive, sometimes humorous portrayal of adolescence with realistic dialogue and excellent characterization. The feelings of the inarticulate, mentally retarded Charlie, in his baffled search for the swans his sister had taken him to see earlier, and his agonized realization that he is lost, are superbly drawn. Newbery Award, 1971. Ages 10–12.

Campbell, Hope. *Why Not Join the Giraffes?* New York: W. W. Norton & Co., 1968.

Teen-age Suzie Henderson is revolted by the Bohemian life-style of her Greenwich village family. Father, a television writer, is home all day instead of nine-to-fiving it like other fathers. Mother paints and refinishes antiques. But worst of all, her brother Sam has long hair and plays the guitar in a group called the Giraffes. Wanting to impress a new boy friend, Suzie makes up a new name and a conformist family. The resulting complications lead to an unexpected, and to Suzie a bewildering, denouement. Though hilariously funny on the surface, the portrayal of adolescent throes is handled ably, without preachiness. Ages 12–14.

Carlson, Natalie. *Ann Aurelia and Dorothy*. Illustrated by Dale Payson. New York: Harper & Row, Publishers, 1968.

A lonely, white foster child, Ann Aurelia, meets a genial Negro girl, Dorothy, on the school playground, and the two become friends. A series of realistic and humorous incidents strengthens the tie between the two fun-loving, imaginative youngsters. The off-again, on-again home situation of Ann Aurelia, who has been shunted from one foster mother to another, is contrasted with Dorothy's stable, happy home. There are no purposeful overtones—the girls' relationship is natural and happy. Ages 9–11.

Caudill, Rebecca. *A Certain Small Shepherd*. Illustrated by William Pene du Bois. New York: Holt, Rinehart and Winston, 1965.

Jamie, a small mute boy, is heartbroken when a blizzard cancels the school Christmas pageant in which he had had the role of a shepherd. A young Negro couple beg for shelter at Jamie's door, and his father puts them in the warm church across the road, where their child is born. Caught up in his part, Jamie gives the child his Christmas orange and speaks for the first time in his life. An inspiring and sensitive Christmas story laid in Appalachia, with clear, soft illustrations. An A.L.A. Notable Book. All ages.

Cavanna, Betty. *Jenny Kimura*. New York: William Morrow & Co., 1964.

Jenny Kimura Smith, a charming girl of mixed parentage, raised in Japan, goes one summer to visit her American grandmother. Her life with her parents in a home that expressed "the best of two worlds" leaves her unprepared for the coolness she encounters, not only from her grandmother, but from almost everyone else she meets. Hurt by the prejudice and often shocked and surprised by customs new to her, Jenny finds solace in the friendship of two boys, one Caucasian and one of Japanese descent. A nearly fatal accident brings about a better understanding between Jenny and her grandmother. Although the ending is somewhat pat, there is perception in the handling of the racial situation. Ages 12–14.

Christopher, Matt. *The Year Mom Won the Pennant.* Illustrated by Foster Caddell. Boston: Little, Brown and Co., 1968.

The Little League Thunderball team, unable to get a father to coach them, reluctantly make do with teammate Nick Vassey's mother. Though at first they are the laughing stock of the league, the Thunderballs silence their hecklers by winning the pennant, much to their own and everyone else's surprise. Characterization is minimal, but humorous situations and play-by-play action add up to popular sports fare for young readers. The mixed racial makeup of the team is taken for granted. Ages 8–10.

Other easy-to-read sports stories by Christopher are: *Tall Man in the Pivot* (1961), *Challenge at Second Base* (1962), *Catcher with a Glass Arm* (1964), *The Counterfeit Tackle* (1965), and *Too Hot to Handle* (1965), all published in Boston by Little, Brown and Co.

Chute, Marchette. *The Wonderful Winter.* Illustrated by Grace Golden. New York: E. P. Dutton & Co., 1955.

Running away to London to seek his fortune and to save his dog from being "disposed of" by his domineering aunt, Robin Wakefield finds the city a cold, unfriendly place until he is befriended by John Heminges, an actor. Through Heminges he meets Will Shakespeare and becomes a member of his company. The Elizabethan setting is authentically protrayed, and a number of the characters are actual historical personages. But the excellent Shakespearian background is only the framework for a warm and appealing story, deftly told. A most entertaining introduction to Shakespeare and his plays by the author of the adult biography *Shakespeare of London* (New York: E. P. Dutton & Co., 1949). Ages 11–13.

Clapp, Patricia. *Constance: A Story of Early Plymouth.* New York: Lothrop, Lee & Shephard Co., 1968.

High-spirited Constance Hopkins comes reluctantly to the rugged wilderness of Plymouth in 1620. The first grim winter, with its many deaths from scurvy, tests her to the limit. Her friendship with an Indian girl, her growing awareness of her stepmother as a person, and the suitors who seek her favor all help her to adjust to the new country. Flirtatious, somewhat vain, she finds true love and marriage in 1626. Told in diary form, the story is historically accurate. Constance emerges as an appealing girl, very like the teenagers of any century, and a fine antidote to the marble image concept of Pilgrims. Ages 12–14.

Cleary, Beverly. *Ramona the Pest.* Illustrated by Louis Darling. New York: William Morrow & Co., 1968.

Spirited, five-year-old Ramona, who has often been a nuisance to Henry Huggins and others in her neighborhood, feels very grown-up when she enters kindergarten. She likes her pretty young teacher, Miss Binney, and enters into classroom activities with zest until an irresistible compulsion to pull another little girl's curls makes her a kindergarten dropout. The author's acute ear for children's dialogue, her strong sense of humor, and her highly believable treatment of children's actions and problems make this a totally captivating book. Ages 9–10.

Other deservedly popular books by Beverly Cleary are *Henry Huggins* (New York: William Morrow & Co., 1950), *Ellen Tebbits* (New York: William Morrow & Co., 1951), and *Beezus and Ramona* (New York: William Morrow & Co., 1965).

Cleaver, Vera, and Bill Cleaver. *Where the Lilies Bloom.* Illustrated by Jim Spanfeller. Philadelphia: J. B. Lippincott Co., 1969.

At her father's death, 14-year-old Mary Call Luther doggedly determines to keep her family—a younger brother and sister and an older sister—together without accepting charity. She is equally bent on preventing pretty, "cloudy headed" Devola (the older sister) from marrying their tight-fisted landlord, Kiser Pease. Burying her father secretly on the mountain side, she drives her family to earning money by harvesting medicinal plants. The back-breaking struggle to survive scares Mary Call, but she refuses to admit defeat until Devola and Kiser take matters into their own hands. Stark realism flavored with humor, and a memorable, gritty heroine. Mary Call is the epitome of the proud, independent mountain people who live in beautiful, but isolated and poverty-ridden Appalachia. Ages 12–adult.

Coatsworth, Elizabeth. *The Princess and the Lion*. Illustrated by Evaline Ness. New York: Pantheon Books, 1963.
In eighteenth-century Abyssinia all the king's sons were kept in isolation to prevent fratricidal conflict. Only the designated successor was allowed to leave the mountain prison and come to court. Princess Mariam, believing that her beloved brother Michael is doomed to life-long imprisonment, plots his escape and then is stunned to learn that he has been chosen heir to the throne. To avert his escape, she travels disguised as a boy and accompanied by her pet lion on a difficult and dangerous journey to the mountain of exile. The exotic setting, good characterization, and delicate but vital illustrations all contribute to this absorbing and unusual story. Ages 10–11.

Crane, Caroline. *Wedding Song*. Illustrated by Kurt Werth. New York: David McKay Co., 1967.
Seventeen-year-old April, the misfit in an academically talented family, feels all her problems will be solved by getting married. After eight months her young husband, fed up with the responsibilities of wedded life, leaves her, and she is forced to realize that her own immaturity placed her in a relationship that was doomed to fail. A realistic, perceptive look at a hasty marriage and why it broke up. Ages 13–15.

Cunningham, Julia. *Burnish Me Bright*. Illustrated by Don Freeman. New York: Pantheon Books, 1970.
In a small provincial village, a mute boy, considered an idiot by his neighbors, is befriended by a retired mime, Monsieur Hilaire. The penniless old man sees a possible artist in Auguste, and the boy, responding to the first affection he has ever known, enters a world of silent music and learns to use his body with skill and grace. When the old man dies, the superstitious country folk vent their fear and hatred on Auguste. Society's reaction to the individual who is "different" is the theme explored here, with compassion but without sentimentality. Ages 9–12.

Danska, Herbert. *Street Kids*. Illustrated by the author. New York: Alfred A. Knopf, 1970.
Seventy-five-year-old Hannibal Serendipity, a night watchman in New York City, was as odd as his name. He conversed with plants and animals, especially with Agamemnon, his pet goat. The neighborhood kids made fun of the old weirdo, but he won them over and got them interested in his flowers. Then a wild idea burgeoned in his mind. Why not beautify the rusting steel skeleton of the strike-abandoned skyscraper with flowers? The kids helped, and when the flowers bloomed, they brought a touch of beauty to the drab neighborhood. But Serendipity faced arrest for trespassing and defacing a building. The New York scene is authentic, the kids lively if improbable in their response to the situation, but Serendipity is such a real character that he compels belief. Ages 10–13.

Dillon, Eilis. *The Coriander*. Illustrated by Vic Donahue. New York: Funk & Wagnalls Co., 1964.

The people of Inishgillan, a tiny, remote island off the west coast of Ireland, have no doctor. When a fine ship, the Coriander, is wrecked, not only do its cargo and its fittings become the prized property of the islanders who salvage it, but so does the ship's doctor. The conflict between the acid-tongued, captive doctor and the apologetic but obdurate villagers is filled with suspense, excitement, and humor. The Irish setting is superb, and the depiction of the life of the hardy, self-sufficient islanders is outstanding. An A.L.A. Notable Book. Ages 12–16.

Ellis, Mel. *Flight of the White Wolf*. New York: Holt, Rinehart and Winston, 1970.

When Gray, a white wolf who has been raised at the Clagg family's dog training kennels, breaks loose and kills a show dog that tormented him, he becomes the object of country-wide pursuit. Panicky residents form posses led by bloodhounds to track him down. Fifteen-year-old Russ Clagg follows, too, but he wants to escort Gray to the safety of a wildlife refuge 250 miles away. To fight the cold, find food, and evade their pursuers taxes the stamina of both boy and wolf. Their relationship is absorbing and credible, and the boy's concern and the animal's dignity shine through convincingly. An engrossing wilderness survival story. Ages 11–14.

Estes, Eleanor. *The Alley*. Illustrated by Edward Ardizzone. New York: Harcourt Brace Jovanovich, 1964.

Ten-year-old Connie Ives, an only child, lives in a community of faculty homes in Brooklyn whose backyards open into an area called the Alley. Here the 33 faculty children play. When Connie's house is burglarized, she and her best friend, Billy Maloon, set out to solve the case with the other youngsters' help. Though the plot is not outstanding, the real delight of the book lies in the characterizations of the Alley's people. With warmth and perceptiveness, the author portrays the thoughts and feelings of two rather shy children and their friends. Ages 10–11.

The same qualities are displayed in *The Moffats* (New York: Harcourt Brace Jovanovich, 1941) and *Ginger Pye* (New York: Harcourt Brace Jovanovich, 1951), a Newbery Award winner.

Fenner, Phyllis, compiler. *Danger Is the Password. Stories of Wartime Spies*. Illustrated by Charles Geer. New York: William Morrow & Co., 1965.

A varied, exciting array of tales about spies, amateur and professional, young—age seven—and old—age 70—ranging from World War I through the Japanese invasion of China to World War II. An Englishman broadcasting from Germany is considered a traitor by all his family except his anguished wife, who must convince the authorities that he is really sending valuable information by code. A small French boy leads the enemy into ambush, and a Chinese brother and sister despise their collaborator father until they learn the truth about him. Among the authors represented are Graham Greene, Pearl Buck, Stuart Cloete, Louis Bromfield, and C. S. Forester. Though the stereotype of the German military in several stories is unfortunate, the overall picture of the spy's loneliness and the unusual type of courage demanded of him is admirably portrayed. One of the best of the Fenner short story collections. Ages 12–14.

Fitzhugh, Louise. *Harriet the Spy*. Illustrated by the author. New York: Harper & Row, Publishers, 1964.

Harriet, a precocious, brash, self-centered city child, wants to be a spy. And since a spy must observe and note all she sees, Harriet keeps a notebook where she jots down her observations about her parents, her neighbors, her teachers, and her classmates. When her journal is discovered by her school friends and her unflattering statements read aloud, Harriet becomes the school pariah. A wry, realistic study of childish cliques and cruelty. Harriet, so unlike the usual "nice child," is a lineal descendant of Burnett's Mary Lennox, but unlike Mary, has no Yorkshire moors or secret gardens to heal a spirit bruised by ostracism and separation from her nurse, "Ole Golly," who had been her only security. A true-to-life character study of a girl most adults find obnoxious but whom most children have a fellow-feeling for. Ages 10–11.

Fleischman, Sid. *Mr. Mysterious and Company*. Illustrated by Eric von Schmidt. Boston: Little, Brown and Co., 1962.

Hoping to buy a ranch in California, a magician and his family travel West by covered wagon. Doing shows in the frontier towns, they add to their income and bring a breath of the exotic to the townspeople. Humor vies with suspense. Mama frightens off some threatening Indians by putting on a magic lantern show, and the children turn in the Badlands Kid during a performance. Lighthearted, amusing, a different and welcome approach to the books on the Westward movement. Ages 10–12.

Equally humorous and fast-paced are Fleischman's *By the Great Horn Spoon* (Boston: Little, Brown and Co., 1963), *Ghost in the Noonday Sun* (Boston: Little, Brown and Co., 1965), and *Chancy and the Grand Rascal* (Boston: Little, Brown and Co., 1966), dealing with the California Gold Rush, pirates, and frontier life, respectively.

Forman, James. *My Enemy, My Brother*. New York: Meredith Press, 1969.

Daniel Baratz, at 16, has survived the siege of the Warsaw ghetto and the horrors of a Nazi concentration camp. His illegal entry into Palestine, before the formation of the state of Israel, does not bring him the peace he longs for. Unwilling to join the Irgun and disturbed by his friend Gideon's implacable hatred of all non-Jews, Daniel becomes a shepherd and makes friends with an Arab shepherd boy. But tensions between Jew and Arab make peace impossible, and Daniel finds himself with Arab blood on his hands. This powerful, realistic, historically accurate account provides insight into the problems of the Middle East and gives consideration to the feeling of the Arabs and their rights as well as to claims of the harassed, driven, and homeless Jews. 1969 winner of the Children's Spring Book Festival Award. Ages 12–17.

Fox, Paula. *Portrait of Ivan*. Illustrated by Saul Lambert. Englewood Cliffs, N.J.: Bradbury Press, 1969.

Motherless Ivan's life with a busy father who travels a lot and a friendly but preoccupied Haitian housekeeper is comfortable but lonely. When he sits for his portrait, the artist brings in an elderly, bookloving friend to read to Ivan during the sittings, and a bond begins to grow among the three. Commissioned to paint in Florida, the artist invites Ivan and Miss Manderly to go along, and there Ivan makes his first real friend, Geneva, a lively, imaginative, talkative girl his own age. When she weeps to see him leave for home, Ivan's circumscribed life has been enlarged, and though they may never meet again there is hope for Ivan now. A subtle, perceptive treatment of the problems of identity and isolation. A young boy's thoughts, feelings, and reactions to people, places, and situations are handled without sentimentality. An A.L.A. Notable Book. Ages 10–12.

Fritz, Jean. *I, Adam*. Illustrated by Peter Burchard. New York: Coward-McCann, 1963.

Fifteen-year-old Adam, fresh from school, is sent to spend the summer on his family's newly acquired farm until his father can retire from whaling. The sea is not in Adam's blood, but neither does he care for farming. His struggles with the former owner, the evil Sharkey, who attempts to regain the farm by fraud, only reflect his own inward struggles to make a decision about his future. The influence of an inspiring teacher enables Adam to see that what he really wants is more education. A sensitive, rather quiet, but thoroughly convincing story of a nineteenth-century teen-ager with crucial decisions to make. Ages 11–14.

Frolov, Vadim. *What It's All About*. Translated by Joseph Barnes. New York: Doubleday & Co., 1968.
Fourteen-year-old Sasha's puzzled wonder at his actress mother's lengthy "tour" away from home is changed into bitterness when a schoolmate tells him his mother has taken a lover. The sensitive and introspective boy, already acutely aware of girls, leaves home to confront his mother and learn the truth. Vigorous writing in the first person, showing details of Rusian family life, the exuberance and warmth of the Russian character, and a continual soul-searching that seems unchanged from the days of Chekhov and Dostoevski. The political system is not attacked, but hypocrisy and inconsistency in handling social problems are. Ages 12–14.

Gard, Joyce. *The Mermaid's Daughter*. New York: Holt, Rinehart and Winston, 1969.
Astria, attuned to the things of the spirit, is chosen to serve the great mermaid goddess as her mortal embodiment. Her life as teen-age bride, wife, and mother is narrated in first person with directness and charm. More than a love story, this recreation of life in the Scilly Isles (known to the ancient writers as the Isles of the Blest) during the Roman occupation is full of rich historical detail. The characterizations are well-rounded and the action believable. Like the author's *Talargain* (New York: Holt, Rinehart and Winston, 1964), this novel skilfully evokes life in early Britain, when the unseen world was very close and could be felt and known by the perceptive. A postscript with sources, bibliography, and a map adds to the value of the book. Ages 11–14.

Garfield, Leon. *Smith*. Illustrated by Antony Maitland. New York: Pantheon Books, 1967.
Seconds after picking the pocket of an elderly man in a London slum, 12-year-old Smith sees him murdered and thereby becomes involved in a mystery that leads him into Newgate and out again. The raffish underworld of eighteenth-century London is magnificently brought to life by a master of pace and suspense with an almost Dickensian ability to create memorable characters. An A.L.A. Notable Book. Ages 12–14.

George, Jean C. *My Side of the Mountain*. Illustrated by the author. New York: E. P. Dutton & Co., 1959.
Told in the first person by 14-year-old Sam Gribley, who decides to escape from life's humdrum routine and see if he can live off the land for one year. A woods in the Catskill mountains becomes his base of operations; a hollow tree becomes his home. He has difficulty at first, but with experience he manages to make an enviable life for himself. An outstanding survival story. The descriptions of animal life, the food Sam learns to prepare, his thoughts and deepening awareness of himself lend conviction to a thoroughly absorbing account. Newbery runner-up. Ages 11–15.

Greene, Constance C. *Leo the Lioness*. New York: Viking Press, 1970.
Thirteen-year-old Tibb, who has big feet and a flat chest, consoles herself by remembering that she was born under the sign of Leo and is therefore strong, forceful, steadfast, and practically everything good. Not that this helps much when her older sister and best friend become boy- and clothes-crazy, but an even worst jolt is handed her when her former baby-sitter and idol, Carla, a college girl, has to get married. A first-person account of an adolescent learning to cope with sex, parents, and siblings.

Excellent dialogue and good characterization, imbued with humor throughout. Ages 10–13.

Grin, Alexander. *Scarlet Sails*. Translated by Thomas P. Whitney. Illustrated by Esta Nesbitt. New York: Charles Scribner's, 1967.
A lovely girl, motherless Asole, is raised in almost complete isolation by her loving but embittered father. In childhood she is told that when she grows up a prince will come for her in a white ship with scarlet sails. Her prince, a wealthy and whimsical young captain, sees Asole, hears the prediction, and makes it come true. This famous Russian classic, first published in 1932, is a tender, romantic story with mystical overtones whose characters seem like figures out of legend. A biographical note describes the author's life and his place in Russian literature. Ages 12–14.

Hamilton, Virginia. *The House of Dies Drear*. Illustrated by Eros Keith. New York: Macmillan Co., 1968.
The Smalls, a Negro family, move into an ancient mansion in Ohio, once a station of the Underground Railroad. Reputedly haunted by Dies Drear, the abolitionist who built it, and two slaves, it has a sinister and unwholesome reputation. Strange things begin to happen, and 13-year-old Thomas Small attempts to get to the bottom of them. Soon he is involved in a puzzling and perilous mystery. Superior characterization and an excellent feeling for Gothic atmosphere distinguish this absorbing story by the gifted author of *Zeely* (New York: Macmillan Co., 1967). An A.L.A. Notable Book. Ages 11–15.

————. *The Time-Ago Tales of Jahdu*. Illustrated by Nonny Hogrogrian. New York: Macmillan Co., 1969.
Mama Luke, an elderly baby-sitter in Harlem, entertains her charge Lee Edwards with stories about Jahdu, a fabulous little boy-hero who uses his magic powers sometimes for good and sometimes for mischief. But in the end, though he gives up most of his power, he retains his pride in himself as "a strong, black boy." The illustrations are subtle and expressive, the writing poetic, and the "black is beautiful" theme treated with dignity and strength. An A.L.A. Notable Book. Ages 8–10.

Haugaard, Erik. *The Little Fishes*. Boston: Houghton Mifflin Co., 1967.
Orphaned by the war, 12-year-old Guido begs on the streets of Naples until he is evicted from his vermin-ridden quarters in a cave. With two younger children, Anna and Mario, he travels north to Cassino in search of safety and a home. Some adults are kind, but others, equally desperate and starving, are indifferent if not hostile to the children's plight. Guido, who is strong without being callous, manages to find some measure of human understanding and compassion even when Mario dies, and he and Anna journey on, still hopeful. A grim, realistic picture of life in a war-ravaged country with no pat solution or happy ending provided. An A.L.A. Notable Book. Ages 11–13.

Henry, Marguerite. *Mustang: Wild Spirit of the West*. Illustrated by Robert Lougheed. Chicago: Rand, McNally & Co., 1966.
Professional killers hunted wild mustangs for pet food with planes and trucks; horse-lovers objected, but no one did anything. Then Annie Brown Johnston stepped in. Raised on a Nevada ranch, where her father instilled in her a love of freedom for all living things, Mrs. Johnston, with her husband's help and the help of neighbors, senators, and horse-lovers all over the nation, got a bill passed in 1959 to protect the wild mustangs from extinction. Now she is known as "Wild Horse Annie." An emotional, heartwarming, true story with a timely theme. The scenes come alive through the vigorous pencil sketches abundantly scattered throughout the book and the many

two-page action paintings in strong earth-tones, which are evocative of the wild country of the mustangs. Ages 10–12.

Hightower, Florence. *Dark Horse of Woodfield*. Illustrated by Joshua Tolford. Boston: Houghton Mifflin Co., 1962.

Humor, suspense, and lively characters round out a family story set in the Depression era. Horse-loving Maggie and her brother Buggsy live at Woodfield, the once magnificent but now run down Armistad family estate, with their grandmother and aunt. To help the family finances Buggsy catches and raises butterflies to sell, while Maggie hopes to win a money prize in a horse show. There is a bit of mystery and a touch of romance. Distinctive characterization is combined with engaging humor in an appealing and diverting story. Ages 10–12.

Hildick, Edmund Wallace. *Manhattan Is Missing*. Illustrated by Jan Palmer. New York: Doubleday & Co., 1969.

Manhattan, a beautiful Siamese cat, comes with the New York apartment sublet to the Clarke family from England. Dreamy Peter Clarke is chief cat-lover and watcher, but despite his care Manhattan disappears. Then the family receives a ransom note demanding money for the cat's return. Peter enlists the aid of an American friend, and together they initiate Operation Catnet to retrieve the missing feline. Lively dialogue, good characterization and a plausible plot make for exciting, humorous reading. Ages 10–11.

Louie's Lot (New York: White, 1968), *Secret Winners* (New York: Crown, 1970) and *Top Boy at Twister's Creek* (New York: White, 1969) —all by the same author— are equally well done.

Hinton, S. E. *The Outsiders*. New York: Viking Press, 1967.

Two gangs—the long-haired "Greasers," who live on the wrong side of the tracks, and the "Socs," or well-to-do kids—engage in open warfare that culminates in murder. The tensions, loyalties, difficulties, and problems that beset the members of each gang are narrated by Ponyboy, a Greaser. The author, a 17-year-old girl, probes the roots of conflict with sensitivity and understanding. Most frightening and most hopeful is her depiction of teen-agers at a crossroads where a nudge from the right or wrong person can mean the difference between the dead-end of delinquency and an encouraging future. Ages 12–17.

Holm, Anne. *North to Freedom*. New York: Harcourt Brace Jovanovich, 1965.

Twelve-year-old David knows life only as an inmate of a concentration camp. Escaping into a world for which he is completely unprepared, he travels across Europe in search of his mother. He encounters kindness, brutality, and indifference. But his gradual awakening to a world of color, beauty, and feeling is narrated with such skill that the reader, like David, sees life as if for the first time. A unique achievement that won the author the Gyldendal Prize for Best Scandinavian Children's Book in 1963. An A.L.A. Notable Book. Ages 10–14.

Hunt, Irene. *Across Five Aprils*. Illustrated by Albert John Pucci. Chicago: Follett Publishing Co., 1964.

Nine-year-old Jethro Creighton, the Benjamin of his family and its pet, does not fully understand the talk of war he hears in April 1861. By the second April, he has watched two brothers march off—one for the Union and one for the Confederacy. In the Aprils that follow, Jethro and his sister Jenny hold the Illinois farm together after their father is felled by a heart attack. A rich and understanding story, not only of battles but of issues and emotions. Newbery runner-up. Ages 12–17.

Hunter, Mollie. *A Pistol in Greenyards*. New York: Funk & Wagnalls Co., 1968.

The tenants in Greenyards, a Scottish Highland valley, are evicted from their homes by an avaricious landlord who wants to use his land to graze sheep. Fifteen-year-old Connal Ross is caught up in the injustice and upheaval of the times when he draws a pistol on the brutal sheriff to protect his mother and becomes a candidate for hanging. The aftermath of the people's futile revolt is arrest, trial, and emigration, with Connal barely escaping capture as he boards the ship that will take him to a new life in America. Based on an actual event and told with zest and speed. Ages 12–14.

Ish-Kishor, Sulamith. *Our Eddie*. New York: Pantheon Books, 1969.

The Raphael children chafe under the domination of their severe, egotistical father. An orthodox Jew, a dedicated Hebrew scholar and teacher, a convinced Zionist, he is willfully blind to his family's physical and emotional needs. The result is tragedy. His eldest son Eddie, a victim of muscular dystrophy, is alienated by his father's inability to understand any viewpoint but his own. But not until Eddie dies on the operating table is there some measure of understanding between Mr. Raphael and the rest of his family. A penetrating, realistic study of a generation gap, partly autobiographical and superbly done. Newbery Award runner-up. Ages 12–14.

Jones, Adrienne. *Sail, Calypso!* Illustrated by Adolph Le Moult. Boston: Little, Brown and Co., 1968.

A partnership between Clay, a Negro boy, and Paul, a Caucasian, is born of necessity as they work on a stranded, derelict sailboat. As the summer passes, their reluctant association develops into friendship. Books on boat repair and sailing taken from the library show them how to bring the Calypso back to life. Realistic dialogue and credible characterization are set against a shore background. The authentic details of boat repair and handling never obtrude. Ages 10–12.

Keith, Harold. *Komantcia*. New York: Thomas Y Crowell, 1965.

Pedro Pavan, captured by the Comanches, suffers barbarous treatment as a captive and slave to the brutal Belt Whip. But under a kinder master, who adopts him, he eventually becomes an honored warrior. His struggles to maintain a Christian mind and soul in the midst of alien savagery—though he learns to recognize the good things in the Indian life and character—are convincing. Based on careful research, the depiction of Comanche ways is rich in detail and completely realistic. An eye-opener to readers accustomed to the "noble savage" or "bloodthirsty fiend" images found in so many books. Pedro's wooing of Willow Girl adds a tender note to the fast action and suspense of this robust tale. Similar action and suspense can be found in the author's Newbery Award winner, *Rifles for Watie* (New York: Thomas Y Crowell, 1957). Ages 12–17.

Konigsburg, E. L. *Altogether, One at a Time*. Illustrated by Gail E. Haley, Mercer Meyer, Gary Parker, and Laurel Schindelman. New York: Atheneum, 1971.

A collection of four short stories full of wry humor, each illustrated by a different artist. Compelled to invite a child he doesn't want to his birthday party in "Inviting Jason," Stanley likes him even less afterwards and for a different reason. A 10-year-old boy learns something about old age when he realizes that his grandmother has lost her last chance to see a shower of stars in "The Night of the Leonids." The spirit of a long-dead camp counselor helps an obese girl make up her mind that she will never have to attend "Camp Fat" again. In "Momma at the Pearly Gates," Momma's superb aplomb when called a "dirty nigger" by a white classmate, and her handling of the situation, are both credible and memorable. Ages 10–11.

The author shows the same empathetic insight into the minds and emotions of children in her earlier books: *Jennifer, Hecate, Macbeth, William McKinley and Me,*

Elizabeth (New York: Atheneum, 1967) and *About the B'nai Bagels* (New York: Atheneum, 1961).

————. *From the Mixed-up Files of Mrs. Basil E. Frankweiler.* Illustrated by the author. New York: Atheneum, 1967.
The eldest of four children, 12-year-old Claudia Kinkaid feels put upon and decides to run away to teach her parents a lesson. Taking her brother, nine-year old Jamie, with her because he has money, she lives undetected with him for a week in the Metropolitan Museum of Art. Their adventure ends when Claudia tries to authenticate a statue attributed to Michelangelo and encounters the acerbic donor, Mrs. Basil E. Frankweiler. Crisp writing, natural dialogue, and believable characterization create a humorous, suspenseful tale of two youngsters whose running away, reprehensible though it is, is something every child has dreamed of doing. Newbery Award 1968. Ages 10–11.

Krumgold, Joseph. *Henry 3.* Illustrated by Alvin Smith. New York: Atheneum, 1967.
Henry Lovering III, who prefers to be known as Henry 3, moves with his parents into an exclusive New York suburb populated by status-conscious executive families. Henry, a brilliant boy, struggles to conform to Crestview standards. He judges his father and his way of life and finds them both wanting. Then a hurricane reveals his father in a new light, and Henry begins to grow in understanding. The theme of maturing youth is a familiar one, but Krumgold's writing is creative and memorable and Henry is more than just another adolescent with growing pains. Ages 12–14.

Lee, Mildred. *The Rock and the Willow.* New York: Lothrop, Lee & Shephard Co., 1963.
Hidden under a willow on a rock in a stream, teen-age Enie Singleton is able to slip away from the barrenness and poverty of her life on an Alabama farm in the 1930s. Longing to escape from her environment, she dreams of becoming a teacher or a writer. During her high school years she copes with death, watching her stern father's inarticulate grief when his favorite child, the small Sue Ann, dies, and seeing her mother succumb to overwork and hard times. Enie's increasing share of work and responsibility, her first brush with love, and her bitter resentment towards her father's new wife are perfectly realized. Outstanding characterization and superb feeling for time and place. Ages 12–17.

Lipsyte, Robert. *The Contender.* New York: Harper & Row, Publishers, 1967.
A 17-year-old drop-out in Harlem takes up boxing as the only way out of the ghetto. As a contender he learns to concentrate on a goal. When others in his crowd drift into drugs and delinquency, he moves toward self-confident manhood, though he realizes he will not make the grade as a fighter. Understanding adults, both black and white, help him, but ultimately it is his own inner strength that keeps him from becoming a quitter. The dialogue is tough, bitter, and natural. The book is more polished and affecting than Bonham's *Durango Street* (New York: E. P. Dutton & Co., 1965) or Vroman's *Harlem Summer* (New York: G. P. Putnam's, 1967). The author's expertise as a sportswriter lends verisimilitude to the tense boxing scenes. An A.L.A. Notable Book. Ages 12–15.

Little, Jean. *Mine for Keeps.* Illustrated by Lewis Parker. Boston: Little, Brown and Co., 1962.
Sal Copeland is afraid she can't cope with living permanently at home. A victim of cerebral palsy, she has spent five years in a school for the handicapped. Her sympathetic but sensible parents, wanting to make her independent, give her a puppy to take care of. His need, Sal's friendship with two classmates, and her interest in a self-pitying sick boy help her to overcome her fears and solve her problems at home and school. A satisfying story of the difficulties faced by a handicapped child.

An independent sequel is *Spring Begins in March* (Boston: Little, Brown and Co., 1966), in which Sal's younger sister Meg feels a misfit in her own family and a failure in school, though she does not have a handicapped body. The promise of a room of her own spurs her on in a determination to improve her grades, but the addition of her grandmother to the Copeland household cancels out this promise. A realistic but sympathetic treatment of the generation gap problem. Ages 9–11.

————. *Take Wing*. Illustrated by Jerry Lazere. Boston: Little, Brown and Co., 1968.
Laurel's protective love for her seven-year-old brother James is clouded by her fear that he is not normal. He shouldn't still be wetting the bed or needing help getting dressed. But only when her mother is hospitalized does the truth about James' condition become apparent—retarded but educable. Freed from her responsibility, Laurel meets a new problem—making friends her own age. A sensitive story of a girl whose shyness and insecurity arise from her difficult role of champion, protector, and nurse to the retarded James. Sympathetic but unsentimental treatment of a once-shunned subject. Ages 10–12.

McGraw, Eloise J. *Greensleeves*. New York: Harcourt Brace Jovanovich, 1968.
The green sleeves of her waitress uniform effectively disguise 18-year-old Shannon Lightly, daughter of famous but divorced parents. Shuttled from one set of guardians to another in Europe and the United States, Shannon must take time out to decide about her future. A lawyer friend of her father's asks her to observe the legatees of a strange will in Portland, Oregon, where she assumes the role of a gum-chewing, elaborately coiffed, small-town girl. As Georgette Smith she becomes involved with the beneficiaries of the will and meets an attractive, tender young man who helps her gain self-confidence and self-acceptance. Lively style and excellent dialogue freshen up a familiar theme. Ages 12–14.
The author's *Moccasin Trail* (New York: Coward-McCann, 1952) and *Golden Goblet* (New York: Coward-McCann, 1961) were runners-up for the Newbery Award.

Macken, Walter. *Flight of the Doves*. New York: Macmillan Co., 1968.
To escape their stepfather's cruel and abusive treatment, the motherless Dove children, 12-year-old Finn and seven-year-old Derval, run away from their English home in search of their grandmother, who lives in Ireland. Though uncertain how to find her, the two plucky youngsters are helped by various people they meet along the way until they reach their goal and are permanently freed from their menacing stepfather. An exciting story with a melodramatic plot made believable by the use of restraint and realism. Ages 10–12.

Montgomery, Jean. *The Wrath of Coyote*. Illustrated by Anne Siberell. New York: William Morrow & Co., 1968.
The tragic confrontation of Indian and white man becomes immediate and personal in this depiction of the struggle between the Miwok Indians and Spanish missionaries and soldiers in the California of 1775. When the people of Coyote, the Miwok, first encounter the Spaniards, Kotola, an Indian boy, watches them with interest. He learns their language and they call him "Marin." Only later do he and his people realize that the strangers are bringers of disease, cruelty, and death. A fictional life of the legendary Chief Marin, rich in Indian lore and well written though sombre in tone. Woodcuts complement the text and a glossary of Miwok words is appended. Ages 12–14.

Mowat, Farley. *Owls in the Family*. Illustrated by Robert Frankenberg. Boston: Little, Brown and Co., 1961.
When Billy brings home a bedraggled owlet whom he names Wol, and later rescues

another from some cruel youngsters who are tormenting it, he adds two unusual pets to his collection. Wol, fiercely independent and mischievous, is also generous and protective. He tries to share a skunk with the family and almost literally takes the pathetic Weeps, the abused owlet, under his wing. Both owls have to be taught to fly, but only Wol does it; Weeps remains on foot. Lively black and white drawings accompany the humorous text, which is based on the author's boyhood experiences. Ages 9–12.

Moyes, Patricia. *Helter-Skelter*. New York: Holt, Rinehart and Winston, 1968.
When Felicity Bell, nicknamed Cat, goes to the English coast to visit relatives at a Naval Research base, she expects an uneventful vacation. But she sights a corpse floating in the water, and its subsequent disappearance makes her do some snooping. Learning that there is a security leak at the base, Cat begins to put two and two together and almost loses her life in the process. A suspense story that combines sailing with light romance, enlivened by a breezy style and natural dialogue. Ages 12–14.

Neufeld, John. *Edgar Allan*. New York: S. G. Phillips, Inc., 1968.
A white minister's family attempts to adopt a black child. Edgar Allan, a bright three-year-old, is received with simple, loving acceptance by the two youngest children, with determined loyalty by Michael, the narrator, and his mother, and with outright resentment and fear by 14-year-old Mary Nell, the oldest. Community pressures add to the minister's burden, and eventually Edgar Allan is returned to the adoption agency. Ironically enough, the minister's resentful daughter and intolerant congregation are disappointed by his failure to live up to his ideals, and Michael finds it difficult to forgive him. Based on fact, this is a moving account of human frailties, failures, and needs. An A.L.A. Notable Book. Ages 11–14.

Neville, Emily. *It's Like This, Cat*. Illustrated by Emil Weiss. New York: Harper & Row, Publishers, 1963.
A perceptive, humorous story about 14-year-old Dave Mitchell, growing up in New York City. Out of sorts with his father, Dave acquires Cat from an eccentric neighbor, Crazy Old Kate, whose apartment swarms with cats. His friend Nick and his first girlfriend Mary help Dave to see his father as a person just as his father comes to recognize Dave's right to a mind of his own. Told in the first-person in teen-age vernacular, the story shows real feeling for the problems of a boy who is no longer a child but not yet a man. Newbery Award 1964. Ages 10–14.

O'Dell, Scott. *Sing Down the Moon*. Boston: Houghton Mifflin Co., 1970.
A young Navajo girl, Bright Morning, describes her capture by Spanish-American slavers, her rescue by Tall Boy, her husband-to-be, and the tragic confrontation of the Navajos and the American soldiers that ended in the 300-mile death-march to Fort Sumner. Here, as in the author's Newbery Award-winning *Island of the Blue Dolphins* (Boston: Houghton Mifflin Co., 1960), the quiet, simple style, with its poetic overtones, reflects the dignity and courage of an Indian girl whose indomitable spirit refuses to accept defeat. She persuades Tall Boy, now her husband, crippled in body and spirit though he is, to return to their old home in the Canyon so that their son can live the life of his ancestors. Newbery Award runner-up. Ages 11–13.

Perrine, Mary. *Salt Boy*. Illustrated by Leonard Weisgard. Boston: Houghton Mifflin Co., 1968.
A Navajo boy, forbidden by his father to continue roping his mother's sheep disobeys him to save a drowning lamb. His father then promises to teach him to rope a horse. A simple story, but the motivations and feelings are universal, and the dramatic illustrations in red, ocher, and black catch the spirit of the Navajo country and its people. Ages 5–8.

The same author's *Nannabah's Friend* (Boston: Houghton Mifflin Co., 1970) follows the quiet adventures a Navajo girl experiences while watching her sheep.

Peyton, K. M. *Flambards*. Illustrated by Victor G. Ambrus. Cleveland: World Publishing Co., 1968.

An orphaned heiress is sent to live at the family estate, Flambards, with her uncle Russell and her cousins Mark and William. Russell and his son Mark are abysmally selfish, violent, interested only in horses and hunting, and totally incapable of understanding or tolerating anyone whose views and tastes differ from theirs. Expected to marry Mark and restore Flambards to its former splendor, Christina is drawn instead to the younger son. William is passionately interested in a new invention, a machine that flies. The conflict between William and his father and brother, the social customs of pre-World War I England, and the growing attachment between Christina and William are vividly brought to life in this well written runner-up for the Carnegie Medal of 1967. An A.L.A. Notable Book. Ages 12–16.

The two sequels are equally outstanding in setting and characterization. In *The Edge of the Cloud* (Cleveland: World Publishing Co., 1969) William and Christina are on their own as newlyweds. William's absorption in flying and his near-fatal accidents terrify Christina but she comes to accept them. *Flambards in Summer* (Cleveland: World Publishing Co., 1970) finds Christina, widowed by World War I, returning to Flambards with her child to begin a new life.

Phipson, Joan. *Threat to the Barkers*. Illustrated by Margaret Horder. New York: Harcourt Brace Jovanovich, 1965.

An Australian family in New South Wales is concerned when an outbreak of sheep stealing occurs in their area. Fourteen-year-old Edward learns that four older boys are the culprits, but he is frightened into silence by their threats. When his older brother's flock of stud sheep is menaced, his loyalty to Jack is stronger than his fear: he informs the police and helps catch the thieves. An independent sequel to *The Family Conspiracy* (New York: Harcourt Brace Jovanovich, 1963), with the same excellent characterization, flavorful dialogue and evocation of locale. Ages 10–12.

Picard, Leonie. *One Is One*. New York: Holt, Rinehart and Winston, 1966.

Scorned as a coward and a weakling by his family, shy, sensitive, 13-year-old Stephen is sent to a monastery and must give up his only friend, his dog Amile. In the monastery his talent as a painter brings him satisfaction, but he still longs to prove his worth to his family. Running away, he is taken in by the wise and understanding Sir Pagan, who trains him for knighthood. But his benefactor is executed—having chosen the wrong side—and Stephen is cast adrift again. In time he achieves his goal and helps a young frustrated squire to find his place, but loses him to the plague. In the end he finds peace of mind by returning to the monastery. A haunting portrait of a misfit in medieval society, where physical strength and hardihood in battle were considered supreme virtues. The title is taken from an old ballad and reflects Stephen's solitary role in life. "One is one and all alone and evermore shall be so." Ages 12–14.

Polland, Madeleine. *To Tell My People*. Illustrated by Richard H. Powers. New York: Holt, Rinehart and Winston, 1968.

Life in a British lake village is harsh to 12-year old Lumna, the chief's daughter. Inarticulate and longing for something she cannot define, she meets Caesar's soldiers, and the encounter plunges her into a new life. A well treated slave in a Roman household, she longs to convince her people that resistance to Rome is futile, and to persuade them to accept Roman ways—so superior to their savage ones. With a fellow slave's help she returns to her village, to be met with hostile disbelief. When the tribesmen ambush a Roman patrol, Lumna flees in terror and heartbreak, knowing the sorrow that will come. A deeply moving presentation of a doomed effort. Less complex than Rosemary Sutcliff's novels, which are set in the same period. This one is for younger readers. Ages 11–13.

Potter, Bronson. *Antonio*. Illustrated by Ann Grifalconi. New York: Atheneum, 1968.
   The familiar theme of the left-out individual who longs to gain status and acceptance, this time in a Portuguese setting. Antonio, a fisherman's son, is barred from his father's calling by a crippled hand. He is the ox-boy who guides the lumbering beasts as they launch and beach the fishing boats. During a great storm, Antonio's quick thinking and his swimming prowess enable him to rescue the fleet, in danger of being smashed on the shore. Spare and direct writing establishes the mood and sustains the pace with its constant reminders of the insignificance of man against the immensity of nature. Complementing the writing are the prints of rough-grained wood representing the sea and sand on which black ink figures are starkly superimposed. An A.L.A. Notable Book. Ages 9–12.

Pyle, Howard. *Men of Iron*. Illustrated by the author. New York: Harper & Brothers, 1891.
   A classic popular romance of chivalry set in England under Henry IV. Trained for knighthood, Myles Falworth restores his family's rank and honor when he engages the cruel enemy of his house in a fight to the death and wins. Boyhood, youth, and manhood unfold against a heroic background of arduous and rigid chivalric codes. Full of character and rich dialogue invoking the very essence of the period. Howard Pyle's illustrations are among the finest in children's literature; perfect in detail and technically outstanding, they are classics of their kind. Meticulous and splendid. Ages 12–14.

Richter, Hans Peter. *Friedrich*. New York: Holt, Rinehart and Winston, 1970.
   Life in Germany from 1925 to 1942 as seen by a boy whose best friend is Jewish. At first, Friedrich is the more fortunate. His father is respected and prosperous, while the narrator's father is unemployed until Hitler comes to power. Then the vise begins to close on eight-year-old Friedrich, who is not allowed to join the Jungvolk, is expelled from school at nine, and becomes motherless at 13 when his home is brutally invaded. He later escapes arrest by being away from home when his father is deported. Denied entrance to an air raid shelter in 1942, Friedrich is killed. "His luck that he died this way," is one man's terse comment as he kicks the body. While his friend and his friend's family deplore the treatment given the Schneiders, they are powerless to prevent it; they can only alleviate it by occasionally offering food and shelter. Neither an apology or a polemic, but a straightforward, episodic account, eloquent in its restraint. A chronological list of the laws, degrees, and regulations affecting the Jews is appended. Ages 11–14.

Robertson, Keith, *Henry Reed, Inc.* Illustrated by Robert McCloskey. New York: Viking Press, 1958.
   Writing in a journal because "girls keep diaries," ingenious Henry Reed records his experiences during a summer visit to his aunt and uncle in a small New England town. With no playmates except a younger girl, Midge, who establishes herself as a person of character, Henry sets himself up in various enterprises. The two sell pigeons, earthworms, and turtles and experiment with a homemade balloon. A series of hilarious incidents, revolving around staid Henry and energetic Midge. Ages 10–12.
   The same deft humor is carried on in the thoroughly entertaining sequels: *Henry Reed's Journey* (1963), *Henry Reed's Babysitting Service* (1966), and *Henry Reed's Big Show* (1970), all published in New York by Viking Press.

Rodman, Bella. *Lions in the Way*. Chicago: Follett Publishing Co., 1966.
   A documentary novel covering a week in a small Tennessee town in 1959, when eight

Negro students enter an all-white high school. The contrast between the black and white communities, the hopelessness felt by the Negroes, the ugliness of the mob, stirred up by professional agitators, and the effect on the town when troops are brought in to keep order are presented with conviction and intensity. Though sermon-like in spots, the over-all effect is gripping. An A.L.A. Notable Book. Ages 12–14.

Rose, Karen. *There Is a Season*. Chicago: Follett Publishing Co., 1967.
Katie Levin's crush on Catholic Jamie McAllister and her feeling for Gary Berg, a popular boy with a dubious reputation, are frowned on by her Jewish family. Doubts about God and religion, concern over her father's sudden illness, her brother's approaching Bar Mitzvah, and her mother's antagonism disrupt Katie's summer, but help her toward maturity. A perceptive treatment of sensitive subjects, handled with a light touch and deft humor. Ages 12–15.

Sachs, Marilyn. *Veronica Ganz*. Illustrated by Louis Glanzman. New York: Doubleday & Co., 1968.
An overgrown, domineering, 13-year-old girl from a broken home bullies other children remorselessly until pint-sized Peter Wedermeyer, a classmate, challenges her tyranny. Through her frustrating feud with Peter, Veronica slowly learns that her femininity is an asset and abandons her bullying ways. Characters and dialogue are realistic, and the writing is lively with humorous insight. An A.L.A. Notable Book. Ages 9–11.

Schaefer, Jack. *Old Ramon*. Illustrated by Harold West. Boston: Houghton Mifflin Co., 1960.
An old shepherd takes the son of his patron on a sheep drive in the Southwest. Together they face a devastating sandstorm and a wolf attack, as well as the many daily minor crises involved in tending sheep. The seasoned old man's wisdom and understanding are contrasted realistically with the eagerness, impatience, and short-sightedness of the boy, who does not always understand what is involved in caring for the flock and the dogs. The relationship between the old man and the boy is a tender one, shown without sentimentality or affectation. The cadenced prose is memorable. Newbery Award runner-up. Ages 11–adult.

Seuberlich, Hertha. *Annuzza, a Girl of Romania*. Illustrated by Gerhard Pallasch. Chicago: Rand, McNally & Co., 1962.
Young Annuzza dreams of a chance to study at the High School in the city. She wins a scholarship there, though her parents feel that anything unconnected with running the farm is a waste of time for a peasant girl. But Annuzza hopes to create a new life for herself away from farm and family. She conceals her peasant status from her schoolmates but finally realizes that her roots are in the country and returns to teach in the village school. A good picture of Rumanian rural life and realistic in its presentation of Annuzza's problems: her father's drinking, which has impoverished his family, and her classmates' coldness when they find out she lied about her background. Ages 12–14.

Skirrow, Desmond. *The Case of the Silver Egg*. Illustrated by Robin Jacques. New York: Doubleday & Co., 1968.
An incredible but funny mystery about a pint-sized James Bond called Mini-Minor Morris. Mini's brilliant father has discovered an astounding energy source which is code-named the Silver Egg. The word gets around and Mini's father is abducted. The Queen Street boys, led by Mini-Minor, set out to retrieve the scientist and his discovery from the unscrupulous gang of baddies that hold him prisoner. Despite the bumbling efforts of the Secret Service and minimal aid from the police, the elder Morris is rescued. Delightful farcical adventure. Ages 10–12.

Snyder, Zilpha K. *The Egypt Game*. Illustrated by Alton Raible. New York: Atheneum, 1967.

A Caucasian girl, April, and her Negro friend, Melanie, share an enthusiasm for imaginative pastimes and devise the "Egypt game," played in the unused backyard of an antique shop. The deserted yard yields statues, altars, and props for the amateur Egyptians, and rituals, hieroglyphic codes, and an oracle are set up. Other neighborhood children are drawn into the game. Then one child is murdered and the others are forbidden to go out. Through Melanie's little brother Marshall and the antique shop owner, the murderer is identified after he attempts to strangle April. The action is convincing and the dialogue is so natural that every child is a distinct character. An exceptional story of contemporary life in an integrated urban community where Negro, Chinese, and Caucasian children mingle with no feeling of forced integration, and race is only casually mentioned. Newbery Award runner-up. Ages 10–11.

Sobol, Donald J. *Encyclopedia Brown, Boy Detective*. Illustrated by Leonard Shortall. Camden, N.J.: Thomas Nelson, 1963.

An observant 10-year-old, Leroy Brown, whose memory retains an astounding collection of facts, is nicknamed Encyclopedia by his peers. Whenever his father, the Chief of Police has a difficult case to solve, Encyclopedia always comes up with the answer. His ability leads him to set up his own detective agency with remarkable success. Each chapter contains a case with all the clues, and the reader is challenged to match wits with Encyclopedia. Solutions are given at the end of the book. Ages 9–10.

The first in a popular series designed for young mystery fans, this book is followed by *Encyclopedia Brown and the Case of the Secret Pitch* (1965) and by others wherein Encyclopedia *Gets His Man* (1967), *Solves Them All* (1968), *Finds the Clues* (1968), *Keeps the Pace* (1969), and *Saves the Day* (1970). All are published in Camden N.J. by Thomas Nelson.

Southall, Ivan. *Hills End*. Illustrated by the author. New York: St. Martin's Press, 1963.

Seven children with their teacher Miss Godwin explore a cave in search of aboriginal drawings. Meanwhile, the rest of the population of Hills End, a remote Australian logging town, is at a picnic in the nearest settlement, 85 miles away. A violent storm washes out Hills End, and the children (Miss Godwin being injured and helpless) have to survive on their own until relief comes. The theme of survival, always a popular subject, is handled here with skill and dispatch. The characterizations are excellent and the action moves fast. Ages 11–13.

Spicer, Dorothy. *The Humming Top*. New York: S. G. Phillips, 1968.

Orphaned Dorcas, who has the gift or curse of ESP, is hired by a wealthy dowager, ostensibly as a companion. Actually her employer hopes Dorcas can explain the mysterious disappearance of her grandson 12 years earlier. Triggered by the humming of a top, her only link with her own past, Dorcas' strange talent begins to operate. As she begins to unravel the mystery, her employer is murdered, and Dorcas is not only a suspect but a potential victim, for the real killer fears her eerie ability. Romance, realism, and suspense blend in this Gothic mystery by a serious researcher into ESP. Ages 13–17.

Steele, William O. *The Year of the Bloody Sevens*. Illustrated by Charles Beck. New York: Harcourt Brace Jovanovich, 1963.

The many Indian raids on the frontier in 1777 caused that year to be called the "year of the bloody sevens." 11-year-old Kelsey Bond, left motherless, starts for Kentucky to join his father. Leaving the slow-moving family of fellow travelers, he joins two hunters who are later killed by the Indians. Haunted by guilt because he had been too frightened to try to save his two companions, Kelsey makes his way alone through the hostile wilderness to his father, and confesses his feelings of shame. In time he is convinced that he could have done nothing and that discretion is indeed the better part of valor. Authentic in background, fast-moving, and told in flawless colloquial style. Ages 10–11.

Other titles by this author (all published by Harcourt Brace Jovanovich in New York) are *The Lone Hunt* (1956), *Far Frontier* (1959), *Trail through Danger* (1965), and *Tomahawk Border* (1966).

Steptoe, John. *Stevie.* Illustrated by the author. New York: Harper & Row, Publishers, 1969.

Small black Robert, an only child, resents the intrusion into his life of Stevie, whose mother works. Though Stevie goes home on weekends, Robert has to share his toys and his mother with him during the week. "I used to have a lot of fun before old stupid came to live with us." But when "crybaby" moves away, Robert misses him. Set in the ghetto, the situation is a familiar one to children everywhere. The striking illustrations in dark brilliant colors are reminiscent of Rouault. An A.L.A. Notable Book. Ages 5–8.

Stevenson, William. *The Bushbabies.* Illustrated by Victor Ambrus. Boston: Houghton Mifflin Co., 1965.

When, an English game warden's daughter, Jackie, leaves her beloved Africa, she wants to take her pet galago or bushbaby with her. Lacking permission to do so, she leaves the ship to return her pet to his native habitat. Guided by her father's African headman, Tembo, she starts for her African home. The hardships of the journey, the danger from fire and flood, the growing affection and mutual dependence of the young girl and the elderly native are handled convincingly and with great sensitivity. The background of the African bush is authentic. A grim picture of white prejudice against the black native believed to have kidnapped the girl adds another dimension to the tale. An A.L.A. Notable Book. Ages 10–adult.

Stiles, Martha Bennet. *Darkness over the Land.* New York: Dial Press, 1966.

Mark Elend, at eight, cannot understand the difference between what his Nazi teachers tell him about the war and what his parents say and do. As he grows older, he watches his government persecute those he knows and loves, until, torn with anguish, he becomes involved in acts of treason. The strain of living under bombing siege, the struggle to find food, the torment of being unable to escape the increasing tyranny of a doomed regime are presented with clarity, realism, and depth. Terrible events are neither glossed over nor dwelt upon. When the war ends, Mark has opportunity to leave his shattered homeland. Now fifteen, he resolves to remain and rebuild it. A powerful study of Germany in World War II. Ages 12–14.

Stolz, Mary. *The Bully of Barkham Street.* Illustrated by Leonard Shortall. New York: Harper & Row, Publishers, 1963.

Martin, the bully who tormented Edward Frost in *A Dog on Barkham Street* (New York: Harper and Row, Publishers, 1960), is the protagonist here. Bigger and fatter than his classmates, longing to be accepted by them, and hoping to be understood by adults, he is continually frustrated. Martin realizes he will have to change, but there is no overnight transformation. A realistic story with touches of humor and emphathic characterization. Ages 9–11.

————. *The Noonday Friends.* Illustrated by Louis S. Glanzman. New York: Harper & Row, Publisher, 1965.

A realistic story of the shabbily poor world of Manhattan's lower middle class, viewed through the eyes of 11-year-old Franny. Franny contrasts her own family of working mother, unemployed artist father, and two brothers with that of her best friend, Simone Orgella, a Puerto Rican. Simone has freedom to come and go because her mother takes care of her household. Because of home responibilities, Franny has time for her friend only at noon. No complicated plot, but rather a stream of life with high and low moments. Newbery Award runner-up. Ages 9–11.

The author's teen-age novels, *To Tell Your Love* (1950), *Because of Madelaine* (1957), and *Wait for Me, Michael* (1961) are written with the same insight into character and conflict. All three published in New York by Harper & Row, Publishers.

Sutcliff, Rosemary. *Warrior Scarlet*. Illustrated by Charles Keeping. New York: Henry Z. Walck, 1958.

Drem, a boy with a withered arm, yearns for warrior status in his tribe. To achieve it, he must slay a wolf single-handed. His efforts to overcome his handicap and pass the test are recounted in this vivid recreation of early Bronze Age Britain. When he fails to kill his wolf, he is sent off to become a keeper of sheep, but some time later, defending a ewe, he kills the leader of the wolf pack. It turns out to be the wolf he failed to kill before, and Drem wins the right to don the scarlet clothing of the warrior. The rugged, grim, arresting illustrations are appropriate to the text. The background of clan and tribal customs, the result of careful research, is typical of an author who brings authenticity to all her books. Ages 12–14.

Sykes, Pamela. *Our Father!* Camden, N.J.: Thomas Nelson, 1969.

Handsome, vain Mark Devonish, a successful author, delights in being unconventional. He castigates the British public school system, sells the ancestral home when he falls heir to it, and jaunts about the continent with a roving eye for pretty girls, though he has a lovely wife and four children. He encounters the "moment of truth" when he and his family spend their annual holiday at a small French resort hotel. Teen-age Margaret tries to elope with an Italian waiter; Jasper, the only son, runs away to an English public school to escape being exploited as a musical prodigy. His twin Josephine "borrows" a baby she considers neglected; mother breaks the news that a fifth child is on the way; and 13-year-old Phoebe, the narrator, makes friends with her father's arch rival. Sophisticated humor and a finely characterized family, all finally loyal to their charming blustery father, feet of clay and all. Ages 11–14.

Taylor, Sidney. *The All-of-a-Kind Family*. Illustrated by Helen John. Chicago: Follett Publishing Co., 1951.

Five little sisters consider themselves an all-of-a-kind family until a baby brother arrives. A delightful, warm story of a Jewish family in New York's East side in 1912. There is not much money but there is an abundance of love and companionship. Going to the library, shopping for the Sabbath dinner, become joyous adventures for the girls. Mamma's understanding makes a game of household dusting; Papa's big heart brings lonely Charlie into the family and reunites him with his lost sweetheart—the library lady! Jewish customs and holiday celebrations are skilfully woven into the story. Deft black and white illustrations are just right for the adventures of this most believable family. Ages 10–12.

The sequels, *More All-of-a-Kind Family* (Chicago: Follett Publishing Co., 1954) and *The All-of-a-Kind Uptown* (Chicago: Follett Publishing Co., 1958), sustain the excellent quality found in the first book.

Taylor, Theodore. *The Cay*. New York: Doubleday & Co., 1969.

Shipwrecked Philip Enright finds himself on a raft with an elderly West Indian sailor. His resentment of Timothy for his blackness, his ugliness and his smell begins to fade when a head injury leaves him blind and totally dependent. The weeks on the cay, a small coral island, trying to stay alive, and the training that Timothy insists Philip undergo so he can survive alone if necessary are at first painful and incomprehensible to the boy. But when Timothy dies in a hurricane protecting Philip he realizes the debt he owes to a wonderful human being. The always popular theme of survival is made memorable by the outstanding characterization of old Timothy and the credible abandonment by Philip of his former prejudice. An A.L.A. Notable Book. Ages 11–13.

Townsend, John Rowe. *Trouble in the Jungle*. Illustrated by W. T. Mars. Philadelphia: J. B. Lippincott Co., 1969.
The grim realities of life in an English slum are vividly depicted in the story of the abandoned Thompson children, who hide in an empty warehouse to escape being placed in an institution. Kevin, who tells the story, learns that their refuge is also the headquarters of a criminal gang with whom his feckless, irresponsible Uncle Walter is involved. A dangerous confrontation with the gang ends when the police arrive, and when the remorseful Uncle Walter and his common-law wife return, the family is reunited, ready to settle back into their old routine. Strong characterization of appealing children and weak adults. The events here precede those in *Good-bye to the Jungle* (Philadelphia: J. B. Lippincott Co., 1967). Both are A.L.A. Notable Books. Ages 10–12.

Watson, Sally. *The Mukhtar's Children*. New York: Holt, Rinehart and Winston, 1968.
Yasmin, the 12-year-old daughter of the headman, or Mukhtar, of an isolated Arab village in Israel, is irresistibly drawn to the new Jewish kibbutz nearby. A rebel against the restrictions of her life, she cannot help contrasting the difference between the freedom and equality given to the kibbutz women and the inferior status of the females of her village. When her twin brother becomes involved, unwillingly at first, with the kibbutz dwellers, the way is opened up for friendship and understanding between the two communities. Though pro-Israel in tone, the author has tried to present the Arab viewpoint. The Mukhtar's final acceptance of the state of Israel and all it implies may seem unrealistic but not so his daughter's. The strength of the book lies in the vivid portrayal of the restless, searching, strong-willed Yasmin. Ages 11–13.

Weik, Mary Hays. *The Jazz Man*. Illustrated by Ann Grifalconi. New York: Atheneum, 1966.
Nine-year-old Zeke, who lives in Harlem, is almost a recluse. He avoids school because he doesn't want to be teased about his lame leg. When his mother leaves because her husband can't hold a job, Zeke is left more and more alone. Only the music of a jazz man across the way gives him any comfort or hope. Increasingly hungry and feverish, he dreams of visiting the jazz man and wakes to find his parents, now reunited, with him. A beautifully and powerfully written mood piece. The interpretation will vary with each reader. Is Zeke's waking only an illusion and his parents' presence a dream that will be extinguished in death? The woodcuts, like the story, are both realistic and lyrical. Newbery Award runner-up. Ages 9–12.

Wersba, Barbara. *The Dream Watcher*. New York: Atheneum, 1968.
Albert Scully, an adolescent loner, the only child of an unhappily married couple, considers himself a failure. His interests—Shakespeare, Brahms, gardening, and recipe-collecting—estrange him from his parents and his contemporaries. Then he meets Orpha Woodfin, an eighty-year-old, self-designated actress, and his friendship with her gives him self-confidence. When she dies he learns that almost everything she told him was a lie. But now he has matured enough to know that she gave him strength to be himself without apology. A moving, first-person account of a credible relationship between a boy and an aged woman. Ages 12–17.

Werstein, Irving. *The Long Escape*. New York: Charles Scribner's, 1964.
Based on an incident that took place during the Nazi invasion of Belgium, this vivid account tells how a dedicated nurse, Justine Raymond, director of a children's convalescent home, took her 50 charges from Heyst to Dunkerque. As they traveled, they wit-

nessed the strafing of the refugee-choked road and the horrors of death and destruction. Space was found for them on a rescue ship when some Tommies gave up their places. The compassionate heroism of the nurse and the Tommies is in shining contrast to the barbarism surrounding them. A gripping, unusually realistic story of courage and self-lessness rising above a hopeless situation. Ages 11–14.

Wibberley, Leonard. *John Treegate's Musket*. New York: Farrar, Straus and Giroux, 1959.
Wealthy merchant and ardent Royalist John Treegate leaves his 11-year-old son Peter alone in Boston as an apprentice when he sails to England on business. Feeling abandoned by his father, Peter becomes involved in the unrest of the period and has to flee the city. His ship is sunk in a hurricane, and, memory gone, Peter is found half dead on the Carolina coast by an exiled Scotsman, the MacLaren of Spey. When he travels to Boston four years later his memory returns, and father and son fight together at Bunker Hill. Well knit, fast moving and written with a discipline and humor that brings the period and the people to life. Ages 11–14.
Peter Treegate's War (New York: Farrar, Straus and Giroux, 1960), an independent sequel, takes Peter back to the Scots colony in the Carolinas, where his love for the MacLaren conflicts with his loyalty to his real father. *The Sea Captain from Salem* (New York: Farrar, Straus and Giroux, 1961) retells the remarkable exploits of Peter's friend, Captain Peace of God Manly, an American privateer who proves to the French that Americans can win battles at sea. In *Treegate's Raiders* (New York: Farrar, Straus and Giroux, 1962), Peter leads the Scottish mountaineers in raids and battles ending with Cornwallis' surrender at Yorktown.

Wier, Ester. *The Loner*. Illustrated by Christine Price. New York: David McKay Co., 1963.
An abandoned, nameless boy, who has been used and abused by adults as he follows migrant workers from camp to camp, finds a friend, only to lose her in a fatal accident. Fleeing from the scene in a state of shock, he is found cold, dirty, and tired by Boss, a hardy woman who herds sheep. His struggles to please Boss are motivated by a wish to live up to the name she has given him—David. The loneliness of the rugged Montana country and the growing bond between the taciturn woman and the insecure boy are described with simplicity and restraint. Newbery Award runner-up. Ages 11–15.

Williams, Jay and Raymond Abrashkin. *Danny Dunn and the Homework Machine*. Illustrated by Ezra Jack Keats. New York: McGraw-Hill Book Co., 1958.
Danny and his friends Joe and Irene are dismayed at the amount of homework they have to do. When Professor Bullfinch leaves his semi-portable computer in Danny's care, Danny decides to program it to do their assignments. At his mother's insistence he obtains his teacher's permission, and then sets to work with grade A results. An entertaining story with an accurate background in computer science. Ages 9–11.
This book is the third in a series beginning with *Danny Dunn and the Anti-gravity Paint* (New York: McGraw-Hill Book Co., 1956) and *Danny Dunn on a Desert Island* (New York: McGraw-Hill Book Co., 1957), and followed by excursions into automated housing, cave exploration and fossils, the laser beam, outer space communication, weather, undersea exploration, a miniaturizing machine, and time travel.

Wojciechowska, Maia. *Shadow of a Bull*. Illustrated by Alvin Smith. New York: Atheneum, 1964.
As the only son of a famous bullfighter, Manolo Olivar is expected to equal his father by the people of Arcangel. Six men, devotees of bullfighting, begin teaching him all he must know about the art in anticipation of his twelfth birthday, when he will face a bull for the first time. Manolo gamely practices, but is afraid, knowing that he lacks

the *aficion* of the true "killer of bulls." Regarding himself as a coward, he faces his trial, and then finds the courage to reject the role forced on him. A sensitive story of a boy becoming a man, written with great feeling for the boy, for bullfighting, and for Spain. A glossary of bullfighting terms is included. Newbery Award, 1965. Ages 11–14.

Wrightson, Patricia. *A Racecourse for Andy*. Illustrated by Margaret Horder. New York: Harcourt Brace Jovanovich, 1968.

Mentally retarded Andy "buys" the racetrack of the Australian town where he lives from a vagrant ragpicker. His friends attempt without success to persuade him that he is not the owner, and then decide to go along with his delusion. The adults at the racecourse gently humor him and tactfully "buy" the property back. The total acceptance of Andy for what he is by friends and grownups alike is unusual and perhaps unrealistic, but the character of Andy is so beautifully realized that the reader will want to believe it. An A.L.A. Notable Book. Ages 10–12.

Zei, Aliki. *Wildcat under Glass*. Translated by Edward Fenton. New York: Holt, Rinehart and Winston, 1968.

The impact on a Greek family of the imposition of a fascist dictatorship is narrated by Melissa, or Melia, its youngest member. Both Melia and her older sister Myrto adore their adult cousin Niko, who tells them enthralling stories about the stuffed wildcat on display in their home. When Niko is forced into hiding because he is pro-democratic, he leaves clandestine messages in the wildcat, and the family has to decide where their allegiance lies. A timeless theme, fine characterization, and a realistic plot. An A.L.A. Notable Book. Ages 11–13.

Zindel, Paul. *The Pigman*. New York: Harper & Row, Publishers, 1968.

Confused, restless, unhappy teenagers, John and Lorraine find a friend in Mr. Angelo Pignati, a lonely, elderly widower who is touchingly proud of his ceramic pig collection. When a heart attack sends him to the hospital, he gives them the key to his house along with his complete trust. A party turns into a drunken brawl, the pig collection is smashed, and at the height of the revelry, Mr. Pignati returns. The remorseful duo try to make amends but when Mr. Pignati dies the next day, they are compelled to face reality. "There was no one to blame anymore. . . . And there was no place to hide. Our life would be what we made of it—nothing more, nothing less." An intensely moving story. Ages 14–18.

Poetry Adoff, Arnold, compiler. *I Am the Darker Brother*. Illustrated by Benny Andrews. New York: Macmillan Co., 1968.

The Negro experience in America—its despair, anger, bitterness, pride, and hope for the future—is powerfully depicted in sixty-four selections by twenty-eight American Negro poets. These include well known writers such as Langston Hughes, Arna Bontemps, and Leroi Jones, and less well known ones such as Ray Durem, Raymond Patterson and Joseph White. Biographical sketches, explanatory notes, and author and title indexes are appended. Charlemae Rollins' brief foreword discusses creativity, the Negro, and poetry. An A.L.A. Notable Book. Ages 12–17.

Arnold Adoff's *Black Out Loud* (New York: Macmillan Co., 1970) contains new poems by new and established poets. It is equally inspirational. An A.L.A. Notable Book.

Aiken, Conrad. *Cats and Bats and Things with Wings*. Illustrated by Milton Glaser. New York: Atheneum, 1965.

Sixteen different creatures are featured in unusual pictures and poems, each poem and picture having a page to itself. The writing is imaginative and whimsical without being outrageous or silly, and the typographical layout is distinctive. The illustrations, astonishingly inventive, employ various media and styles and alternate between color and black and white. The author, a Pulitzer Prize winner and a distinguished poet, is making his first foray into the children's field. A remarkably handsome book is the result. An A.L.A. Notable Book. Ages 5–9.

Arbuthnot, May Hill, compiler. *Time for Poetry*. Illustrated by Rainey Bennett. Chicago: Scott, Foresman and Co., 1959.

A durable collection intended for teacher use, this book should appeal to any adult who wants his child to find "an exhilaration that comes from compatibility of ideas and form, from the melody and movement of the lines, from the little shivers of delight these qualities induce." There are ten subject areas, ranging from "all sorts of people" to "wisdom and beauty," and the contents range from very simple, tumpety-tump nursery rhymes to rich, mature poems for older children. The foreword, "Why take time for poetry?" is an inspirational assessment of the value of poetry in children's lives and stresses the necessity of reading it aloud. An invaluable aid to any adult who wants to bring poetry to children. Ages 5–11.

Baron, Virginia O., compiler. *The Seasons of Time: Tanka Poetry of Ancient Japan*. Illustrated by Yasuhide Kobashi. New York: Dial Press, 1968.

The five-line Tanka is a basic Japanese form that predates the Haiku. Like the Haiku, it mirrors the profound Japanese interest in nature imagery as an expression of human emotions. From two classic anthologies, 78 poems have been collected and arranged by theme, each of the four seasons and "This World." The black, gray, and white wash drawings reflect the fanciful delicacy of the text. There is a helpful introduction explaining the history and nature of Tanka, the difficulty of translation, and the symbolism involved. An A.L.A. Notable Book. Ages 10–adult.

Behn, Harry, compiler and translator. *Cricket Songs*. New York: Harcourt Brace Jovanovich, 1964.
A poet in his own right and a lover of Japanese haiku, Mr. Behn has retained all the beauty and simplicity of the originals in his translations. He tries to do "what the author might have done if English had been his language," and he succeeds superbly. These fleeting glimpses of the marvels of nature, momentarily captured in the words of great Japanese poets, are seen fresh, pure, and new. The accompanying pictures, selected from the works of Sesshu and other Japanese artists, increase the appeal of the haiku and add their own flavor to the book. Ages 9–adult.

————. *Golden Hive*. Illustrated by the author. New York: Harcourt Brace Jovanovich, 1966.
Some of these poems are mellifluous but unmemorable hum-alongs of the "summer, bees, crickets" variety. But there are others, like "Two Views of the Planet Earth" and "The Blackfoot Chieftains," that evoke the thrill of reponse a true poem inspires. An A.L.A. Notable Book. Ages 9–10.

Bierhorst, John, editor. *In the Trail of the Wind*. Illustrated, with engravings from various sources. New York: Farrar, Straus & Giroux, 1971.
A comprehensive collection of Amerindian poems and ritual orations. Sources range from the northern Eskimos to the tribes of Central and South America. Arranged by theme and mood rather than by location and culture, the selections begin with poems of origin in "The Beginning." Other subjects are prayer, home, hunting, war, love, death, and dreams. The book ends with the affecting "The Arrival of the Whites" and "We Shall Live Again"—where pathos, tragedy and hope combine. The compiler uses appendices to explain the selections and their sources. A glossary of tribes, cultures, and languages, with suggestions for further reading, is also included. Regardless of subject, these poems all have a lyric and emotional quality in common. They can be read not only as poetry but as history, and as a plea to conserve the land and its people. A unique combination of scholarship, research, beauty, and historical record. Ages 10–adult.

————. *The Ring in the Prairie: A Shawnee Legend*. Illustrated by Leo and Diane Dillon. New York: Dial Press, 1970.
A skilful young hunter, Waupee or White Hawk, discovers a strange circle worn in the grass of the prairie. Hiding, he observes twelve beautiful skymaidens descend and dance in it. Captivated by their loveliness, he steals and woos the youngest. In time his star wife becomes homesick and returns to the sky with her son. Her star father then invites Waupee to come to the sky country. Finally he and the star people assume the forms of birds and animals and return to earth. A poetic retelling from a collection of Indian tales gathered by Henry Rowe Schoolcraft in the nineteenth century. The stylized illustrations, with their subtly superimposed and varied hues, provide a glowing accompaniment to the text. Ages 7–9.

Blake, William. *Songs of Innocence*, 2 vols. Illustrated by Ellen Raskin. New York: Doubleday & Co., 1966.
To many readers Blake's poetry is opaque, yet much of it is well known and widely quoted, notably *Songs of Innocence*. Ellen Raskin's imaginative woodcuts in warm, muted tones endow each poem in this book with irresistible appeal. An excellent introduction to a poet whose mystic feeling for innocence and wonder is expressed most clearly in this, his early work. In a companion volume the artist has set the poems to music. The melodies are haunting and there are simple accompaniments with guitar chords indicated. The two volumes form a unique set. Ages 8–adult.

Blishen, Edward, compiler. *The Oxford Book of Poetry*. Illustrated by Brian Wildsmith. New York: Franklin Watts, 1963.

A tightly-packed treasure trove of limericks, ballads, story poems, lyrics, and songs. Chiefly English poets, including Shakespeare, Shelley, and Yeats—and *Anon.*, to whom Gelett Burgess' "Purple Cow" is erroneously attributed. In the foreword the compiler explains his selections, discusses the place of poetry in his own life, and encourages children not to worry immediately about meaning; rather, he tells them to feel the flow of the words when they listen to or read a poem. Tantalizingly inexact titles mark off each section of the book. Many of the selections are standard fare and may be found in other anthologies, but few are illustrated in such glowing, vibrant colors. One small criticism: the binding is too stiff. Ages 9–12.

Bogan, Louise, and William Jay Smith, compilers. *The Golden Journey*. Illustrated by Fritz Kredel. Chicago: Reilly and Lee, 1965.

One hundred major and minor poets, past and present, provide something for every age and taste. The selections contain familiar and unfamiliar poems ranging from simple rhymes to soaring imaginative flights; the compilers have included only those poems they themselves have "read, enjoyed and remembered with pleasure—poems fresh, delightful, and perennially new." An outstanding anthology for family use. The dignified woodcuts set the tone of each section. An author and title index and a brief introduction discussing the nature and enjoyment of poetry add to the value of this book. An A. L. A. Notable Book. All ages.

Bontemps, Arna, compiler. *Hold Fast to Dreams: Poems Old and New*. Chicago: Follett Publishing Co., 1969.

A poet's own selection of poems he could not forget. Such heavily anthologized poets as Frost, Dickinson, Keats, Millay, and Hughes are represented next to less well-known ones, including many black writers. They dream, sing, observe nature, lose and win, love, weep, remember, and hope for freedom, brotherhood and a happier world. A browsing collection. The author explains his own feelings about poetry in a short introduction. Author, title, and first line indexes. An A.L.A. Notable Book. Ages 12–adult.

Brewton, Sara, and John E. Brewton, compilers. *Shrieks at Midnight*. Illustrated by Ellen Raskin. New York: Thomas Y Crowell, 1969.

A collection of macabre, eerie, humorous poems by Lewis Carroll, Ogden Nash, Hilaire Belloc, Langston Hughes, Dorothy Parker and the familiar "Author unknown," among others. Ballads, puns, and epitaphs recounting fatal accidents, murder, suicide, ghosts, indigestion, shiverous beasts, funerals, graves, and the hereafter appear, from the old "From Ghoulies and Ghosties, / And long-leggity Beasties, / And all things that go bump in the night, / Good Lord deliver us," to the up-to-date "Here he lies moulding; / His dying was hard— / They shot him for folding / An IBM card." The ghoulishly grinning illustrations add the right touch of mock ferocity to the goings-on. Index of authors, titles, and first lines. An A. L. A. Notable Book. All Ages.

Ciardi, John. *I Met a Man*. Illustrated by Robert Osborn. Boston: Houghton Mifflin Co., 1961.

A successful and delightful foray into the limited vocabulary field. Wanting "to write the first book my daughter read herself," Mr. Ciardi uses riddles, puns, rhymes, and guessing and drawing games all on the central theme "a man," to lead young beginning readers through and even beyond the original four hundred basic word list. The cartoon-like drawings blend perfectly with the fun and humor of the text. Ages 6–8.

Coatsworth, Elizabeth. *The Sparrow Bush*. Illustrated by Stefan Martin. New York: W. W. Norton & Co., 1966.

How did a certain moment look or feel or sound? These light and lilting, varied rhymes recall nature with its creatures, seasons, moods, and musings as well as other familiar childhood experiences. In the preface the author defines the role of poetry, observing that her own rhymes are not formal poems but "poetry in petticoats." Attractive black and white woodcuts, sculptural in feeling, accompany the text. Ages 8–10.

In *Down Half the World* (New York: Macmillan Co., 1968) the author is concerned with "the quality of history and places." In her lively, imaginative character studies of Columbus, Mary Tudor, Bathsheba, and Lincoln and in her sketches of nature the poet's acute eye is very evident. Ages 10–12.

Cole, William, compiler. *Beastly Boys and Ghastly Girls*. Illustrated by Tomi Ungerer. Cleveland: World Publishing Co., 1964.

A collection of humorous poems about naughty children. Milne, Ciardi, Belloc, Nash, Burgess, Carroll, Anonymous, and others exaggerate the mischief inherent in every child. Nearly always the hilarious antics bring speedy retribution. The mock serious style of the selections is admirably complemented by Tomi Ungerer's droll sketches. An A.L.A. Notable Book. Ages 9–11.

Colum, Padraic, compiler. *Roofs of Gold: Poems To Read Aloud*. Illustrated by Thomas Bewick. New York: Macmillan Co., 1964.

The selections, mostly from English poets, were chosen "for certain qualities—visualness, striking imagery, picturesqueness, action, humor." Himself a poet, Padraic Colum has included a plea for learning poetry in his eloquent introduction. A section entitled "Notes" gives the historical background of some of the poems. The decorative wood engravings are those of the famous late eighteenth-century printmaker. Indexed by first line and author. An A.L.A. Notable Book. Ages 10–14.

De Forest, Charlotte B., adapter. *The Prancing Pony: Nursery Rhymes from Japan*. Illustrated by Keiko Hida. New York: Walker and Co., 1967.

A collection of delightful rhymes freely adapted from Japanese folk sources. The subjects—snow, springtime, butterflies, elves, and animals—have universal appeal. The unusual and captivating collage illustrations are called "kusa-e"; they employ handmade papers whose soft, muted colors are produced by natural plant dyes. Their simple shapes and sparse detail are graceful in keeping with the rhymes. The elegant endpapers in textured gold add distinction to the format. A visual treat. An A.L.A. Notable Book. Ages 5–8.

Doob, Leonard W., compiler. *A Crocodile Has Me by the Leg*. Illustrated by Solomon Irein Wangboje. New York: Walker and Co., 1967.

A collection of authentic African folk poems about everyday concerns from birth to death. An unlucky man mourns that "a crocodile has me by the leg," a young girl informs her friends, "I refused, of course I did, / I do not want to get married. / But father and mother compel me to, / And so I am willing to give it a try." A bit of sage observation is found in, "To become a chief's favorite / Is not always comfortable; / It is like making friends / With a hippopotamus." "Hail, let happiness come" greets a new baby, and mother is appealed to as one "Who freely gives of what she has: / Fresh food and cooked meals alike. / Mother who never deserts the hearth. . .". Distinctive, eye-catching woodcuts in brown and orange by a Nigerian artist reflect the strength, dignity, humor, and beauty of the selections. Ages 10–14.

Dunning, Stephen, Edward Lueders, and Hugh Smith, compilers. *Reflections on a Gift of Watermelon Pickle . . . and Other Modern Verse*. Illustrated with photographs. New York: Scott, Foresman and Co., 1966.

From 1200 modern poems, three perceptive English teachers have selected 114. Such familiar poets as Ezra Pound, Walter de la Mare, and Robert Frost are included, but most are relatively unknown. The variety of subjects—fresh looks at creatures of fur and feather, plant life, the inanimate but astonishing machine, and the activities of young and old—reflect tenderness, irony, humor, satire, shock, wonder, joy, and tragedy in kaleidoscopic progression. The sharp, significant photographs paired with many of the poems will tempt the reader to linger and perhaps change him from a looker at pictures to a lover of poetry. An A.L.A. Notable book. Ages 12–adult.

—————. *Some Haystacks Don't Even Have Any Needles and Other Complete Modern Poems*. New York: Scott, Foresman and Co., 1969.
Twentieth-century life reflected in a wide selection of modern poems. The old themes of love, anger, loneliness, and compassion are recast in the context of today, in images fresh and full of surprises. Familiar poets like Frost, Dandburg, Roethke, and Yevtushenko are included along with new young poets whose work has appeared in literary journals and magazines. The use of full color reproductions of modern paintings perfectly complements the text. Ages 12–adult.

Ferris, Helen, compiler. *Favorite Poems, Old and New*. Illustrated by Leonard Weisgard. New York: Doubleday & Co., 1957.
Over 700 poems, chiefly British and American, remembered and loved by the former editor of the Junior Literary Guild. "Myself and I," the family, the seasons, play, birds, animals, this country, the world, and many other subjects are included. All are poems of high quality, many of them standard titles. The introduction, recounting the Ferris family's pleasure in reading together, adds a nostalgic but pleasant note to this large (over 500 pages) browsing collection. Author, title and first line indexes. Ages 6–adult.

Frost, Robert. *You Come Too*. Illustrated by Thomas W. Nason. New York: Holt, Rinehart and Winston, 1959.
A very wise and understanding introduction by Hyde Cox prepares the young reader for the wisdom and beauty of Robert Frost's poetry. The poet's selections are meant for young people to read or have read to them. Some of the poems are long, some sharp and brief, some serious, some light, and they range from the simple to the sophisticated. Distinguished wood engravings blend in naturally with the text. Ages 12–adult.

Gregory, Horace, and Marya Zaturenska, compilers. *The Crystal Cabinet: An Invitation to Poetry*. Illustrated by Diana Bloomfield. New York: Holt, Rinehart and Winston, 1962.
The title of this fine anthology is taken from William Blake's strange, lovely poem. The selections, varied in mood and excellent in quality, were chosen in the hope of encouraging the appreciation of poetry. The emphasis is on youthful moods and emotions. Avoiding, for the most part, the well-worn anthologized favorites, the compilers have preferred to include less well-known works by American and English poets. There is also a section of notes on poems and authors. The wood engravings suitably mirror the attractive selections. First line, title, and author indexes. Ages 12–17.

—————. *The Silver Swan: Poems of Romance and Mystery*. Illustrated by Diana Bloomfield. New York: Holt, Rinehart and Winston, 1966.
Ballads, elegies, spells, charms, and songs—both sad and joyful—reflect the moods of mystery, longing, gloom, nostalgia, and joy common to the adolescent. The sources vary from traditional to modern, and the emphasis is on the less known works of English and American poets. Helpful notes give brief information about the author

and sometimes the poem. A companion to the compilers' *Crystal Cabinet,* with the same distinguished format. Author, first line and title indexes. Ages 12–17.

Hannum, Sara, and Gwendolyn E. Reed, compilers. *Lean Out of the Window.* Illustrated by Ragna Tischler. New York: Atheneum, 1965.

A collection of unfamiliar poems by familiar contemporary British and American poets, from Amy Lowell, Vachel Lindsay, and A. E. Housman to Dylan Thomas, Ezra Pound, Richard Wilbur and Theodore Roethke. Diverse in theme, mood, and form, unified only by their twentieth-century origin, they spur the reader's imagination and his curiosity. Some are deceptively simple; others are enigmatic and sophisticated. An inviting introduction to modern poetry. An author and title index. Ages 10–adult.

Sara Hannum's anthology, *To Play Man Number One* (New York: Atheneum, 1969), explores the condition of modern man in a time of social crisis and change as seen by contemporary poets. It resembles the modern poetry collections of Stephen Dunning.

Larrick, Nancy, compiler. *Piping Down the Valleys Wild.* Illustrated by Ellen Raskin. New York: Delacorte. 1968.

A most attractive collection. It includes selections from the Old Testament, folk song lyrics, familiar classical English poetry, and such modern authors as Cummings, Ciardi, Updike, and Hughes. The range of subjects is unusually wide. Each section is illustrated with humorous, imaginative vignettes. Author, title and first line indexes are appended. Ages 8–11.

Lear, Edward. *The Scroobious Pip.* Illustrated by Nancy Ekholm Burkert. New York: Harper & Row, Publishers, 1968.

A mysterious creature, part fish, part insect, part bird, and part beast, firmly refuses to identify himself with any of the creatures who challenge him. He is uniquely himself and answers only, "Chippety flip! Flippety chip! My only name is the Scroobious Pip!" An incomplete poem by the master of nonsensical verse is ably finished by Odgen Nash in Lear's own style. The imaginative, intricately detailed and richly textured illustrations are in complete harmony with the text. Ages 5–adult.

Lewis, Richard, compiler. *In a Spring Garden.* Illustrated by Ezra Jack Keats. New York: Dial Press, 1965.

Twenty-three haiku presenting moods and moments from morning to evening of a day in spring. The delicate Oriental illustrations that usually accompany haiku are replaced here by vibrant colors, rich textures, and patterns of paint and cut paper in an endlessly inventive series of double-page pictures of frogs, leaves, insects, and dewdrops. The poems are superimposed over these collages, one per picture. Despite the intensity of pictorial image, the poems are not overwhelmed; each element serves to reinforce the effect of the other. A very beautiful introduction to this particular form of Japanese poetry. All ages.

—————. *Miracles: Poems by Children of the English-speaking World.* New York: Simon and Schuster, 1966.

A remarkable collection of almost two hundred poems written by children between five and thirteen. The child's creative impulse and his perception of his life and his surroundings are expressed in a wide variety of ways. Each selection is printed on a separate page, and the author's name, age, and home city are included. The illustrations, one for each section, are also by children. All ages.

—————. *The Moment of Wonder; A Collection of Chinese and Japanese Poetry.* New York: Dial Press, 1964.

Poems from all periods of Chinese and Japanese literature are divided into four sections, each with a short preface: "The family of nature," "Landscapes of the sky and earth," "The passage of seasons," and "The ages of man." Brief expressions of awe and delight inspired by nature and by life. Classical Chinese and Japanese paintings accompany the text. An appreciative introduction is included. An A.L.A. Notable Book. Ages 12–adult.

——————. *Out of the Earth I Sing.* New York: W. W. Norton & Co., 1968.
A distinguished array of poems, chants, and songs in which various primitive groups around the world express their basic thoughts and feelings. The Bushmen of the Kalahari and other peoples of Africa, the Indians of North America, the Australian aborigine, and the primitive tribes of India are represented. Translated from the original languages by writers able to retain the originality and freshness of the source material, the selections "sing of the joys, fears, dreams and cares of humanity as a whole—and it is in this singing, in these words, that we may renew our link to a people, who, from the earth, must sing." The striking illustrations are photographs of drawings, paintings, carvings, masks, and other primitive artifacts. A first-line index and a list of the art objects and the museums in which they may be found. An A.L.A. Notable Book. Ages 9–11.

Livingston, Myra Cohn, compiler. *A Tune beyond Us.* Illustrated by James Spanfeller. New York: Harcourt Brace Jovanovich, 1968.
From her own wide reading and from her experience in introducing students to poetry, Myra C. Livingston has compiled a distinguished anthology. International in scope and ranging in time from the eighth century to the present day, it contains not only English, but Russian, Chinese, Spanish, Latin, German, and French poetry, both in the original languages and in translation. Less known works by great poets and works by little known writers were chosen to reflect the interests of active and alert young people. Fresh and individual in selection and presentation. Indexes of titles, first lines, authors, and translators and an editorial foreword. An A.L.A. Notable Book. Ages 12–adult.

——————. *Speak Roughly to Your Little Boy.* Illustrated by Joseph Low. New York: Harcourt Brace Jovanovich, 1971.
A collection of parodies and burlesques of poems loved or loathed by generations of schoolchildren. Most of the subject poems, by such familiar authors as Shakespeare, Blake, Wordsworth, Tennyson, Poe, and Lewis Carroll are well known, but their parodies, generally, are not. Consider " 'Twas brillig, and the slithy toves . . ." imitated in: " 'Twas Euclid, and the theorem pi/Did plane and solid in the text./ All parallel were the radii, /And the ang-gulls convex'd." The original poems appear in Roman type and the parodies follow immediately in italics. There are brief notes at the end of the book as well as an index of titles, first lines and authors. The illustrations are suitably whimsical. Ages 12–adult.

——————. *Whispers and Other Poems.* Illustrated by Jacqueline Chwast. New York: Harcourt Brace Jovanovich, 1958.
Brief, pleasant, often delightful verses for the very young child. The experience and thoughts of a lively, imaginative girl or boy are presented with childlike directness. Healthy joy in living is the predominant mood, accompanied by engaging illustrations. "The winter is an ice-cream treat,/ All frosty white and cold to eat./ But summer is a lemonade/ Of yellow sun and straw-cool shade." Clarity of image distinguishes the poet's work. Ages 5–7.

McCord, David. *Every Time I Climb a Tree.* Illustrated by Marc Simont. Boston: Little, Brown and Co., 1967.

From three of the author's earlier books, *Far and Few, Take Sky,* and *All Day Long,* 25 of the "youngest verses" have been selected. Plants and animals and the simple pleasures of childhood are described in verses which range from amusing nonsense to serene loveliness. Marc Simont's delightful drawings shift with the mood of the poems from the cartoonlike to the delicately beautiful. Ages 5–9.

McDonald, Gerald D., compiler. *A Way of Knowing: A Collection of Verse for Boys.* Illustrated by Clare and John Ross. New York: Thomas Y. Crowell, 1959.
A vigorous collection designed to appeal to the boy reader who likes strong, straightforward verse untinged by sentimentality. "Fur, fin and feather," "Live and learn," "Wondering," "Rise and go" are some of the section-titles and the back includes lyric, humorous, and traditional verse. The variety of poetic style from Blake, Coffin, and Emerson to Sandburg, de la Mare, and Thomas provides something for a variety of tastes. A short introduction sets the pace of the book and gives useful information on how to present poetry to a group. Author, title and first line indexes. Ages 11–15.

Merriam, Eve. *It Doesn't Always Have to Rhyme*. Illustrated by Malcom Spooner. New York: Atheneum, 1964.
A captivating collection of sixty poems in which a variety of verse patterns are used to show that rhyming is not always necessary. The place of mnemonics, homonyms, and onomatopoeia in poetry is demonstrated with skill and feeling. An enjoyable introduction to the beauty of words—wonderful words that tingle on the tongue and linger in the ear. A must for reading aloud. "How To Eat a Poem" and " 'I' Says the Poem" are an invitation to any reader who has shied away from poetry. Small amusing drawings are sprinkled through the text. Ages 10–adult.

Moore, Lilian. *I Feel the Same Way*. Illustrated by Robert Quackenbush. New York: Atheneum, 1967.
Twenty small poems of city and suburb whose simple imagery captures the child's feelings about fog, wind, rain, insects, flowers, seasons, and so on. The soft pastel pictures accompanying each verse emphasize the concept that beauty may be encountered in the most unlikely places. Bright, perceptive writing. Ages 5–8.

Morrison, Lillian. *Remember Me When This You See*. Illustrated by M. Bauernschmidt. New York: Thomas Y Crowell, 1961.
A companion volume to the author's *Yours Till Niagara Falls* (New York: Thomas Y Crowell, 1950), this book takes its title from a sentiment often found in autograph albums. Clever, catchy rhymes and rhythms contributed to such albums by friends, relatives, and ancestors are arranged by topic: friendship, graduation, love, and so forth. The lively text is mirrored by equally lively illustrations. Ages 8–11.

O'Neill, Mary. *Hailstones and Halibut Bones*. Illustrated by Leonard Weisgard. New York: Doubleday & Co., 1961.
Twelve colors are evoked and described in gay, humorous, and often subtle verses. The title comes from the opening lines of "What Is White?" "White is a dove/ And lily of the valley/ And a puddle of milk/ Spilled in an alley—/ A ship's sail/ A kite's tail/ A wedding veil/ Hailstones and/ Halibut bones/ And some people's telephones." The illustrations, each in the appropriate color, are delectable. For reading aloud and to stimulate the imagination. Ages 10–adult.

Parker, Elinor, compiler. *The Singing and the Gold*. Illustrated by Clare Leighton. New York: Thomas Y Crowell, 1962.
An outstanding anthology of world poetry in thirty-four languages ranging from Arabic to Zulu and including Egyptian, Greek, and Shoshone Indian. Arranged by subject rather than language to show the universality of man's thoughts and emotions.

The translations have been chosen for their beauty of expression. Distinguished wood engravings enhance the text. In addition to the standard author, title, and first line indexes, there are indexes by language and translator. Ages 12–17.

Plotz, Helen, compiler. *The Earth Is the Lord's: Poems of the Spirit*. Illustrated by Clare Leighton. New York: Thomas Y Crowell, 1965.
"Man's long struggle with the idea of God" as expressed in poetry is the theme of this discriminating compilation. Beginning with an affirmation of faith in Bynner's "I Need No Sky" and concluding with Thomas Merton's work, the selections are arranged in five groups: the search for God; rebellion, despair, and triumph of the search; saints; brotherhood of man; prayers of praise. Designed for the thinker and philosophical reader but rewarding to anyone who will take the time to contemplate. Illustrated with attractive wood engravings. Author, title, and first-line indexes. An A.L.A. Notable Book. Ages 12–17.
Two earlier anthologies by Helen Plotz, *Imagination's Other Place: Poems of Science and Mathematics* (New York: Thomas Y Crowell, 1955) and *Untune the Sky: Poems of Music and Dance* (New York: Thomas Y Crowell, 1957), are compiled with the same discrimination.

Rasmussen, Knud, compiler. *Beyond the High Hills: A Book of Eskimo Poems*. Illustrated by Guy Mary-Rousseliere. Cleveland: World Publishing Co., 1961.
A Danish explorer and ethnologist has gathered this unique collection of Eskimo songs. They express the exultation of hunting, the joyous welcome of a new day, fear and respect for the Arctic's fierce climate, and acceptance of old age and death. The striking, dramatic color photos reflect the beauty, strength, wisdom, and vigor of Eskimo thought and character. Ages 10–adult.

Reed, Gwendolyn, compiler. *Bird Songs*. Illustrated by Gabriele Margules. New York: Atheneum, 1969.
The blackbird, blue jay, wren, robin, swallow, heron, owl, and other feathered creatures are described by poets of various countries and ages. Of the wren, Walter de la Mare writes: "Never was sweeter seraph hid/ Within so small a house—/ A tiny, inch-long, eager, ardent,/ Feathered mouse." A pleasing format with wide margins and small pen-and-brush sketches. An author and title index. An A.L.A. Notable Book. Ages 11–adult.

Reed, Gwendolyn, compiler. *Out of the Ark*. Illustrated by Gabriele Margules. New York: Atheneum, 1968.
The title indicates the scope of this anthology. The verses range through the animal kingdom from termite to buffalo, with a few mythical beasts tossed in for good measure. The myriad moods of poets, beginning with the Greeks, are represented, though British and American authors predominate. The random arrangement and impressionistic sketches invite browsing. Difficult or unusual words are defined at the end of each selection, and background notes on some poems are included, along with an author-title index. An A.L.A. Notable Book. Ages 12–15.
William Cole's *The Birds and the Beasts Were There* (Cleveland: World Publishing Co., 1963) though similar in coverage, includes more light verse and more poems for younger readers, and has striking woodcuts by Helen Siegl. Only seven selections are duplicated.

Sandburg, Carl. *Wind Song*. Illustrated by William A. Smith. New York: Harcourt Brace Jovanovich, 1960.
Poems selected by the poet himself after over forty years of writing for young people. In addition to familiar old favorites, sixteen new poems have been added. A rich treasury of images, sounds, and ideas about nature and people grouped under such headings as "Night," "Blossom Themes," "Wind," "Corn Belt," and "Little People."

A suitable drawing precedes each section. A brief foreword by the poet informs the reader that "some poems may please you for half a minute . . . other poems you may feel to be priceless and you hug them to your heart . . . in this book poems of each kind may be found: you do the finding." Ages 10–adult.

Stevenson, Robert Louis. *A Child's Garden of Verses*. Illustrated by Brian Wildsmith. New York: Franklin Watts, 1966.
　　Stevenson's beloved and familiar poems, freshly interpreted in the lavish, glowing color characteristic of Brian Wildsmith's style. The illustrations may seem bombastic and overbearing to some, exciting and imaginative to others. Nostalgic adults may feel the Victorian mood of the poems is best expressed by Jessie Wilcox Smith, *A Child's Garden of Verses* (New York: Charles Scribner's, 1905) ; or they may prefer the delicate pastels of Tasha Tudor, *A Child's Garden of Verses* (New York: Henry Z. Walck, 1947) . An A.L.A. Notable Book. Ages 5–8.

Tagore, Rabindranath. *Moon, For What Do You Wait?*. Illustrated by Ashley Bryan. New York: Atheneum, 1967.
　　A small book of great distinction containing seventeen brief poems chosen from Tagore's *Stray Birds* (New York: Macmillan Co., 1916) . Each poem is set against a striking woodcut in red, yellow, blue, and black. The poet is struck afresh by the wonders of nature; in their clarity, simplicity, brevity, and joyfulness, the poems are reminiscent of Haiku. Chiefly adult in appeal, but a guided interest will make Tagore a friend forever to the young reader. Ages 7–adult.

Thompson, Blanche Jennings, compiler. *All the Silver Pennies*. Illustrated by Ursula Arndt. New York: Macmillan Co., 1967.
　　Silver Pennies and *More Silver Pennies*, two children's classics, are combined here in one appealing, attractive anthology. Though objections have been raised to the introductory remarks preceding each selection—some of which tend to be coy—they may help the less imaginative child to find his way into the poem. The great poets of the twenties and thirties, both British and American, are well represented. Author, title, and first-line indexes are appended. Ages 9–11.

Untermeyer, Louis, compiler. *Golden Treasury of Poetry*. Illustrated by Joan Walsh Anglund. New York: Golden Press, 1959.
　　A welcome collection of over four hundred poems from Chaucer to Ogden Nash. Familiar and lesser known poems have been arranged by themes such as animals, people, humor, nature, seasons etc. Brief comments on a poet's life or style, the period in which he wrote or the meaning or purpose of a poem are interjected here and there but do not obtrude. Anglund's illustrations in black and white and color lend charm to every page. For the family, the classroom, the poetry lover and to introduce poetry to the poem deaf. Indexed by author, title and first line. All ages.
　　Other fine anthologies edited by Louis Untermeyer include *This Singing World* (New York: Harcourt, Brace, World, 1926) , *Rainbow in the Sky* (New York: Harcourt, Brace, World, 1935) , and *Stars To Steer By* (New York: Harcourt, Brace, World, 1941) .

Withers, Carl, compiler. *A Rocket in My Pocket*. Illustrated by Susanne Suba. New York: Holt, Rinehart and Winston, 1948.
　　An utterly fascinating compilation of over four hundred rhymes, chants, tongue-twisters, and riddles current among youngsters in the U.S.A. The bouncing, rolling, rhythmic nonsense of the verses is perfectly expressed in line drawings. The sequel, *I Saw a Rocket Walk a Mile* (New York: Holt, Rinehart, and Winston, 1965) , contains nonsense tales, chants, and songs from many lands. Two vibrant collections with sure-fire appeal. Ages 8–10.

Picture books and
picture storybooks

Briggs, Raymond, compiler and illustrator. *The Mother Goose Treasury*. New York: Coward-McCann, 1966.

Four-hundred eight rhymes, nearly all selected from the Iona and Peter Opie collection, and accompanied by 897 exuberant illustrations. The latter, in both black and white and color, are clever, sophisticated, and amusing, done with imagination and a tinge of the grotesque. Index of first lines and titles. Ages 5–8.

Brooke, Leslie, compiler and illustrator. *Ring O'Roses*. New York: Warne, 1922.

Twenty-one nursery rhymes set against the English countryside. The detailed illustrations are done in pastel colors. Extra action spills over onto several pages, expanding the verses in a delightful way reminiscent of the work of Randolph Caldecott, whom Brooke greatly admired. Characters, both human and animal, usually have something humorous in either their posture or their facial expression. An unforgettable interpretation of *Mother Goose*. Ages 5–8.

De Angeli, Marguerite, compiler and illustrator. *Marguerite De Angeli's Book of Nursery and Mother Goose Rhymes*. New York: Doubleday & Co., 1954.

A Mother Goose for the entire family to pore over. Over 350 rhymes, including all the well known ones and many that are less well known. The illustrations, 32 in full color (half of which are full-paged), and over 200 scattered throughout the text, are enchanting. Backgrounds and costumes reflect the period flavor of the verses. A first-line index and a foreword by the artist. All ages.

Spier, Peter, compiler and illustrator. *And So My Garden Grows*. New York: Doubleday & Co., 1969.

Traditional nursery rhymes, many unfamiliar, acquire new lustre when set in the beautiful Italian countryside. Two children in nineteenth-century dress wander through the Florentine garden of Fiesole ("Mistress Mary, quite contrary . . ."), the fourteenth-century city "of the fine towers," San Gimignano ("This is the key to the Kingdom / In that Kingdom is a city . ."), and the water garden of the Villa Gamberaia ("A hedge between keeps friendship green."). "Mother, may I go and bathe? / Yes my darling daughter . . ." is set in the world-famous Avenue of the Hundred Fountains in the Tivoli gardens. The lively water color paintings are full of captivating details that invite a lingering perusal. Notes identifying the locales will interest adults, artists, and travelers. A fourth in Spier's outstanding Mother Goose Library series, which includes *London Bridge Is Falling Down* (New York: Doubleday & Co., 1967), *To Market! To Market!* (New York: Doubleday & Co., 1967), and *Hurrah, We're Outward Bound* (New York: Doubleday & Co., 1968). Ages 5–8.

Wildsmith, Brian, compiler and illustrator. *Brian Wildsmith's Mother Goose*. New York: Franklin Watts, 1964.

Approximately 75 rhymes, many of them traditional, but with a sprinkling of the unfamiliar to lend variety to the whole. The arrangement of one rhyme per page lends itself to a casual, unhurried reading and an appreciation of each rhyme on an individual basis. Wildsmith's illustrations are striking yet sensitive and embody vivid, glowing colors that complement each verse, capturing the fun as well as the dramatic action. Ages 4–6.

Other Picture Books

Alexander, Martha. *Bobo's Dream*. Illustrated by the author. New York: Dial Press, 1970.

An amusing picture story without words. Bobo, a little dachshund, has his bone stolen from him by a large dog. Bobo's master retrieves it for him. The grateful Bobo dreams that he returns the favor when some big boys seize his master's football. He grows to heroic size and cows the mean youngsters. Waking from his dream, Bobo bravely stands off the big dog when it comes back. The unpretentious, humorous, three-color drawings need no words to underscore the message that might does not make right. Ages 3–6.

Anderson, Lonzo. *Two Hundred Rabbits*. Illustrated by Adrienne Adams. New York: Viking Press, 1968.

A peasant boy wishes to entertain the king but is a failure at singing, playing the fiddle, and juggling. An old woman suggests that he make a whistle of slippery elm, which she then enchants so that he can summon 199 rabbits by playing a tune. He leads them to the castle in parade formation, 20 rows of ten each except for the last row of nine rabbits. When the king, reviewing the procession, is upset by the uneven last line, the narrator of the tale reveals himself. He is the two-hundredth rabbit! Delicate but lively pastel illustrations accompany this gently humorous story. Read aloud. An A.L.A. Notable Book. Ages 6–8.

Balet, Jan. *Joanjo: A Portuguese Tale*. Illustrated by the author. New York: Delacorte, 1967.

A small boy, weary of the prospect of spending his life as a hardworking fisherman, dreams that he leaves his village. Remaining child-sized, he becomes a merchant, the mayor, and finally governor. He then marries a beautiful wife and plans to become king, but wakes up. His loving family are around him, food is waiting, and he decides he is better off at home. A much-used theme saved by the rich and striking stylized illustrations. An A.L.A. Notable Book. Ages 5–7.

Barrett, Judi. *Animals Should Definitely Not Wear Clothing*. Illustrated by Ron Barrett. New York: Atheneum, 1970.

The absurdity of dressing animals is shown in this humorous picture book. The sheep perspires in a wool sweater, scarf and cap; the moose's suspenders get caught on his antlers; the hen in figured slacks has problems laying eggs; the giraffe looks ridiculous with seven neckties, and the porcupine's quills come right through the polka dots. Uncluttered drawings and brief text make this book a natural for picture book storytelling. Ages 4–8.

Benchley, Nathaniel. *A Ghost Named Fred*. Illustrated by Ben Shecter. New York: Harper & Row, Publishers, 1968.

A small, imaginative, and self-reliant boy enters an old house to get out of the rain and encounters an absent-minded ghost. The ghost cannot remember the whereabouts of the treasure he is supposed to be guarding and asks the boy to help him find it. More humorous than scary, with engaging illustrations in color. A pleasant ghost story for the beginning reader. Ages 6–7.

Benchley's *The Strange Disappearance of Arthur Cluck* (New York: Harper & Row, Publishers, 1967) is an equally pleasant offering for the beginning mystery fan.

Bolognese, Don. *A New Day*. Illustrated by the author. New York: Delacorte, 1970.

The Nativity story in modern dress. Jose and Maria, Mexican migrant workers, can find no room in the local motel. They take refuge in the garage of an open-all-night gas station, where Maria has her baby. A band of hippie musicians plays for the little family; other people, attracted by the music, come and bring food, and soon there is dancing. The party breaks up when a policeman warns Jose that the chief wants to arrest him for disturbing the peace. A truck driver offers the family a ride across the border and they leave. Although there is no mention of God or Christmas, the spirit is there, with ordinary people helping one another. The pictures, striking and warm, eloquently expand the sparse text. Ages 5–7.

Bonsall, Crosby. *Whose Eye Am I?* Illustrated by Ylla. New York: Harper & Row, Publishers, 1969.
   A slight story of a boy who sees an eye through a hole in a fence and searches among the barnyard animals for its owner. In turn the rooster, turkey, horse, cow, bull, and others disclaim all knowledge of the mysterious eye. Finally a soft, shy rabbit reveals himself. The superb photography completely overshadows the text. Ideal for picture book browsing and reading aloud. Ages 4–8.

Brown, Marcia. *How, Hippo!* Illustrated by the author. New York: Charles Scribner's, 1969.
   A baby hippo spends peaceful days dozing by Mama and placid nights eating by Mama, snug and secure. He learns how to make the appropriate hippo sounds, practicing "how" in a variety of tones, each with a special meaning. Attacked by a fearsome crocodile, he "hows" with all his might, and Mama bites the crocodile in two. Mama's expression is extraordinarily fierce for this gentle animal, but the marvelous night spread of the herd, the awkward spontaneity of Baby, and the African background are beautifully caught in woodcuts of blue, pink and green. An A.L.A. Notable Book. Ages 5–6.

Burningham, John. *ABC*. Illustrated by the author. New York: Bobbs-Merrill Co., 1967.
   An ABC that eschews the bizarre approach. Each object is a familiar one—with the possible exception of "volcano." An apple, birds, a clown, dogs, flowers, and a girl succeed one another in full color. Each occupies a full page with the accompanying letter in upper and lower case, and the word itself, on the facing page. Many of the illustrations are imbued with quiet humor. Ages 3–6.

Chalmers, Mary. *Be Good, Harry*. Illustrated by the author. New York: Harper & Row, Publishers, 1967.
   A "child in kitten's clothing," three-year-old Harry, faces his first stay with a baby sitter. He prepares for his visit by piling all his favorite toys and three books into a wagon. When mother leaves Harry cries, but the wise old baby sitter (a comfortable grandmotherly cat) consoles him with milk and cookies, cuddles him and all his toys in her ample lap, and reads each book three times! Beautifully simple and direct, this book speaks reassuringly and tenderly to the small children who face this situation. Ages 3–6.
   Previous titles about Harry are *Throw a Kiss, Harry* (New York: Harper & Row, Publishers, 1958) and *Take a Nap, Harry* (New York: Harper & Row, Publishers, 1964).

Clifton, Lucille. *Some of the Days of Everett Anderson*. Illustrated by Evaline Ness. New York: Holt, Rinehart and Winston, 1970.
   The thoughts and actions of a lively, six-year-old black boy from Monday morning to Sunday night are expressed in nine short poems. Though a city child, Everett Anderson knows the joys of climbing and kite flying as well as the sound of the siren and the noise of traffic. "Being six / is full of tricks / and Everett Anderson knows it. / Being a boy / is full of joy / and Everett Anderson shows it." Black, brown, and yellow line and wash drawings interpret the vigor of the text. Ages 5–8.

DeRegniers, Beatrice Schenk. *May I Bring a Friend?* Illustrated by Beni Montresor. New York: Atheneum, 1964.

When the king and queen invite a small boy to tea on Sunday, he asks if he may bring a friend. Permission granted, he brings a giraffe. On Monday—a hippo, on Tuesday—monkeys, and so on, until on Saturday the courteous royal couple are invited to tea at the zoo in return for their generous hospitality. Simple, repetitive rhymes that children will enjoy as well as the situations. Luminous drawings, richly detailed, with something of the feeling of tapestries, accompany the text. Caldecott Award. Ages 5–7.

Emberley, Barbara. *Drummer Hoff*. Illustrated by Ed Emberly. Englewood Cliffs, N.J.: Prentice-Hall, 1967.

A bouncy, repetitive folk rhyme describes the building of a cannon. From "Private Parriage brought the carriage, Corporal Farrell brought the barrel" on up the military hierarchy to General Border, who "gave the order," each verse ends with "but Drummer Hoff fired it off." A magnificent "Kahbahbloom" explodes across a crimson double page when Drummer Hoff finally does his duty. But the ending—the cannon has become a nesting place for birds, insects crawl upon it, grass and flowers grow round it—is a surprise. Bright colored, modern woodcuts with a Napoleonic flavor fit the staccato text. An A.L.A. Notable Book. Winner of the Caldecott Award. Ages 4–7.

Feagles, Anita. *Autun and the Bear*. Illustrated by Gertrude Barrer-Russell. New York: Young Scott Books, 1967.

An Icelandic farmer's single-minded determination to present a bear to the king of Denmark brings him into conflict with the king of Norway, with whom Denmark is at war. But Autun's steadfastness wins royal favor and rich gifts from both kings. This ancient Icelandic legend not only shows the Vikings as great travelers—Autun sails from Iceland to Greenland to Norway and Denmark and travels on foot to Rome as well—but also shows their unabashed, independent, and fearless qualities. The stark, bald simplicity of the saga-like text is wonderfully enhanced by the striking three-color illustrations, which combine medieval detail with impressionistic beauty. Ages 8–10.

Fontane, Theodor. *Sir Ribbeck of Ribbeck of Havelland*. Illustrated by Nonny Hogrogrian. New York: Macmillan Co., 1969.

An old German ballad relates the tale of a kindly, generous knight who gives away "sweet pears" to all who come by. His miserly heir has no intention of carrying on the old man's generosity, but Sir Ribbeck's last request that a pear be planted by his grave foils the heir. It takes root, grows, and blossoms, "until one autumn as of old, the tree was rich with pears of gold" and once more free to passersby. Fine woodcuts in black, green and orange-gold complement the somewhat pedestrian text. An A.L.A. Notable Book. Ages 4–6.

Freeman, Don. *The Guard Mouse*. Illustrated by the author. New York: Viking Press, 1967.

The Petrini family of *Pet of the Met* (New York: Viking Press, 1953) and *Norman the Doorman* (New York: Viking Press, 1953) come to visit cousin Clyde, who stands guard at Buckingham Palace. Leaving the younger mice to rest in his bearskin hat, Clyde shows their parents the city. The resulting mouse-eye view of London is a delightful introduction to its most famous sights. Among the bright water color scenes, the double spread of the Thames as seen from the hour hand of Big Ben is especially notable. Ages. 5–8.

Galdone, Paul. *Henny Penny*. Illustrated by the author. New York: Seabury Press Inc., 1968.

A master at endowing familiar stories with fresh life, Paul Galdone, in vigorous, bold color, depicts the well known quintet of Henny Penny, Cocky Locky, Ducky Lucky, Goosey Loosey and Turkey Lurkey on their way to tell the king the sky is falling. But, alas, crafty Foxy Loxy entices them into his cave and the king never receives the message. Each character is portrayed as an individual with most expressive facial features. The last picture, showing Foxy Loxy as a family man surrounded by his wife and seven bright offspring, is a gem. Ages 5–8.

Another fine example of Paul Galdone's work is his version of the famous Jataka tale, *The Monkey and the Crocodile* (New York: Seabury Press, 1969).

Goodall, John S. *The Ballooning Adventures of Paddy Pork*. Illustrated by the author. New York: Harcourt Brace Jovanovich, 1969.

When Paddy Pork sets out on a balloon trip, he sails over a tropical island, rescues a charming feminine pig from a cauldron about to boil, views a snowy forest, and barely escapes a raging sea. A sequel to *The Adventures of Paddy Pork* (New York: Harcourt Brace Jovanovich, 1968) and, like it, is textless. The beautifully detailed pictures on full and half pages provide suspense and fun for all youngsters, especially those of preschool age. Ages 3–7.

Graham, Lorenz. *Every Man Heart Lay Down*. Illustrated by Colleen Browning. New York: Thomas Y Crowell, 1970.

A retelling of the Christmas story in the speech patterns of African people newly acquainted with English. The author's introduction tells how he first heard the stories in Liberia and describes their transformation into the rhythmical cadence of the story-teller. The stylized African designs in blue, black, yellow, and orange form a perfect background for Joseph, Mary, and "the small pican" who came to earth for the people so that "Bye-m-bye they savvy the way." The familiar and beloved story takes on new freshness and vitality in this African interpretation, which ends with the wise men and the country folk looking "on the God pican and every man heart lay down." All Ages.

In the same idiom Lorenz Graham tells the story of the Deluge in *God Wash the World and Start Again* (New York: Thomas Y Crowell, 1970) and Exodus in *A Road Down into the Sea* (New York: Thomas Y Crowell 1970).

Graham, Margaret Bloy. *Be Nice to Spiders*. Illustrated by the author. New York: Harper & Row, Publishers, 1967.

Informative fun about a pet spider given to a zoo by a small boy who cannot keep pets in his new apartment. The animals, plagued by flies, are relieved of them by Helen, as she spins her web in cage after cage. But when a zealous zoo keeper orders a clean-up, Helen's webs are destroyed and the flies return. Then the zoo keeper realizes what a contribution Helen has made. He permits her to weave undisturbed and the animals are happy once more. Cheerful sketches make a *Charlotte's Web* appeal on a primary level. Ages 5–8.

Hutchins, Pat. *Rosie's Walk*. Illustrated by the author. New York: Macmillan Co., 1968.

When Rosie the hen goes for a walk across the yard, around the pond, over the haystack, past the mill, through the fence, under the beehives, and back in time for dinner, she is completely unaware that a fox, with the worst of intentions, is trailing her. However, the unfortunate animal meets with a series of disasters—stepping on a rake, falling in the pond, stifling in a haystack, being routed by angry bees—while oblivious Rosie walks on. Double spread, stylized pictures, brightly colored, are in perfect accord with the nonsensical tale of Nemesis in the barnyard. An A.L.A. Notable Book. Ages 3–6.

————. *The Surprise Party*. Illustrated by the author. New York: Macmillan Co., 1969.

Rabbit confides to owl in a whisper that he is having a party tomorrow. Owl whispers to Squirrel that Rabbit is "hoeing the parsley tomorrow," and the message becomes more and more garbled as it is whispered on through Duck, Mouse, Fox, and Frog. The following day each one rejects Rabbit's overtures until he announces loudly, "I'm having a party." And so they have a wonderful party that is indeed a surprise. An amusing rendition of the game of "gossip" with stylized illustrations in yellow, orange, brown, and green. Each animal is given a distinct personality. Ages 5–7.

Kantrowitz, Mildred. *Maxie*. Illustrated by Emily A. McCully. New York: Parent's Magazine Press, 1970.

The pitiable lot of a solitary old person is shown here in picture book format. The heroine, an old woman, is not the well-adjusted happy grandmother of many stories. She lives alone with her cat and canary on the top floor of an old brownstone house and becomes more and more lonely and depressed, finally taking to her bed. Her neighbors, who depended on the song of her canary, the whistle of her teakettle, and her unvarying routine to send them off to their various days' activities, crowd in to see if she is all right. Maxie is assured that she is needed and recovers. A happy, idealistic, and unfortunately unrealistic ending, but it may give young readers and their parents something to think about. Ages 5–8.

Keats, Ezra Jack. *The Little Drummer Boy*. Illustrated by Ezra Jack Keats. New York: Macmillan Co., 1968.

A simple, sentimental Christmas song that has become a popular modern favorite is transformed into a striking picture book. The story of a poor boy who can bring no gift to the Child but a solo on his drum is illustrated in a bright array of colors with an occasional collage effect. The result is a visual feast. The one-line melody together with the words is given at the end of the book. Ages 5–7.

Another carol beautifully interpreted by an outstanding artist is *Bring a Torch, Jeanette, Isabella* (New York: Charles Scribner's, 1963), in which Adrienne Adams completely captures the Old French background of the song.

Kessler, Leonard. *Kick, Pass, and Run*. Illustrated by the author. New York: Harper & Row, Publishers, 1966.

Before the curious eyes of Rabbit, Duck, Cat, Dog, Owl, Frog, Turtle, and three birds, the game of football is played by two teams of youngsters. The fascinated animals attempt to play it themselves, though their first ball, an apple, is eaten by Frog, and their second, a paper bag, is broken by the Duck's kickoff. The temporary possession of a real football enables Cat to make a touchdown and the game ends. Slight but enjoyable sports fare for beginning readers. Ages 6–8.

Kijima, Hajime. *Little White Hen*. Illustrated by Setsuko Hane. New York: Harcourt Brace Jovanovich, 1969.

A fresh interpretation of the well-known story of the hen who outwits the fox. A plump, clever, white hen takes refuge in a tree to escape a hungry fox. When he fails to sweet-talk her out of the tree, he circles round it so fast that the hen becomes giddy, falls, and is popped into the fox's sack. The resourceful hen happens to have scissors, needle, and thread with her and cuts her way out of the sack while the fox sleeps. Refilling the sack with rocks and sewing up the cut, the little white hen goes on her way. The surprise and frustration of the fox when he empties the sack and the events leading up to that are delightfully drawn in bright crayon colors. An A.L.A. Notable Book. Ages 4–7.

Kraus, Robert. *Whose Mouse Are You?* Illustrated by Jose Aruego. New York: Macmillan Co., 1970.

A forlorn mouse is nobody's mouse because mother is inside the cat, father is inside a trap, sister is on a faraway mountain top, and no little brother exists. But the little mouse sheds his sadness and shakes his mother out of the cat, saws his father out of the trap, and rescues his sister from the mountain top by balloon. Last of all, to the reunited family a mouseling is born, and nobody's mouse has a little brother. Bright orange and yellow line and wash drawings with contrasting touches of mouse gray make this an utterly delightful book. Ages 5–7.

Lent, Blair. *From King Boggen's Hall to Nothing-at-all.* Illustrated by Blair Lent. Boston: Little, Brown and Co., 1967.
Old English nursery rhymes, Edward Lear, and Mother Goose yield 14 such fascinating and unconventional dwelling places as Peter's pumpkin shell and the jar of the Old Person of Bar. The bright, distinctive woodcuts, showing in detail the furnishings of each odd domicile, are sure to delight small children. Ages 5–7.

Lexau, Joan M. *Crocodile and Hen.* Illustrated by Joan Sandin. New York: Harper & Row, Publishers, 1969.
A crocodile about to snap up a fat hen cannot do so when she calls him, with perfect aplomb, brother. The perplexed saurian wonders and wonders how he could possibly be related to a creature so different in appearance and habits from himself. Enlightenment comes when a lizard tells him that, as he and Hen are both hatched from eggs, they must be related. Though still hungry, the baffled crocodile accepts Lizard's logic and Hen is safe forevermore. A hilarious African tale with bold, colorful illustrations that capture the humor of Crocodile's ridiculous predicament. Ages 5–7.

Lionni, Leo. *Alexander and the Wind-up Mouse.* Illustrated by the author. New York: Pantheon Books, 1969.
Alexander, a lonely mouse, thinks he will be safer as a toy mouse like Willy. But when Willy is to be junked, Alexander begs the magic lizard to save him from the scrap heap by making him real. A lesson in friendship. The collage technique is handled to such effect that the characters' eyes are even given various expressions. Ages 5–7.
Other books by the same author, like this one, runners-up for the Caldecott award, are: *Inch by Inch* (New York: Ivan Obolensky, 1960); *Swimmy* (New York: Pantheon, 1963); and *Frederick* (New York: Pantheon, 1967).

————. *The Biggest House in the World.* Illustrated by the author. New York: Pantheon Books, 1968.
A small snail's desire for a big house fades when his father tells him the story of a foolish young snail who grew his house so big that he could not move and died of slow starvation. Large illustrations in color give a snail's-eye view of small creatures moving about among the vegetation. The biggest house in the world is a huge shell, encrusted with numerous superstructures. Picturing it, the young, listening snail resolves to keep his shell small and mobile. Ages 3–7.

Lobel, Arnold. *Frog and Toad Are Friends.* Illustrated by the author. New York: Harper & Row, Publishers, 1970.
A long-legged green frog and a squat brown toad are featured in five adventures depicting the joys and frustrations of friendship. In one of these, Toad is reluctant to awaken from his winter's sleep, and lonesome Frog pulls month after month off the calendar until he reaches wide-awake May and can rouse his friend. Told in short, easy-to-read sentences with droll, very expressive illustrations in soft green and brown. An I CAN READ BOOK. An A.L.A. Notable Book. A Caldecott Award runner-up. Ages 5–8.

Lord, Beman. *A Monster's Visit.* Illustrated by Don Bolognese. New York: Henry Z. Walck, 1967.

A shy, candy-loving monster hiding in a closet is lured out of his retreat by a boy and his sister, who offer him sweets. In return, he entertains them by changing shapes. The full-color pictures blaze with vitality. The story evokes a mood of companionship and may help allay the night fears of small children. For many youngsters the monster theme has popular appeal. Ages 5–8.

Mahy, Margaret. *A Lion in the Meadow.* Illustrated by Jenny Williams. New York: Franklin Watts, 1969.

A little boy with an over-active imagination tells his mother that there is a lion in the meadow. Mother fights fire with fire by giving him a matchbox which she says contains a tiny dragon. That when released, it will grow enormous and frighten the lion away. The lion, who is really friendly, runs from the dragon and takes refuge in the closet. Mother, protesting that she made the dragon up, is told that he has come true. Bright and lively illustrations combine humor and color in this fanciful tale, which is sure to appeal to young pretenders. Ages 5–7.

Mari, Iela, and Enzo Mari. *The Apple and the Moth.* Illustrated by the authors. New York: Pantheon Books, 1970.

First green and then bright red, an apple hangs from a green bough. A cutaway picture shows a tiny red dot inside the apple. A small worm emerges from the red dot, eats its way out of the apple, spins a cocoon, and sleeps through fall and winter. In the spring a moth emerges and flies to a blossoming apple tree. It deposits an egg in an apple blossom and the cycle begins all over again. A most attractive picture book in which bright, distinct drawings describe a natural process without a single word. Ages 3–7.

Equally eye-catching, wordless, and informative is *The Chicken and the Egg* (New York: Pantheon Books, 1970), by the same authors. Iela Mari's solo title, *Magic Balloon* (New York: S. G. Phillips, 1969), is a slight, wordless fantasy.

Mayer, Mercer. *A Boy, a Dog, and a Frog.* Illustrated by the author. New York: Dial Press, 1967.

A humorous picture story without words in which a boy and a dog try to catch a frog, who escapes in a pond. When the dejected boy and dog leave frogless for home, the frog follows them there and into the bathtub. Diverting pen and ink line drawings. The sequel, *Frog, Where Are You?* (New York: Dial Press, 1969) finds frog back in the pond with a family, one of whom becomes the new pet. Small book for small hands. Ages 3–5.

Miles, Miska. *Nobody's Cat.* Illustrated by John Schoenherr. Boston: Little, Brown and Co., 1969.

He slept on a box of papers in an alley and scrounged for his food—a house cat's milk, a butcher's bones, the school custodian's lunch box—and when children let him into the classroom and fed him, he left a mouse at the schoolhouse door. A realistic picture of the life of a cat who knew when to run, when to fight, and how to survive in city traffic. Strong illustrations match the text. Reminiscent of Tom Robinson's *Buttons* (New York: Viking Press, 1938) but harsher than that old favorite. An A. L. A. Notable Book. Ages 6–9.

Minarik, Else Homelund. *A Kiss for Little Bear.* Illustrated by Maurice Sendak. New York: Harper & Row, Publishers, 1968.

Little Bear asks Hen to take a picture he drew to Grandmother, who sends him a kiss in return. It passes from animal to animal but comes to a standstill when two little skunks exchange it. The haze of romantic delight that follows leads to a wedding with Little Bear as the best man—after all, it was his kiss that began it. The endearing pictures are among Maurice Sendak's most captivating. The detail shows the influence of Leslie Brooke. An I CAN READ BOOK. An A.L.A. Notable Book. Ages 5–7.

Mosel, Arlene. *Tikki Tikki Tembo.* Illustrated by Blair Lent. New York: Holt, Rinehart and Winston, 1968.
When Tikki Tikki 'Tembo-no Sa Rembo-chari Bari Ruchi-pip Peri Pembo, eldest son of a widow, falls into a well, it takes so long for his little brother to tell what happened that he almost drowns. Based on an Oriental legend explaining why short names are preferable to long. Stylized color drawings reflect the Oriental setting. Excellent for storytelling use with or without the pictures. An A.L.A. Notable Book. Ages 5–9.

Oxenbury, Helen. *Numbers of Things.* Illustrated by the author. New York: Franklin Watts, 1968.
A tall counting book with pictures depicting a variety of objects from one lion to 50 ladybugs. All are brightly colored and full of detail and humor. The layout, combining numerals with words, affords the youngster using the book ample opportunity to count and read together. The details are ingenious: for the number "seven," seven chairs are shown, but they are all different, ranging from a rocker containing an old lady to high chair with a baby in it. Ages 4–7.

Peet, Bill. *Capyboppy.* Illustrated by the author. Boston: Houghton Mifflin Co., 1966.
A South American capybara, the largest rodent in the world, becomes a pet in the Peet family. Though he is not an ideal household pet, Capy's engaging ways and harmless appearance—he resembles a giant guinea pig—make him a favorite with the Peet family and their friends. But as the spoiled animal grows larger, his pranks becomes less funny, and he is finally sent to the zoo. A true story accompanied by hilarious illustrations. The appalled expression on the faces of the three Peet cats when they see Capy bearing down on them is priceless. Ages 8–9.

Politi, Leo. *Moy Moy.* Illustrated by the author. New York: Charles Scribner's, 1960.
Small Chinese–American Lily, who is called Moy Moy or "little sister" by her three older brothers, participates in the excitement of the Chinese New Year festivities in Chinatown, Los Angeles. The shops, the kites, the games, the splendid dragon, the adults, and above all the children are shown with clarity and deep affection. The glowing colors reflect the artist's love of children wherever he finds them. He shows them full of guileless charm and innocence. Ages 5–8.
Los Angeles is also the setting of *Pedro, the Angel of Olvera Street* (New York: Charles Scribner's, 1946), *Juanita* (New York: Charles Scribner's, 1948), *Piccolo's Prank* (New York: Charles Scribner's, 1965) and *Mieko* (Los Angeles: Golden Gate, 1969).

Preston, Edna Mitchell. *Pop Corn and Ma Goodness.* Illustrated by Robert Andrew Parker. New York: Viking Press, 1969.
A rollicking, rural ballad with water color illustrations in a modern vein. Sliding "all down the [muddy] hill," the twain meet, their heads crack, and they are on their way to wedded bliss in the country. A "skippety skoppety" folksy rhyme, ideal for reading aloud. Caldecott Award runner-up 1970. Ages 4–8.

Raskin, Ellen. *And It Rained.* Illustrated by the author. New York: Atheneum, 1969.
An original and unusual tale about a pig, a parrot, and a potto who are determined to have tea every afternoon at four. Unfortunately it rains at five past daily, making the tea weak and the biscuits soggy, and ruining the party. One attempt after another

is made to get around the problem, but without success—until the potto deliberately brews the tea too strong and serves biscuits that are too hard. The rain, arriving on schedule, weakens the tea and softens the biscuits to the precise degree of perfection and the party is a success. Stylized illustrations in blue, green, and yellow depict the zany protagonists. An A.L.A. Notable Book. Ages 5–7.

Schoenherr, John. *The Barn*. Illustrated by the author. Boston: Little, Brown and Co., 1968.
A realistic, unsentimental picture story. A skunk living in an old barn searches for food and almost falls prey to a hungry owl, who has three small owlets to feed. The struggle for survival is shown in double-page stark black and white pictures. An A.L.A. Notable Book. Ages 6–8.

Scott, Ann H. *Sam*. Illustrated by Symeon Shimin. New York: McGraw-Hill Book Co., 1967.
Sam, a small Negro boy, begins to cry after unintentionally annoying every member of his family. Finally a project is found for him, one for which he is not too small or too big but just right. A common childhood problem is lifted from the ordinary by outstanding, sensitive black and white pictures, which reflect Sam's hurt and disappointment when his family rebuffs him. An A.L.A. Notable Book. Ages 5–7.

Selsam, Millicent E. *Benny's Animals and How He Put Them in Order*. Illustrated by Arnold Lobel. New York: Harper & Row, Publishers, 1966.
Benny, an extremely neat boy who likes everything labeled and classified, is puzzled by a collection of sea creatures he brings home. With the help of his parents and a kindly museum professor he learns how to divide animals into those with and without backbones and from there on into the major zoological divisions. Scientific information is skilfully combined with a pleasing humor-tinged plot. A book from the I CAN READ series. Ages 6–8.

Sendak, Maurice. *In the Night Kitchen*. Illustrated by the author. New York: Harper & Row, Publishers, 1970.
A small boy's dream drops him out of bed, out of pajamas, and into the cake batter of the Night Kitchen, where three bakers who look exactly like Oliver Hardy mistake him for the milk and begin to stir. Up and out pops Mickey, to construct an airplane out of the batter. He flies to the Milky Way, a huge bottle of milk, and sends some of it to the Night Kitchen, saving the day for the bakers. Maurice Sendak draws heavily on the impressions of his childhood to create the dream city of the Night Kitchen, whose skyline is composed of kitchen utensils. His triple bakers are reminiscent of the Sunshine Bakery symbol, and the Mickey Oven is lettered in Mickey Mouse style. Sendak's birthdate, his childhood addresses, the out-of-context names of his dog Jennie and of his parents, Philip and Sadie, are integrated into superb pictures that combine meticulous draughtsmanship with softly colored but diamond-clear line. Adults seeing Mickey's nakedness may read Freudian overtones into the action, but children will find it funny and intriguing. A Caldecott Award runner-up. Ages 3–8.

Dr. Seuss. *Horton Hatches the Egg*. Illustrated by the author. New York: Random House, 1940.
The zany genius of Theodore Geisel, whose pen name is Dr. Seuss, has never shown to better advantage than in this tale of a good-hearted elephant who promises a lazy mother bird that he will sit on her nest and keep her egg warm until she returns from a short rest. Thoroughly bored with egg sitting, she does not return at all, but Horton remains at his post as he has promised, because "I meant what I said, and I said what

I meant. An elephant's faithful one hundred percent!" Horton is vindicated a year later, when an elephant bird hatches out ("it had ears, and a tail, and a trunk just like his!"), in a totally satisfying ending. Ages 5–adult.

————. *The Cat in the Hat*. Illustrated by the author. New York: Random House, 1957.

A story in Dr. Seuss' inimitable style for readers who have finished the primer level in school. A cat comes to entertain two lonesome children on a rainy day and completely upsets every room in the house. But just before mother comes homes, he swishes everything back into place. Fantastic fun and a boon to beginning and reluctant readers everywhere. Ages 5–7.

Other equally good books by Dr. Seuss are: *The Bat in the Hat Comes Back*, (1958), *Green Eggs and Ham*, (1960), *Hop on Pop*, (1963), and *Fox in Socks* (1965), all published in New York by Random House.

Shecter, Ben. *Conrad's Castle*. Illustrated by the author. New York: Harper & Row, Publishers, 1967.

A little boy, accompanied by his dog, picks up a rock and tosses it up into the sky, where it remains, defying the law of gravity. Mounting a ladder, Conrad builds an elaborate castle in the air, while his chums attempt to bring him down to earth and reality by offering to let him view a dead mouse, be captain of the team, or watch a spanking. A gentle fantasy, with illustrations reminiscent of Maurice Sendak's in subdued colors. Ages 5–7.

Shulevitz, Uri. *One Monday Morning*. Illustrated by the author. New York: Charles Scribner's, 1967.

A small boy in a dreary neighborhood finds refuge in daydreaming about the visitors to his dingy apartment. "One Monday morning the king, the queen, and the little prince came to visit me. But I wasn't home." The royal party, increasing its retinue by one new member daily, comes everyday for the rest of the week without success, until Sunday, when the boy is finally in. Reality and imagination merge as the boy plays contentedly with a deck of cards that his fancy has brought to life. The cortege in glowing colors contrasts with the drab apartment house setting. An A.L.A. Notable Book. Ages 4–7.

Steig, William. *Sylvester and the Magic Pebble*. Illustrated by the author. New York: Simon and Schuster, 1969.

His chance discovery that a red pebble is magic puts Sylvester, a boy donkey, in a most unfortunate situation. He changes himself into a large rock to escape a lion. The seasons pass over him, but all ends well when his parents, picnicking on him, find the pebble and reverse the magic. The daily and seasonal changes in the countryside, the neighborly animals, and Sylvester's parents are shown in lovely water color. All the characters are animals, and when Sylvester's parents seek help at the police station, the police are shown as pigs, a choice that has aroused unfavorable comment though the author has disclaimed any intention of insulting the police. Caldecott Award, 1970. Ages 3–8.

Tolstoi, Alexei. *The Great Big Enormous Turnip*. Illustrated by Helen Oxenbury. New York: Franklin Watts, 1969.

A simple tale imbued with folklore flavor. An old man plants a little turnip. It grows so large that it takes the old man, his wife, his granddaughter, the dog, the cat, and finally the mouse to pull the turnip out of the ground. The deft, humorous, colored illustrations showing the turnip pullers in various positions and from various perspectives underscore the repetitive text. Ages 3–6.

The Tale of the Turnip (New York: Whittlesey, 1961) by Anita Hewett is fuller than the basic Tolstoi version but lacks the pictorial excitement engendered by the Oxenbury illustrations.

Turkle, Brinton. *Thy Friend, Obadiah.* Illustrated by the author. New York: Viking Press, 1969.

A small boy in Nantucket has an unsought "friend"—a seagull who accompanies him daily wherever he goes, even to First Day Meeting, and perches near his window at night. Obadiah is embarrassed by these attentions until he is able to help the seagull by freeing him from a fishing line wound around his bill. "Since I helped him, I'm *his* friend too," says Obadiah happily, reconciled to the situation. The author's illustrations depict an old-fashioned Quaker Nantucket with freshness and charm. A sequel to *Obadiah the Bold* (New York: Viking Press, 1965). Caldecott Award runner-up, 1970. Ages 4–7.

Waber, Bernard. *An Anteater Named Arthur.* Illustrated by the author. Boston: Houghton Mifflin Co., 1969.

Though Arthur is an anteater, his behavior is strikingly similar to any small boy's. Arthur is by turns logical, lazy, helpful, exasperating, forgetful, and endearing. He scorns his mother's offer of delicious, tasty red ants, with or without sugar and lemon, and demands the brown variety. He forgets his speller, sneakers, and pencil case, but remembers to kiss his mother good-by. Children will chuckle over this picture story with its brown, red, and black illustrations. Ages 3–5.

Wildsmith, Brian. *Fishes.* Illustrated by the author. New York: Franklin Watts, 1968.

In 14 double-page paintings of fish with their collective names, Wildsmith continues what he began in *Wild Animals* (New York: Watts, 1967) and *Birds* (New York: Watts, 1967). In rich, gorgeous color the dazzled viewer sees a cluster of porcupine fish, a school of butterfly fish, a battery of barracuda, a flotilla of swordfish, and a spread of sticklebacks among other piscine dwellers of lake, stream, and sea. An A.L.A. Notable Book. Ages 5–adult.

Zemach, Harve. *The Judge.* Illustrated by Margot Zemach. New York: Farrar, Straus and Giroux, 1969.

A hard-headed judge becomes more and more annoyed as each prisoner warns him of an approaching monster. Confronted at last by the beast itself, who resembles something out of the Apocalypse, the scoffing judge gets his come-uppance—the monster devours him. The illustrations that accompany the delightful cumulative refrain are excellent in their delineation of stuffy judge, anxious prisoners, and horrendous monster. Caldecott Award runner-up 1970. Ages 5–8.

The same pair did *Mommy Buy Me a China Doll* (Chicago: Follett Publishing Co., 1966), in which the illustrations perfectly reflected the homespun quality of the verse.

Zion, Gene. *Harry the Dirty Dog.* Illustrated by Margaret B. Graham. New York: Harper & Row, Publishers, 1956.

Harry, a white dog with black spots, escapes a hated bath by running away and then plays in the dirtiest possible places until he changes into a black dog with white spots. When he comes home, his family fails to recognize him, and Harry dejectedly prepares to leave. Then he thinks of a foolproof way to prove his identity. Large, clear pictures full of action and humor. Ideal for browsing and picture book story-telling use. Ages 3–6.

No Roses for Harry (New York: Harper & Row, Publishers, 1958) and *Harry by the Sea* (New York: Harper & Row, Publishers, 1965) are popular sequels.

Zolotow, Charlotte. *Mr. Rabbit and the Lovely Present.* Illustrated by Maurice Sendak. New York: Harper & Row, Publishers, 1962.

A little girl's search for a perfect birthday present for her mother is solved when she meets a strapping, oversized rabbit and asks him for help. She knows her mother likes red, yellow, green, and blue. Mr. Rabbit suggests a beautiful fruit for each color, and at the end of the story the little girl has a full basket and a lovely present. Mr. Rabbit appears to fade away as he waves good-by to the little girl, his task complete. She waves too, looking out on a landscape of shining stars and impressionistic, shadowy greens and blues. The feathery, dream-like trees, doll-sized houses, soft-looking grass, and star-filled sky all have an other-worldly charm in this runner-up for the 1963 Caldecott Medal. Ages 4–6.

Biography Angell, Pauline K. *To the Top of the World.* New York: Rand, McNally & Co., 1964.

An engrossing dual biography of Robert E. Peary and Matthew A. Henson, his black colleague, who were in 1909 the first explorers to reach the North Pole. Their lives prior to their meeting shows Henson, self-educated and alone, in contrast to Peary's advantages of family, education, and acceptance. Peary's moodiness, obsession, persistence, far-sightedness, and ability to learn from his failures are complemented by Henson's fidelity, equal persistence, versatility, and remarkable rapport with the Eskimos. A mutually dependent but impersonal relationship between the two grows up. Vivid descriptions of the voyages, the struggles, the thrill of accomplishment as well as the controversy, the feuds, and the frauds are detailed with accuracy and authority. Peary's rejection of Henson after the expedition was reprehensible but typical of the times, when a black was not considered equal to a white. Henson's achievement was recognized posthumously in 1945 when Congress awarded him a medal. Maps, photos, source materials, and an index. Ages 12–17.

d'Aulaire, Ingri, and Edgar Parin d'Aulaire. *Abraham Lincoln.* Illustrated by the authors. New York: Doubleday & Co., 1939.

"Abraham Lincoln first saw the world on a Sunday Morning. It wasn't much of a house in which he was born, but it was just as good as most people had in Kentucky in 1809." The text and distinguished lithographs create a very human Abraham Lincoln—the small, solemn toddler following his father's plow, the vigorous rail-splitter, the tall, lanky president who "held together the great nation brought forth upon this continent by his forefathers." The details of clothing, furniture, and setting reflect much research into Lincoln's life and period. Caldecott Award, 1940. Ages 5–9.

Other d'Aulaire titles include *George Washington* (New York: Doubleday & Co., 1936) and *Benjamin Franklin* (New York: Doubleday & Co., 1950); they are outstanding picture book introductions to the lives of great Americans.

Becker, Beril. *Jules Verne* New York: G. P. Putnam's, 1966.

A complete life of the man called the father of science fiction. Foiled in an attempt to go to sea as a cabin boy, young Jules promised his mother he would travel only in his imagination. His keen interest in science and literature led him to abandon law and devote himself to writing despite his father's strong disapproval. His thorough study of the science of his time and his fertile imagination led him to forecast the future and brought him fame as an author of the fantastic. His writings anticipated the submarine, space travel, helicopters, the guided missile, and artificial satellites. Becker tells only enough about Verne's books to arouse the desire to read them. Ages 12–14.

Bernard, Jacqueline. *Journey toward Freedom* New York: W. W. Norton & Co., 1967.

Isabelle Hardenbergh, born a slave in New York state around 1797, knew hardship, privation, and many masters. With freedom at age 46, she took a new name Sojourner—"because I want to travel up and down the land"—and Truth—"because I was to deliver the truth unto the people"—and set out to preach her religious convictions as well as her views in favor of women's rights and the abolition of slavery. Lecturing where and when she could draw a crowd, she appealed to all who sympathized with her convictions and was a thorn in the side of those who did not. During the Civil War, she helped the soldiers. Afterwards she helped homeless and jobless freedmen. Though a bit dry at the beginning, this book's historical background is well researched, and Sojourner Truth is presented as a compellingly interesting figure. Illustrated with photos. Bibliography and index. An A.L.A. Notable Book. Ages 12–17.

Bixby, William. *The Universe of Galileo and Newton*. New York: Harper & Row, Publishers, 1964.
This is a splendid dual biography of two great geniuses whose scientific contributions laid the foundation of our space age. Fiery tempered Galileo's valiant fight to teach and write about the universe as he perceived it through his telescope is in contrast to the reticent Newton's tireless experiments and calculations. The political, philosophical, economical, social, and religious background of their respective ages is shown with excerpts from the writings of Galileo and Newton and their contemporaries. Profusely illustrated with photos and paintings, many in color. Index and bibliography. An A.L.A. Notable Book. Ages 11–adult.
Sidney Rosen's *Galileo and the Magic Numbers* (Boston: Little, Brown and Co., 1958) and Harry Sootin's *Isaac Newton* (New York: Messner, 1955) are fine individual biographies of these scientists.

Brandenberg, Aliki. *A Weed Is a Flower*. Illustrated by the author. Englewood Cliffs, N.J.: Prentice-Hall, 1965.
A most attractive introductory biography of George Washington Carver. Main events in his life and his outstanding contributions are shown in colorful impressionistic illustrations with a straightforward, very simple text. Designed for the primary grade reader. Ages 6–9.
Shirley Graham's *Dr. George Washington Carver: Scientist* (New York: Messner, 1944) and Anne T. White's *George Washington Carver: The Story of a Great American* (New York: Random House, 1963) are well-written accounts of this famous man for the Junior High School reader.

Braymer, Marjorie. *The Walls of Windy Troy: The Biography of Heinrich Schlieman*. New York: Harcourt Brace Jovanovich, 1960.
A well drawn portrait of the father of modern archaeology, a brilliant, eccentric man whose childhood ambition to find Homer's Troy spurred him on to become a millionaire so he could retire and spend the balance of his life digging for cities mentioned in the *Iliad*. Each chapter, appropriately enough, begins with an excerpt from Homer related to the subject of the chapter. Well documented with many excellent photographs. Index, time chart, and bibliography. Ages 12–15.

Busoni, Rafaello. *The Man Who Was Don Quixote*. Illustrated by the author. Englewood Cliffs, N.J.: Prentice-Hall, 1958.
Miguel de Cervantes y Saavedra was a soldier who fought in the Battle of Lepanto; was imprisoned by pirates and sold into slavery; he was an actor and playwright; was twice imprisoned by the Inquisition; and is today remembered as the author of one of the great literary masterpieces of all time, *Don Quixote*. Cervantes' wisdom, attitudes, and flavorsome observations come through vividly and intimately in this biography. An outstanding recreation of a period and a man. Lively black and white drawings enhance almost every page. Ages 13–adult.

Campion, Nardi Reeder. *Look to this Day!* Boston: Little, Brown and Co., 1965.

Born in 1882, one of 12 children in a close-knit Southern family, Connie Guion had to finance her own education and help with that of her younger brothers and sisters before she could, at 31, achieve a cherished goal—entering medical school. Her internship at Bellevue was the beginning of a long, distinguished career, climaxed 50 years later by being the first woman doctor to have a hospital building named in her honor. A homey, folksy account in which the doctor's hearty, independent personality shines through. Not so much a serious medical biography as a lively family chronicle and a look at the development of higher education for women. An A.L.A. Notable Book. Ages 12–15.

Chase, Alice. *Famous Artists of the Past*. Bronx, N.Y.: Platt, 1964.

A handsome biographical survey of 25 master painters and sculptors plus a discussion of the Indian Mughal school of painting. Each brief sketch describes the subject's life and analyzes the themes and techniques he used as well as his goals and achievements. A generous sampling of each artist's work—many illustrations are in color—is excellently reproduced. The location and ownership of each work of art is listed in the index. Renoir, Tintoretto, Hokusai, El Greco, Bosch, Rodin, and Michelangelo are among artists considered by the author who writes from her experience as a lecturer at Yale's Art Gallery. An excellent companion volume to her *Famous Paintings* (Bronx, N.Y.: Platt, 1962). An A.L.A. Notable Book. Ages 11–14.

Coit, Margaret. *Andrew Jackson*. Illustrated by Milton Johnson. Boston: Houghton Mifflin Co., 1965.

A superior biography by a Pulitzer Prize winner that shows Andrew Jackson's strengths and weaknesses. Jackson emerges as a dynamic exponent of the common man. The personalities and issues of his two administrations with their pros and cons and the essence of Jacksonian democracy are thoughtfully appraised without fictionalizing, even though specific facts are omitted. An A.L.A. Notable Book. Ages 12–14.

Genevieve Foster's *Andrew Jackson* (New York: Charles Scribner's, 1951) and Clara Judson's *Andrew Jackson, Frontier Statesman* (Chicago: Follett Publishing Co., 1954) are for younger readers.

Coolidge, Olivia. *Makers of the Red Revolution*. Boston: Houghton Mifflin Co., 1963.

The historical and social forces that shaped world communism and its ideological basis are explored through the lives of seven communist leaders—Marx, Lenin, Trotsky, Stalin, Tito, Khrushchev, and Mao. A well-written, clear presentation of a complex subject ending with an analysis of communism's place in today's world. Ages 12–15.

————. *Tom Paine, Revolutionary*. New York: Charles Scribner's, 1969.

A complex man ahead of his time and greatly maligned for his too-advanced ideas. Paine advocated universal suffrage, believed rational thinking should be applied to religion, expected the government to protect the rights of the individual, and was against complex institutions, which he felt dehumanized people. His flawed life and difficult personality are portrayed without exaggeration or bias and his period is depicted with accuracy. Indexed. An A.L.A. Notable Book. Ages 14–17.

Denzel, Justin F. *Genius with a Scalpel: Harvey Cushing*. New York: Messner, 1971.

Harvey Cushing, a man whose accomplishments merit the appellation of genius, was the father of modern neurosurgery; he performed over 2,000 brain tumor operations. His book, *The Life of Sir William Osler* (New York: Oxford University Press, 1940) won him the 1926 Pulitzer prize in biography. He excelled in research, teaching, public health care, book collecting, hospital procedure, athletics, and illustrating. His childhood, his achievements in medicine, his fifteen-year courtship of "loyal" Kate, and his work on the battlefields of World War I are described. Excerpts from his journals and correspondence are included and add vivacity. A man of feeling (distress over a patient's death when a student at Harvard almost caused him to abandon medicine), he had a warm relationship with his patients, friends, and family. Eminently readable. Bibliography. Ages 11–14.

Dewey, Ann P. *Robert Goddard: Space Pioneer.* Boston: Little, Brown and Co., 1962.
The builder and firer of the first liquid-fuel rocket, Robert Goddard, was the first American scientist to investigate the theory and practice of rocketry. A warm, interesting, and often humorous account showing the development of the scientist from his youthful experiments in chemistry and physics to his outstanding achievements in his chosen field. Illustrated with diagrams and photos. Ages 11–14.

Douglass, Frederick. Adapted by Barbara Ritchie. *Life and Times of Frederick Douglass.*
New York: Thomas Y Crowell, 1966.
A masterly abridgment of the final revision of Douglass' autobiography, completely faithful to its spirit. By judicious pruning and rearrangement of the original, a simple, eloquent narrative results, covering Douglass' experiences as a slave, a fugitive, and a forceful, articulate Negro spokesman whose words are as applicable to today's racial upheaval as they were in his lifetime. An A.L.A. Notable Book. Ages 11–adult.
Arna Bontemps' *Frederick Douglass: Slave-Fighter–Freeman* (New York: Alfred A. Knopf, 1959) is a somewhat fictionalized and easier to read version of Douglass' life than Ritchie's adaptation. Bontemps concentrates on the boyhood and youth of Douglass and summarizes his career and later years in the last two chapters. Ages 10–11.

Douty, Ester M. *Forten the Sailmaker.* Chicago: Rand, McNally & Co., 1968.
James Forten was born 10 years before the American Revolution to freeborn Negro parents in Philadelphia. He fought in the Revolution as a powder boy on a privateer, was imprisoned by the British, and came home to make a fortune in sailmaking. He spent his life and his wealth helping the cause of his people, both slave and free. This pioneer champion of Negro rights is deservedly rescued from obscurity in this thoughtful, scholarly study. This biography offers what little information is available about the situation of free blacks in the North at this time and about white attitudes toward them. Illustrated by prints and engravings. Bibliography and index. An A.L.A. Notable Book. Ages 12–17.

Fisher, Aileen. *We Alcotts.* Illustrated by Ellen Raskin. New York: Atheneum, 1968.
This is the story of the Alcott family as if told by Mrs. Alcott, the "Marmee" of *Little Women.* In an appropriately old-fashioned style, she records her courtship and marriage to the impractical, idealistic philosopher Bronson Alcott whose ideas were ahead of his time. Their friendship with Emerson and Thoreau, their stand against slavery, the disastrous experiment in communal living, the constant moving from place to place, the loving and mentally stimulating home life in spite of poverty, hard work, and struggle are vividly projected. The book ends soon after the publication of *Little Women*—the turning point in the family's fortunes with a short postscript following the Alcotts to the deaths of Bronson and Louisa. An excellent, unsentimental recreation based on the journals and letters of the Alcotts and their friends. Ages 11–15.

Foster, Genevieve. *George Washington's World.* Illustrated by the author. New York: Charles Scribner's, 1941.
A horizontal view of the life and times of George Washington; as the title implies, this is a world-wide coverage of outstanding events that occurred and the prominent people who lived at the time of Washington's birth, childhood, youth, maturity, and

death. Significant incidents showing historical, religious, cultural, social, and economic developments are highlighted. Numerous lively drawings as well as maps and charts graphically carry out parallel themes. This unusual approach grew from the author's reaction to the textbook presentation of history during her school years, which left her wondering what was happening in the rest of the world at the same time. Runner-up for the Newbery Award. Ages 10–14.

The same pattern is used in *Abraham Lincoln's World* (1944), *Augustus Caesar's World* (1949), *The World of Captain John Smith* (1959), and *The World of Columbus and Sons* (1965), all published in New York by Charles Scribner's. These titles give a breadth of dimension valuable to the reader who wants to see a favorite historical personage in relation to the rest of his world.

Freedgood, Lillian. *Great Artists of America*. New York: Thomas Y Crowell, 1963.

The development of art in the United States is surveyed through the lives of 15 American painters from Gilbert Stuart to Jackson Pollock. Their early lives, struggles, accomplishments, and influence on the development of American painting are presented with quotes and lively anecdotes. Technique, theory, and media of each artist are discussed alongside a fine color reproduction of his work. Recommended readings, bibliography, and index. Ages 12–17.

Gardner, Jeanne de Monnier. *Mary Jemison: Seneca Captive*. Illustrated by Robert Parker. New York: Harcourt Brace Jovanovich, 1966.

A sensitive account spanning Mary Jemison's life with the Seneca Indians from her capture at age 15 to her death in 1883 at 90. Her gradual understanding and acceptance of Indian ways after her initial shock and fear wore off is realistically described with action, adventure, and an appreciation of the Indian culture. Though much shorter than Lois Lenski's *Indian Captive* (Philadelphia: J. B. Lippincott Co., 1941), which is a fictional treatment and now lamentably out of print, it carries on beyond the early years Lenski covers. Atmospheric black and white drawings, a map, and notes are included. Both Lenski's and Gardner's books are based on Mary Jemison's recollections at age 80. Ages 10–12.

Gurko, Miriam. *Clarence Darrow*. New York: Thomas Y Crowell, 1965.

A complete, well-rounded biography based on Darrow's autobiographical *Story of My Life* (New York: Charles Scribner's, 1932). Darrow emerges as a colorful, shrewd character whose championship of unpopular causes made him a controversial figure. The author describes Darrow's small town origin and slow-to-start legal career and then concentrates on his famous cases—the Scopes trial, the Pullman strike, the Haymarket affair, Leopold and Loeb, and others. The principles and background of the issues involving Darrow and the defendants are clearly described in each case. Index and bibliography. An A.L.A. Notable Book. Ages 12–adult.

Hautzig, Esther. *The Endless Steppe; Growing Up in Siberia*. New York: Thomas Y Crowell, 1968.

Exiled to Siberia by the Russians in 1941 for being "capitalists," 11-year-old Esther and her family, Polish citizens, spend a harrowing five years in a forced labor camp. Her memories of the struggle to stay together and keep alive through near-starvation and arctic winters are recorded with simplicity, candor, and lack of bitterness. An outstanding recital of courage, endurance, and strength of character, worthy of being compared to *The Diary of Anne Frank*. An A.L.A. Notable Book. Ages 12–adult.

Hume, Ruth Fox. *Great Men of Medicine*. Illustrated by Robert Frankenberg. New York: Random House, 1961.

In an entertaining and informative manner, 10 leading figures in the history of medicine—Vesalius, Paré, Jenner, Laennec, Morton, Pasteur, Lister, Koch, Banting, and Fleming—are presented with emphasis on intelligent innovation and persistence. Their contributions to knowledge of anatomy, surgery, vaccination, diagnosis, anesthesia, pasteurization, antiseptics, and the discovery of insulin and penicillin are detailed. An attractive edition with bibliography, index, and author's note. Ages 12–14.

Ruth Hume's complementary biography, *Great Women of Medicine* (New York: Random House, 1964), deals with the distaff side of medicine, including Florence Nightingale, Elizabeth Blackwell, Elizabeth Garrett Anderson, Sophia Jex–Blake, Mary Putnam Jacobi, and Marie Curie.

Isenberg, Irwin. *Caesar*. New York: Harper & Row, Publishers, 1964.

Julius Caesar's many sides—soldier, politician, dictator—are revealed in an account that "brings together the facts and myths of Caesar's life with pertinent art, documents, and photographs and reconstructions of significant sites." Well researched with interesting information on the Gallic Wars and the arms, dress, rank, and duties of the Roman soldier. As in other books of the Horizon Caravel series, the wealth of illustrative material adds to the appeal and usefulness of the text. Ages 12–17.

Kennedy, John F. *Profiles in Courage*. New York: Harper & Row, Publishers, 1964.

A special edition for young people, slightly abridged, of this Pulitzer Prize winning book. A stirring and inspirational account of eight American statesmen, each of whom "chose to act according to his beliefs even though to do so meant unpopularity and criticism and often defeat in elections": John Quincy Adams, who placed national interest before party and section; Daniel Webster, who compromised with slavery to preserve the Union; Thomas Hart Benton and Sam Houston, who broke with their states and their parties; Edmund G. Ross, whose single vote to save President Andrew Johnson from impeachment resulted in his own fall to political oblivion, Robert A. Taft, who condemned the Nuremberg Trials and lost his party's presidential nomination. In each case, a description of background pressures culminates in an outstanding act of courage. A foreword by Robert F. Kennedy and a preface by John Kennedy add to the outstanding quality of the book. Ages 12–adult.

Kroeber, Theodora. *Ishi, Last of His Tribe*. Illustrated by Ruth Robbins. Berkeley: Parnassus Press, 1964.

The peaceful, gentle Yahi Indians of California were no match for the restless, encroaching white men. In 1908 the last survivor, Ishi, walked into the Kroeber's life, the primitive and the modern confronted one another. Ishi's tale shows him as a child—happy, ambitious, faithful—growing into a man who sees the beauty of his childhood and youth replaced by sorrow as gradually his family and friends die. A long, beautiful, philosophic story which should lead the interested reader to the story of Ishi as an adult, *Ishi In Two Worlds* (Berkeley: Parnassus Press, 1961). An A.L.A. Notable Book. Ages 10–adult.

Latham, Jean Lee. *Drake, the Man They Called a Pirate*. Illustrated by Frederick Chapman. New York: Harper and Row, Publishers, 1960.

A well-written, exciting biography about the most famous Elizabethan sea captain. His swift, bold, imaginative raids on Spanish shipping and his astonishing defeat of the Spanish Armada made him a legend in his own time and a fearsome figure to the Spanish, who called him El Draque—"the dragon." Modern standards would label him a pirate, but the author's view is that he was trying to save England from Spain by taking the offensive and to avenge tragic earlier losses due to Spanish treachery. Humane towards his prisoners and magnanimous in victory, unlike many of his contemporaries, he also was a magnetic and inspiring leader of men. Ages 11–14.

Ronald Syme's *Francis Drake* (New York: Morrow, 1961) is a much briefer treatment of the same subject; it is an attractive, easier-to-read biography for ages 9–11.

McNeer, May. *Give Me Freedom*. Illustrated by Lynd Ward. New York: Abingdon Press, 1964.

Brief biographies of seven Americans who have been concerned with freedom for themselves and others. Included are William Penn, Thomas Paine, Elijah Lovejoy, Elizabeth Cady Stanton, Edwin Markham, Marian Anderson, and Albert Einstein. Sensitive and insightful writing and striking illustrations produce a distinguished inspirational work which should lead to further reading about these outstanding individuals. Ages 10–12.

Armed with Courage (New York: Abingdon, 1957), a companion volume, is concerned with such outstanding humanitarians as Florence Nightingale, Jane Addams, George Washington Carver, Father Damian, Sir Wilfred Grenfell, Mahatma Gandhi, and Albert Schweitzer. Notable individuals in Mexican history from the legendary Mayans to Pancho Villa and the modern Mexican are described in *The Mexican Story* (New York: Ariel Press, 1953). Both books are vibrantly illustrated by Lynd Ward.

Meltzer, Milton. *Langston Hughes, a Biography*. New York: Thomas Y Crowell, 1968.

The poet laureate of his race, a gifted and prolific writer of more than 40 volumes of poetry, stories, plays, songs, history, translations, articles, and autobiography, Langston Hughes' portrait is penned with vigor and clarity. The emphasis is on the early half of his life, from boyhood in Kansas to manhood in Harlem. Proud to be black and dedicated to freedom, he opened the way to realism and honesty in Negro literature and reflected the feelings, struggles, defeats, and hopes of the people of Harlem. A complete bibliography of his works is included. Ages 12–adult.

————. *A Light in the Dark*. New York: Thomas Y Crowell, 1964.

Undeservedly obscured by the fame of his wife Julia Ward Howe, who wrote "Battle Hymn of the Republic," Samuel Gridley Howe's achievements are recognized in this excellent biography. A nineteenth-century idealist with a strong social conscience, he founded the Perkins Institute for the Blind, engaged in prison reform, aid for the psychotic, and help for fugitive slaves. He was a soldier, surgeon, educator, reformer, abolitionist, and editor. While his wife shared his interests, the marriage was not a happy one. Julia's independent spirit and income were hard for Samuel to accept, but concern for their six children kept them together. A well done portrait of a great but very human man. Extensive bibliography, chronology, and index. An A.L.A. Notable Book. Ages 12–17.

Mercer, Charles. *Alexander the Great*. New York: Harper & Row, Publishers, 1962.

An intriguing study of a man who is one of the foremost conquerors of all time. The times in which he lived, his character, his campaigns, and the military victories that carried him from Macedon to India are treated with authority and authenticity. The Horizon Caravel format, with its wealth of paintings, maps, and pictures of artifacts, compels interest. Index and bibliography. Ages 12–17.

Charles Robinson's *Alexander the Great* (New York: Franklin Watts, 1963) is a scholarly depiction of Alexander's influence on the development of western civilization. It stresses his hopes for uniting those under his rule; he regarded non-Greeks without prejudice, most unusual in his day.

Mirsky, Reba. *Beethoven*. Illustrated by W. T. Mars. Chicago: Follett Publishing Co., 1957.

A full account of the remarkable musical genius whose career was plagued by poverty, privation, and poor health culminating in deafness. The author, herself a musician, has carefully researched Beethoven's life and treats him with a sympathy that does not overlook the composer's difficult personality. Attractive format. Ages 9–11.

For younger readers, see the admirable *Beethoven, Master Musician* (New York: Holt, Rinehart and Winston, 1946) by Madeleine Goss.

Noble, Iris. *Leonardo Da Vinci: The Universal Genius*. New York: W. W. Norton & Co., 1965.
An absorbing fictionalized full biography of Leonardo showing all facets of his activities as artist, scholar, inventor, and experimenter. His contempt for the jealous quarrels of the artists and nobles of his day and his loneliness, resulting from his illegitimate birth, are discussed in a straightforward manner. Black and white illustrations include his paintings, drawings, and inventions. Bibliography and index with location of major works. Ages 12–14.
Noble's work is better written than Henry Gillette's *Leonardo Da Vinci* (New York: Franklin Watts, 1962) which emphasizes his scientific bent, more inclusive than Elizabeth Ripley's *Leonardo Da Vinci* (New York: University Press, 1952), which concentrates on the artist. Jay Williams' *Leonardo Da Vinci* (New York: Harper & Row, Publishers, 1965) is lavishly illustrated and invites browsing but is more limited in its biographical data, while Richard McLanathan's *Images of Universe* (Garden City, N.Y.: Doubleday & Co., 1966) is for more mature readers.

Peare, Catherine Owens. *The Woodrow Wilson Story*. New York: Thomas Y Crowell, 1963.
A complete biography of a much misunderstood man whose refusal to compromise his principles brought him bitter heartache. Wilson's boyhood in Atlanta, his student days at Princeton and later presidency there, his career as an educator, and his life as President of the United States are well delineated. Serious, fine writing reveals the more human side of Wilson's nature in relation to his family and friends; it shows how "his personal traits contributed to his success, both as an educator and as a statesman." Bibliography and index. Ages 12–15.

Petry, Ann. *Tituba of Salem Village*. New York: Thomas Y Crowell, 1964.
The hard-working, skillful Negro slave Tituba is uprooted from her life in Barbados when she and her husband are sold to the minister of Salem village. As she successfully adjusts to the cold climate and difficult work, forces of ignorance, superstition, and religious fanaticism close in upon her. Because she is different, because her household prospers through her industry, she is suspect. The collaboration—inexplicable to the modern mind—of the community against her during the witchcraft hysteria is shown to be both pitiable and contemptible. Told from Tituba's point of view, this book offers insight into social psychology and Puritan American history as well as into a woman of strong character. It is not, however, as outstanding as the author's *Harriet Tubman* (New York: Thomas Y Crowell, 1955). An A.L.A. Notable Book. Ages 12–16.

Robinson, Jackie, and Alfred Duckett. *Breakthrough to the Big League*. New York: Harper & Row, Publishers, 1965.
A departure from the usual formula sports biography is this personal recounting by Jackie Robinson of his childhood, his early career in professional baseball, and the challenge of his entry into a major league. As the first Negro player, he had to face jeering fans, uncooperative teammates, hostile adversaries, dubious reporters, and his own hot temper. He credits the support of his family and friends of both races for his success and acceptance in the sports world. An honest, readable autobiography. Photographs and index. Ages 11–14.

Roosevelt, Eleanor, and Helen Ferris. *Your Teens and Mine*. Garden City, N.Y.: Doubleday & Co., 1961.
With warmth and common sense, Mrs. Roosevelt discusses the problems of teenagers. Being afraid, getting along with others, learning to think, being one of a family,

and getting married are some of the topics covered. From her own experience as a shy, awkward ugly duckling, she shows that, though she lived in a different time, her problems were basically the same as the modern adolescent's. How she faced her difficulties and resolved them and her philosophy of life come through without preachiness or long-windedness. Ages 12–17.

Selvin, David. *Eugene Debs: Rebel, Labor Leader, Prophet.* New York: Lothrop, Lee & Shephard Co., 1966.
An objective portrait of controversial labor leader Eugene Debs and his role in union history. He organized and headed the American Railway Union and was sent to jail when he defied a court injunction against the Pullman strike. His championship of pacificism during World War I sent him to jail again on charges of sedition. Based on primary sources, the book insightfully describes an American figure of worldwide influence. Ages 12–17.
Iris Noble's *Labor's Advocate* (New York: Messner, 1966) is a more fictionalized and romantic treatment.

Shirer, William L. *The Rise and Fall of Adolph Hitler.* New York: Random House, 1961.
A chilling portrait of a man obssessed with a desire for power based on the author's personal experience, observation, and study of captured German documents. Though based on the research from which he wrote the massive adult work, *The Rise and Fall of the Third Reich* (New York: Simon and Schuster, 1960), this is not an abridgment of that volume but a much simpler presentation of a complex man and his times. In crisp reporterial style, the background of Hitler's rise to power, his crafty personality, his ability to sway people by his words, and his growing megalomania are shown in a straightforward, almost documentary, approach. Hitler is quoted extensively, adding dimension to the narrative. Photos and index. Ages 10–12.

Sterling, Dorothy. *Lucretia Mott, Gentle Warrior.* Garden City, N.Y.: Doubleday & Co., 1964.
A timely biography, since many of the problems that aroused Lucretia Coffin Mott's concern are still relevant. An eloquent Quaker preacher and reformer prominent in the antislavery movement from the 1830s to the Civil War, she worked tirelessly for civil rights for Negroes and women after the war. Excitement, pathos, humor, romance, and many details of Quaker family living are found in this inspiring narrative. The lengthy bibliography attests to thorough research and authenticity; a number of contemporaries are identified in an appendix. Ages 12–14.

Sterne, Emma G. *I Have a Dream.* Illustrated by Tracy Sugarman. New York: Alfred A. Knopf, 1965.
Describing the lives of nine Negro leaders, the history of Civil Rights in the twentieth century is shown up to the 1963 March on Washington. Forceful presentation of the dreams, goals, and actions of such lesser known figures as Hugh Mulzac, first Negro merchant ship captain; Rosa Parks, who triggered the Montgomery bus boycott; Daisy Bates, who guided Little Rock school desegregation; and such notables as Marian Anderson, A. Philip Randolph, Thurgood Marshall, James Farmer, Fred Shuttlesworth, and John Lewis. Biographical sketches precede the stories of each individual's role. Index and background reading list. Ages 12–17.

Syme, Ronald. *Bolivar, the Liberator.* Illustrated by William Stobbs. New York: William Morrow & Co., 1968.
A well written, objective, balanced presentation of a great patriot. Without adulation, the author shows Bolivar change from the wealthy Venezuelan whose spendthrift

ways shocked Paris into the leader of a ragged army against Spanish domination of his homeland. He gave all he possessed to the cause of independence and became president of five countries only to die a pauper exiled from his home. The political, military, social, and geographical complications facing Bolivar are treated with an insight that makes present-day conditions in South America more understandable. Quotations from Bolivar's letters and speeches shed light on his character and personality. Ages 9–12.

Trevino, Elizabeth Borton. *I, Juan de Pareja*. New York: Farrar, Straus & Giroux, 1965.
    The Negro slave boy, Juan de Pareja, becomes the property of the great Spanish painter Diego Velasquez. Taught to grind and mix colors and to prepare canvases, he becomes fascinated with art and longs to become a painter. However, the law forbids a slave to paint; Juan is forced to follow his calling in secret. When Velasquez, who has become his friend, discovers this, he frees Juan and accepts him as a colleague. Based on meager but authentic facts, the story, written like an autobiography, gives a vivid picture of aristocratic and court life in seventeenth century Spain. The personality and character of both Velasquez and Juan and their strong friendship are treated with sensitivity and conviction. Newbery Award, 1966. Ages 11–15.

Warner, Oliver. *Nelson and the Age of Fighting Sail*. New York: Harper & Row, Publishers, 1963.
    The colorful, dramatic career of England's greatest naval hero, Horatio Nelson, is covered from his entry into the navy at 12 to his death at Trafalgar at 47. His revolutionizing of the strategy and tactics of the British Navy to make it supreme and the political consequences of his imagination and daring are ably described. The Napoleonic background is authentic. No less an authority than Admiral Chester W. Nimitz was consulted to insure accuracy and authenticity in the naval scenes. Nelson's love affair with Lady Hamilton is handled with restraint. A wealth of drawings, prints, battle charts, photos, and an index accompany the text. Ages 12–adult.
    Commander Herbert J. Gimpel's *Lord Nelson* (New York: Franklin Watts, 1966) stresses Nelson's naval career, not his personality.

Webb, Robert N. *Leaders of Our Time: Series I*. New York: Franklin Watts, 1964.
    The policies, philosophy, and the national and international role of 12 important world leaders: Adenauer, Ben-Gurion, Castro, De Gaulle, Kennedy, Krushchev, Macmillan, Mao Tse-tung, Nasser, Nehru, Nkrumah, and U Thant. Still timely and relevant, this is as much a thoughtful commentary on world power politics and curent events as it is a focus on key men. In *Series II* (New York: Franklin Watts, 1965), Webb adds thirteen additional figures including Queen Elizabeth II, Ludwig Erhard, Emperor Hirohito, Lyndon Baines Johnson, Martin Luther King, Robert Gordon Menzies, Pope Paul VI, Hyman G. Rickover, Sargent Shriver, Achmed Sukarno, Tito, Earl Warren, and Harold Wilson. Webb's *Series III* (New York: Franklin Watts, 1966) includes Leonid Brezhnev, Arthur Goldberg, Hubert Humphrey, Robert Kennedy, Ayub Khan, Aleksei Kosygin, John Lindsay, Robert McNamara, Thurgood Marshall, Lester Pearson, Walter Reuther, and George Romney. Death and retirement have removed some of these individuals from the world scene, and time has either increased or decreased their influence, but all three volumes are currently useful. Photos and index. Ages 11–14.

Wibberley, Leonard. *The Life of Winston Churchill*. New York: Farrar, Straus & Giroux, 1965.
    Beginning with his birth at Blenheim Palace in 1874 until his honorary United States citizenship in 1963 and death in 1965, Winston Churchill's life reads like an action-packed adventure story. His inability to learn Greek and Latin at Harrow was more than compensated for later in life by his magnificent command of his native tongue. A graduate of Sandhurst, he served in the Boer War and World War I. His

career in Parliament was a turbulent one, but during World War II as Prime Minister he became the symbol of British resistance against the Nazi juggernaut. An absorbing biography written in a smooth fast-moving style and illustrated by photos. Ages 11–15.

Olivia Coolidge's *Winston Churchill and Two World Wars* (Boston: Houghton Mifflin Co., 1960) is also a complete biography for somewhat older readers, while Quentin Reynolds' *Winston Churchill* (New York: Random House, 1963) is briefer, ending with Churchill's resignation as Prime Minister in 1955. It includes 12 pages of the great man's personal recollections.

————. *Young Man from the Piedmont: The Youth of Thomas Jefferson.* New York: Farrar, Straus & Giroux, 1963.

A fictionalized biography of Thomas Jefferson, beginning with his birth and ending with his authorship of the Declaration of Independence. The description of the social, intellectual, and political world of his day shows the influences that helped shape Jefferson's mind and character. In this first of four volumes the author is more detailed than other biographies: Clara Judson's *Thomas Jefferson, Champion of the People* (Chicago: Wilcox and Follett, 1952); Gene Lisitzky's *Thomas Jefferson* (New York: Viking Press, 1933); or American Heritage's *Thomas Jefferson and His World* (New York: American Heritage Publishing, 1960).

————. *A Dawn in the Trees: Thomas Jefferson, the Years 1776–1789.* New York: Farrar, Straus & Giroux, 1964.

This title continues with an excellent portrayal of Jefferson as a family man and covers the debate on the Declaration and Jefferson's diplomatic mission to France.

————. *The Gales of Spring: Thomas Jefferson, the Years 1789–1801.* New York: Farrar, Straus & Giroux, 1965.

Jefferson's career as Secretary of State and the conflict between him and Alexander Hamilton is objectively covered, citing strengths and weaknesses of both men.

————. *Time of Harvest: Thomas Jefferson, the Years 1801–1826.* New York: Farrar, Straus & Giroux, 1966.

From his presidency to his retirement at Monticello and death this concluding volume emphasizes the Louisiana Purchase and the Burr conspiracy. All four combine to show Jefferson the man, but without detracting from his greatness. All volumes are indexed. Ages 12–14.

Wise, William. *Alexander Hamilton.* New York: G. P. Putnam's, 1963.

A short but full biography of the enormously gifted, energetic, and ambitious young man from the West Indies. Adopting America as his country, he served it well on the field of battle, and even better in his writings and as Secretary of the Treasury under Washington. His friends, his enemies, and his differences with Jefferson—who is described in an unflattering light—and his own character with its foibles are shown with authentic detail. Indexed. Ages 10–12.

The Reynolds affair, omitted in Wise's book, is included in Milton Lomask's *Odd Destiny; A Life of Alexander Hamilton* (New York: Farrar, Straus & Giroux, 1969) for older readers. It focuses more on the period and its politics than on the man. Ages 12–14.

John F. Roche's *Illustrious Americans: Alexander Hamilton* (Palo Alto, Calif.: Silver Burdett, 1967) includes the Reynolds affair in its biographical information. In addition, there is a lavish picture portfolio and a section entitled "His Own Words." Ages 14–adult.

Wood, James Playsted. *The Snark Was a Boojum: A Life of Lewis Carroll.* Illustrated by David Levine. New York: Pantheon Books, 1966.

An erudite man, a brilliant mathematician, a Christ Church Don, a member of the clergy, a gifted photographer, and author of the immortal Alice books, Lewis Carroll was also eccentric and unhappy. The author presents a mature, thoughtful portrait interspersed with quotations from Carroll's prose and rhymes as well as critical comments on them. Sophisticated, humorous drawings and a bibliography. Ages 12–17.

James Playsted Wood has written other biographies of writers: *Trust Thyself: A Life of Ralph Waldo Emerson* (New York: Pantheon Books, 1964), *The Lantern Bearer: A Life of Robert Louis Stevenson* (New York: Pantheon Books, 1965), *The Man Who Hated Sherlock Holmes: A Life of Sir Arthur Conan Doyle* (New York: Pantheon Books, 1965), and *A Hound, a Bay Horse, and a Turtle Dove* (New York: Pantheon Books, 1963) about Henry David Thoreau. In all of them, Mr. Wood displays a remarkable ability to lose himself in the life, philosophy, and environment of each of his subjects, infusing them with life without introducing fictitious scenes or dialogue.

Wyatt, Edgar. *Cochise: Apache Warrior and Statesman*. Illustrated by Allen Houser. New York: McGraw Hill Book Co., 1953.

An authoritative account of a great Indian leader and his dealings with the white man. His feelings about peace and the reasons for his warfare against the "white eyes" are presented with sympathy but without sentimentality in a lively, well-documented way. There is excellent feeling for Apache customs and culture. The illustrations by an Apache artist add interest. This is a companion title to the earlier *Geronimo* (New York: McGraw-Hill Book Co., 1952), which describes a contemporary of Cochise. Bibliography and a guide to Spanish and Indian pronunciation. Ages 11–14.

Yates, Elizabeth. *Amos Fortune: Free Man*. Illustrated by Nora Unwin. New York: E. P. Dutton & Co., 1950.

Captured by slavers, a 15-year-old African prince is taken to the American colonies in 1725. In Boston, his Quaker master educates and trains him as a weaver; he learns to tan leather from another master. Thrifty, hardworking, literate, and a devout Christian, he buys his freedom and dedicates his life to buying the freedom of others. A thoughtful, inspiring portrait of a courageous, patient man who hoped the future life of his people would be brighter than his own life had been. Newbery Award. Ages 12–14.

Information books Abbott, R. Tucker. *Sea Shells of the World*. Illustrated by George Sandstrom and Marita Sandstrom. New York: Golden Press, 1962.

A handy portable guide for the shell collector. Colored illustrations are labeled with both the scientific and popular name of the shell, and the size is indicated. The shells are divided into classes: snails, bivalves, cephalopods, Tusk shells, Chitons, and monoplacophora. Though information on finding and storing shells is brief, its small size makes it ideal for carrying on shell hunting expeditions. Ages 11–adult.

Kathleen Johnstone's *Sea Treasure* (Boston: Houghton Mifflin Co., 1957) is a much fuller discussion of shells and shell collecting but lacks portability. Ages 11–adult.

Asimov, Isaac. *Realm of Measure*. Illustrated by R. Belmore. Boston: Houghton Mifflin Co., 1960.

Asimov begins with the first simple measurements based on the human body and proceeds to Einstein's theory of relativity in discussing the history of measures. Various kinds of measures and the tools used to calculate them are discussed with enthusiasm and authority. The metric system for measuring length and the highly complex units used to measure force, energy, and viscosity are included in this eminently readable survey. Graphs, charts, and drawings clarify the text. Indexed. Ages 12–14.

Sam Epstein and Beryl Epstein's *First Book of Measurement* (New York: Franklin Watts, 1960) is good introductory fare for ages 10–11 though it is not as comprehensive. Jeanne Bendick's *How Much and How Many* (New York: McGraw-Hill Book Co., 1947) is also introductory. Melvin Berger's *For Good Measure* (New York: McGraw-Hill Book Co., 1969) is less technical and detailed than Asimov's but includes information on masers, lasers, and the measurement of radiation, which are not included in Asimov's earlier book.

Aylesworth, Thomas G., editor. *It Works like This: A Collection of Machines from Nature and Science Magazine*. Garden City, N.Y.: Doubleday & Co., 1968.

A compilation of short articles on the operation and structure of various appliances, household gadgets, measuring devices, and transportation and photographic equipment. How they tick, click, flash, or flush, as the case may be, is clearly described with diagrams and drawings in black, white, and sienna. It duplicates to some extent and updates Herman Schneider's *Everyday Machines and How They Work* (New York: McGraw-Hill Book Co., 1950), but includes such popular items as the tape recorder and record player—not found in Schneider's book. It is more detailed and inclusive that Herbert Zim's brief *Things around the House* (New York: William Morrow & Co., 1954), which is for younger readers, aged 8 to 10. Ages 11–14.

Baity, Elizabeth Chesley. *Americans before Columbus*. Illustrated by C. B. Falls. New York: Viking Press, 1961.

An enthusiastic but well-grounded exposition of the origin and history of prominent Indian cultures of the Americas from the Ice Age to the sixteenth century A.D. The facts and theories presented are in line with 1960 archaeological evidence. Authentic drawings and many photos from museums and anthropological collections lend color and verification to the text. This beautifully designed book is a tribute to the knowledge, skill, and resourcefulness of the many anthropologists who patiently pieced together the pre-Columbian history of the Americas. Imaginative stories based on factual information are interspersed among the direct accounts of life among the Amerindians. Ages 14–adult.

Bartlett, Susan. *Books: A Book To Begin On.* Illustrated by Ellen Raskin. New York: Holt, Rinehart and Winston, 1968.
A concise introduction to the story of books and bookmaking from the clay tablets of Assyria, the papyrus rolls of Egypt, Gutenberg's movable type, to modern high-speed printing. Though the contribution of the Phoenicians is ignored, the narrative is consistently interesting and accurate throughout. Illustrations printed in nutmeg and black include facsimiles, woodcuts, and distinctive drawings; they are in perfect harmony with the lucid text. A companion to Bartlett's *Libraries* (New York: Holt, Rinehart and Winston, 1964) . Ages 9–10.

Bendick, Jeanne. *Space and Time.* Illustrated by the author. New York: Franklin Watts, 1968.
The dynamics of space, form, distance, and time are illustrated through familiar objects and situations in this beginning concept book. With the aid of cartoon-like illustrations, simple experiments, and leading questions, the child is encouraged to observe, classify, and infer. An easy introduction to a complex subject. Ages 8–9.

Blow, Michael. *The History of the Atomic Bomb.* New York: Harper & Row, Publishers, 1968.
An objective, well-written, often exciting survey beginning with the Greek Democritus, who first postulated the atom as a unit of matter, and recounting the contributions of many others—including Newton, Roentgen, Becquerel, the Curies, and Rutherford—to the first successful splitting of the atom. The scientists involved in the development of the bomb, the decision to use it, and the destruction of Hiroshima and Nagasaki are graphically portrayed in text, diagrams, and the profuse illustrations typical of the American Heritage format. A brief look at postwar developments. A scientifically accurate presentation written in consultation with William W. Watson, Professor of Physics at Yale, who participated in the Manhattan Project. A fine bibliography, glossary, and index. Ages 12–17.

Borgeson, Griffith. *Grand Prix Championship Courses and Drivers.* New York: W. W. Norton & Co., 1968.
A brisk, definitive guide to the great international road races that test cars and the men who drive them. Arranged by country, a brief history of the race is given, then each course is described with a diagram of the track, statistics covering types of cars used, winning speeds and lap times, and winners. Capsule biographies of famous drivers are included. Photos and index. Ages 12–17.
Bruce Carter's *Jimmy Murphy and the White Dusenberg* (New York: Coward-McCann, 1968) and *Nuvolari and the Alfa-Romeo* (New York: Coward-McCann, 1968) are dramatic, low vocabulary, high interest, "you are there" approaches to two Grand Prix winners with brief biographical information, car specifications, and illustrations by Raymond Briggs. Ages 9–13.
Hal Butler's *Roar of the Road* (New York: Messner, 1969) adds memorable sports car, stock car, midget car, and oval racing to the Grand Prix accounts in a fast-moving recital that supplements Borgeson and Carter's books. Ages 11–adult.

Bowen, J. David. *The Island of Puerto Rico.* Philadelphia: J. B. Lippincott Co., 1968.
An informative, readable overview of Puerto Rican history and geography, with em-

phasis on the island today. The people, life in city and country, economics, politics, education, and culture are all accurately described. A section on literature presents such island folk heroes as Juan Bobo (Silly John) and Juan Cuchilla (John the Knife). The relationship of Puerto Rico to the United States and the workings of Operation Bootstrap are factually detailed. One of the useful "Portraits of a Nation" series. Indexed. Ages 12–adult.

M. M. Brau's *Island in the Crossroads* (Garden City, N.Y.: Doubleday & Co., 1968) is a complete history of Puerto Rico emphasizing the unique contributions of different races in the formation of Puerto Rican history. Ages 12–adult.

Bowen, David. *The Struggle Within: Race Relations in the United States*. New York: W. W. Norton & Co., 1965.

A survey of race relations from colonial times to the events in Selma, Alabama, in 1965. A study of Negro and White, Southern and Northern attitudes, how and why they developed, and their influence on the legal, economic, political, scientific, ethical, emotional, and social aspects of present confrontation. A lucid, impartial account that advocates nonviolence and combines information from periodicals, books, and other sources. Indexed. Ages 12–adult.

Bradford Chambers' *Chronicles of Negro Protest* (New York: Parents' Magazine Press, 1968) and Janet Harris' *Black Pride* (New York: McGraw-Hill Book Co., 1969) emphasize the role and history of the Black Power movement, which is largely ignored in the Bowen title. Ages 12–adult.

Branley, Franklyn. *The Earth: Planet Number 3* Illustrated by Helmut K. Wimmer. New York: Thomas Y Crowell, 1966.

The nature of the earth, its origin, age, and probable end, its motion, gravity, geomagnetism and radiation belts, its atmosphere, its land, and its water are presented scientifically but understandably by a well-known science writer. Charts, graphs, drawings, photos, a data table, and suggestions for further reading. Indexed. Ages 12–14.

Gerald Ames' *Planet Earth* (New York: Golden Press, 1963) is for younger readers, ages 10–11.

Bronowski, J., and Millicent E. Selsam. *Biography of an Atom*. Illustrated by Weimer Pursell. New York: Harper & Row, Publishers, 1965.

A succinct explanation of the atom. Telling the story of a carbon atom, the author begins with its structure then describes its birth eons ago in a new star, its dispersal into space, and its arrival on earth to become part of the carbon cycle, where it may have been part of coal, carbon dioxide, or even a human chromosome. Clearly stated and informatively illustrated with diagrams and photographs. An A.L.A. Notable Book. Ages 9–12.

Bulla, Clyde R. *Stories of Favorite Operas*. Illustrated by Robert Galster. New York: Thomas Y Crowell, 1959.

A useful retelling of the plots of 23 famous operas. Action on the opera stage is described scene by scene, though no excerpts or descriptions of the arias, choruses, duets, or trios are included. A prefatory note to each opera tells when and how it came to be written and first performed. Brief biographies of the composers and selected casts of characters, stating the type of voice—soprano, mezzo-soprano, tenor, and so on—the role requires. Ages 10–14.

Bulla's *More Stories of Favorite Operas* (New York: Thomas Y Crowell, 1965) is a companion volume which adds 22 more plots. His *Ring and the Fire* (New York: Thomas Y Crowell, 1962) is a dramatic retelling of the stories from the four operas of Wagner's "Ring" cycle with starkly appropriate woodcuts, with the musical themes appended. Bulla's *Stories of Gilbert and Sullivan Operas* (New York: Thomas Y Crowell, 1968) lack the sprightly illustrations of the Curtain Raiser series published by Franklin Watts, but does keep them all in one volume and has more complete texts of the lyrics.

Bulman, Alan D. *Model-Making for Physicists*. New York: Thomas Y Crowell, 1968
A physics teacher tells how to build apparatus for science experiments and demonstrations using commonly available materials. Prefaced by chapters on the tools, methods, and safety measures involved, the student learns to construct a bimetallic or air-expansion thermostat, a water motor and alternator, a polariscope, a Tesla coil, a Wilson cloud chamber, and many other devices useful for illustrating scientific principles on all levels of experience. Indexed. Ages 12–17.

Burton, Virginia Lee. *Life Story*. Illustrated by the author. Boston: Houghton Mifflin Co., 1962.
The story of life on earth is staged as a drama beginning with a prologue in which the universe is introduced, and continues through five acts and an epilogue. Each geologic era occupies an act, and the epilogue brings man on stage. A novel presentation which, though lacking specific, detailed information, does give the reader an understanding of the sweep of time and the continuity of life. The striking illustrations in color, each framed by a proscenium arch, are the outstanding feature of the book. Ages 8–10.

Carr, Albert Z. *A Matter of Life and Death: How Wars Get Started—Or Are Prevented*. New York: Viking Press, 1966.
A thoughtful, provocative discussion of the causes, consequences, and prevention of war with maps and notable cartoons on the subject. By analyzing the events that led to the Spanish–American War, the Russo–Japanese War, and World Wars I and II and examining the propaganda of all sides, the economic and political pressures involved, and the psychology of the militant and the conservative the economist author offers some answers, if not solutions, to the problem of war. Korea and Vietnam are discussed, though not extensively. Footnoted with bibliography and index. Ages 12–17.

Carson, Rachel. *The Sea Around Us*. Adapted by A. T. White. New York: Simon and Schuster, 1958.
A skillful adaptation of the highly praised adult book, which has been abridged almost by half. The author's language has largely been retained, but long sentences have been broken up, and easier words have occasionally been substituted. This discussion of the sea in all its infinite variety has been immeasurably enhanced by the addition of diagrams and colorful photos. An engrossing presentation that will attract many readers who would have been put off by the length and plain format of the original. Ages 12–adult.
James Fisher's *Wonderful World of the Sea* (Garden City, N.Y.: Doubleday & Co., 1970) is an introduction to the sea for younger children, aged 8–11. Maxwell Reed's *Sea for Sam* (New York: Harcourt Brace Jovanovich, 1960) covers much of the same information as the Carson's book but lacks its memorable text. Ages 12–adult.

Chute, Marchette. *Stories from Shakespeare*. Cleveland: World Publishing Co., 1956.
A superb introduction to the comedies, tragedies, and histories of Shakespeare. The 36 plays from the first folio are retold in fresh twentieth-century language in Lamb's venerable collection, which describes only 20 plays, each nevertheless conveys a great deal of the humor, action, and emotion of the drama. Interspersed quotations give a glimpse of the beauty and power of the language with explanations of the intentions and point of view of the characters. The author's enthusiasm for her subject is shown in her preface, which explains why "in all the world of storytelling, [Shakespeare's] is the greatest name." Ages 12–adult.

Coolidge, Olivia. *Women's Rights; the Suffrage Movement in America 1848–1920*. New York: E. P. Dutton & Co., 1966.

A history of 72 years of struggle before women won the right to vote. Women's interest in temperance, abolition of slavery, and equality before the law is also discussed. Considered the physical and mental inferiors of men, discriminated against in education, law, and labor, their efforts brought them ridicule, notoriety, imprisonment, and abuse. Outstanding stalwarts include Lucy Stone, Susan B. Anthony, Elizabeth Cady Stanton, Alice Paul, and Carrie Chapman Catt. Economic and social factors of this movement are discussed as well. A well-written survey of an important historical achievement and its personalities. A chronology of dates, suggestions for further reading and index. Ages. 12–14.

Coombs, Charles. *Motorcycling*. New York: William Morrow & Co., 1968.

An easy-to-read introduction to various types of power-driven two-wheelers: motorcycles, scooters, bikes, and others. The emphasis is on their care, safety precautions, information on the selection of a motorcycle, camping, and competitions. The large-size print and clear black-and-white photographs enhance the popular appeal of the subject. Ages 10–14.

Ed Radlauer's *Motorcycles* (Glendale, Calif.: Bowmar Publications, 1967) is briefer and definitely geared to the high-interest, low-vocabulary reader. Illustrated with color photographs, as are other Radlauer books on surfing, custom cars, drag racing, Dune buggies, Dune buggy racing, karting, slot car racing, and so on. Ages 9–13.

Coy, Harold. *The Mexicans*. Illustrated by Francisco Mora. Boston: Little, Brown and Co., 1970.

Using the device of a Mexican student writing to an American friend, the history of Mexico is recounted from prehistoric times to the present, emphasizing the advancement of Indian culture at the time of the Spanish Conquest and the subsequent blend of cultures and races to form the present-day Mexican people. Fascinating differences emerge between the Mexican view of relations with the United States and our view of them. This salutary and sometimes abrasive glimpse of ourselves as others see us is heightened by the epistolary presentation. An extremely useful and readable title by an author who lives in Mexico. A fine bibliography and a pronunciation guide. Ages 12–17.

Cromer, Richard. *The Miracle of Flight*. Illustrated by Joseph Cellini. Garden City, N.J.: Doubleday & Co., 1968.

An outstanding and detailed exposition on flight. Beginning with gravity, the physics of flight—mechanical and avian—are discussed to show how the bird's form is adapted to flight, while man can fly only with elaborate navigational devices. An intriguing, clear, readable, informative, and accurate treatment which was expanded from a "Wild Kingdom" television program. Effective illustrations and diagrams and an index. Ages 10–14.

Cummings, Richard. *101 Masks; False Faces and Make-up for All Ages*. Illustrated by the author. New York: David McKay Co., 1968.

Excellent easy-to-follow directions for simple, quickly made masks using handkerchiefs, paper plates, and grocery bags as well as masks of professional quality requiring plaster of paris, papier-mâché, and claycrete. Among his creations are the Scarecrow, Cowardly Lion, and Tin Woodman of Oz, the Beatles, the classical Harlequin, No masks of Japan, and the Iroquois False Faces. Three short plays, a history of masks, and suggestions for mask entertainments are included. Indexed. Ages 9–adult.

Equally useful and valuable is Cummings' *101 Hand Puppets* (New York: David McKay Co., 1962).

Ellis, Harry B. *Ideals and Ideologies: Communism, Socialism, and Capitalism.* Cleveland: World Publishing Co., 1968.

An experienced foreign correspondent compares the three chief economic systems operating in the world today. Concentrating mainly on the socialism of Great Britain and Sweden, the capitalism of the United States and Western Europe, and the communism of Russia and Eastern Europe (with brief reference to China), he enlivens facts with pertinent firsthand anecdotes and observations. The differences between the theory and practice of each form of government are shown as well as their similarities. Clear, objective presentation with no hysterical overtones. Numerous photographs, bibliography and index. Ages 12–17.

Feigenbaum, Lawrence H., and Kalman Seigel. *Israel: Crossroads of Conflict.* Chicago: Rand, McNally & Co., 1968.

After the initial historical chapters, the emphasis is on present-day Israel—its people, government, education, economy, military and social organization, language, archaeology, and its role in international relations. Pro-Israeli in tone, it imparts a strong feeling for the vital young nation as a homeland for the Jews. The 1967 war is briefly mentioned. Photos, index, and a chronology of events from ancient times to present. Ages 11–14.

More complete than Joan Comay's *Israel* (New York: Macmillan Co., 1964), which it updates.

Feistal, Sally, and Leonard Meshover. *The Guinea Pigs That Went to School.* Chicago: Follett Publishing Co., 1968.

First-grader Wendy brings her pet guinea pig Theo to school, and the teacher provides him with a mate. The entire class has the fun of observing the two and learning about pregnancy, gestation, birth (resulting in two offspring), and care of the young. Based on a real first-grade class project, the writing is simple and direct. Photos by Eva Hoffman are clear and unposed and show youngsters in their missing-front-teeth stage. Ages 5–9.

Fisher, Aileen. *Easter.* Illustrated by Ati Forberg. New York: Thomas Y Crowell, 1968.

An explanation of the customs, legends, and symbols of Easter: the Easter egg, Easter bunny, egg tree, and wearing new clothes on Easter Sunday. The pre-Christian celebrations of the annual renewal of life in spring lead to the story of Jesus and the Christian belief in his resurrection. Attractive illustrations on alternate yellow and white pages accompany the simple, straight-forward text. Ages 8–10.

E. H. Sechrist's *It's Time for Easter* (Philadelphia: Macrae, 1961) is a distinguished mature presentation of the subject for older readers from 12–adult.

Fitch, Florence Mary. *Allah: the God of Islam.* New York: Lothrop, Lee & Shephard Co., 1950.

This companion volume to *One God* and *Their Search for God* begins with the story of Mohammed and his rise as the prophet to Allah, the One God. It presents the beliefs and history of the faith, an evaluation of Moslem art, architecture, music, social customs and culture, a brief analysis of the roots of Israeli and Arab conflict, and the hopes for the future. Written with grace and charm and enhanced by many excellent photographs. Ages 11–14.

————. *A Book about God.* Illustrated by Leonard Weisgard. New York: Lothrop, Lee & Shephard Co., 1953.

A picture book which draws an analogy between the concept of God and the beauty and power of nature—the sky, sun, sea, and air: "The air is like God. Air is all around us; even though we do not see it we feel its warmth and its coolness. Without air outside us and within us we cannot live. Without God we cannot live." The pictures in exquisite color, full of delicacy and symmetry, perfectly match the quiet beauty and poetic quality of the text. No denominational position, but a simple, serene affirmation of theism. Ages 3–8.

————. *One God: The Ways We Worship Him*. New York: Lothrop, Lee & Shephard Co., 1944.
Beliefs, festivals, traditions, and observances of Jews, Catholics, and Protestants are described clearly in text and expressive photographs that stress the beauty and similarity of these three religions. Approved by the governing bodies of each of these three faiths, this informative, useful presentation is written out of a lifetime of study by the author. Ages 9–11.

————. *Their Search for God: Ways of Worship in the Orient*. New York: Lothrop, Lee & Shephard Co., 1944.
The author presents what is most distinctive and valued in Hinduism, Confucianism, Taoism, Shinto, and Buddhism. The deep sense of religious reverence and its supreme place in the Oriental's life is shown through vivid depiction of the ceremonies, festivals, and religious teachings in India, China, and Japan. Outstanding photographs. Ages 9–11.

Fleming, Thomas. *The Battle of Yorktown*. New York: Harper & Row, Publishers, 1968.
The culminating battle of the American Revolution which ended in Cornwallis' surrender is handsomely mounted in the typical American Heritage format of profuse illustrations—many in color—and helpful maps. The events leading up to the battle and the battle itself have been carefully researched. Numerous quotations about the personal experiences of those involved lend color and vitality to the chronicle. Ages 11–14.

Foster, G. Allen. *Communication: From Primitive Tom-Toms to Telstar*. New York: Criterion Books, 1965.
Speech, writing, postal service, newspapers, telegraph, telephone, wireless telegraph, radio, television, and Telstar each fill a chapter in this lively, compact history of communication. The social and technical factors which affected their development, the usefulness of each medium, and a look into the future are presented. The hope that good communication will bring world understanding and consequently peace is stressed. Photos. Ages 12–17.
Hal Hellman's *Communications in the World of the Future* (Philadelphia: J. B. Lippincott Co., 1969) is more technical, while the approach of Etta Ress' *Signals to Satellites* (Bronx, N.Y.: Creative Education Press, 1965) appeals to younger readers.

Freeman, Mae B., and Ira M. Freeman. *Fun with Chemistry*. New York: Random House, 1962.
Over 25 interesting experiments introduce the beginner to some of the basic principles of chemistry. By using material found in the kitchen, laundry, or the medicine cabinet, a minimum of outside equipment is needed. Crystallization, combustion and oxidation, flame tests, acids and bases, soap, electricity and other phenomena are studied. None of the experiments is dangerous. Black-and-white photos add interest to this easy, entertaining, inexpensive introduction. Ages 10–12.

Fuchs, Erich. *Journey to the Moon*. Illustrated by the author. New York: Delacorte, 1969.
Apollo 11's epochal voyage appears in picture book form without words (a descriptive, keyed text is in the beginning of the book) so the art can speak for itself. An atmos-

phere of tension, silence, and wonder is evoked by the wash and watercolor paintings that show the blue and green of earth, and the silver, gray, and black of space. The double-page spreads range from the count-down against the orange sky of Cape Kennedy to the blue and white cratered moon, the walk itself, and the splashdown near the awaiting carrier Hornet. A distinguished presentation. Ages 5–7.

Glubok, Shirley. *The Art of Africa*. New York: Harper & Row, Publishers, 1965.
    An introduction to African life and customs through outstanding photographs of the art of its people: wooden masks and headdresses, bronze and sculpture, pottery, rock paintings, golden weights, and other works. The brief text touches on each object's history, the techniques used to make it, its description. An A.L.A. Notable Book. Ages 7–12.
    The Art of Africa is seventh in a series of art books that includes *The Art of the Eskimo* (New York: Harper & Row, Publishers, 1964) and *The Art of Ancient Peru* (New York: Harper & Row, Publishers, 1966), both A.L.A. Notable Books for the same age group.

Goldston, Robert. *The Negro Revolution: From Its African Genesis to the Death of Martin Luther King*. New York: Macmillan Co., 1968.
    Beginning with a survey of ancient African civilizations, this is a chronicle of the history of the American Negro from the beginning of the slave trade to the late 1960s. His thesis that the black struggle is an economic one is supported by his well-documented analysis of the causes and methods of Negro exploitation and exposes the myths created by the white man to justify his past and current attitudes. Bibliography, reading list, and index. An A.L.A. Notable Book. Ages 12–17.

Gray, Robert. *Children of the Ark*. New York: W. W. Norton & Co., 1968.
    A study of over 30 species of land mammals, birds, and reptiles now threatened with extinction by our world's increasingly shaky ecological balance. Where they live, the dangers they face, and what can or is being done to save them is clearly and simply related. The American Bison, the Great Indian Rhinoceros, the Panda, the Puma, and the Whooping Crane are the better known endangered species discussed, along with the less familiar California Condor, Galapagos turtle, and others. Each is introduced in a fictionized episode with a photograph. Easier to use and more attractive than Robert Silverberg's *The Auk, the Dodo, and the Oryx* (New York: Thomas Y Crowell, 1967) which is for ages 11–13. Index. Ages 8–11.

Hawkes, Jacquetta, and B. V. Bothmer. *Pharoahs of Egypt*. Cleveland: American Heritage, 1965.
    The history of Egypt from predynastic to Roman times, with emphasis on the rulers. The unique role of the pharaoh in ancient Egyptian religious, political, and cultural life stresses the close relationship between the political power of the ruler and his divine status. The reigns of Tuthmosis III, Hatshepsut, and Akhenaten are treated in detail, but the book's outstanding feature is its numerous excellent reproductions of reliefs, sculptures, wall paintings, and monuments in black and white and in color. A chapter on Egyptology, a list of books for further reading, museum locations of Egyptian antiquities, and index. Ages 11–14.

Helfman, Elizabeth S. *Signs and Symbols around the World*. New York: Lothrop, Lee & Shephard Co., 1967.
    A fascinating, well-written survey of signs, symbols, and ideographs that have persisted as essential parts of human communication and culture in many fields and are important as a universal method of imparting vital information. From pictographs, alphabets, and numerals the author turns to the symbols in religion, astrology, and astronomy,

musical notation, mathematics, chemistry, biology, earth sciences, engineering, and the international travel and traffic symbols which may find worldwide use. Trade marks and hobo signs are not neglected. Profusely illustrated, bibliography, and index. Ages 11–14.

Hellman, Hal. *Light and Electricity in the Atmosphere.* Illustrated by Nancy Etheredge and Gilbert Etheredge. New York: Holiday House, 1968.
The historical background and current study of atmospheric phenomena including primitive explanations, religious and folk beliefs, modern scientific investigations, and a look into the future. Under scrutiny are lightning, St. Elmo's Fire, airglow, radiation belts, thunderstorms, auroras, the ionosphere, and UFO sightings. A lively, comprehensive account. A section on instructive, safe experiments, a list of suggested books and periodicals for further reading, and an index. Ages 12–17.

Hess, Lilo. *The Remarkable Chameleon.* New York: Charles Scribner's, 1968.
Brilliant, detailed black and white photographs by the author show the chameleon in various poses. The misconceptions about this unusual and fascinating lizard are dispelled, its habits are explored, and its ability to change skin pattern and color is explained in a particularly interesting way. The care and feeding of this delicate pet is included in the well written text. Ages 9–11.
The author's photographic skill is also displayed to advantage in her *Curious Raccoons* (New York: Charles Scribner's, 1968), *Foxes in the Woodshed* (New York: Charles Scribner's, 1966), *Pigeons Everywhere* (New York: Charles Scribner's, 1967), and *Sea Horses* (New York: Charles Scribner's, 1966).

Hirsch, S. Carl. *On Course! Navigating in Sea, Air, and Space.* Illustrated by William Steinel. New York: Viking Press, 1967.
Beginning with the ancient Phoenician sailors venturing into the Mediterranean sea and ending with today's astronauts venturing into space, this history of navigation is a superb blend of fine writing, organization, printing, and illustration. The navigational instruments of each period and their effect on man's ability to travel farther from home are described. The contributions of explorers, inventors, astronomers, physicists, and mathematicians to this complex science are presented in informal, understandable terms. Suggestions for further reading and an index. Ages 12–adult.
More technical but less inclusive is Jack Coggins' *By Star and Compass* (New York: Dodd, Mead & Co., 1967).

Hutchins, Ross E. *Plants without Leaves.* New York: Dodd, Mead & Co., 1966.
Excellent photomicrographs add depth to a lively study of algae, fungi, slimemolds, lichens, liverworts, mosses, and horsetails. Their growth, reproduction, and survival in the sea, on earth, and on rocks from the tropics to the polar regions is well covered. Annotated further study suggestions and index. Ages 11–13.
Lucy Kavaler's *Wonders of Algae* (New York: John Day, 1961) and *Wonders of Fungi* (New York: John Day, 1964) do not have the scope of the Hutchins book, but are very informative and more detailed.

Hyde, Margaret O., and E. S. Marks. *Psychology in Action.* Illustrated by Carolyn Cather. New York: McGraw-Hill Book Co., 1967.
A readable overview of psychology emphasizing its practical aspects. Case studies of adolescents are included to show its application to problems common among young people. Brief information on schools of psychology, the use of experiments and tests, and the various kinds of psychologists. Descriptions of how a psychologist can choose the man best suited to go into space or determine the extent of one's racial prejudice

add interest to the book. A well-balanced look at an extremely complex subject. Index and list of suggested further readings. Ages 12–17.

Jennings, Gary. *Black Magic, White Magic*. Illustrated by Barbara Begg. New York: Dial Press, 1965.

The history of magic and its influence on religion, science, and medicine from prehistoric times to the present. Famous magicians, witchcraft and witch hunts, the research of the alchemist, rain making and fertility rites, intriguing recipes for potions, and incantations are discussed in a scholarly but pleasing style. An excellent list of suggested further reading and an index. Ages 12–14.

Benjamin Appel's *Man and Magic* (New York: Pantheon Books, 1966) covers somewhat the same information but deals more with primitive man in all parts of the world and the American Indian, while Jennings deals mainly with Europe and colonial America.

Johnson, Gerald W. *America Is Born: A History for Peter*. Illustrated by Leonard Everett Fisher. New York: William Morrow & Co., 1959.

The first of a trilogy written to give the author's grandson an understanding of what being an American means. His interpretation of the ideas and ideals, events, and people of the period between 1492–1787 is presented objectively in clear, arresting prose. Shameful incidents as well as praiseworthy ones are shown because, "if you leave out the bad parts you never understand it all. Yet you must understand it if you are to make your part one of the fine parts." Dramatic pen and ink drawings accompany the text. Newbery Award Runner-up. Ages 10–14.

Johnson's *America Grows Up* (New York: William Morrow & Co., 1960) carries on from 1787 through expansion, civil conflict, and World War I. *America Moves Forward* (New York: William Morrow & Co., 1960) finishes the trilogy, carrying the reader from the crucial period following World War I through the Eisenhower administration. Newbery Award runner-up.

————. *The Congress*. Illustrated by Leonard Everett Fisher. New York: William Morrow & Co., 1963.

A companion volume to Johnson's *The Presidency* (New York: William Morrow & Co., 1962) and *The Supreme Court* (New York: William Morrow & Co., 1962) —all are direct and readable. This one explains how Congress works: the formation of committees and their functions; how a bill is passed; the qualifications for a Congressman; the origin and meaning of gerrymandering and filibustering; the ideology of the Congress from its inception to the present; and the system of checks and balances as it applies to famous cases. Lists of vice-presidents, speakers of the House, and names of the standing committees of both houses as well as an index. Ages 9–12.

Jordan, June. *Who Looks at Me*. New York: Thomas Y Crowell, 1969.

An eloquent, poetic statement on the black experience: the predicament of the black individual who finds himself invisible and unfree, though cruelly visible to bigots and extremists. Twenty-seven paintings dealing with the history of slavery and the present-day life of blacks show bitterness and frustration as well as the magnificent rediscovery of African heritage. Ends with a hope for future acceptance and freedom. Biographical notes on the painters, both black and white, are included. Ages 12–adult.

Kadesch, Robert R. *The Crazy Cantilever and Other Science Experiments*. New York: Harper & Row, Publishers, 1961.

An excellent collection of 40 physics experiments covering electricity, magnetism, gravity, light, optics, color, atomic fission, sound, and crystals. Inexpensive or easily available materials are suggested; directions are clear and accompanied by helpful diagrams and photographs. Designed by the author, a science teacher, to provide practice in careful observation, sound experimentation, and clear thinking. No index. Ages 11–16.

Don Herbert's Mr. *Wizard's Science Secrets* (New York: Hawthorn Books, 1965) is a popular presentation which can be used with a younger group, ages 9–11. George Barr's *Research Ideas for Young Scientists* (New York: McGraw-Hill Book Co., 1964) is for younger readers, ages 11–14. Like Herbert's book, it is confined exclusively to physics experiments.

Karp, Walter, and J. W. Burrow. *Charles Darwin and the Origin of Species*. Cleveland: American Heritage Press, 1968.

A stimulating history of an idea as well as the biography of a man whose five-year sea voyage on the Beagle gave him an invaluable opportunity to observe nature and led him to propound a discovery that rocked the Victorian world's conceptions of man's place in the universe. Much of the background essential to understanding the impact of evolution and the furor it roused is carefully supplied by the author, and his explanation of Darwin's theories is well done. Profuse illustrations from contemporary sources plus color photos of plants, animals, and other natural history subjects relating to Darwin's findings are important additions to the text. Ages 11–adult.

Klein, Richard M. *Discovering Plants*. Garden City, N.Y.: Doubleday & Co., 1968.

The activities and functions of plants are explored through experimental investigation of their growth, nutrition, metabolism, and diseases. How to collect and preserve plants, how to set up experiments, what materials are required, and how to record data are explained in a lucid technical text accompanied by clear, well-labeled drawings. Ages 10–adult.

Millicent Selsam's *Play with Plants* (New York: William Morrow & Co., 1949) and *Play with Seeds* (New York: William Morrow & Co., 1957) introduce plant experimentation on a very simple level. A. Harris Stone's *Plants Are like That* (Englewood Cliffs, N.J.: Prentice-Hall, 1968) is more advanced but less technical than the Klein title. It refers to books and magazine articles throughout and includes a list of laboratory supply houses and additional titles. Ages 12–adult.

Lavine, David. *Outposts of Adventure: The Story of the Foreign Service*. Garden City, N.Y.: Doubleday & Co., 1966.

A highly informative, well-written account of the history and activities of the United States Foreign Service. A discussion of diplomacy, the daily routine of the five sections—executive, consular, political, economic, and administrative—of a typical embassy, the training of foreign service officers, and career information is enlivened by illustrative anecdotes. An introduction by Dean Rusk. Ages 11–14.

Lawson, Robert. *Watchwords of Liberty: Pageant of American Quotations*, rev. ed. Illustrated by the author. Boston: Little, Brown and Co., 1957.

Beginning with "So they commited themselves to the will of God & resolved to proseede" from William Bradford's *The Voyage of the Mayflower,* this unique contribution to the field of American history traces, through more than 50 famous quotations, our nation's struggle and development. Short, vivid accounts of the circumstances surrounding each quotation with superb black and white sketches give an inspiring overall view of United States history. Ages 9–adult.

Lens, Sidney. *Working Men: The Story of Labor*. Illustrated by David Collier. New York: G. P. Putnam's, 1960.

Labor's role as a social and political force in America's growth is delineated from colonial times through the 1950s. The artisan, the farmer, the indentured servant, the slave, the immigrant, and the capitalist embody the changing forms of labor and management from creative entrepreneurship to unskilled drudgery to automation. The rise of labor parties, unions, and cooperatives is well researched and integrated with historical events to give a balanced picture. Though a union official sympathetic to labor, the author is unbiased and fair in his criticism of big business. A valuable glossary of terms and index. Ages 11–13.

Shippen's *This Union Cause* (New York: Harper & Row, Publishers, 1959) has similar coverage.

Lent, Henry B. *Agriculture U.S.A.: America's Most Basic Industry*. New York: E. P. Dutton & Co., 1968.

A survey of American agriculture covers information about varieties of crops (mainly soybeans, corn, wheat, and cotton), livestock production, methods of food processing, farm equipment and supplies, research, mechanization, and electrification in the United States. The problems of poverty, marginal farming, and surpluses and government attempts to solve them are considered. Career opportunities are explored, and a state-by-state rundown of farming is followed by a preview of rural America and agriculture in the year 2000. Photos throughout, an index, and list of state agricultural colleges and universities. Ages 11–14.

Lester, Julius. *To Be a Slave*. Illustrated by Tom Feelings. New York: Dial Press, 1968.

Dragged from their homes, cramped in stifling holds, sold at auction, worked, abused, beaten, violated, and, when finally freed, still segregated, still exploited, and still the underdog—this seems to be the burden of this revealing survey of the black man's history. These extracts from reminiscences, experiences, and evaluations by ex-slaves, gathered before and after the Civil War, are heartbreaking in their simplicity and dignity. Julius Lester's accompanying commentary is both lucid and forceful and the black and white drawings are masterful. Newbery Award runner-up. Ages 12–adult.

Lewis, Anthony. *The Supreme Court and How It Works*. New York: Random House, 1966.

Based on the author's adult book *Gideon's Trumpet*, this use of a case history to explain the function and power of the Supreme Court emerges as a drama of compelling interest. Clarence Earl Gideon, a penniless Florida convict claimed unjust denial of the right to counsel, resulting in a Court ruling that all defendants have the right to legal counsel in criminal actions thus reversing an earlier decision on the same issue. The human and legal aspects of American justice are shown in the personalities, events, and ideas discussed. Ages 12–17.

Robert A. Liston's *Tides of Justice* (New York: Delacorte, 1966) lacks Lewis' insight but covers a number of landmark cases as well as breaking down each Justice's view by topic. Ages 12–17.

Johnson's *The Supreme Court* (New York: William Morrow & Co., 1962) is for younger readers than the former titles. Ages 10–14.

Lubell, Winifred. *In a Running Brook*. Illustrated by the author. Chicago: Rand, McNally & Co., 1968.

A lively description of what one may encounter while wading in and watching a freshwater stream. The plants, insects, amphibians, and crustaceans are shown chiefly during the warmer months, though the final chapter tells about winter. Instructions on how to look, a one-page rebus titled "How To Collect," and index. Profusely illustrated in water color with artistry and accuracy the entire book is an inspiring invitation to go outdoors and observe nature. Ages 9–11.

Harriet Huntington's *Let's Go to the Brook* (Garden City, N.Y.: Doubleday & Co., 1952) uses photographs and is for younger readers, aged 8–10. Margaret Buck's *In Ponds and Streams* (Nashville: Abingdon Press, 1955) is more detailed and lends itself to better identification, but her writing is less appealing than Lubell's. Index. Ages 9–14.

McKendrick, Melvenna J., and J. H. Elliott. *Ferdinand and Isabella.* Scranton, Pa.: American Heritage Press, 1968.
An absorbing historical and biographical portrait of the rulers who unified Spain, expelled the Moors from Granada, and sponsored Columbus. Set against the splendor and formality of Renaissance court life, the characters of the two sovereigns—the devoutly religious Isabella and the wily Ferdinand—lack depth, but the customs and conventions of the period, the political intrigues, and what motivated the Inquisition are clearly shown. Numerous striking contemporary illustrations, some in color, reproductions of paintings, artifacts, and buildings. Ages 12–17.

Maloney, Terry. *Telescopes; How To Choose and Use Them.* New York: Sterling, 1968.
A well written, practical explanation of how telescopes function, how to choose the best type for different locations, price range, how to judge the telscope's accuracy, how to make its accessories, and how to view the heavenly bodies and what to see. A chapter on radio telescopes is included. All presented in detail and illustrated with photos and diagrams. Ages 12–14.

Matthews, William H. *The Story of the Earth.* Illustrated by John E. Alexander. Irvington-on-Hudson, N.Y.: Harvey, 1968.
Beginning with the earth as a planet and treating successively its minerals, mountain building, erosion, fossils, and geologic eras, the result is an outstanding, concise introduction to geology. Helpful drawings and photographs amplify the text. Index, glossary, and suggestions for further reading. Ages 10–13.

May, Julian. *The First Men.* Illustrated by Lorence Bjorklund. New York: Holiday House, 1968.
A simplified introduction to evolution, reflecting current thinking. Focusing on the development of man as reconstructed from the discoveries at the Olduvai Gorge in East Africa in preference to the well-known Asian and European forms, the concepts of archeological stratigraphy and culture are presented clearly and understandably. Latin nomenclature is included in a separate section at the end of the book. Superb pencil drawings. Ages 8–9.

Meltzer, Milton. *Brother, Can You Spare a Dime? The Great Depression, 1929–1933.* New York: Alfred A. Knopf, 1969.
Through diaries, songs, and observations of contemporary authors, the effects of the Great Depression on those who lived through it are shown in depth. The plight of each group—Negroes, children, farmers, factory workers, vagrants, and others—is painfully described. Photos and contemporary prints are included as well as an annotated bibliography of books, periodicals, photography, and songs.
For Wyman Boardman's *The Thirties; America and the Great Depression* (New York: Henry Z. Walck, 1967) and Robert C. Goldston's *The Great Depression* (New York: Bobbs-Merrill Co., 1968) cover much the same period except that Boardman takes in the entire decade whereas Meltzer and Goldston focus specifically on the depression years. Ages 12–adult.

Milne, Lorus, and Margery Milne. *The Phoenix Forest.* Illustrated by Elinor Van Ingen. New York: Atheneum, 1968.
The legendary phoenix's power to rise anew from its ashes becomes the symbol of the renewal of a forest destroyed by fire. Plant and animal life are minutely described before and after the holocaust, pointing out the effects of the fire on the area's ecology. The

beneficial effects of fire are also considered. An excellent informative presentation that nature lovers and conservationists will enjoy. Suggested readings. Ages 10–13.

Moore, Janet Gaylord. *The Many Ways of Seeing: An Introduction to the Pleasures of Art*. Cleveland: World Publishing Co., 1968.

Drawing on her background as a painter, art teacher, and lecturer, the author attempts to cultivate an awareness of the best in art by exploring its techniques "to develop a selective and discriminating eye" in an age of visual bombardment. Anecdotes, quotations from such authors as Proust, Thoreau, and Andrew Marvell, and lively observations emphasize the message that the pleasures of art are infinite and a lifetime isn't long enough to encompass them all. Thirty-nine illustrations in color and many in black and white. A Newberry Award runner-up. All ages.

Morris, Richard. *First Book of the Constitution*. Illustrated by Leonard Everett Fisher. New York: Franklin Watts, 1958.

An authority on American history and editor of the Encyclopedia of American History presents a succinct, lucid survey of the Constitution from inception in 1780 to ratification in 1787 describing the personalities of its authors and discussing its basic values. The text is not reproduced, but a simplified outline of the document and its amendments are included. Dramatic, strong black and white drawings. Ages 10–11.

Morrison, Sean. *Armor*. Illustrated by the author. New York: Thomas Y Crowell, 1963.

A comprehensive and authoritative survey of armor from Sumerian times (c. 4000 B.C.) through Greek and Roman times, the Middle Ages, and the Renaissance, with a brief final chapter on modern armor. How armor was made and used and the historical events and economic and social conditions in which it evolved are related with skill and humor. Black and white drawings throughout the text clearly present the armor and weapons involved. Ages 10–14.

Helmut Nickel's *Warriors and Worthies: Arms and Armor through the Ages* (New York: Atheneum, 1969), though somewhat meager in text, is lavishly illustrated with black and white and colored photographs of the art objects and historical pieces found in the Metropolitan Museum of Art.

Morrow, Betty. *A Great Miracle; the Story of Hanukkah*. Illustrated by Howard Simon. Irvington-on-Hudson, N.Y.: Harvey House, 1968.

A dignified retelling of the Jewish triumph over the oppressive Syrians, the recapture of Jerusalem, the cleansing of the Temple, and its rededication with the miraculous kindling of the Temple Menorah in the days of the heroic Maccabees. What happened afterwards and how Hanukkah is celebrated today concludes this very readable and tellable version. More depth than Norma Simon's *Hanukkah* (New York: Thomas Y Crowell, 1966), which is for younger readers. Ages 9–11.

Morton, Miriam, editor. *A Harvest of Russian Children's Literature*. Berkeley: University of California Press, 1967.

A superb anthology showing what Russian children from five to 15 read. Divided by age groups and kinds of stories, the nearly 100 selections consist of nursery rhymes, fables, folktales, poetry, classical and modern stories, and excerpts from several novels. Original Soviet illustrations are reproduced. Since the traditions, values, ideals, and nationalistic qualities of any country are reflected in its literature, this "pioneering effort" (as the preface states) provides an invaluable way to study not only the children's literature of the USSR but also the social and political background of those children. Ages 5–17.

Neal, Harry Edward. *Money*. Illustrated with photographs. New York: Messner, 1967.

An exceptionally interesting and vividly written account of the history of money from barter to the printing of paper currency. There is detailed information about the U.S. Federal Reserve System, the gold standard; balance of payments; foreign exchange; counterfeiting and present-day consumer spending. More comprehensive in scope than John Joseph Floherty's *Money-Go-Round* (Philadelphia: J. B. Lippincott Co., 1964) and older in appeal than Walter Buehr's *Treasure* (New York: G. P. Putnam's, 1955). Ages 11–13.

North, Sterling. *Rascal*. Illustrated by John Schoenherr. New York: E. P. Dutton & Co., 1963.

Living alone with his permissive and absent-minded widower father, 11-year-old Sterling had freedom to roam the countryside. He finds a tiny motherless raccoon who becomes a cherished pet and is the subject of heartwarming reminiscence. The year he spends with Rascal is described with loving nostalgia that gives a thoroughly entertaining picture of a vanished era before the twenties. For young readers, the author has shortened and simplified the original story into *Little Rascal* (New York: E. P. Dutton & Co., 1965). Newbery Award runner-up. Ages 12–adult.

Paine, Roberta M. *Looking at Sculpture*. New York: Lothrop, Lee & Shephard Co., 1968.

An informed, handsome, and inviting introduction to sculpture from ancient Egypt to twentieth-century America. The use of stone, wood, clay, bronze (either in the round or in relief), the modern mobiles, and string compositions are reproduced in clear photographs with a discussion of techniques and design by the author, a lecturer at the Metropolitan Museum of Art. Biographical notes on the sculptors, an illustrated glossary, and suggestions for further reading. An A.L.A. Notable Book. Ages 10–adult.

Phleger, Fred. *You Will Live under the Sea*. Illustrated by Ward Brackett. New York: Random House, 1966.

A believable peek into the future for the novice reader; from an undersea lodge he can watch the herding of fish on the Finnegan Fish Ranch, visit the Kelly Kelp farm, ride a turtle, watch miners at work on the sea bottom, and plan an undersea career. Handsome, clear pictures accompany the "I Can Read it All by Myself" text. Ages 7–9.

Similar in appeal and usefulness to Mae Freeman and Ira Freeman's *You Will Go to the Moon* (New York: Random House, 1959).

Rappaport, Uriel. *The Story of the Dead Sea Scrolls*. Illustrated by Milka Cizid. Irvington-on-Hudson, N.Y.: Harvey House, 1967.

A comprehensive account of the discovery and deciphering of the Dead Sea Scrolls, including a history of the times in which they were written. The author, an Israeli scholar, has benefited from recent information gained from the Masada archaeological expedition and the 1967 unification of Jerusalem. Numerous photographs, drawings, and charts accompany the factual account. Ages 12–17.

Geoffrey Palmer's *Quest for the Dead Sea Scrolls* (New York: John Day, 1965) is on a comparable reading level but lacks Rappaport's depth and detail. Alan Honour's *Cave of Riches* (New York: McGraw-Hill Book Co., 1956) and Azriel Eisenberg's *The Great Discovery* (New York: Abelard-Schuman, 1956) presents facts in story form; these two are for younger readers.

Raskin, Edith. *The Fantastic Cactus: Indoors and in Nature*. (New York: Lotnrop, Lee & Shephard Co., 1968.

An enthusiastic approach to cacti and related succulents narrowing to a study of 30 varieties that can be grown indoors. Suggestions for experimenting with seeds and grafts, advice on care of the plants (each with its own black and white photograph), and a list of books, magazines, and commercial sources. Accurate, practical information attractively presented. Ages 10–12.

Sanderlin, George. *1776: Journals of American Independence*. New York: Harper & Row, Publishers, 1968.

An excellent source book that combines excerpts from letters, speeches, resolutions, and other documents of colonial America showing the tenor of the times from the French and Indian War to the signing of the Declaration. A chapter entitled "Guidelines from History" shows the influence of such personages as Pericles, Thucydides, Tacitus, Rousseau, and John Locke on the political thinking of the colonists as well as the inspiration engendered by the Magna Carta. Bibliography, chronology, and index. Ages 12–14.

Richard Morris' *The Colonies and the New Nation* (New York: E. P. Dutton & Co., 1963) for the same age has wider scope, covering the period between 1607 and 1829 but Sanderlin discusses the philosophy of the colonists more fully.

Sasek, Miroslav. *This Is Paris*. Illustrated by the author. New York: Macmillan Co., 1959.

A delightful picture-book introduction to the famous "City of Light" showing famous landmarks—Notre Dame, Pont de Neuf, the Louvre—as well as everyday modern scenes using techniques reminiscent of Monet, Seurat, and Modigliani. The well known Czech painter conveys a potpourri of information in a concise, lively text that matches his full-color illustrations. The first in a series encompassing cities, states, and countries, *This Is Paris* is followed by London, New York, Rome, Munich, Edinburgh, Israel, San Francisco, Ireland, Cape Kennedy, Hong Kong, Greece, Texas, the United Nations, and Washington, D.C. Pleasurable reading and viewing for the entire family. Ages 9–adult.

Schwartz, Alvin. *What Do You Think?* New York: E. P. Dutton & Co., 1966.

A clear, unbiased analysis of the factors that mold public opinion: market research, consumer education, propaganda, pressure groups, and reasoning. The role of the teen-ager as consumer and his attitudes and opinions are recognized. The techniques of public opinion polling are described using timely examples drawn from politics and current issues. Charts, tables, and photos of advertising media and propaganda samples. Indexed. Ages 12–17.

Shippen, Katherine. *Portals to the Past*. Illustrated by Mel Silverman. New York: Viking Press, 1963.

An informative, well-written survey of archaeology from its beginnings to the present. Such familiar discoveries as the Rosetta Stone, the tomb of Tutankhamen, the site of Troy, the Ziggurat of Ur, Pompeii, and Herculaneum are concisely discussed. Then the author moves into current investigations, beginning with the effect of carbon dating and how the new methods of aerial photography and skin diving are being used. Stonehenge, the Dead Sea scrolls, Zimbabwe in Africa, and recent discoveries in China, Russia, and Pakistan occupy the last half of the book. A list of suggested readings and an index. Ages 12–15.

Showers, Paul. *Before You Were a Baby*. Illustrated by Ingrid Fetz. New York: Thomas Y Crowell, 1968.

This simple, easy-to-read text describes the conception, growth, and birth of a baby. The appearance and function of the male and female sex organs are also included. Delicate, schematic drawings add to the accuracy of the text and help adults answer the inevitable question, "Where do babies come from?" More frank and easier to read than Marie Hall Ets' *Story of a Baby* (New York: Viking Press, 1939). Showers' *A*

Baby Starts To Grow (New York: Thomas Y Crowell, 1969) mainly duplicates the earlier title but omits the process of conception. Adult use with children is recommended. Ages 5–8.

Shuttlesworth, Dorothy E. *The Story of Spiders.* Illustrated by Su Zan N. Swain. Garden City, N.Y.: Doubleday & Co., 1959.

Spiders of all shapes, sizes, and habits including common garden varieties found in eveyone's back yard. This volume is filled with authentic and fascinating facts about these misunderstood, mysterious, maligned creatures, whose consumption of insects, beetles, and caterpillars plays a major part in keeping hunger at bay, not to mention its reduction of the mosquito and fly population. The descriptive text is accompanied by clear diagrams and superb color paintings, almost photographic in detail, with line sketches showing the spider's natural size. An outstanding introduction to the arachnid class. Scientific and common names are included. Ages 10–adult.

Simon, Irving B. *The Story of Printing: From Woodblocks to Electronics.* Illustrated by Charles E. Pont. Irvington-on-Hudson, N.Y.: Harvey House, 1965.

The men, the methods, and the machines involved in the technological development of printing from early times until today. An authority on graphic arts explains the history of printing clearly and logically and includes a chapter on printing as a career. An abundance of clear drawings and photos reinforce the text. A glossary, list of further reading, and an index. Ages 12–17.

Broader in scope and more detailed than Sam Epstein's *The First Book of Printing* (New York: Franklin Watts, 1955), which is for younger readers, ages 8–10.

Smith, Moyne R. *Seven Plays and How To Produce Them.* Illustrated by Don Bolognese New York: Henry Z. Walck, 1968.

An experienced children's theater director shows how plays may be adapted from fairy tales and other fanciful stories. Using Andersen's "Swineherd," the Grimms' "The Elves and the Shoemaker," and an episode from Lucretia Peabody Hale's *Peterkin Papers,* the author gives advice on costume, sets, and props and shows how requirements of setting, cast, or time may compel changes. Some general advice on production and construction of simple sets precedes the plays themselves. Clear and lively presentation, with a list of books on theatrical subjects appended. Ages 10–12.

An earlier title by Smith, *Plays and How To Put Them On* (New York: Henry Z. Walck, 1961) is equally useful.

Sobol, Donald J. *Lock, Stock, and Barrel.* Illustrated by Edward J. Smith. Philadelphia: Westminster Press, 1965.

Forty dramatic moments of the American Revolutionary era as they were lived by heroes and villains on both sides of the Atlantic, including the background of the period, the personality, virtues, and faults of each character. The crucial incidents are based on scrupulous research and careful selection of detail. The writing is pithy and vital. Along with Washington, Lafayette, Revere, and Arnold are included such lesser known figures as William Howe, Henry Knox, Frederick von Steuben, Casimir Pulaski, Walter Butler, Banastre Tarleton, John Burgoyne, Francis de Grasse, and Frederick North. Bibliography of suggested readings and an index. Ages 12–17.

Stevens, Carla. *The Birth of Sunset's Kittens.* Chicago: Scott, Foresman and Co., 1969.

A small girl watches with awe and wonder as Sunset, the family cat, gives birth to four kittens. Black and white photos of the process follow each stage in detail, while the straightforward text compares the procedure with human birth. Scientific terms such as amnion, uterus, and umbilical cord are used with accompanying explanations. Good for family sharing. Ages 5–8.

Swindler, William F. *Magna Charta*. Illustrated by Mitchell Hooks. New York: Grosset
    & Dunlap, 1968.
    A detailed history of the events leading up to the signing of the Magna Charta in
1215 and the subsequent development of the English Constitution in 1688. The men
involved—from unstable, treacherous King John and his rebellious, grasping nobles to
the parliamentarians of a later day—are shown in their relationship to the great
document. The influence of the charter's principles on the framing of the United
States Constitution, the Bill of Rights, and other freedom-expanding documents are
traced. In the appendix are a facsimile of the Charta and its text, a list of books for
further reading, selected documents that contributed to English constitutional development, a table of monarchs, and an index. Ages 12–14.
    James Daugherty's *Magna Charta* (New York: Random House, 1956) is a more
general, fictionalized book for younger readers, ages 10–12; Walter Hodges' *Magna
Charta* (New York: Coward-McCann, 1966) is a distinguished, informative, superbly
illustrated account also for younger readers, ages 6–11.

Trease, Geoffrey. *This Is Your Century*. New York: Harcourt Brace Jovanovich, 1965.
    A survey of twentieth-century world history from the death of Queen Victoria in
1901 to the uneasy years of the sixties. The first World War, the coming of Stalin,
Hitler, and Mussolini; World War II, the rise of new nations in Africa, and the
awakening of China are included with significant particulars about the personalities
and social changes involved. The emphasis is British, but the United States is not
neglected, especially in social details. All in all, a vividly written, useful overview of
the first two thirds of the twentieth century. Plentifully illustrated with photos throughout and some maps. A postscript, key dates, and index. Ages 12–adult.

Tunis, Edwin. *Frontier Living*. Illustrated by the author. Cleveland: World Publishing
    Co., 1961.
    A well researched, detailed account of life on the American frontier from 1710 to the
opening of the Cherokee Strip in 1889. The many aspects of pioneer life—food, clothing, weapons, houses, tools, religion, education, transportation, and law—are presented
in a highly readable text. Most significant are the more than 200 meticulous drawings
of pioneer artifacts by the author. The same skillful treatment and painstaking
sketching are evident in Tunis' *Wheels* (Cleveland: World Publishing Co., 1955),
Colonial Living (Cleveland: World Publishing Co., 1957), and *Colonial Craftsmen*
(Cleveland: World Publishing Co., 1965), and other titles. A Newbery Award runner-
up and an A.L.A. notable book. Ages 10–adult.

Untermeyer, Louis. *Tales From the Ballet*. Illustrated by Alice Provensen and Martin
    Provensen. New York: Golden Press, 1968.
    The plots of 20 ballets—including the classic *Swan Lake, Giselle, Coppelia,* and
Les Sylphides (listed as *The Wood Nymphs*) as well as some of the more modern
offerings such as *Rodeo, Fancy Free,* and *Billy the Kid*—are delineated. The readable
synopses use dialogue and description to give some idea of the action conveyed by the
combination of pantomime, music, setting, and movements of the dancers. Large,
brilliantly colored illustrations suggest the mood of each selection. A brief history of
this art form and production, notes about the choreographer, composer, and history of
each ballet round out an excellent presentation. Ages 10–14.

Van Loon, Hendrik Willem. *The Story of Mankind*. Illustrated by the author. New
    York: Liveright, 1921.
    A breakthrough when first published, Van Loon wrote a sweeping overview of world
history from prehistoric times to 1920. His emphasis on ideas, movements, and personalities instead of dry-as-dust facts and dates still impresses the reader with its freshness

and originality. The fourth edition in 1951 was updated by the author's son, Gerard Willem Van Loon. It includes World War II, the Atlantic Charter, and the United Nations. The current edition has been further updated by Professor Edwin C. Broome of New York University. Profusely illustrated in pen and ink animated sketches. Winner of the first Newbery Medal in 1922. Ages 12–15.

Van Wormer, Joe. *The World of the Coyote*. Philadelphia: J. B. Lippincott Co., 1964.
   The life cycle of the coyote from birth in early spring to maturity in winter. His habits and his relationship to his world and man's world are depicted through many fine, clear black and white photographs and a well-written, informative text. The author appreciates the cleverness of the animal, his ability to defy extinction, and his adaptability to diverse habitats. One of the handsome Living World Series to which Van Wormer has contributed *The World of the Black Bear* (Philadelphia: J. B. Lippincott Co., 1966), *The World of the Pronghorn* (Philadelphia: J. B. Lippincott Co., 1969), *The World of the American Elk* (Philadelphia: J. B. Lippincott Co., 1969), *The World of the Bobcat* (Philadelphia: J. B. Lippincott Co., 1964), and *The World of the Canada Goose* (Philadelphia: J. B. Lippincott Co., 1968). Wilfrid Bronson's *Coyotes* (New York: Harcourt, Brace Jovanovich, 1946) is for younger readers aged 9–10. Bibliography and index included in each book. Ages 11–14.

Voss, Carl H. *In Search of Meaning: Living Religions of the World*. Illustrated by Eric Carle. Cleveland: World Publishing Co., 1968.
   A comparison of the origins, history, and beliefs of nine contemporary faiths with a concluding chapter on some modern substitutes, including existentialism and antionalism. The emphasis is on the living religions and man's spiritual expressions from primitive times to the Roman period, including the beliefs and practices of the Incas, Mayas, and Aztecs. Joseph Gaer's *How the Great Religions Began* (New York: Dodd, Mead & Co., 1956) appeals to slightly younger readers; it deals with religion as man's explanation of the universe, whereas Voss treats religion as primarily an ethical system with overtones of faith and spiritual impact. More detailed and factual than Time-Life's *World's Great Religions* (New York: Simon and Schuster, 1961). An excellent index and bibliography. Ages 12–17.

Werstein, Irving. *The Uprising of the Warsaw Ghetto*. New York: W. W. Norton & Co., 1968.
   An affecting account of the last-ditch stand of Warsaw's Jews who resolved to fight rather than go meekly to the gas chambers of Treblinka. Drawn from trial records, contemporary sources, and interviews. The depravity and brutality of the Nazis, the anti-Semitism of the Poles, and the initial timidity of the Jews themselves are dramatically portrayed. An unflinching, almost unbearable, account of courage. Ages 12–17.

Yates, Elizabeth. *Someday You'll Write*. New York: E. P. Dutton & Co., 1962.
   Drawing on her own experiences as a writer, Newbery Medal winner Yates has written an informal guide to creative writing. Answering an 11-year-old friend's questions on how books are written and how to become a writer, she gives step-by-step advice on plot, dialogue, characterization, observation, research, and good writing habits. Examples from various well-known books point up her suggestions. Ages 11–13.

Zim, Herbert Spencer. *Dinosaurs*. Illustrated by James Gordon Irving. New York: William Morrow & Co., 1954.
   The dinosaur's appearance on earth through its extinction is described with informative details on species, size, habits, and habitat. The differences between reptiles,

amphibians, and mammals are clarified, as well as how fossils were formed, how they were discovered and how to preserve them. The large print and simple text, accompanied by clear and well-labeled illustrations, have made this an extremely popular book on a perennially popular subject. Nonreaders can gain much information from the excellent black-and-white line drawings alone. Accuracy, readability, and clarity in text and illustration are characteristic of Zim's prolific pen. Almost from A to Z—from *Alligators and Crocodiles* (New York: William Morrow & Co., 1952) to *Your Heart and How it Works* (New York: William Morrow & Co., 1959)—he has authored over 50 science books—all of them useful and popular. Ages 8–12.

Major Book Awards

The John Newbery Medal Named in honor of the first English-language publisher of books for children, this prize is awarded annually by the American Library Association to "the author of the most distinguished contribution to American literature for children." The selection is made by a committee of 23 members of the Children's Services Division of the Association and is presented at the summer conference to the designated author of the prize book, which must have been published in the preceding year. The author must be either a citizen of the United States or a permanent resident. The award has been given since 1922 and is considered of such quality that many states require elementary school children to read at least one Newbery Award book each year. In addition to the winner, several runners-up are usually mentioned.

The Caldecott Medal This prize, named for the noted English illustrator Randolph Caldecott, is awarded annually to "the artist of the most distinguished picture book for children." Like the Newbery Medal, this award is presented by the American Library Association and is chosen by the same committee which chooses the Newbery Award. The Caldecott Medal was first awarded in 1938.

The National Book Award First given in 1969, The National Book Award joins the 20-year history of similar awards for outstanding literature. This prize is selected by the Children's Book Council and is administered by the National Book Committee. The prize of $1000 is awarded annually by the panel to the most distinguished work written by an American citizen and published in the United States in the preceding year. It is a significant step toward placing children's literature and children's book awards within the same context as awards for adult literature.

Sources of Reviews of Children's Books

These journals, containing reviews of children's books, can be found in most large libraries:

Bookbird
The Booklist and Subscription Books Bulletin
Book Review Digest
The Bulletin of the Center for Children's Books, the University of Chicago
Calendar
Childhood Education
Elementary Education
Elementary English
The Grade Teacher
The Horn Book Magazine
The Instructor
Library Journal and the portion called *School Library Journal*
Publisher's Weekly
Saturday Review
Science Books
Science and Children
Wilson Library Bulletin
Young Readers' Review

Index

Author Index

A Glossary of Literary Terms

Allegory A prose or poetry narrative in which objects and persons directly represent general concepts or abstractions. For example, in John Bunyan's *The Pilgrim's Progress*, Christian represents salvation.

Archetype Universal images, situations, characters, plots, and themes found in myths and folktales and repeated in literature, either consciously or unconsciously. The fairytale prince and princess, the wicked stepmother, the orphan child, the threatened maiden, the test and quest of a hero on a journey are examples of archetypes used in children's literature.

Characterization The creation of an imaginary personage in literature to simulate reality. Among the methods of characterization are: (1) description of a character's appearance and thoughts by the author; (2) portrayal of personality through distinctive speech patterns and dialect; (3) using archetypal attributes (saying a character is a witch, goblin, or elf); and (4) portrayal through deeds and actions—noble actions showing a hero, stealth and deceit portraying a villain.

Climax The highest point of interest in a story; the resolution of the problems in the plot and the point of greatest emotional response in the reader.

Denouement The final resolution of the plot; implies the solution to a suspenseful plot, as in an intrigue or mystery.

Didactic Primarily intended to teach a moral lesson, with any entertainment or amusement value remaining secondary. "A stitch in time / Saves nine" is didactic. The main purpose of children's literature until the middle of the nineteenth century was didactic.

Dramatic Irony An effect in which the reader, aware of facts in a plot unknown to the characters, either notes a discrepancy between what a character says and what is actually the case or sees a special significance in the character's actions. Dramatic irony creates a sense of power and omniscience in the reader.

Epic A long narrative poem of a grand and elevated style presenting noble, godlike characters engaged in quests that are of central importance to the survival of a nation or civilization.

Fable Brief didactic stories in prose or verse derived from folklore, with characters—usually animals—allegorically representing moral concepts: the cunning fox, the patient tortoise, and the industrious ant.